Witnessing the Disaster

Witnessing the Disaster

*Essays on Representation and
the Holocaust*

Edited by
Michael Bernard-Donals
and
Richard Glejzer

THE UNIVERSITY OF WISCONSIN PRESS

The University of Wisconsin Press
1930 Monroe Street
Madison, Wisconsin 53711

www.wisc.edu/wisconsinpress/

3 Henrietta Street
London WC2E 8LU, England

1   3   5   4   2

Printed in the United States of America

Library of Congress Cataloging-in-Publication Data
Witnessing the disaster : essays on representation and the Holocaust
[edited by] Michael Bernard-Donals and Richard Glejzer.
        p.   cm.
ISBN 0–299–18360–2 (cloth)
ISBN 0–299–18364–5 (paper)
1. Holocaust, Jewish (1939–1945), in literature—Study and teaching.
I. Bernard-Donals, Michael F.   II. Glejzer, Richard R.
PN56.H55 W58   2003
809´.93358—dc21   2002010203

Publication of this book has been made possible in part by the generous support
of the Anonymous Fund of the University of Wisconsin–Madison.

Contents

Witnessing the Disaster

Introduction

Representations of the Holocaust and the End of Memory

MICHAEL BERNARD-DONALS AND RICHARD GLEJZER

In spite of Adorno's dictum of over forty years ago that to make art from the suffering of the Holocaust is barbarity, the event of the Holocaust can be and has been effectively represented. Even if Lawrence Langer had not pointed this fact out in 1976, the proliferation of novels, plays, films, and other representations of the event seems to have mooted Adorno's point altogether, though the fact of that proliferation also raises serious questions about the culture industry's prurience. But we wonder whether a more complicated and troubling facet of Adorno's point has been missed altogether: while it is true that representations of the event, and scholarly work on those representations, have experienced something of a boom in the last decade, it is unclear to what extent those representations—and the academic industry that has grown up around them—provide a knowledge of the Shoah, and to what extent they provide (or perhaps better, present) something other than knowledge, something akin to a flash of horror that precedes and disturbs our ability to know, the barbarism that Adorno concludes must be the ultimate poetic object after Auschwitz. So he may have been right after all: the demand to know and to remember the events may well simply replicate the rationality of the Final Solution, if that demand translates to the will to knowledge, whereby each representation is ultimately reduced to a moral imperative or to the need to square memories of the survivors—what they saw—with history.

Dori Laub makes just this point about witness testimony in the face of the historian's demand for authenticity. He gives us the testimony of a woman bearing witness to the short-lived uprising in Auschwitz in which she remembers seeing four crematoria exploding in flames, and the subsequent reaction by historians after viewing her testimony. That reaction was dismissive: what she says is completely flawed, since we know that only one of the crematoria was destroyed, not four; "Since the memory of the testifying woman turned out to be, in this way, fallible, one could not accept—nor give credence to—her whole account of the events. It was utterly important to remain accurate, lest the revisionist in history discredit everything."[1] Further, Laub reports one particular reaction: "'Don't you see,' one historian passionately exclaimed, 'that the woman's eyewitness account of the uprising that took place at Auschwitz is hopelessly misleading in its incompleteness? She had no idea what was going on. She ascribes importance to an attempt that, historically, made no difference.'"[2] But Laub sees something in this woman's testimony that the historians do not, something that the focus of squaring what she reports with a historical record ultimately occludes. For Laub, what was important was not the number of chimneys that exploded but rather the way in which the witness enacted the memory, the way her testimony resists the silence that Auschwitz itself attempted to enact: "The woman's testimony, on the other hand, is breaking the frame of the concentration camp by and through her very testimony: she is breaking out of Auschwitz even by her very talking. She had come, indeed, to testify, not to the empirical number of the chimneys, but to resistance, to the affirmation of survival, to the breakage of the frame of death."[3] Laub concludes that there is a more important—and indeed more authentic—knowledge at work in this particular testimony, a knowledge that is passed over in the attempt at historical authenticity. It is this woman's experience of resistance and survival that is the ultimate object of her bearing witness. The survivor's testimony and the reactions to it show what happens when one joins questions of representation to questions of history, questions of accuracy to questions of authenticity. And yet while the testimony is at the very least problematically connected to the event it purports to narrate, it is transmitted (horror; fascination; an act of witnessing) just as in other contemporary representations of the Holocaust. The question that must be asked is just what is being presented, whether what the writer witnesses and writes and what the reader sees in testimony amount to the same thing.

It is not only the question of authenticity that is at issue in Holocaust testimonies; so is the problem of memory. During a conference at the Yad Vashem International School for Holocaust Studies two years ago, at a session on history led by Michael Marrus, a survivor stood up to take issue with something Marrus had said about transports to one of the camps. A large man whose voice boomed a strongly accented English said, "No, that was not how it was. From Warsaw to Treblinka my family was taken in trains with compartments, not boxcars," and he cited the month and year during which his family was destroyed. Marrus responded, "Yes, they were green cars with seats facing each other down the aisle, and that ran for three weeks in May." Marrus went on to mention the names of the towns at which the train stopped on the way to the camp, and as he did so, the survivor, who had by this time sat down, nodded his head in amazement, remembering—or was he really recalling a story?—the time and the place, and the train on which his family went to its end.

It is likely that in twenty years, this survivor, along with his wife, whom he met in the Russian Army, all of the other survivors who met in that room in a building on the outskirts of Jerusalem, and the woman who testified to the Auschwitz revolt, will be dead. And along with them will go the memories, the palpable remainders of events whose imprint is indelibly written as history. This story is worth retelling because we wonder about statements that equate the death of survivors with the end of memory and of history, for we see in this story another possibility. Marrus, a historian who was not in Warsaw and did not travel in the train about which he knew so much, was able to "remember" the details of an event that seemed lost even to the individual who experienced it. But living memory is not history; witnessing the event, and having been in the train, does not guarantee that its representations will not be inaccurate, or ineffective, or simply wrong. In fact, living memory is not so much the recuperation of events as it is an imprint of the loss of the event, and narrative histories, built as a bulwark against memory's loss, stand in for and replace the event. Two conclusions result from this claim. The first is that the end of memory does not mean the end of history, but instead marks history's beginning. The second, which follows from the first, is that written histories need to be aware of—and indicate—their status as substitutes for, and supplements to, a deep loss. Historians like Marrus may remember more clearly than those who were there; but their memories mark, and should indicate, the loss of the event to its witnesses, and its effect on subsequent witnesses.

We consider history as that which can be preserved as a memory and written. But the event that serves as the object of history—in the case of the survivor at Yad Vashem, the journey by train that led to the destruction of his family; in the case of the survivor of the uprising at Auschwitz, her resistance to the fact of annihilation—cannot be made unavailable. This is true as much for the historian as it is for the one who was there. Maurice Blanchot writes, in *The Writing of the Disaster,* about the "immemorial" nature of the disaster and suggests that once an experience occurs, it is forever lost; it is at this point—"upon losing what we have to say,"[4] the point of forgetfulness—that writing begins. The loss of the event is the source of memory, writing, and history.

This is especially true in the case of horrible events such as those recollected by Marrus and the survivor in attendance at his lecture or by the witness to the destruction at Auschwitz. The witness saw the deed or the circumstance that presented itself (as trauma). But the event, as witnessed, gets in the way of what can be known or said about it. In Cathy Caruth's terms, the event registers on the witness as a void; to survive—to "get away apparently unharmed," in Freud's terms—the witness testifies, though the narrative of the event bears at best an oblique relation to what the witness saw. You could argue that there is no history—a knowledge of what happened—available to either the survivor or the historian. Between the horrible memory of loss whose image the survivor cannot seem to shake and the stunningly complete knowledge of the timetable on which this particular train ran that is available to the historian is something unavailable to knowledge, lost "to what we were to say."[5]

Caruth's point is that testimonial narratives do not disclose history; instead, they disclose—where the narrative most clearly shows its seams—the effect of events upon witnesses. The survivor's correction of the historian functions as an interjection more than an argument, and it likely interrupts the survivor's knowledge of history and the memory of his place in it as much as it intervenes in Marrus's narrative. The effect of what the witness saw—in the presence of an audience of scholars and survivors, and those who have no historical connection to the event at all—is not knowledge, nor is the inconsistency between Marrus's narrative and the survivor's memory evidence of an error or bad faith. In Caruth's terms, the interjection—the testimony—preserves the event in its disruptive effect; but the gap between the historical record and the irretrievable event cannot be filled by memory or testimony.

We do not remember a traumatic event so much as we "take leave of it," in Caruth's terms, though it leaves an indelible mark on everything we say, including the subject of the narrative of the event. It is at the point of "losing what we have to say" that we speak,[6] and writing begins. The distance between what has been witnessed and what can be committed to testimony—what was seen and what can be said—is often wide and always palpable: not only in the witness's statements but in the shrugged shoulders, the winces, the tears, and the silences that punctuate written and oral testimonies. The survivor's insistence, at Yad Vashem, that his family had seats in a compartment and did not stand in boxcars was an insistence upon the facts of history. But the urgency in the interjection—and Marrus's equally insistent focus on the timetable of the Reichsbahn—registers an element of history that is unavailable to knowledge. We may understand, through the testimonies of these two very different men, the nature of the transport during some weeks in May 1943 in Poland, and we may enumerate at least a few of its victims from this memory, but what is perhaps most chilling about this exchange (and the one described by Laub) is not the content of the story—of the experience—itself but of what cannot be placed into the narrative: the witness's sense of horror, or resignation, or loss at the sight of the green passenger cars, or his anger over the historian's error. They find no place in the language of narrative, though they register in the interjection. Here, in the no-place of the narrative, is the disaster of experience seen by the survivor but available only as the incommensurable narratives: one the product of footnotes, as Raul Hilberg has called his and other historians' work, and one the product of the loss of the event. What was witnessed by a roomful of people in Jerusalem, or those who view any number of testimonies from the Fortunoff video archive, is not living memory—a window onto the events of the Shoah—but its end.

The essays in this book examine the ways in which writing and representation of the Shoah—in survivor testimonies, fiction, film, museums, and memorials, among other forms—involve problems of witnessing.

Since the Holocaust is represented in spite of Adorno's dictum, what is the relation in such representations between what one sees and what cannot be seen or remembered? Clearly the survivor at Yad Vashem and the one described by Laub were there on the spot: they saw what they saw, and whether we understand memory as a receptacle or a void, some aspect of what they saw has made itself apparent to them. The question that remains, however, concerns the extent to which what they saw can be made visible to other, secondhand witnesses, and by what means it can be made visible. The problem, of course, is that Marrus's representation of what the witness saw is more accurate than the witness's, but it may not make Marrus's representation more effective. To cite another, more controversial example that is treated in some detail later, Stefan Maechler's representation of what Binjamin Wilkomirski (as Bruno Doesseker, the clarinet maker born in Switzerland rather than the Jewish survivor born in Riga) saw is more accurate as a testament to the events that occurred in the years from the subtitle of *Fragments* (1939–1948) than the author's. But Maechler's representation is no more effective as an indication of what Doesseker/Wilkomirski saw than the "fiction" of the memoir. The distance between what is said and what cannot be said may be small, as in the former cases, or vast, as in the latter, but in all three cases you have representations that "write" the Holocaust that present what exceeds writing and representation— some kernel of the event as it makes itself present to the witness that cannot be transmitted because it is not knowledge. And all three cases involve problems including, but not limited to, investigations of memory, the problematization of history, and a complication of the notion of mimesis.

Over the last ten years, dozens of books addressing the subject of representation of the Holocaust have been published. Many of these studies begin with the problem laid out in Lawrence Langer's seminal study, *The Holocaust and the Literary Imagination*, and his subsequent books on memoir and poetry *(Versions of Survival)* and on survivor testimonies *(Holocaust Testimonies)*. While Langer's studies deal specifically with the formal properties of Holocaust representation, and while they carefully trace the characteristics visible in fiction, in poetry, and in the recollections of survivors, only the book on testimonies considers the problem of witnessing itself. Even there, witnessing and testimony are often conflated, and despite the "conflict among selves" that Langer uses as a metaphor to explain the gaps and impasses in survivor testimonies that he found in the Fortunoff archive at Yale, it remains only a metaphor. James Young's *Writing and Rewriting the Holocaust* studies the narrative structure of memory but not the narrative structure of the works that are written about the event; his later work on Holocaust memorials goes farther to examine what he calls the anti-redemptory context for a generation whose memory is at a remove from the events and must create their own.[7] Both Langer's and Young's books ask questions about the nature of the language and modes of representation that are used, often problematically, to create what amounts to a collective memory that is often at odds with the individual memories impressed upon the survivors. Both conclude where we begin in this book by suggesting that the Holocaust, as a catalyst for literary representation, may provide a glimpse of the structure of knowledge. This same impulse drives Daniel Schwarz's *Imagining the Holocaust*, which analyzes a number of more or less literary representations of the Shoah and draws conclusions about how they may provide ways to imagine, if not know, the event by means of their generic constraints; and it underwrites Sue Vice's project in *Holocaust Fiction*, in which she examines the controversies surrounding the publication of books like Kosinski's *The Painted Bird* and Keneally's *Schindler's List* and the cultural context in which such controversies could take place. But rather than see fiction, memoir, film, and other representations as interventions in the production of knowledge of the Shoah, the contributors to this book take the glimpse of the structure of knowledge as a point of departure and examine how our confrontation with representations of the Shoah also provides a way to investigate what comes before language (trauma; history; witness) and what comes after it (testimony; pedagogy). In other words, this book is less about what literary representations do than about how they function as a testimony of what can and cannot be seen, and as a result of what can and cannot be known.

Of course, several scholars in recent years have made the same point that, because the Holocaust—as an event—is traumatic, and because writing about it is affected by that trauma, we need a new understanding of knowledge and discourse. Geoffrey Hartman has gone some way toward establishing such a theory in a series of essays in a number of different books and journals. Dominick LaCapra's essays, collected in *Representing the Holocaust* and *History and Memory after Auschwitz*, theorize the way Holocaust representations exceed or work beyond meaning, though in terms of the psychosocial Freudian unconscious rather than the sublime. We would agree with Hartman's thesis about the need to theorize the sublime and connect it to representations of the Holocaust (a task he continues to pursue in his essay on Blanchot included here). We also include in this collection analyses of representations themselves (through testimony and mimetic means), though they are seen by the authors as complicating notions of representation, the sublime, and the Holocaust as an event that can be remembered or represented. Most of the essays in the book fall between studies that see themselves as primarily descriptive and those that see themselves as theoretical, examining the ways in which individual representations put a good deal of pressure on what we think we know about events and about the dynamics of seeing and knowing that lie at their foundation.

It will come as no surprise to readers of this book that many of the most significant studies on the Holocaust over the last several years have been done in the field of history (see Friedlander's *Probing the Limits of Representation;* Lang's *Writing and the Holocaust* and *Act and Idea in the Nazi Genocide;* Novick's *The Holocaust in American Life;* and Cole's *Selling the Holocaust*). Countless journal articles on the subject of history and historiography have taken on the problem of the status of (testimonial) evidence in studies of the Holocaust. Most historians suggest either that the evidence (including written records and objects from the ghettos and camps) speaks for itself, giving it a status beyond question, or that it is mediated by the historian's or curator's ideologies and choices. Our concern here is less about how evidence should or should not count in our assessment of events, or how the evidence can be read as a text; rather, we are interested in the possibility that, though it is mediated, evidence provides traces of the event that leave a mark on the viewer or reader.

In short, we want to get past the notion that the Holocaust is an "event" that defies representation and yet which is represented successfully. Instead we move on to consider specific, contemporary instances of witnessing the Holocaust; how those instances are made apparent in testimonies and other writing; how those testimonies are structured aesthetically, historically, and culturally; and how they are cut across by contemporary debates about authenticity, what counts as documentary evidence, and the limits of art and of knowledge. To do so, we take up two separate but related conceptual issues that are involved in understanding Holocaust representation in terms of witnessing: memory and ethics. Three questions concerning memory are generally associated with the Holocaust. The first, the idea of Jewish memory and the question of how to contextualize the Shoah, profoundly affects the historical narrative of Judaism, Jewish culture, and—specifically—a definition of "the Jew" in contemporary literature. The second, the question of National Socialist cultural memory, particularly as it relates to Jews and the "Jewish question," tends to focus on how a German cultural and historical memory was created through which to marginalize Judaism and which led eventually to the Final Solution. But posing these questions together presents a final difficulty: in what ways does the desire to create a post-Holocaust (Jewish) cultural memory tend also to marginalize the particularities of the individual Jewish lives, to integrate them (in Adorno's words) in the disaster of the Holocaust? The essays included here will try to answer that question and suggest ways in which literary representations of Jews, Judaism, and the events comprising the Holocaust trouble the notion of memory. Our working hypothesis is that the creation of a subaltern Jewish subject in literary representations of the Holocaust alters both Jewish history/memory as well as the cultural memory that led to the ovens. If memory's effect upon historical and literary narratives is transformative as well as potentially dangerous—in that it led to the disaster of the Holocaust—then it is possible that the creation of a Jewish memory of the events of the Shoah also integrates the particularities of those events into an imaginary—and manageable—narrative.

What this suggests, then, is that the insistence upon "authentic" memories—testimonies from survivors that accord with the historical record; representations that hew to the horrible logic of the Final Solution—may replicate the logic that promulgated the Shoah by eliminating that which defies logic or system. The debates surrounding *The Painted Bird* and *Fragments* are debates over the authenticity of these "testimonies": did the witness really see what he claims to have seen? The problem with posing the question this way is that it ignores the extent to which the representations indicate a site of trauma that may or may not be available in the historical record at all. While the narratives may prove to be historically inauthentic, in dismissing them from the "Holocaust archive" we lose what capacity they have for causing the reader—the secondhand witness—to see that traumatic kernel (whether or not it squares with the event we believe we know as "the Holocaust"). Put another way, if memory is a way to integrate lived events into a historical series of (remembered) events—whether in National Socialist ideology

or in the continuum of the history of the Jewish people—then that integration potentially evacuates the particularity of the events and renders
them marginal (or altogether absent) in any literary (or other) representation. Adorno was right: "genocide is the absolute integration" in both
material and literary terms. We investigate how and whether contemporary literary representations of the Shoah manage to work against integration by carving out what amounts to a subaltern Jewish subject.
And we will examine how some contemporary literary representations
of the Shoah disintegrate cultural memory—in some cases in their enactment of trauma, in some cases by brushing historical representation,
in Walter Benjamin's terms, against the grain—and call into question
the notions of both a Jewish cultural memory and a coherent National
Socialist (or, later and more broadly, anti-Semitic) sense of "the Jew."

We move from the question of memory to the question of ethics by
taking up the two imperatives generally connected to Holocaust writing
and representation: first, to produce knowledge of the event so that
something like it not recur; second, to produce in the reader an effect
that forces him or her not simply to recognize the event but to confront
it. The first imperative is founded on the assumption that mimesis is not
only possible but that there is a direct correspondence between aesthetic object and the object of representation. The second imperative is
founded on the assumption that the knowledge produced in the relation
with a work translates into universal ethical action. The essays in this
book critically examine these and other ethical imperatives attached to
the Shoah by suggesting that the effects of representations of the Holocaust are what could be called excessive, in that they exceed our ability
to bring them into accord with knowledge, and that efforts to work
through the effects of witnessing the Holocaust—or of bearing witness
to others' testimonies—cannot be mapped as simply as some (like Shoshana Felman and Dominick LaCapra, to mention only two) have suggested. If witnesses to the Shoah present a kernel of the event in testimony but fail to represent the event in a language adequate to history,
then establishing the effects of those testimonies upon subsequent witnesses is a complicated affair. Any attempt to produce knowledge from
that testimony—to obey the ethical imperative by writing a version of
what the witness has seen—risks emptying it of the horror of the event.
It may be possible to produce knowledge *from* the Holocaust, but this is
not to say that we produce knowledge *of* the Holocaust. The question
worth asking—and the essays in this book ask it—is whether it is better

to engage in an ethics of trauma, in which what is transmitted is something other than knowledge, a radical sense of the event's horror and unreason rather than a reasonable map of the event as history. One of the most significant shortcomings in much of the contemporary scholarship on Holocaust representation is that in its concern for the adequacy of representation to the event it ignores the effects of those representations in specifically ethical (that is, particular) terms. These essays will begin to redress this shortcoming.

The book falls into three sections, each of which includes four or five essays. The sections roughly follow the argument laid out above to explore the issues of witness and testimony, the complexities of memory, and the problem of ethics. Each section includes essays that examine the pedagogical implications of these issues, with particular attention devoted to what, if anything, we hope to teach when presenting students with histories and representations of the Shoah. The hypothesis that begins the first section, "The Epistemology of Witness," is that the recent debates over representations of the Shoah like *Schindler's List* are telling because they inevitably fall back on an unnecessarily simplistic view of mimesis (that is, the truth can be told). This is borne out by comments written by visitors to the U.S. Holocaust Museum: "I didn't know what happened until I came here." By examining recent representations of the Holocaust as representations of witness rather than of the event itself, we can trace the distance between seeing and knowing both in intellectuals' uneasiness over what we should see in representations of the Holocaust and in the peculiar forms of those representations themselves. James E. Young's essay "The Holocaust as Vicarious Past: Art Spiegelman's *Maus* and the Afterimages of History" examines how Spiegelman acts as a witness by providing his experiences through expression and textual actuality, while in order to make his testimony seem true he "objectivizes" it by effacing himself as witness. This double act, of effacing the self and foregrounding the self in the telling of the tale, goes past the debates about how Spiegelman did or did not get history right and instead examines the nature and structure of history and of its witnesses. The difficulty, of course, is that this double act also suggests a space between them: how are the "histories" of Artie on the one hand and Vladek on the other related, and what chasm separates these two survivors? One of Young's points is that the historical trauma that seems to tie the two witnesses together is incidents and moments that appear only as a trace in the book itself—as when Vladek, in one of his last interviews with his son, mistakenly identifies the latter as Richieu, the son he lost during the maelstrom. Alan Rosen's essay is interested in the intersection not just of witnessing—what the witnesses saw and their difficulties in bringing it to language—but of the languages with which it becomes testimony. In "'The Language of Dollars': Multilingualism and the Claims of English in *Hasidic Tales of the Holocaust*" Rosen examines the extent to which Yaffa Eliach's compilation, rendered in English—coin of the realm for Holocaust representation—acts as something of a bulldozer to the act of witnessing itself. But, like the images that linger just at the edge of the comic frame in Spiegelman's work, the multilingual traces of the *Hasidic Tales* interrupt and question the validity of such a unified view. It seems to point to traces of a language, and a world, to which few, if any, living witnesses can provide testimony in the wake of the destruction of the Shoah.

The implications of writing from the position of the witness are potentially troubling. Shoshana Felman warned about this difficulty a decade ago in "Education and Crisis; or, the Vicissitudes of Teaching," in which she examined a crisis of witnessing in a graduate class she taught at Yale, in which her students, traumatized by the images and testimonies of atrocity they encountered, became witnesses to another trauma. But what Felman ignored, and what Janet Alsup takes up in her essay, "A Pedagogy of Trauma (or a Crisis of Cynicism): Teaching, Writing, and the Holocaust," is whether trauma can always be "worked through," particularly given the constraints within which undergraduate students work. In an examination of a writing course for undergraduate students whose focus was the events (and representations) of the Shoah, Alsup notes that one path students may follow is that of resistance, which made itself apparent in a version of Holocaust denial. Though this was hardly what she or the members of the class would have expected, it is a possible outcome in a course that takes seriously the problems inherent in writing the position of the witness to a traumatic event. Sharon Oster, in "The 'Erotics of Auschwitz': Coming of Age in *The Painted Bird* and *Sophie's Choice*," wonders whether fiction—with its individuation of character—is the most ethical way of presenting a sense of the events of the Shoah, since it presents the voice of the writer as the voice of the witness, whereas histories, in their drive to present knowledge, create a disembodied and authoritative account that empties the event of its horror. Oster examines novels by Styron and Kosinski as case studies, and she suggests—like Alsup—that narratives of testimony can have effects that may work against our expectations (and knowledge) of the Shoah. Finally, Richard Glejzer, in "*Maus* and the Epistemology of Witness," confronts the representation of witnessing as an epistemological shift traceable in the movement between viewed and viewer, where we become subject to witnessing itself through breaks in representation. *Maus* alienates readers from themselves by placing them in the position of both the witness and, through identification with its characters, the witnessed. The reader as witness recognizes the events represented but also understands that he or she stands at a distance from them. Picking up where Young leaves off, Glejzer suggests that what lies at the crux of witnessing is a trace of the real, the double-edged and horrifying sense that what you see is both much like what you know and completely alien to knowledge.

The second section, "Memory, Authenticity, and the 'Jewish Question,'" takes as its point of departure work on Jewish memory that begins with David Roskies's *Against the Apocalypse,* work that places the possibility of Holocaust representation into a historical sequence of disasters that have been made part of the imaginative fabric of Jewish memory for millennia. Recent work on survivor testimonies as representations of the events of the Shoah has also focused upon the possibility of rendering memory—and its traumatic excess—so that it "does justice" to the survivors and to the dead. These studies—including work on the representations of trauma—tend to treat the memories of survivors as interruptions in a personal narrative—a story that is part of a cultural/historical past—or as a radical departure into a secular (and often Americanized) future. The focus on the National Socialist (and European anti-Semitic) memory of Judaism and "the Jew," on the other hand, tends to focus on the ideological formations that made their way into literature, propaganda, law, and popular mythology immediately prior to, and twenty years after, the war. Here, the "Jewish question"— and the complex history of Judaism in central Europe—is subsumed by a cultural memory that treats Jews as members of a marginalized category of other, easily objectified and disposable. This focus is seen in the work of Saul Friedlander, Dominick LaCapra, and (in an examination of its effects in France after the war) Alain Finkielkraut and in work by survivors such as Primo Levi, Jean Améry, and Tadeusz Borowski, to name only the obvious cases. The question for us is how cultural memories both create a memory of Jews, Judaism, and the Shoah that stands in and substitutes for individual memories that bear no trace of the Final Solution, and how those cultural memories prevent forms of representation—by insisting upon "authenticity" or "historicity"—that would otherwise allow the second and third generations to act as witnesses themselves, witnesses to the Shoah's aftereffects.

In "Promiscuous Reading: The Problem of Identification and Anne Frank's Diary," Susan David Bernstein examines the recent controversy over the existing multiple versions of the diary and the responses to their proliferation. She argues that if we see the diary as a testimony of witness, subsequent "stagings" of the testimony will suffer the consequences inherent in the move from witness to testimony, the most profound being the necessary mismatch between what the witness sees and what the reader or secondhand witness sees. In its most problematic form, promiscuous identification allows the reader to identify with the subject without accounting for the complexities of the subject's position. This process effectively eliminates the problem of the witness by eliding the "Jewish question" of Anne Frank and of the Shoah, and it has the effect of eliminating the specificity of Anne (and, as a consequences, the "Jewish problem") in much the same way as the National Socialists did in Germany. Also in the American context, Elizabeth Jane Bellamy examines how Saul Bellow confronts the American memory of the Holocaust—its Jewish question—by painstakingly avoiding it altogether. In "*Humboldt's Gift* and Jewish American Self-Fashioning 'After Auschwitz,'" Bellamy suggests that it is that novel—and not the more obvious *Mr. Sammler's Planet*—in which the death camps, though only available as absences or interruptions in the imagined poet's life, effectively render the protagonist subjectless, marginal, and eventually silent. The memory of the Holocaust here is suppressed only to return as destroyer.

But in some appropriations of the trope of Auschwitz, that return is made difficult. Reinhold Hill's essay, "Mormon Literature and the Irreducible Other: Writing the Unspeakable in Holocaust Literature," takes on the peculiarities of the Mormon appropriation of Jewish identity and the events of the Shoah as an unusual case of a communitarian act of "working through." The posthumous conversion of Jews killed during the Holocaust is one notorious example of how one chosen people may co-opt another; but this is not the only way in which the history of the Mormon Other—its diasporic and marginal existence in the United States—is seen as a mirror image of the Jewish Other. The question Hill asks is how, precisely, such an appropriation maintains a distinction between what the witness sees and what a religious tradition must see in order to survive. In effect, Hill's answer is much like Hayden White's: some emplotments of history (and in the cases cited by Hill, it is not just the history of the Holocaust but also individual histories of conversion, survival, and ritual in both their Mormon and Jewish versions) simply cannot bear the weight of history, and they creak under it. It is accounts that, in Lyotard's terms, are willing to account for the incommensurability of events by other, perhaps non-narrative means, that indicate the unspeakable events, though perhaps they do not represent them as such. Michael Bernard-Donals's "Beyond the Question of Authenticity: Witness and Testimony in the *Fragments* Controversy" makes plain the consequences of such a conclusion. Though apparently "inauthentic," Binjamin Wilkomirski's account of a child in the camps provides an instance of a text whose language nonetheless indicates what cannot be made whole by memory. The irony, of course, is that the book's success in calling up the trauma of specific events of the Shoah is undermined by the author's claim to have suppressed his memories and the international media's documentation of the historical falseness of the author's stories. As in the injunction in Exodus to constantly remember to blot the memory of Amalek from Jewish history, *Fragments* presents a figural instance of the forgetting inherent in memory and the desubjectification inherent in representation.

In the book's third and final section, entitled "The Ethical Imperative," contributors address the question of an (appropriate) ethical response to the Shoah. Following Augustine, Benjamin, and Blanchot, who argue that teaching as the dissemination of knowledge is a retelling of things that the hearer already knows, they suggest that seeing representation as a retelling or a teaching of the Holocaust impoverishes not just the event but also the human capacity to think the event, because it forecloses the incommensurable in favor of a secure position from which to speak or be spoken. Humans have a tendency to elide incommensurabilities by inserting them into systems that have already been devised, into positions of identifying or naming (and therefore misrecognizing) trauma. This is the danger in Holocaust education: learning the Holocaust as a named event will not prevent future Holocausts, since we will think we can see it coming. The ethics presented in this section is not the universal ethics (capital "E") of system but rather a particular ethics, one that insists that the impact of the Holocaust as a human event is that it resists such a universal ethics. This does not mean, of course, that we turn our backs on the ethical imperative to teach the Holocaust; rather, we want to rethink that imperative so that, in teaching it, the event's capacity to traumatize and to allow for the intervention of the divine through a different sort of redemptive power is not lost.

Contributors in this section ask whether it is true, as James Young suggested in an earlier essay, that memories are more fruitfully said to be "created" than retrieved in writing on and in testimonies of the Shoah; whether knowing the Holocaust (in Kant's terms) and understanding the Holocaust are the same thing; whether we can use the term "mimesis" in Holocaust representations and what the implications of the answer are; whether it is possible to "work through" the Holocaust, and if so, how we do so; and—this is the point all the contributors address directly—what the ethical implications of the answers to all of these questions are. Geoffrey Hartman's essay, "Maurice Blanchot: Fighting Spirit," takes on the controversy surrounding Blanchot's silence in the face of anti-Semitism and the eventual destruction of the Jewish remnant in Europe. The term "fighting" can be understood to mean working against the fascist and Nazi concept of "spiritual revolution," and how that resistance involved a new understanding of Judaism's dependence upon texts (defamed, previously, as literalism). That resistance also involved a different understanding of the literary element in language, and its defense against a Sartrean notion of "engagement." Hartman sees in Blanchot's disavowal of such an engagement the beginnings of another sort of ethics, one that owes a good deal more to Levinas and Ahasuerus—a burdensome and inescapable sense of rootlessness and the imperative to act responsibly (rootedly) nonetheless—than to Kant or Sartre. David Metzger's essay, "Shoah and the Origins of Teaching," takes up the question of Levinasian responsibility to ask what a pedagogy of the Holocaust might look like. If the ethical imperatives of the last twenty years are not enough, Metzger suggests, neither is the statement attributed to Levi, "Here there is no why." In fact, Metzger says that (*pace* Levinas) this is the very question that pedagogy begins with, particularly a pedagogy of the Holocaust: rather than begin with the proposition that a knowledge of the event is possible, we ought rather to ask about origins, about what resides at the heart of knowledge. For Levinas, this was knowledge's other, which, like Bernard-Donals's notion of forgetfulness, is as horrifying and perilous as it is unavoidable. As Alsup suggested earlier, teaching provides the tempting proposition that we may finally know the object under scrutiny; Metzger's point is that in the case of the Shoah such a proposition is misleading and that we would be better off, and more honest, if we were to ask instead about the limit of knowledge and the precariousness of ethics. Michael Bernard-Donals and Richard Glejzer's essay, "Teaching (after) Auschwitz: Pedagogy between Redemption and Sublimity," advances a similar thesis: that teaching the Holocaust is impossible under contemporary theories of pedagogy, and that by examining how a post-Auschwitz theory of representation works, we can do something perhaps more valuable than teach: we can examine the limits of language in the face of a paradigmatic instance of trauma, namely, the Shoah. Finally, Dominick LaCapra's essay, "Approaching Limit Events: Siting Agamben," addresses the previous essays and the difficulties involved in creating an ethics out of the remnants of Auschwitz. LaCapra wonders whether the question of ethics is the right one to ask, given the Holocaust's utter destruction of the norms that guided human behavior, and suggests that we recuperate sublimity not as a replacement for ethics but as a mode of representation that troubles it. In an analysis of Giorgio Agamben's *Remnants of Auschwitz*, LaCapra suggests that if it is true—as Agamben argues—that Auschwitz shows the potential of humans for inhumanity rather than the inhuman exception, then we need to be careful about drawing ethical lessons from the camps at all. We may, in fact, learn nothing at all from Auschwitz: the *Muselmann*, after all, has no voice and must be spoken for by those who survived. And yet in the destruction, and in the *Muselmann*'s absent testimony, we may nonetheless be forced to see—to witness—the underside, or perhaps the excess, of ethics.

Notes

1. In Shoshana Felman, *Testimony: Crises of Witnessing in Literature, Psychoanalysis, and History*, ed. Shoshana Felman and Dori Laub (New York: Routledge, 1992), 59–60.

2. Ibid., 61.

3. Ibid., 62.

4. Maurice Blanchot, *The Writing of the Disaster* (Lincoln: University of Nebraska Press, 1980), 21.

5. Ibid.

6. Ibid.

7. See Young, *At Memory's Edge* (New Haven: Yale University Press, 2000), 5.

1

The Epistemology of Witness

I

The Holocaust as Vicarious Past

Art Spiegelman's Maus *and the Afterimages of History*

JAMES E. YOUNG

Despite the brilliant example of his own work, *Nazi Germany and the Jews*, Saul Friedlander is still not convinced that an anti-redemptory historiography of the Holocaust is possible.[1] For even that narrative, which integrates something akin to the deep, unassimilated memory of survivors as a disruption of "rational historiography," also seems to mend these same disruptions with the inexorable logic of narrative itself. The question arises: to what extent will the introduction of the survivors' memory into an otherwise rational historiography add a destablizing strain to this narrative, and to what extent will such deep, unassimilable memory be neutralized by the meaning generated in any and all narrative? Or will such a working through always remain the province of artists and novelists, whose imaginative flights bridge this contradiction even as they leave it intact? Friedlander is not sure. "Even if new forms of historical narrative were to develop," he says, "or new modes of representation, and even if literature and art were to probe the past from unexpected vantage points, the opaqueness of some 'deep memory' would probably not be dispelled. 'Working through' may ultimately signify, in Maurice Blanchot's words, 'to keep watch over absent meaning.'"[2]

Here Friedlander also draws a clear distinction between what he terms "common memory" and "deep memory" of the Holocaust: common memory is that which "tends to restore or establish coherence, closure and possibly a redemptive stance," whereas deep memory remains essentially inarticulable and unrepresentable, that which continues to exist as unresolved trauma just beyond the reach of meaning. Not only are these two orders of memory irreducible to each other, Friedlander says, but "Any attempt at building a coherent self founders on the intractable return of the repressed and recurring deep memory."[3] That is, to some extent, every common memory of the Holocaust is haunted by that which it necessarily leaves unstated, its coherence a necessary but ultimately misleading evasion.

As his sole example of deep memory, Friedlander refers to the last frame of Art Spiegelman's so-called comic book of the Holocaust, *Maus: A Survivor's Tale*, in which the dying father addresses his son, Artie, with the name of Richieu, Artie's brother who died in the Holocaust before Artie was even born.[4] The still apparently unassimilated trauma of the first son's death remains inarticulable—and thereby deep—and so is represented here only indirectly as a kind of manifest behavior. But this example is significant for Friedlander in other ways as well, coming as it does at the end of the survivor's life. For Friedlander wonders— profoundly, I think—what will become of this deep memory after the survivors are gone. "The question remains," he says, "whether at the collective level . . . an event such as the *Shoah* may, after all the survivors have disappeared, leave traces of a deep memory beyond individual recall, which will defy any attempts to give it meaning."[5] The implication is that, beyond the second generation's artistic and literary representations of it, such deep memory may be lost to history altogether.

In partial answer to this troubling void in Holocaust history, Friedlander proposes not so much a specific form but a way of thinking about historical narrative that makes room for a historiography that integrates deep and common memory. For the uncanny historian, this means a historiography whose narrative skein is disrupted by the sound of the historian's own, self-conscious voice. In the words of Friedlander, such "commentary should disrupt the facile linear progression of the narration, introduce alternative interpretations, question any partial conclusion, withstand the need for closure."[6] These interruptions would also remind readers that this history is being told and remembered by someone in a particular time and place, that it is the product of human hands and minds. Such narrative would simultaneously gesture both to the existence of deep, inarticulable memory and to its own incapacity to deliver it.

Perhaps even more important for Friedlander, though he gives it equal weight in his argument, is the possibility that such commentary "may allow for an integration of the so-called 'mythic memory' of the victims within the overall representation of this past without its becoming an 'obstacle' to 'rational historiography.'"[7] Here, it seems, Friedlander would not only answer Martin Broszat's demand that the mythic memory of victims be granted a place in "rational historiography," but he would justify doing so not on the basis of "respect for the victims" (as Broszat had suggested) but as a necessary part of an integrated history.[8] Such history necessarily integrates both the contingent truths of the historian's narrative and the fact of the victims' memory, both deep and common. In this kind of multivocal history, no single, overarching meaning emerges unchallenged; instead, narrative and counternarrative generate a frisson of meaning *in* their exchange, in the process of working through that they now mutually reinforce.

The Commixture of Image and Narrative

Here I would like to return to Art Spiegelman's *Maus*, not because it actually answers Friedlander's call for an integrated history of the Holocaust but because it illustrates so graphically the very dilemmas that inspire Friedlander's call. At the same time, I find that by embodying what Marianne Hirsch has aptly termed an aesthetics of post-memory, it also suggests itself as a model for what I would like to call "received history"—a narrative hybrid that interweaves both events of the Holocaust and the ways they are passed down to us.[9] Like Hirsch, I would not suggest that post-memory takes us beyond memory, or displaces it in any way, but rather that it is "distinguished from memory by generational distance and from history by deep personal connection. Post-memory should reflect back on memory, revealing it as equally constructed, equally mediated by the processes of narration and imagination. . . . Post-memory is anything but absent or evacuated: It is as full and as empty as memory itself."[10]

Born after Holocaust history into the time of its memory only, a new, media-savvy generation of artists rarely presumes to represent these events outside the ways they have vicariously known and experienced them. This postwar generation, after all, cannot remember the Holocaust as it actually occurred. All they remember, all they know of the Holocaust, is what the victims have passed down to them in their diaries, what the survivors have remembered to them in their memoirs. They remember not actual events but rather the countless histories, novels, and poems of the Holocaust they have read, the photographs, movies, and video testimonies they have seen over the years. They remember long days and nights in the company of survivors, listening to their harrowing tales, until their lives, loves, and losses seem grafted onto their own life stories.

Coming of age after—but indelibly shaped by—the Holocaust, this generation of artists, writers, architects, and even composers does not attempt to represent events they never knew immediately; instead, they portray their own, necessarily hypermediated experiences of memory. It is a generation no longer willing, or able, to recall the Holocaust separately from the ways it has been passed down to them. "What happens to the memory of history when it ceases to be testimony?" asks Alice Kaplan.[11] It becomes memory of the witness's memory, a vicarious past. What distinguishes many of these artists from their parents' generation of survivors is their single-minded knack for representing just this sense of vicariousness, for measuring the distance between history-as-it-happened and their "post-memory" of it.

As becomes clear, then, especially to Art Spiegelman himself, *Maus: A Survivor's Tale* is not about the Holocaust so much as it is about the survivor's tale itself and the artist-son's recovery of it. In Spiegelman's own words, "*Maus* is not what happened in the past, but rather what the son understands of the father's story. . . . It is an autobiographical history of my relationship with my father, a survivor of the Nazi death camps, cast with cartoon animals."[12] As his father recalled what happened to him at the hands of the Nazis, his son Art recalls what happened to *him* at the hands of his father and his father's stories. As his father told his experiences to Art, in all their painful immediacy, Art tells his experiences of the storytelling sessions themselves—in all of their somewhat less painful mediacy.

"In 1970 I drew a short comic strip called 'Maus' for a San Francisco artists' comic book," Spiegelman has written. "It was based on my parents' experiences as Jewish survivors of the ghettoes and death camps of Nazi Europe. In that early work I represented the Jews as mice and the Germans as cats. (Kafka's tale, 'Josephine the Singer, or the Mouse Folk' offered a precedent, as did the Saturday morning cartoons and comics of my childhood)."[13] That Spiegelman has chosen to represent the survivor's tale as passed down to him in what he calls the "commix" is neither surprising nor controversial. After all, as a commix artist and founder of *Raw Magazine*, Spiegelman has only turned to what has always been his working artistic medium. That the "commix" would serve such a story so well, however, is what I would like to explore here. On the one hand, Spiegelman seems to have realized that in order to remain true to both his father's story and his own experience of it, he would have to remain true to his medium. But in addition, he has also cultivated the unique capacity in the "commix-ture" of image and narrative for telling the double-stranded tale of his father's story and his own recording of it.

While Spiegelman acknowledges that the very word *comics* "brings to mind the notion that they have to be funny, . . . humor itself is not an intrinsic component of the medium. Rather than comics," he continues, "I prefer the word commix, to mix together, because to talk about comics is to talk about mixing together words and pictures to tell a story."[14] Moreover, Spiegelman explains, "The strength of commix lies in [its] synthetic ability to approximate a 'mental language' that is closer to actual human thought than either words or pictures alone."[15] Here he also cites the words of the person he calls the patron saint of commix, Swiss educational theorist and author Rodolphe Topffer (1799–1846): "The drawings without their text would have only a vague meaning; the text without the drawings would have no meaning at all. The combination makes up a kind of novel—all the more unique in that it is no more like a novel than it is like anything else."[16] For unlike a more linear historical narrative, the "comix-ture" of words and images generates a triangulation of meaning—a kind of three-dimensional narrative—in the movement between words, images, and the reader's eye. Such a form also recognizes that part of any narrative will be this internal register of knowledge—somewhere between words and images—conjured in the mind's movement between itself and the page. Such a mental language may not be reproducible, but it is part of any narrative just the same.

Thus, in describing Winsor McKay, another pioneering cartoonist, Spiegelman further spells out what he calls the "storytelling possibilities of the comic strip's unique formal elements: the *narrative* as well as design significance of a panel's size and shape, and how these individual panels combined to form a coherent visual whole."[17] That is, the panels convey information in both vertical and horizontal movements of the eye as well as in the analogue of images implied by the entire page appearing in the background of any single panel. The narrative sequence of his boxes, with some ambiguity as to the order in which they are to be read, combines with and then challenges the narrative of his father's story—itself constantly interrupted by Art's questions and his own neurotic preoccupations, his father's pill-taking, the rancorous father-son relationship, his father's new and sour marriage. As a result, Spiegelman's narrative is constantly interrupted by—and integrative of—life itself, with all its dislocutions, associations, and paralyzing self-reflections. It is a narrative echoing with the ambient noise and issues surrounding its telling. The roundabout method of memory-telling is captured here in ways unavailable to more linear narrative. It is a narrative that tells both the story of events and its own unfolding as narrative.

Other aspects of Spiegelman's specific form and technique further incorporate the process of drawing *Maus* into its finished version. By drawing his panels in a 1:1 ratio, for example, instead of drawing large panels and then shrinking them down to page size, Spiegelman reproduces his hand's movement in scale—its shakiness, the thickness of his drawing pencil line, the limits of miniaturization—all to put a cap on detail and fine line and so keep the pictures underdetermined. This would be the equivalent of the historian's voice—not as it interrupts the narrative, however, but as it constitutes it.

At the same time, *Maus* resonates with traces of Spiegelman's earlier, experimental foray into anti-narrative. According to Spiegelman, at the time of his first *Maus* narrative, in 1972, he was actually more preoccupied with deconstructing the commix as narrative than he was in telling a story. As Jane Kalir has observed, Spiegelman's early work here grew more and more abstruse as he forced his drawings to ask questions such as "How does one panel on a page relate to the others? How do a strip's artificial cropping and use of pictorial illusion manipulate reality? How much can be elided from a story if it is to retain any coherence? How do words and pictures combine in the human brain?"[18]

Later, with the 1977 publication of *Breakdowns,* an anthology of strips from this period of self-interrogation, the artist's overriding concern became how to tell the story of narrative's breakdown in broken-down narrative.[19] His answer was to quote mercilessly and mockingly from mainstream comics like "Rex Morgan" and "Dick Tracy," even while paying reverently parodic homage to comics pioneers like Winsor McKay and his "Dream of the Rarebit Fiend" ("Real Dream" in Spiegelman's nightmarish versions). In *Breakdowns,* Spiegelman combined images and narrative in boxes but with few clues as to whether they should be read side to side, top to bottom, image to narrative, or narrative to image; the only linear narrative here was that generated in the reading process itself, a somewhat arbitrary reassembling of boxes into sequential order. In his introductory panels to *Breakdowns,* Spiegelman even rejects the notion of narrative as story, preferring to redefine story as the "complete horizontal division of a building . . . [From Medieval Latin HISTORIA . . . a row of windows with pictures on them.]" But while he exploded commix narrative into a kind of crazy-quilt to be read in all directions, Spiegelman deliberately maintained a linear narrative for the Holocaust segment of *Breakdowns.* When I asked why, he replied simply that he was not interested in breaking the story of the Holocaust itself into incoherence, only in examining the limits of this particular narrative for telling such a story.

In fact, what Spiegelman admires in the form itself, he says, he once admired in Harvey Kurtzman's *Mad Magazine:* "It was *about* something—reality, for want of a better word—and was also highly self-reflexive, satirically questioning not only the world, but also the underlying premises of the comics medium through which it asked the questions."[20] For Spiegelman, there is no contradiction between a form that is about reality, on the one hand, and that which questions its own underlying premises, on the other. It is clear that part of the world's reality here is the artist's own aching inadequacy in the face of this reality.

As for possible objections to folding the deadly high-seriousness of the Holocaust into what some regard as the trivial low-seriousness of comics, Spiegelman merely points to the ways in which the medium itself has always raised—and dismissed—issues of decorum as part of its raison d'être. Here he recalls that even the distinction between the high art of the masters and the low art of cartoonists is challenged by the manner in which "modern masters" such as Lyonel Feininger, George Grosz, Kathe Kollwitz, and Juan Gris divided their time between painting and cartoons. Indeed, as Adam Gopnik has suggested, the comics in the twentieth century have served as a "metalanguage of modernism, a fixed point of reference outside modern painting to which artists could refer in order to make puns and ironic jokes."[21] As an unusually retentive mirror and caricature of styles in modern art, the comics have at once cataloged and mocked modern art with its own high-seriousness, making them the postmodern art par excellence.

Written between 1972 and 1985, the first volume of *Maus* thus integrated both narrative and anti-narrative elements of the comics, embedding the father's altogether coherent story in a medium ever threatening to fly apart at the seams. The result is a continuous narrative rife with the discontinuities of its reception and production, the absolutely authentic voice of Spiegelman's father counterposed to the fabular images of cartoon animals. In its self-negating logic, Spiegelman's commix also suggests itself as a pointedly anti-redemptory medium that simultaneously makes and unmakes meaning as it unfolds. Words tell one story, images another. Past events are not redeemed in their telling but are here exposed as a continuing cause of the artist's inability to find meaning anywhere. Meaning is not negated altogether, but the meaning created in the father's telling is immediately challenged in the son's reception and visualization of it.

In fact, the "story" is not a single story at all but two stories being told simultaneously: the father's story and Spiegelman's imaginative record of it. It is double-stranded and includes the competing stories of what his father says and what Artie hears, what happened during the Holocaust and what happens now in Artie's mind. As a process, it makes visible the space between what gets told and what gets heard, between what gets heard and what gets seen. The father says one thing as we see him doing something else. Artie promises not to betray certain details, only to show us both the promise and betrayal together. Indeed, it may be Artie's unreliability as a son that makes his own narrative so reliable.

Throughout *Maus*, Spiegelman thus confronts his father with the record of his telling, incorporating his father's response to Art's record of it into later stages of *Maus*. Like any good postmodern memory-art, *Maus* thereby feeds on itself, recalling its own production, even the choices the artist makes along the way (would he draw his French wife, who converted to Judaism, as a frog or as an honorary *Maus*?). The story now includes not just "what happened" but how what happened is made sense of by father and son in the telling. At the same time, it highlights both the inseparability of his father's story from its effect on Artie and the story's own necessarily contingent coming into being, all of which might be lost to either images or narrative alone, or even to a reception that did not remark its own unfolding.

By weaving back into his narrative the constant reflection on his own role in extracting this story from his father, Spiegelman graphically highlights not only the ways that testimony is an event in its own right but also the central role he plays in this event. Moreover, as Dori Laub has noted, "The listener is a party to the creation of knowledge *de novo*."[22] That is, what is generated in the interaction between father and son in this case is not a revelation of a story already existing, waiting to be told, but a new story unique to their experience together. This medium allows the artist to show not only the creation of his father's story but also the necessary grounds for its creation, the ways his father's story hinges on his relationship to the listener. Artie is not just a shaper of testimony during its telling, or after in his drawings, but an integral part of its very genesis, part of its very raison d'être. By making this telling and receiving the subject of *Maus*, Spiegelman acknowledges the multiple levels of creativity and knowledge-making here: that in the telling and that in his subsequent drawing. In this way, Spiegelman is both midwife to and eventual representer of his father's story.

Maus as Side-Shadowed History

Throughout its narrative, *Maus* thus presumes a particular paradigm for history itself, a conception of past historical events that includes the present conditions under which they are being remembered. The historical facts of the Holocaust, in this case, include the fact of their eventual transmission. This is why the "autobiographical history of the survivor's tale" necessarily begins, then, not in the father's experiences but in Artie's own. Neither the three-page 1972 version of "Maus" in *Breakdowns* nor the later two-volume edition of *Maus* opens in the father's boyhood Poland; rather, both open with the son's boyhood in Rego Park, Queens. The 1972 version begins with Poppa mouse sitting on the edge of his adoring little boy's bed, telling him "bedtime stories about life in the old country during the war": ". . . and so, Mickey, *die Katzen* made all the mice to move into one part from the town! It was wery crowded in the ghetto!" "Golly!" says little mouse in his pajamas. Hence the "real dreams" that follow in *Breakdowns*.

Maus: A Survivor's Tale also opens in Rego Park, Queens, in 1958, with the young Artie's relationship to his father. Indeed, every detail of his childhood life is already fraught with his father's memory, already shaped by his father's experiences. In the opening panel, something as innocent as being ditched by friends in childhood sparks the father's indignant comparison: "Friends? Your friends? If you lock them together in a room with no food for a week, THEN you could see what it is, friends" (1:6). *Maus* thus opens with the father's seemingly inexplicable response to his young son's tears, a deep memory that becomes sensible only over the course of the narrative that follows.

After this preamble, Artie appears again, now grown, to visit his father for the first time in nearly two years. He is on a mission, a self-quest that is also historical. "I still want to draw that book about you," Artie says to his father, who answers, "No one wants any way to hear such stories," to which Artie answers, "*I* want to hear it." And then he asks his father to begin, in effect, with his own implied origin: "Start with Mom," he asks. "Tell me how you met" (1:12). He did not ask him to start with the war, deportation, or internment, but with his mother and their union—that is, his *own* origins. But even here, Art's needs are frustrated by his father's actual memory: he begins not with Artie's mother, Anja, but with another earlier girlfriend, Lucia, where *his* memory of Anja begins.

Though Vladek tells his son that Lucia and his other girlfriends had nothing to do with the Holocaust, Spiegelman includes them nevertheless. In so doing, Spiegelman extends the realm of Holocaust history not only forward, to include its effects on the next generation, but also backward, to include the rich, prewar tangle of lives lost. For Spiegelman, the very period of Holocaust was not merely the sum of Jews murdered or maimed but also the loss of all that came before. By including the quotidian and messy details of his father's love affairs before the war (against the father's wishes), he not only restores a measure of the victims' humanity but also, and more importantly, preserves the contingency of daily lives as lived and perceived then—not only as they are retrospectively freighted with the pathos and portent we assign them now. At the same time, the artist shows how the victims themselves, for perfectly understandable reasons, are occasionally complicit in the kind of "back-shadowed history" Spiegelman now rejects.[23]

It is as if Spiegelman realizes that at least part of his aim here as skeptical son, as teller of "side-shadowed" history, will be to show the ways his father has made sense of his Holocaust experiences through many tellings, even as he would sabotage the ready-made story with his questions, his search for competing and contradicting details. The father might prefer a polished narrative, one with beginning, middle, and end, but Artie wants to know the forks in the road, the paths not taken, how and why decisions were made under those circumstances, mistakenly or otherwise. In the nearly fifteen hundred interlocking frames that follow, therefore, the survivor's tale includes life before the war: leaving Lucia; marrying Anja for a mixture of love and money; going to work for his father-in-law; having a baby boy, Richieu; taking Anja to a spa for treatment of severe depression; being called up by the Polish army in the weeks before war.

As a Polish soldier, Vladek sees combat on the front when Germany invades Poland, and he even kills a German soldier. But the Polish army is overrun, and Vladek is captured. He survives a POW camp, and through a combination of guile and luck he makes his way home again to Sosnowiecz. The details of the Polish Jews' ghettoization follow: hiding from selections, the gradual loss of hope and breakup of the family, various acts of courage and betrayal by Jews and Poles, the painful sending of Richieu into hiding with a relative. The first volume ends with Vladek and Anja being caught and deported to Auschwitz-Birkenau.[24]

The second volume opens in Auschwitz, where Vladek and Anja are separated. Intercut repeatedly with scenes depicting the day-to-day circumstances of his telling, Vladek recounts the arbitrariness of day-to-day life and death in Auschwitz, finding work and learning new skills for survival, making and losing contact with Anja, liberation, the postwar chaos of refugees in Europe, and his search for Anja. The book literally ends with Vladek's description of his joyous reunion with Anja ("More I don't need to tell you. We were both very happy, and lived happy, happy ever after"). Two final panels follow: "So . . . let's stop, please, your tape recorder . . . I'm tired from talking, Richieu, and it's enough stories for now . . ." (2:136). At the bottom of the last page, Art has drawn a picture of a single tombstone for Vladek and Anja, with their names and dates of life. Beneath the tombstone, Art has signed his own name and the dates 1978–1991, not his life span but the span of his writing. "Which is the true historical project," Alice Kaplan has asked, "the pinpointing of an empirical cause or the trickier, less disciplined attempt to make links between past and present?"[25] In *Maus*, not only are past and present linked, but they constantly intrude and occasionally even collapse into each other. In Vladek's relating, for example, the fate of his cousin, Haskel, an infamous *Kombinator* (schemer), the very memory seems to stop his heart as he grabs his chest. The narrative is one thing, the heart-stopping anxiety it produces in the teller is another. Both are portrayed here—the story and the effect of the teller himself—a kind of deep memory usually lost to narrative alone (1:118).

Earlier, as the father was recounting the days in August 1939 when he was drafted, he gets to the outbreak of war itself: "[A]nd on September 1, 1939, the war came. I was on the front, one of the first to . . . Ach!" His elbow knocks two bottles of pills onto the floor. "So. Twice I spilled my drugstore!" He blames his lost eye and cataracts for not seeing so well and launches into the story of eye operations and neglectful doctors. On that day and in that chapter of the book, he does not finish his story of the Nazi invasion and says it's enough for the day: "I'm tired and must count my pills" (1:40). This is fine with Artie, whose writing hand is sore from note-taking. Both teller and listener need to recover from the storytelling session itself, though whether it is the activity of telling and listening or the content of the narrative that has worn them out is not clear. Throughout the course of *Maus*, the content of the father's tale of survival is balanced against the literal process of its recovery, the circumstances under which it is received and then retold.

By making the recovery of the story itself a visible part of *Maus*, Spiegelman can also hint darkly at the story not being recovered here, the ways that telling one story always leaves another untold, the ways common memory masks deep memory. In Spiegelman's case, this deep, unrecoverable story is his mother's memory of her experiences during the Holocaust. Vladek does not, cannot volunteer this story. It takes Artie to ask what Anja was doing all this time. "Housework . . . and knitting . . . reading . . . and she was writing always in her diary" (1:84). The diaries did not survive the war, Vladek says, but she did write her memoirs afterward. "Ohmigod! Where are they? I need those for this book!" Artie exclaims. Instead of answering, Vladek coughs and asks Artie to stop with the smoking because it is making him short of breath. What seems to be a mere interruption turns out to be a prescient delaying tactic. Vladek had, after all, burned Anja's memoirs in a fit of grief after her suicide. Was it the memory of smoke from the burned memoirs or Artie's cigarettes that now made him short of breath?

At the end of the first volume, Spiegelman depicts the moment at which his father admits not only destroying his mother's memoirs but leaving them unread. "Murderer," the son mutters. Here he seems to realize that his father's entire story is haunted by Anja's lost story. But worse, it dawns on the son that his entire project may itself be premised on the destruction of his mother's memoirs, their displacement and violation. Spiegelman does not attempt to retell Anja's story at all, but leaves it known only by its absence; he is an accomplice to the usurpation of his dead mother's voice. It is a blank page, to be presented as blank. Nancy Miller has even suggested that "It's as if at the heart of *Maus*'s dare is the wish to save the mother by retrieving her narrative; as if the comic book version of Auschwitz were the son's normalization of another impossible reality: restoring the missing word, the Polish notebooks."[26] As a void at the heart of *Maus*, the mother's lost story may be *Maus*'s negative center of gravity, the invisible planet around which both the father's telling and Spiegelman's recovery of it revolve.

Here Spiegelman seems also to be asking how we write the stories of the dead without filling in their absence. In a limited way, the commixture of image and narrative allows the artist to do just this, to make visible crucial parts of memory-work usually lost to narrative alone, such as the silences and spaces between words. How to show a necessary silence? Art's therapist, Pavel, suggests at one point that because "life always takes the side of life" (2:45), the victims who died can never tell their stories. Maybe it's better not to have any more stories at all, Pavel says. "Uh, huh," Art nods in agreement and adds, "Samuel Beckett once said, 'Every word is like an unnecessary stain on silence and nothingness.'" "Yes," Pavel answers. And then we have a panel without words, just an image of Art and his therapist sitting in silence, a moment in the therapeutic context as fraught with significance as narrative itself. For this is not silence as an absence of words but rather as something that actively passes between two people—the only frame in the two volumes without words or some other sign denoting words. On the other hand, Art points out in the next frame, "he said it." "Maybe you can include it in your book," the therapist replies.

The need to show the unshowable may also underpin Spiegelman's use of animals for humans here. When Spiegelman is asked, "Why mice?" he answers, "I need to show the events and memory of the Holocaust without showing them. I want to show the masking of these events *in* their representation."[27] In this way, he can tell the story and not tell it at the same time. As ancient Passover Haggadoth used to put birds' heads on human forms in order to both show and not show humans at the same time, Spiegelman has put mouse heads on the Jews. By using mouse masks, the artist also asks us not to believe what we see.

They are masks drawing attention to themselves as such, never inviting us to mistake memory of events for events themselves.

At one point, Adam Gopnik echoes Spiegelman's words, but with a slightly different twist. It is not just that Spiegelman wants to show this story by masking it, says Gopnik, but that the story itself "is too horrible to be presented unmasked." Moreover, Gopnik finds that Spiegelman may even be extending an ancient Jewish iconographic tradition, if for very untraditional reasons:

> The particular animal "masks" Spiegelman has chosen uncannily recall and evoke one of the few masterpieces of Jewish religious art—the Bird's Head Haggadah of 13th-century Ashkenazi art. In this and related manuscripts, the Passover story is depicted using figures with the bodies of humans and heads of animals—small, common animals, usually birds.
>
> Now, in one sense the problems that confronted the medieval Jewish illuminator and the modern Jewish artist of the Holocaust are entirely different. The medieval artist had a subject too holy to be depicted; the modern artist has a subject too horrible to be depicted. For the traditional illuminator, it is the ultimate sacred mystery that must somehow be shown without being shown; for the contemporary artist, it is the ultimate obscenity, the ultimate profanity, that must somehow be shown without being shown.[28]

Though Gopnik goes on to suggest that this obscenity has also become our sacred subject, we might do better to keep in mind not this apparent (and mistaken) conflation of sacred and profane but rather the medium's essential indirection, its simultaneous attempt at representing and its self-declared inadequacy.

Indeed, as Spiegelman attempted to ironize narrative, he also uses images against themselves. By adopting the mouse as allegorical image for Jews, he is able to caricature—and thereby subvert—the Nazi image of Jews as vermin. Subjugated groups have long appropriated the racial epithets and stereotypes used against them in order to ironize and thereby neutralize their charge, taking them out of the oppressors' vocabulary. In this case, the images of mice led in turn to other animal figures insofar as they are related to mice: the wily and somewhat indifferent cat is the obvious natural enemy of the mouse and, as German, the principal killer of mice here. The hapless Poles are saddled with a more ambiguous figure: while not a natural enemy of the Jews during the

Holocaust, as pigs they come to symbolize what is *treif* or non-kosher. They may not be as anti-Jewish as the cats, but they are decidedly un-Jewish. The only other animal to resonate a Nazi cast would be the friendly (if none too bright) dogs as stand-in for Americans, regarded as a mongrel people by Hitler but pictured here as the natural and more powerful enemy of the cats. The rest of the animals are more literally benign: reindeer for the Swedes, moths for Gypsies. But none of these, aside from the mouse, is intrinsic, witness Art's deliberations over whether to make his French-born wife, Francoise, who converted to Judaism, a frog or an honorary mouse (technically speaking, she has to be a mouse).

Though he has tried to weave the process of drawing *Maus* back into its narrative, Spiegelman is also aware that as a finished text, *Maus* may not truly capture the process at its heart. This is why two exhibitions, one at the Galerie St. Etienne and the other in the projects room at the Museum of Modern Art in New York were so central to Spiegelman's project at the time. In these exhibitions, each entitled "The Road to *Maus*," the artist mounted the originals of his finished panels sequentially in a horizontal line along the walls of the gallery. Each panel in turn had all of its earlier drafts running vertically down into it, showing the evolution of each image from start to finish. Cassette players and earpieces were strategically interspersed along the walls of the gallery so that viewers could listen to Art's original interviews with his father. In this way, Spiegelman hoped to bring into view his true object of representation: the process by which he arrived at a narrative, by which he made meaning in and worked through a history that has been both public and personal. Though the ostensible purpose of the exhibition was, according to Robert Storr, "to illuminate the final entity—a mass-produced work—by showing its complex genesis in the artist's mind and on the draftsman's page,"[29] the artist himself preferred to see the exhibition *as* the total text. "If I had my way," he told me, "this would be the text of *Maus*, replete with how I got to the so-called final panels."

With the advent of CD-ROM, the artist has had his wish at least partly fulfilled, for here is an interactive text in which the panels of *Maus* are accompanied by complete genealogies of their origins. Where did a particular story or set of images come from? How did they first enter the artist's consciousness? It's all here. We press the interactive screen on one of the colored boxes, and up comes a complete (pre-)history of that panel: Vladek's tape-recorded voice tells one version, with Art's interruptions. The artist's early sketches done as his father spoke tell another version. Photographs and drawings from Art's library that inspired certain images appear one after the other, even video footage of Art's trip to Poland and Auschwitz. By making visible the memory of this memory-text's production, the CD-ROM version of *Maus* reveals the interior, ever-evolving life of memory—and makes this life, too, part of its text.

The Ambivalence of Memory

Finally, like other artists in his anti-redemptory generation, Spiegelman cannot escape an essential ambivalence he feels toward his entire memory enterprise. For he recognizes that both his father's story and his own record of it have arisen out of a confluence of conflicting personal, professional, and not always heroic needs. Vladek tells his story, it seems, more for the sake of his son's company than for the sake of history; it is a way to keep his son nearby, a kind of tether. Indeed, as survivor par excellence, Vladek is not above bartering the story itself to get what he wants: first, as leverage to keep his son nearby, and then later as part of an exchange for food at the local market, where he receives six dollars' worth of groceries for one dollar, a partially eaten box of Special K cereal, an acknowledgment of his declining health, and, of course, a little about "how it was in the camps" (2:90). In a pinch, as it turns out, the savvy survivor can trade even his story of survival for food.

While this kind of self-interested storytelling might drive the son a little crazy, Art must face the way he too has come to the story as much to learn about his origins, his dead mother, and his own mishugas as he does to learn Holocaust history. In fact, the Holocaust-telling relationship literally redeems the father-son relationship for Artie. "I'll get my tape recorder, so today isn't a total loss, okay?" he says after a particularly trying visit with Vladek (2:23). Moreover, he recognizes not only that he too has capitalized on his father's story but also that in so doing he has delayed the rest of the story's publication. What with all the business and promotional deals surrounding the first volume of *Maus*, Art could hardly find time to continue what had been a single project, now broken into two parts for the sake of publication. The Holocaust has been good to a starving artist who admits choosing his life's work partly to spite his father with its impracticality. And now it has made him quite comfortable, as well, which becomes part of the story in the second volume of *Maus*—a recognition of his debt to his father's story, the way Art has traded it for his own survival. In this way, history is received as a gift and as a commodity to be traded, the sole basis for any relationship between father and son.

All of this generates a certain self-loathing in the artist, even as it saps the author of his desire to continue telling the story. The first five frames of the second chapter in volume 2 open with Art's morbid reflections on the production and success of volume 1. With flies buzzing around his head, he contemplates the stages of his parents' life weighed against the stages of his own, while trying to make sense of the yawning gap between their life experiences and his own:

> Vladek died of congestive heart failure on August 18, 1982. . . . Francoise and I stayed with him in the Catskills back in August 1979. Vladek started working as a tinman in Auschwitz in the spring of 1944. . . . I started working on this page at the very end of February 1987. In May 1987 Francoise and I are expecting a baby. . . . Between May 16, 1944 and May 24, 1944 over 100,000 Hungarian Jews were gassed in Auschwitz. . . . In September 1986, after 8 years of work, the first part of MAUS was published. It was a critical and commercial success. At least fifteen foreign editions are coming out. I've gotten 4 serious offers to turn my book into a T.V. special or movie. (I don't wanna.) In May 1968 my mother killed herself. (She left no note.) Lately I've been feeling depressed. (2:41)

Out of his window, where one of New York City's signature water towers might be standing, we see what Art sees: a concentration camp guard tower (its base and outline not unlike that of the water towers). Now, flies buzz around crumpled mouse corpses littering his floor as Art slumps dejectedly onto his drafting board.

Part of what gets Art down, of course, is that he is not an innocent bystander in all this, a grateful vessel into which his father has poured his story. When he remembers his father's story now, he remembers how at times he had to wring it out of him. When his father needed a son, a friend, a sounding board for his *tsouris*, Art demanded Holocaust. Before rejoining his father's story in Auschwitz, Art draws himself listening to the tape-recorded session he is about to tell. "I was still so sick and tired," Vladek is saying about his return from a bout in the hospital.

"And to have peace only, I agreed to make [my will] legal. She brought right to my bed a NOTARY." To which Art replies, "Let's get back to Auschwitz . . ." "Fifteen dollars he charged to come! If she waited only a week until I was stronger, I'd go to the bank and take a notary for only a quarter!" "ENOUGH!" screams the son. "TELL ME ABOUT AUSCHWITZ!" Artie shrinks in his seat and sighs as he listens again to this exchange. Defeated, his father returns to the story (2:47).

Indeed, Spiegelman is both fascinated and repelled by the way he can actually assimilate these stories so seamlessly into the rest of his life. At one point, his wife peeks into Art's studio and asks cheerfully, "Want some coffee?" Art is replaying the tape recording in which his father describes the moments before his brother was killed: "And then she said, 'No! I will not go in the gas chambers. And my children will not . . . ' [clik]." Art turns off the cassette and answers eagerly, "You bet!" (2:120). What do these stories do to the rest of the lives in which they are embedded? Shouldn't they foul everything they touch with their stench? Can we keep such stories separate, or do they seep into the rest of our lives— and how corrosive are they? Maybe, just maybe, we can live with these stories, after all.

"Why should we assume there are positive lessons to be learned from [the Holocaust]?" asks Jonathan Rosen in an essay that cuts excruciatingly close to the bone of Spiegelman's own ambivalence. "What if some history does not have anything to teach us? What if studying radical evil does not make us better? What if, walking through the haunted halls of the Holocaust Museum, looking at evidence of the destruction of European Jewry, visitors do not emerge with a greater belief that all men are created equal but with a belief that man is by nature evil?"[30]

As we see in the case of Vladek's own racist attitudes toward African Americans, the Holocaust may have made him even worse. And if the Holocaust does not enlighten its victims, how will its story enlighten the next generation? It is an irony with a very clear judgment built into it: the Holocaust was an irredeemably terrible experience then, had a terrible effect on many survivors' lives, and endows its victims with no great moral authority now. Categories such as good and evil remain, but they are now stripped of their idealized certainties. Neither art nor narrative redeems the Holocaust with meaning—didactic, moral, or otherwise. In fact, to the extent that remembering events seems to find any meaning in them, such memory also betrays events by blinding us with our own need for redemptory closure.

Post-Memory and the Evasions of History

At no place in or out of *Maus* does Spiegelman cast doubt on the facts of the Holocaust. Moreover, he is positively traditional in his use of documentary artifacts and photographs as guides to describing real events. When his book made the *New York Times* best-seller list in 1991, he was surprised to find it on "the fiction side of the ledger." In his letter to the *Times*, Spiegelman wrote,

> If your list were divided into literature and nonliterature, I could gracefully accept the compliment as intended, but to the extent that "fiction" indicates that a work isn't factual, I feel a bit queasy. As an author I believe I might have lopped several years off the 13 I devoted to my two-volume project if I could only have taken a novelist's license while searching for a novelistic structure.
>
> The borderland between fiction and nonfiction has been fertile territory for some of the most potent contemporary writing, and it's not as though my passages on how to build a bunker and repair concentration camp boots got the book onto your advice, how-to and miscellaneous list. It's just that I shudder to think how David Duke—if he could read—would respond to seeing a carefully researched work based closely on my father's memories of life in Hitler's Europe and in the death camps classified as fiction.
>
> I know that by delineating people with animal heads I've raised problems of taxonomy for you. Could you consider adding a special "nonfiction/mice" category to your list?[31]

In the end, the editors at the *Times* did not add this special "nonfiction/ mice" category to their list, but they did agree to move *Maus* over to the nonfiction list. But in this context, it is not surprising that the author sees no contradiction between his fabular medium and his devotion to fact in *Maus*. For his positivist stance is not a negation of the vagaries of memory but rather that which makes the recognition of memory necessary. The facts of history and their memory exist side by side, mutually dependent on one another for sustenance and meaning.

Thus will a received history like *Maus* also remain true to the mistaken perceptions and memory of the survivor. What might appear as historical errors of fact in *Maus*, such as the picture of Poles—one in a Nazi uniform (1:140) and others saying "Heil Hitler" (1:149), when it would have been almost impossible to find any Pole saluting Hitler to another Pole during the war or to find a Polish Nazi—are accurate representations of his father's possibly faulty memory. The truth of such memory is not that Poles actually gave the Nazi salute to each other but that Vladek remembered Poles to be Nazi-like in their hatred of Jews. Whether accurate or not, such a perception may itself have played a role in Vladek's actions during the war—and so deserves a place in the historical record.

On the one hand, issues of historical accuracy and factuality in a medium like *Maus* are bound to haunt its author, raised as they are by the medium but impossible to resolve in it. Nancy Miller has put the question most succinctly: "The relationship between accuracy and caricature for the cartoonist who works in a medium in which accuracy is an *effect of exaggeration* is a vexed one."[32] But in an era when claims to absolute truth are under assault, Spiegelman's *Maus* also makes a case for an essentially reciprocal relationship between the truth of what happened and the truth of how it is remembered. The facts of the Holocaust here include the facts surrounding its eventual transmission to him. Together, what happened and how it is remembered constitute a received history of events.

No doubt, some will see such work as a supremely evasive, even self-indulgent art by a generation more absorbed in their own vicarious experiences of memory than by the survivors' actual experiences of real events. Others will say that if the second or third generation wants to make art out of the Holocaust, then let it be about the Holocaust itself and not about themselves. The problem for much of these artists' generation, of course, is that they are unable to remember the Holocaust outside the ways it has been passed down to them, outside the ways it is meaningful to them fifty years after the fact. As the survivors have testified to *their* experiences of the Holocaust, their children and children's children will now testify to their experiences of the Holocaust. And what are *their* experiences of the Holocaust? Photographs, film, histories, novels, poems, plays, survivors' testimony. It is necessarily mediated experience, the afterlife of memory, represented in history's afterimages: the impressions retained in the mind's eye of a vivid sensation long after the original, external cause has been removed.

Why represent all that? Because for those in Spiegelman's generation, to leave out the truth of how they came to know the Holocaust would be to ignore half of what actually happened: we would know what happened to Spiegelman's father but miss what happened to the artist-son. But isn't the important story what happened to the father at Auschwitz? Yes, but without exploring why it is important, we leave out part of the story itself. Is it self-indulgent or self-aggrandizing to make the listener's story part of the teller's story? This generation doubts that it can be done otherwise. They can no more neglect the circumstances surrounding a story's telling than they can ignore the circumstances surrounding the actual events' unfolding. Neither the events nor the memory of them takes place in a void. In the end, these artists ask us to consider which is the more truthful account: that narrative or art which ignores its own coming into being, or that which paints this fact, too, into its canvas of history? Art Spiegelman's *Maus* succeeds brilliantly not just for the ways it sideshadows the history of the Holocaust but also for the ways it sideshadows memory itself, the ways it makes visible why such history is worth recalling in the first place.

Notes

1. See Saul Friedlander, *Nazi Germany and the Jews,* vol. 1 (New York: Harper Collins, 1997).

2. Saul Friedlander, "Trauma, Transference, and 'Working Through' in Writing the History of the *Shoah*," *History and Memory* 4 (Spring/Summer 1992): 55. In his earlier *Reflections of Nazism: An Essay on Kitsch and Death* (New York: Harper & Row, 1984), Friedlander was more skeptical of what he would later call postmodern responses to the Holocaust and more deeply ambivalent toward the very motives for such art (see citation in introduction).

3. Friedlander, "Trauma, Transference, and 'Working Through,'" 41.

4. Art Spiegelman, *Maus: A Survivor's Tale,* 2 vols. (New York: Pantheon, 1986, 1991), 2:135. Hereafter cited parenthetically in the text by volume and page number.

5. Friedlander, "Trauma, Transference, and 'Working Through,'" 41.

6. Saul Friedlander, *Memory, History, and the Extermination of the Jews of Europe* (Bloomington: University of Indiana Press, 1993), 132.

7. Friedlander, "Trauma, Transference, and 'Working Through,'" 53.

8. Martin Broszat and Saul Friedlander, "A Controversy about the Historicization of National Socialism," in *Reworking the Past: Hitler, and Holocaust, and the Historians' Controversy,* ed. Peter Baldwin (Boston: Beacon Press, 1990), 129.

9. See Marianne Hirsch, "Family Pictures: *Maus*, Mourning, and Post-Memory," *Discourse* 15, no. 2 (1992–93): 8. For more on my own notion of

"received history," see James E. Young, "Toward a Received History of the Holocaust," *History and Theory* 36, no. 4 (1997): 21–43.

10. Hirsch, "Family Pictures," 8–9.

11. Alice Yeager Kaplan, "Theweleit and Spiegelman: Of Mice and Men," in *Remaking History: DIA Art Foundation Discussions in Contemporary Culture, Number 4,* ed. Barbara Kruger and Phil Marian (Seattle: Bay Press, 1989), 160.

12. From author's interview with Art Spiegelman, as well as from Art Spiegelman, "Commix: An Idiosyncratic Historical and Aesthetic Overview," *Print* (November/December 1988): 61.

13. Art Spiegelman, "Artist's Statement," in *Jewish Themes/Contemporary American Artists II,* ed. Susan Tumarkin Goodman (New York: The Jewish Museum, 1986), 44.

14. Spiegelman, "Commix," 61.

15. From Jane Kalir, "The Road to *Maus*," at Galerie St. Etienne, November 17, 1992, through January 9, 1993, 2.

16. Spiegelman, "Commix," 61.

17. Ibid.

18. Kalir, "The Road to *Maus*," 1.

19. Art Spiegelman, *Breakdowns: From Maus to Now: An Anthology of Strips by Art Spiegelman* (New York: Nostalgia Press, 1977).

20. Ibid.

21. For an overview of the comics' place in modern art, see Kirk Varnedoe and Adam Gopnik, *High and Low: Modern Art and Popular Culture* (New York: Museum of Modern Art, 1991), 153–229.

22. Dori Laub, "Bearing Witness, or the Vicissitudes of Listening," in Shoshana Felman and Dori Laub, *Testimony: Crises of Witnessing in Literature, Psychoanalysis, and History* (New York: Routledge, 1992), 57.

23. For a full elaboration of this kind of "side-shadowed" history-telling, see Michael Andre Bernstein, *Foregone Conclusions: Against Apocalyptic History* (Berkeley: University of California Press, 1994).

24. Though Spiegelman wrote and conceived of *Maus* as a single work from the beginning, he agreed to allow Pantheon Books to divide it into two volumes, the first published in 1986. This was partly to preempt possible copy-cat "comics" and animated cartoons by those familiar with the sections of *Maus* already published in *Raw Comics,* the journal Spiegelman and his wife, Françoise Mouly, coedit.

25. Kaplan, "Theweleit and Spiegelman," 162.

26. See Nancy Miller's deeply insightful essay, "Cartoons of the Self: Portrait of the Artist as a Young Murderer—Art Spiegelman's *Maus*," *M/e/a/n/i/n/g* (Fall 1992): 49.

27. From author's interview with Spiegelman.

28. Adam Gopnik, "Comics and Catastrophe," *New Republic,* June 22, 1987, 33.

29. Robert Storr, "Making Maus," pamphlet for projects room exhibition, Museum of Modern Art, 1.

30. Jonathan Rosen, "The Trivialization of Tragedy," *culturefront* (Winter 1997): 85.

31. Letters, *New York Times Book Review*, December 29, 1991, 4.

32. Miller, "Cartoons of the Self," 46.

"The Language of Dollars"

Multilingualism and the Claims of English *in* Hasidic Tales of the Holocaust

ALAN ROSEN

Introduction

This essay assumes that, in two significant and related domains—
American literary history on the one hand and Holocaust writing on the
other—the position of English is contested, uncertain, and undergoing
transformation. In American letters, scholars have noted the almost ex-
clusive attention given to English-language writing in recent accounts of
literary history, and they have attempted to redress this predicament by
attending to American literature written in languages other than English. According to this view, works written in America in Spanish,
French Creole, Chinese, Norwegian, and Yiddish, among others, are
crucial to include in the canon of American literature.[1] While those who
propose this revision assert that works in English should remain integral
to this canon, the precise cultural position of English is left unclear; one
cannot take for granted that English is the language that essentially represents American literature.[2]

Writing on the Holocaust, in contrast, conventionally positions English on the margins: few would presume that English, a primary language of neither victim nor persecutor, is a language essential to representing the Holocaust. And indeed, during the war years and in their aftermath, the bulk of writing on the Holocaust was in Yiddish, Hebrew, German, and other continental European tongues.[3] When claims were made for a language or languages appropriate to responding to these events, English was rarely if ever deemed a front-runner.[4] Yet in the past few decades writing on the Holocaust has turned with increasing frequency to English, such that, in most types[5] of literary production, the majority of material on the Holocaust has come to appear in English. Moreover, parallel to this escalating production of material in English, claims have even been advanced that English is the preferred language in which to write about the Holocaust.[6]

These two tendencies, then, pull in contrary directions. In the first case, English, formerly entrenched as the primary tongue of America, has been deposed from a singular position of authority; in the second case, English, an outsider to the Holocaust and the responses to it, has been conscripted as a central language. As if to compensate for a reversal in fortunes, English has been recruited to tend to the Holocaust at the same time that its preeminent stature in American letters has been challenged.

Yaffa Eliach's *Hasidic Tales of the Holocaust,* an English-language text that incorporates intensive multilingual concerns, simultaneously anticipates, engages, and contravenes both trends.[7] Drawing on a variety of languages, Eliach and her students at Brooklyn College interviewed Jewish survivors of the Holocaust from approximately 1974 to 1981; Eliach then translated, edited, and rewrote the material of the interviews into a "unified form" of eighty-nine tales. She arranged the tales in four sections, with the first three sections narrating events that took place during the Holocaust, the final section those occurring in its aftermath. Most of the tales are set in Poland, Russia, Germany, and Austria, with a smaller number in the last section taking place in postwar America. Though the interviews were conducted in multiple languages, Eliach rendered the tales derived from the interviews exclusively in English.

Although Eliach's project progresses from a multilingual universe to a monolingual one, I will argue that, by making explicit its foundational ties to multilingual traditions even while enshrining an English-only narrative, *Hasidic Tales* anticipates the present critique of an English monolingualism. And, while seeming to acquiesce in the current trend by writing in English about the Holocaust, *Hasidic Tales* stages scenes of linguistic exchange in the tales that interrogate the status of English and incorporate its unstable position into the representation of the Holocaust.

More Than Nine Languages

In the foreword to *Hasidic Tales*, Eliach makes multilingualism a key programmatic feature. "The original interviews [on which the tales are based]," she writes, "were conducted in more than nine languages and numerous dialects."[8] While Eliach never fully explicates the significance of the multilingual basis, the multiplicity of languages appears to authorize the tales, positing a kind of primal linguistic verisimilitude to counteract the dislocated venue (America) and language (English) in which the tales have ultimately been rendered. In other words, given that America lies at such a geographic and cultural distance from the setting in which the Holocaust took place, and given that English was a language neither of victim nor of persecutors, the plethora of languages, Eliach seems to be saying, may restore some sense of place and hence may facilitate some closer connection to the people who endured the atrocities that occurred there. Whatever distance has been traversed from that time and place, and in spite of the American veneer, Eliach wants to emphasize that her English reworking of the tales has not compromised the voices of those who relate them.

Indeed, Leon Wieseltier, noting the special contributions that *Hasidic Tales* makes to the literature of the Holocaust, speaks of restoring the vital context of Eastern European life: "Eliach has recovered the destruction of the Hasidim of Poland as it was for those who were being destroyed, and she has done so because she knows who they actually were. She knows their philosophical and social and religious particulars, and how they appeared in adversity."[9] The "more than nine languages" seems to go hand in hand with this project of recovery. Moreover, Eliach's reference in her foreword to the plethora of languages probably makes more of the languages than the archive of interviews actually warrants; though many languages were involved, most of the interviews were conducted in

Yiddish or English.[10] That the actual number of interviews in languages other than English may have been quite small makes Eliach's attention to the issue of languages that much more telling.[11]

According to Michael Berenbaum, this attention to the original languages shapes Eliach's strategy of representation. In *Hasidic Tales*, Berenbaum suggests, "each tale is beautifully written and has narrative vitality. Yiddish and many other foreign tongues are captured and transmitted in a literate English that carries a trace of the original language but does not read like an awkward translation."[12] In noting the creative interplay between English and the original languages, Berenbaum is here clearly praising Eliach's balancing act, her ability to fuse Old World with New World, to devise an English that can "carry a trace" without being itself made less "literate"—presumably less beautiful, less aesthetically pleasing, less readable. The stakes of Berenbaum's praise for Eliach's synthesis are heightened when we note that he uses decidedly colonialist terms to characterize her achievement: the original languages "are captured" in English; if they were not quite so domesticated, the foreign tongues could impair her English, undermining the aesthetic effect.

Berenbaum (and perhaps, by implication, Eliach) is not alone, of course, in fearing what can happen to English if a foreign language (particularly Yiddish) leaves too much of an imprint. Kathryn Hellerstein, for instance, in the course of chronicling the "Yiddish voices in American literature," has chastised such notables as Bernard Malamud and Phillip Roth for what she regards as the unseemly manner in which they Yiddishize their English.[13] Closer to the Hasidic orbit, Arthur Green has emphasized how he was at pains to steer clear of "accent" when rendering into English the homilies of a great Hasidic leader, R. Menachem Nahum of Chernobyl. In Green's English rendition, "the hasidic master speaks without a Yiddish accent. He is thus liberated to address his English-reading audience with the message that truly concerns him, that of religious enthusiasm and the spirit of revival. . . . [T]oo rigid an attempt to preserve the original voice of the Yiddish/Hebrew source would lead to a borscht-circuit parody, utterly belying the authors' great seriousness of tone."[14] Accenting here is understood to vulgarize, to contaminate the English, wrenching it inexorably from its appropriate rhetorical register. Indeed, Green's purifying strategy seems to describe that of Eliach as well: even with her desire to celebrate the multilingual universe out of which the tales emerge, in rewriting the tales she too opts for an English without an accent, without that which would most conspicuously testify that the speaker hails from elsewhere.[15]

Eliach also connects multilingualism with genre and gender, two of the most important dimensions of her revisionary project, and dates the connection back to the beginning of the Hasidic movement in the late eighteenth century: "Since most of the [early Hasidic] tales were written in Yiddish, which was the vernacular, as opposed to Hebrew, the language of scholarship, they attracted many women to Hasidism and made Hasidic tales 'best sellers' of their time."[16] For those unfamiliar with the history of Hasidism (and the historiography thereof), Eliach's emphasis on the connection of Hasidism and women seems far-fetched. Hasidism today is rarely viewed as the champion of women's participation in central facets of religious or social life. As part of the ultra-orthodox wing of Jewish religious observance, it rather appears to keep women in the background, with all of the main religious functions, at least in the public sphere, devolving upon men. But Eliach's view of the special draw that Hasidism had for women follows a well-established line of scholarship on the Hasidic movement that found its most important expression in the work of S. A. Horedezky, a twentieth-century Israeli scholar who claimed that Hasidism revolutionized the role of women in religious Judaism. According to Horedecsky, Hasidism elevated women's spiritual experience, made writings (particularly in Yiddish) available to women, and provided opportunities for women to serve as spiritual leaders of Hasidic communities.[17] These claims, including the one concerning the pivotal role of Yiddish writing, have been pointedly challenged, although the main rebuttal came some years after Eliach published her collection.[18] But even in the wake of criticism that voiced skepticism about the central role of Yiddish, other scholars have continued to assert the connection between publication in Yiddish and the audience of women.[19]

For her part, Eliach clearly overstates the case: Hasidic tales were generally published both in Yiddish and in Hebrew, occasionally in bilingual editions, more often under separate covers.[20] So the opposition between Hebrew and Yiddish that Eliach invokes—"most of the tales were written in Yiddish, which was the vernacular, as opposed to Hebrew, the language of scholarship"—is not strictly accurate. And the exact audience of Hasidic literature (or literature about Hasidim) in Yiddish has been (and continues to be) the subject of controversy.[21] But for our purposes, what is crucial is that Eliach views multilingualism at the center of the history—the collecting and editing of Hasidic tales—that she carries forward.

Assuredly, Eliach's provocative observation regarding the historical role of women in Hasidism bears specifically on the nature and evolution of her own collection. Eliach claims—and the stories bear this out—that this particular collection of Hasidic tales is special because "not only Hasidic men but Hasidic women, too, are often protagonists" and "play a major role here, not merely because they are the daughters, sisters, or wives of Hasidic personalities but because of their own faith, convictions, and moral courage."[22] Hence, Eliach's book intensifies what she takes to be the Hasidic movement's foregrounding of women, a prominence that was catalyzed by the importance of the vernacular Yiddish. But the pivotal role that women assume is not simply a shift of focus on Eliach's part (though it is likely that too). Women assume these roles in the tales because, in the terms set forth in *Hasidic Tales*, the Holocaust precipitated a set of unique conditions wherein the usual hierarchies were under siege, the common institutions of authority rendered powerless or paralyzed.

Indeed, in the collection women often replace rebbes as the source of decision and wisdom. In "The Vision of the Red Stars," for instance, the tale begins by having Rebbetzin Bronia Koczicki, on the advice of the Radomsker rebbe, prepare to join her husband in Warsaw, even though to go to Warsaw in 1941 went against her own sense of what was best. At this point in the story, traditional hierarchies are still firmly in place, indeed remain unchallenged, for "who was she, she [Bronia] thought to herself, to question a [rebbe's] advice?" But soon questions do arise. After telling how she dreamed a horrible dream, the tale ends by describing how Bronia reversed her decision, refusing to go to Warsaw, and concludes by quoting her words: "At times one must follow one's own dreams."[23] Subsequent tales show that Bronia's refusal to go to Warsaw was an important step in her surviving the war; her husband, trapped in Warsaw, did not. Hence the intuitive wisdom of a personal dream comes to supplant the learned authority of a rebbe. By 1941, the tale suggests, the usual coordinates can no longer be followed; that shift is signaled by the elevation of women's experience over against the words of male authority.[24]

To be sure, multilingual issues are not always conspicuous in these episodes, though, as we will come to see, they are forcefully present in many. But the issue of languages, already linked by Eliach in her fore-word to women's prominence in the Hasidic movement, shadows the female protagonists of the tales even when the issue itself remains on the margins.

The unusual role of women in Hasidism generally and in *Hasidic Tales* specifically bears on Eliach's own role in the process of obtaining the tales, for Eliach associates the "breakthrough" that enabled the project to come into being with her own role as a woman: "After the students [who were Hasidim] established my credentials I faced no dif-ficulties within the Hasidic community. For a woman, that was an im-portant breakthrough which opened many doors."[25] The breakthrough might well have occurred because, though a religious Jew, Eliach herself is not a Hasid and thus is not a member of the communities from whom she hoped to obtain her material. Nonetheless, it is a breakthrough chiefly because she, a woman, managed to interview Hasidic men — something most women would not be permitted to do, given the prac-tice of many ultra-orthodox men not to converse with women who are not family members.[26] Her own breakthrough then mirrors the break-through of the women who are protagonists in the *Hasidic Tales*. In both cases, women who regularly follow certain rules that orchestrate depen-dent behavior instead act independently, even iconoclastically. In one case — the Hasidic women during the time of the Holocaust — they be-come the subject of chronicles; in the other case — that of Eliach — she herself serves as the chronicler.[27]

The Interview as Urtext

It took a breaking through, then, to circumvent conventional barriers that would have impeded the collection of material. Only by means of these interviews could Eliach chronicle the fate of Eastern European Jewry through the medium of the Hasidic tale. The collection is clearly a synthesis of interview and tale, one that rests on a creative interplay between a plurality of continental languages, on the one hand, and En-glish, on the other. Indeed, the interview distinguishes Eliach's book from most other collections of Hasidic tales, collections that have usu-ally compiled the material from preexisting oral or written sources.[28] Here, interviews serve as a basis for the tales, supplying the larger urtext out of which the tale emerges and from which it derives its authority.

One important assessment of *Hasidic Tales* has missed entirely its composite nature, preferring to treat the collection exclusively as "legend."[29] But for a variety of reasons, the interviews are anything but legendary. Eliach and her students conducted the interviews from 1974 to 1981, years that marked the onset of a serious role for survivor interviews in Holocaust research.[30] Indeed, Eliach's interviews, among the earliest of their kind, served a definite polemical task. In the early 1970s, research on the war years was dominated by historians whose inquiry was exclusively based on Nazi documentation. Eliach established her Center for Holocaust Studies, Documentation and Research in order to undertake the kind of work that would counter the prevailing paradigm. According to Bonnie Gurewitsch, archivist of the center, "Documentation available . . . did not reflect the experiences of either survivors or liberators, but rather the German perspective of the executioner. It was clear that there was a need to seek out eyewitnesses who could testify to the experiences of the victims, as well as of the liberators and other bystanders."[31] The interviews were meant to challenge the monolithic position that historians gave to Nazi documents, offering instead the voice and experience of the victims.[32] This task was hardly simple. As Daniel Goldhagen has recently claimed, the skepticism with which historians of the Holocaust treated the testimony of victims was—and perhaps still is—considerably greater than that which historians generally bring to witness accounts of other events of collective trauma.[33] In the face of such skepticism, it was important to emphasize through every means the intimate link between victim and event. Hence, as the interview attempted to wrest a place for the voice of the victim, we can understand Eliach's insistence on the importance of the languages and dialects of those victims, languages that were part and parcel of the events of the Holocaust.

Eliach's efforts helped to set in motion a focus on the interview in Holocaust research that culminated in the 1980s and 1990s with the Yale Video Archive Project and the work of the Shoah Foundation.[34] Yet there is an extraordinary precedent to Eliach's multilingual interview project: David Boder's "Topical Autobiographies of Displaced People," a project executed between 1945 and 1957. Though driven by different goals in a different era, Boder's project illuminates Eliach's own. In the summer of 1946, psychologist Boder and his staff traveled to Europe to interview victims in the DP camps and what he called "shelterhouses" of Europe. He carried out 109 interviews, 70 of which were eventually transcribed, resulting in a manuscript of over 3,100 pages. Boder, himself an émigré from Latvia, felt that it was imperative to interview the victim/survivors while the memories were fresh and, in addition, to interview victims in "their own language." This equation of language and voice was essential for Boder: "it appears of utmost importance that the impressions still alive in the memories of displaced persons of their sufferings in concentration camps and during their subsequent wandering, be recorded directly not only in their own language but in their own voices."[35] Insisting that the interviews be in the victims' own language was Boder's way to make sure that the victims would speak in their own voice.

Strikingly, the insurmountable multilingual task that faced the interviewer moved Boder to find a more precise technology: "It seems impossible to assume that there were or are enough newspaper correspondents versed in the languages of Russian, Polish, Jewish, French, Latvian, Lithuanian, Dutch, Flemish, and even German sufferers in concentration camps . . . so that such reports could be recorded with sufficient detail and precision for contemporaries as well as posterity by the usual 'paper and pencil' method of interview." Since that is impossible, Boder continues, "the exact recording of their tale in their own voice seems the nearest and most feasible alternative."[36] For Boder, the daunting plurality of languages compels a change in the process of the interview itself.

Despite Boder's insistence on fidelity to original languages as a path toward "the exact recording of their tale," the interviews were printed only in English, disseminated in two different versions: one version was an abridged volume published in 1949 by the University of Illinois Press, entitled *I Did Not Interview the Dead*; the other version was the monumental set of transcriptions. In both, the linguistic plurality at the center of Boder's work remains solely in the indication of the language in which the interview occurred and, at times, in the foreign words that erupt into the English, often moving Boder to list two different words as the best approximation. Thus, his radically multilingual project also devolved into a monolingual artifact. Yet this English-only memorial was clearly far from Boder's ideal: "The work is far from completed," he writes in 1957, noting that "the transcription of all the interviews in their original languages as recorded remains a task for the future."[37] His death four years later kept Boder from completing the envisioned task.

Both Boder and Eliach have at their core the quest for fidelity through languages. And yet in both, paradoxically, there remains a gap between the languages of testimony and the English that narrates that testimony. This gap cuts in several ways. First, the English in which the stories are told remains accountable to the primary languages; Boder and Eliach keep before their reader—through stylistic "traces," through insistent reference to primary sources and their importance—the awareness that English serves to translate not only language but also experience. And second, the gap between languages of testimony and English narration generates a special kind of linguistic elegy: whatever traces there may be in the literate English that Eliach pens, these traces also intimate what has been erased; they convey, in Hana Wirth-Nesher's telling phrase, the "felt presence of an absent source language,"[38] languages that indubitably fuel the tales but which also exist solely as echoes. In this way, the felt echoes of these languages register linguistic losses and memorialize the brutal elimination of an audience for whom the primary languages would have been enough.

This gap, then, defines the multilingual condition of *Hasidic Tales*. As we will see, Eliach, for her part, conscripts a formidable range of strategies in the tales in order to negotiate—to draw attention to as well as to circumvent—this gap.

"Perfect German": Languages in *Hasidic Tales of the Holocaust*

While multiple languages circulate mainly in the urtext of *Hasidic Tales*, the issue of languages also infiltrates the tales themselves in surprising and ironic ways. In the first three sections of *Hasidic Tales*, languages enable survival but also place one in peril. Paradoxically, facility in German either made it possible to pass or allowed for intimate connections with the enemy that proved essential in saving life. Assuredly, for readers of Holocaust literature this paradox is well known, receiving one of its most moving expressions in Primo Levi's essay "Communicating." There he details how surviving in Auschwitz was crucially dependent on one's knowledge of German; those who lacked such knowledge or who spoke a language unrelated to German fared poorly, because they simply could not understand what was asked of them.[39]

Eliach's tales drive home this point, but they also add to it. In one set of stories—"Honor Thy Mother" and "God Is Everywhere . . .

But . . ."—the "special Berlin ring" of Bronia Koczicki's German is a crucial factor in survival.[40] In one instance, while Bronia masquerades as a non-Jew, German soldiers are so impressed with her conversation that, even though they pride themselves on their ability to "sniff out" Jews, they never suspect her, but instead compare Rebbetzin Bronia and her young son, of all things, to "a madonna and child."[41] In another instance Bronia is recognized as a Jew, but her "perfect German" is able to bring admiration from members of the Gestapo and to help procure their collaboration in saving her nieces.[42] Strikingly, even when she is known for the Jew she is, her "perfect German" can seemingly convince Nazis that Jews are not what anti-Semites claim they are. In disguise and out of it, Jews are able to use German for their own purposes, making the lines of demarcation between German and Jew much more difficult to trace.

German again plays this salvific role in the tale where it figures most prominently, "For the Sake of Friendship." Forced into hiding, Rabbi Israel Spira—a great Polish Hasidic leader, often referred to as the Bluzhover rebbe, who is a central figure in Eliach's collection—happens to overhear a conversation in German, remembers the beauty of the German language, and recalls his own facility and the friendship with a German which it garnered him in the prewar days. Compelled to visit the nearby Gestapo office, the rabbi comes face to face with the same friend of prewar days, who, recognizing the rabbi, does everything in his power to help him survive. In terms of the fate of the victim, the rabbi's "perfect command of the German language" thus forged the friendship that now enables survival; in terms of Eliach's narrative strategy, the chance hearing of a German conversation sets in motion the recollection that links past and present, providing the reader with a sense of ironic continuity wherein the German spoken casually in the prewar period comes during the war to mean the difference between life and death.

For German to play such a role also suggests its durability in the midst of the Holocaust, a virtue commentators have often questioned. George Steiner, among others, has asserted that the Nazis debased German during the time of the war to a degree that rendered permanent damage.[43] To be sure, Eliach is not unaware of this side of the equation. Indeed, the Bluzhover rebbe reflects on how strange it is to hear a German spoken "without orders, without commands," as if that kind of imperial German is all that may be left.[44] But in the polyglot world of the

Hasidic Tales, the offense that the Nazis committed against German does not corrupt the German language per se.

This complex representation of German as salvific also implies the rewards of acculturation, the benefits of Jews being able to speak well the languages of the non-Jewish world. Such a facility is usually, of course, associated with Jews who championed Enlightenment principles, seeing integration or assimilation into non-Jewish society as the preferred goal. Clearly, such assimilation was not the aim of the Hasidic Jews who figure centrally in Eliach's tales. It is thus all the more powerful that these Jews, too, benefit from such linguistic facility, suggesting that, in terms of languages, the usual oppositions—between enlightenment and tradition, between secular and religious—do not strictly obtain. It suggests, moreover, that salvation, when it comes, often comes by the apparatus of acculturation, commandeering the very tools that seem to run counter to the Hasidic spirit.[45]

"The Language of Dollars": English and the Holocaust

In the first three sections of *Hasidic Tales of the Holocaust,* then, non-English languages work ironically to further the possibilities of salvation or imperil them. Fittingly, it is only in the volume's fourth section—the one devoted to the postwar period—that English comes to be an active character in the process of representation. Indeed, the first tale in this section, "The Plague of Blood," takes up issues of identity, otherness, and language through the prism of immigration and the shifting position of English. Arriving in New York in 1946, the Bluzhover rebbe is met by an American Jewish soldier, who "pointed out with great pride the Statue of Liberty, which welcomes the immigrants to shores of freedom. He told the rabbi: 'On its pedestal is an inscription written by a Jewish-American poet, Emma Lazarus: "Give me your tired, your poor, your huddled masses yearning to breathe free."' The GI translated the words into Yiddish for the rabbi's benefit."[46]

By framing the tale in the shadow of the Statue of Liberty, Eliach sets the arrival of Holocaust survivors in the context of classic scenes of welcome to America. Yet, making explicit the irony of the scene, Eliach notes how the rebbe reinterprets the poem to bring out the distinctive tragedy of the Holocaust. Survivors are tired, poor, and yearning for freedom, but the few who now come are no longer "masses." "We are remnants," says the rebbe, "a trickle of broken individuals who search for a few moments of peace in this world, who hope to find a few relatives on these shores. For we survived, 'One of a city, and two of a family,'"[47] concludes the rebbe, quoting the Book of Jeremiah and thus linking the fate of the survivors of the Holocaust to the fate of the survivors of the destruction of the first temple almost twenty-five hundred years before. The rebbe uses the words of the ancient text to undercut the modern one, invoking the voice of prophetic lamentation to challenge that of liberal optimism.[48]

This scene is particularly striking in terms of language, for Eliach makes sure to emphasize that the American soldier who serves as the rebbe's guide "translated" Lazarus's "words into Yiddish for the rabbi's benefit." The immigrant himself, Eliach shows us, cannot read the words that are meant to describe his plight and which serve as his welcome to America. The immigrant, in other words, faces an opacity, an English motto that, at least for many like the rebbe, is simply a foreign language. In this immigrant encounter between Holocaust victim and American icon, the English that is designed to appeal to foreigners is itself rendered foreign, in need of translation.[49] In the context of current developments in multilingual America, Mary Louise Pratt has proposed "expunging the term *foreign* to refer to [American] languages other than English."[50] The notion evoked by Eliach of making English itself foreign constitutes a yet more radical revision of America's languages, not so much reclaiming other languages as estranging English.

And yet it is when Lazarus's words are made "foreign" that they can be interpreted properly. By means of the intertextual commentary of the rebbe—through Yiddish translation, set against the Hebrew text of the prophet—Lazarus's English words are reread, thereby proclaiming the distance that lies between the "masses" envisioned some years earlier and the "isolated individual" who now arrives in the wake of the Holocaust.[51]

The surprising opacity of the statue's iconic poem hence generates a fitting response to the legacy of the Shoah. In a later postwar tale, "To Marry a Baker," English is made, not foreign, but rather intimate with Holocaust-era Europe. The story's heroine is a survivor, Tula Friedman, who has a talent for languages and also for telling stories. Seated with Eliach at a bar mitzvah party in Brooklyn, Tula is moved to tell how, while in Auschwitz, her ear was damaged: "She recalled the event," writes Eliach, "blow by blow, in German, Yiddish, Hebrew, and

English, telling it in the appropriate language with direct quotations, describing various episodes related to that beating and its aftermath."[52]

Strikingly, Tula's mode of recounting events of the Holocaust is resolutely mimetic, and it is the multiplicity of languages at her disposal that enables this uncompromising fidelity to the reality of Auschwitz.[53] Even more astonishing is that English is given a role equal to that of the languages central to the Holocaust (German, Yiddish, Hebrew). On some level, this goes against the mimetic grain, since few in Auschwitz knew English; it rather remained on the periphery of the events.[54] But here, in this listing, English aggressively claims a spot for itself as a language of the Holocaust.

There is also a self-reflexive dimension at work in this tale: Tula's linguistic and narrative prowess clearly resembles Eliach's own, yet her tale inverts Eliach's representational strategies. Able to invoke any language she chooses, Tula does what Eliach cannot do in America: she presents the tales in the multiple languages in which they were originally experienced. Nevertheless, the fact that English can assume a place among the most formidable of the languages of the Holocaust strengthens Eliach's own compensatory project, making it seem natural for these tales, set in Europe, to be written in English.

Tula's extraordinary multilingual performance serves as a prelude to the defining event of the tale. As bread is delivered to the tables, Tula reminisces how in the camp she would "dream alot about bread"; she would even dream of marrying a baker "so there would always be an abundance of bread." Other survivors at the table confirm the value and obsession with bread, even though they choose not to eat from the bread in the basket before them on the table. Yet as the waiter attempts to take the apparently unwanted bread, he is asked to leave it: "There is nothing more reassuring in this world," says yet another survivor, "than having a basket of freshly baked bread on the table in front of you."[55]

Bread here serves as a sign of a normal world; superfluous but necessary, its fixed presence at the table testifies to the abundance that America provides over against the deprivation from which the survivors have come. Indeed, Tula's dream of marrying a baker is never literally realized but is symbolically enacted in her "marriage" to America, to the "baker" that provides abundance and normalcy. English enters the story in a similar manner, a language whose very presence reassures one of the power of America, its inclusion in the list of Tula's eminent languages paradoxically signaling the distance that lies between present-day America and Europe of a generation past.

If "The Plague of Blood," set in the shadow of the Statue of Liberty, on the liminal border between America and Europe, showed English to be foreign and only able to register the force of the Holocaust through the filter of Yiddish and Hebrew, and if "To Marry a Baker," set firmly on the soil of America, claims for English unconstrained powers to represent these events, the final tale I will consider, "God Does Not Live Here Anymore," set outside America and on the terrain of the Holocaust, represents English as having both extraordinary powers and definite constraints. It is also the only tale in which English is explicitly viewed as a problem.

Eliach's title of the story focuses on displacement, and, accordingly, the tale conveys a sense of quest for the proper place(s) and language(s) with which to address the Holocaust. Set in Cracow, Poland, in 1979, in the context of an official visit by President Carter's commission on the Holocaust, the events of the tale unfold on the evening of Tisha B'Av, the time designated in the Jewish calendar for commemorating by rites of collective mourning the destruction of the Temple. But, in postwar Cracow, mourning becomes electrifying. A member of the American contingent, Miles Lerman, speaking in English, interrupts the traditional service and proposes instead to put God on trial for the damage rendered in the Holocaust.[56] The scene is linguistically surreal: a Polish Jewish partisan who now lives in America returns to Poland and, instead of speaking Polish or Yiddish, the tongues of postwar Cracow, or Hebrew, the language of prayer, pleads his case against God in English.

Assuredly, Lerman invokes English here to permit the members of the commission, made up of a number of native-born Americans, to understand what he says and to follow the proceedings of the case against God. But that the Americans appropriate the synagogue to carry out their own agenda reinforces the invasive associations around the unlikely use of English. That Lerman's English protest, moreover, arises within the context of an official United States delegation visit gives the prosecution of the case an American seal, as if judgment can be exacted only under the jurisdiction of American authority.

Eliach's narrative delicately negotiates the subversive events and the association with English. She lets Lerman set forth the argument, as he counters the "How"/*Echah* with which the Book of Lamentations begins with his own human (and English) "How" — "how could you [God] stay here [in Cracow, in Poland, in Europe, in the synagogue?] when next door are Auschwitz and Plaszow?"[57] If the questions are to the point, Eliach shows that the English in which he voices them is distinctly "foreign," distinctly out of place, even opaque: "The holy ark remained sealed like the faces of the old people, remnants of Cracow's Jews, listening to the foreign language that they did not understand."[58] That the native audience cannot understand what is being said in their own milieu hints at the linguistic absurdity of Lerman's endeavor. Moreover, Eliach's simile, likening the holy ark containing the Torah to the uncomprehending faces, intensifies the skepticism around English, implying that English does not partake of holiness but rather belongs to the realm of the profane.

At the end of the tale, the profane and intrusive nature of English becomes clear as Eliach quotes a question asked by one of the Cracovian Jews: "What did your American friend say in the language of dollars?"[59] English now becomes explicitly characterized as inappropriate, a language of the street and market rather than of the synagogue and religious court.[60] The opacity of English comes out of a misapplication, a confusion of registers. And, seemingly out of place and misapplied, English cannot, according to the terms of the tale, properly address the terms of God's displacement. For Eliach gives the Cracovian the final word, responding to Lerman's accusations: God did not stay in one place and the people go to another; God is with the people, displaced from the synagogue that they once shared.

Burdened with associations of the profane, the market, and the absurd, English seems at best intrusive, at worse fallacious. Trying to usurp the stage in an arena central to Jewish life (the Rema synagogue) and to the legacy of the Holocaust (Cracow/Auschwitz), English is put in its place, reassigned to the margins. To bring the terrible events of the Holocaust to America and render them in English may be one thing, but to try to take English, even (or especially) under the auspices of the American president, to the site of the Holocaust itself is quite another. In Eliach's tale, then, the question of God's place is displaced onto the question of English. Moreover, this tale, perhaps more than any other in the collection, leads us to wonder about Eliach's English as well, to feel the irony of her mobilizing English to encompass the many languages in which these tales were told.

And yet there is a way that the nature of this tale vindicates, at least to some degree, the use of English to address the Holocaust: the very rapscallion nature of English may well enable it to defy traditional modes; of all the languages at his disposal, in other words, Lerman may have chosen English as the language most apt to pose questions that go against the grain. Its very intrusiveness, its coming from the outside—geographically, culturally, religiously—may have energized Lerman's defiant questions, having them, at least to some ears, dwarf any answers that can be supplied.

Conclusion

Hasidic Tales is not, to be sure, the only work that problematizes the relation of English to the Holocaust by emphasizing multilingual strategies.[61] But no other work, so far as I am aware, demands that English assume so many contrasting positions in relation to this event—positions of weakness and strength, of opacity and transparency, of dependence on other languages and assertions of independence from them. These three tales play out a variety of options whereby English is estranged, wrenched out of or freed from its taken-for-granted roles. Notably, the tales accomplish this by progressively taking English through a journey into and out of America, from immigrant to resident to ambassador. On the face of it, this dynamic makes English increasingly into a language authorized to engage the Holocaust. But at each point English is made to do something more, or less, than it was expected to, and this inflation or deflation thematizes the anomalous role of English in relation to the Holocaust.

Finally, in terms of American literary history, *Hasidic Tales* is remarkable as a uniformly English-language text that displays so incisively the multilingual context that makes possible such tales. For *Hasidic Tales* simultaneously conforms to monolingual pressures and contests them, eliminates a play of languages only to filter them back in. On one level, then, *Hasidic Tales of the Holocaust* both allows for and, in some ways, invites the fantasy of an America fully at home with English—an English, moreover, that is spoken by everyone (or almost everyone), everywhere, and that is prepared to address any experience imaginable, including the Holocaust. On a second level, however, *Hasidic Tales* exposes the compromised postures that English assumes in its quest to master every experience and dramatizes its uncertain—that is, shifting, decentered, opaque, misaligned—status. Yet this predicament may be salutary. By constantly embedding English in the soil of originary languages, by showing how it records echoes and bears traces, by letting English serve as a foreign tongue—foreign to much of America, to the world at large, and to the event it tries to encompass—*Hasidic Tales* exemplifies an English-language text that speaks the idiom of multilingual America.

Notes

I wish to thank the following colleagues for their readings of and comments on various stages of this essay: Ruth Clements, Bonnie Gurewitsch, Michael Kramer, Herb Levine, and Nehemiah Polen. In addition to her careful reading of the essay, Bonnie Gurewitsch, in her capacity as archivist at the Museum of Jewish Heritage in New York, made available aural tapes of selected interviews that served as a basis for the tales in *Hasidic Tales of the Holocaust.*

I have benefited greatly from a conversation with Yaffa Eliach, who, upon my request, also generously provided numerous reviews of *Hasidic Tales of the Holocaust.*

I first presented this material at the 1999 MLA session chaired by Hana Wirth-Nesher on "Representation of Other Discourse in Multilingual America" and, I am grateful for that opportunity as well.

1. Werner Sollors sets forth this position in his introduction to a collection of essays that includes critical writing on American literature in these languages. While guided by Sollors's work on these issues, I am not fully persuaded by his "English Plus" formula, presuming a harmonious fusion of English with non-English tongues in the study of American literature. In the aftermath of such a transformed canon, the ensuing position of English writing seems to me much less stable than he envisions. See "Introduction: After the Culture Wars; or, From 'English Only' to 'English Plus,'" in *Multilingual America: Transnationalism, Ethnicity, and the Languages of American Literature*, ed. Werner Sollors (New York: New York University Press, 1998), 1–13. The essays in the collection can be supplemented by the preceding 1997 INTERROADS Internet discussion on the topic of English and multilingualism. An essay by Sollors (an earlier version of his introduction for *Multilingual America*) initiates the discussion, followed by invited responses, list responses, a counterresponse from Sollors, and, finally, a postscript from Robert Allison. See http://www.georgetown.edu/crossroads/interroads/. Marc Shell's even more encompassing manifesto, arguing for a wholesale reconsideration of American history that would take seriously its polyglot self-perception and aspirations, appeared some years earlier. See "Babel in America; or, The Politics of Language Diversity in

the United States," *Critical Inquiry* 20 (1993): 103–27. Sollors and Shell codirect Harvard University's Longfellow Institute, which is dedicated to reclaiming and publishing the non-English contributions of American literature.

2. Part 6 of *Multilingual America,* entitled "Multilingualism and English-Language Writing," briefly addresses these issues. See pp. 311–12. Although concerned with global rather than national implications, colonial and postcolonial criticism has also addressed the hegemony of English and attempted to work out what a "decentered" English would (or does) look like. See Robert Phillipson, *Linguistic Imperialism* (Oxford: Oxford University Press, 1992); and Bill Ashcroft, Gareth Griffiths, and Helen Tiffin, *The Empire Writes Back: Theory and Practice in Post-Colonial Literatures* (London: Routledge, 1989), particularly chapter 2, "Re-placing Language: Textual Strategies in Post-Colonial Writing."

3. In a bibliography on the Warsaw ghetto published in 1953, for example, Philip Friedman refers to some six thousand items on the Warsaw ghetto; only several hundred of them, he notes, were available in English—original or translation. "The Bibliography of the Warsaw Ghetto (on the Tenth Anniversary of the Uprising in the Warsaw Ghetto)," *Jewish Book Annual* 11 (1952–53): 121–28. For further confirmation of this predicament, see the Yad Vashem–YIVO Bibliographical Series; perusal of even the initial volume, completed in 1959, brings home this point. See Jacob Robinson and Philip Friedman, *Guide to Jewish History under Nazi Impact* (Jerusalem: Yad Vashem and Yivo, 1960).

That said, the secondary or tertiary status of English in relation to the Holocaust does not mean that there was not English-language writing at the early stages. For many examples thereof see Jacob Robinson, *The Holocaust and After: Sources and Literature in English,* Sidrah Bibliografit Meshtefet, no. 12 (Jerusalem: Israel Universities Press, 1973). Having compiled a vast inventory of English sources up through its date of publication, Robinson nonetheless feels obliged to spell out in an afterword that attention to English-language sources cannot constitute serious study of the Holocaust.

4. Writing in the 1946 edition of the *Jewish Book Annual*—a trilingual American journal initiated in 1942 as a response to the perilous situation of European Jewry—Yudel Mark assumes that Yiddish is the appropriate language in which to render the events of the period of Treblinka. Even in the late 1960s, Israel Knox, introducing an authoritative English-language anthology of primary sources in translation on the Holocaust, emphasizes that the principal languages are Hebrew and Yiddish. See *Anthology of Holocaust Literature,* ed. Jacob Glatstein, Israel Knox, and Samuel Margoshes (New York: Atheneum, 1968). I comment on Knox's symptomatic response and other critical approaches to the position of English in relation to the Holocaust in "The Language of Survival: English as Metaphor in Spiegelman's *Maus,*" *Prooftexts: A Journal of Jewish Literary History* 15 (1995): 249–63, reprinted in *Considering Maus,* ed. Deborah Geiss (Urbana: University of Illinois Press, forthcoming).

5. And not, to be sure, only in literary production. For example, of the 50,686 interviews conducted by the Shoah Foundation in the past seven years, English has served as the primary language in almost 49 percent. Russian is a distant second (nearly 14 percent) and Hebrew third (close to 12 percent). I am grateful to Michael Engel, the foundation's associate executive director, for providing me with a list of the primary interview languages.

6. In Anne Michaels's 1995 novel, *Fugitive Pieces,* the protagonist, a Polish Jewish survivor, chooses English as the language in which to write his lyrical memoir, explaining that he wishes to write the "events of my childhood in a language foreign to their happening" (110). I analyzed this surprising predilection in "Strong Enough to Carry Experience: Writing about the Holocaust in English," a paper delivered in June 2000 at the United States Holocaust Memorial Museum.

7. Yaffa Eliach, *Hasidic Tales of the Holocaust* (New York: Oxford, 1982). All subsequent citations refer to this edition.

8. Ibid., xxiii.

9. Leon Wieseltier, "The Life before the Death," review of *Hasidic Tales of the Holocaust, New Republic* 188 (21 February 1983): 38.

10. Personal communication from Bonnie Gurewitsch, an associate of Eliach's at the Center for Holocaust Studies. Gurewitsch is presently an archivist at the Museum of Jewish Heritage, New York, the institution that now houses the collection formerly at the Center for Holocaust Studies. See also note 15, below.

11. Eliach's attention to multilingual issues is also of a piece with the history of Jewish writing. For reflections on this theme, see Baal-Makhshoves, "One Literature in Two Languages," trans. Hana Wirth-Nesher, reprinted in *What Is Jewish Literature?*, ed. and intro. Hana Wirth-Nesher (Philadelphia: Jewish Publication Society, 1994), 69–77; and Shmuel Niger, *Bilingualism in the History of Jewish Literature,* trans. Joshua Fogel (New York: University Press of America, 1990).

12. Michael Berenbaum, review of *Hasidic Tales and the Holocaust, Simon Wiesenthal Annual* (1983): 237.

13. Kathryn Hellerstein, "Yiddish Voices in American English," in *The State of the Language,* ed. Leonard Michaels and Christopher Ricks (Berkeley: University of California Press, 1980). Hellerstein does not, however, simply rule out such "Yiddish voices"; she rather argues that some authors (Cynthia Ozick, for example) integrate them more authentically than those who, to her mind, exploit Yiddish for sentimentality.

14. Arthur Green, "On Translating Hasidic Homilies," *Prooftexts: A Journal of Jewish Literary History* 3 (1983): 67. Green's translation appears in *Upright Practices: The Light of the Eyes,* by R. Menachem Nahum of Chernobyl (New York: Paulist Press, 1982).

15. To be sure, perception of accent is also in the eye (and/or ear) of the beholder: Bonnie Gurewitsch has communicated to me that she believes the

English of *Hasidic Tales* is clearly accented. For a searching analysis of the issue of perception of accents, see Mari J. Matsuda, "Voices of America: Accent, Antidiscrimination Law, and a Jurisprudence for the Last Reconstruction," *Yale Law Journal* 100 (1991): 1329–1407. While Matsuda particularly argues for legal reform with regard to cases that discriminate against accent—for example, the refusal to hire an otherwise competent candidate as a teller because his (substantial or minimal) Filipino accent was perceived by his Hawaiian interviewers as too great a liability—she addresses general issues and cites an extraordinary range of pertinent studies.

16. *Hasidic Tales*, xvi. On the history and context of Hasidic tales, including issues of audience and language, see Joseph Dan, *Ha-Sipur ha-Hasidi* (Jerusalem: Bet Hotsa'ah Keter Yerushalayim, 1975); Mendel Piekarz, *Hasidut Braslav* (Jerusalem: Mosad Byalik, 1972); Gedaliah Nigal, *Ha-siporet ha-Hasidit toledotei-hah ve-nose'eihah* (Jerusalem: Hotsa'at Mosad ha-Ravkuk, 1981); and Martin Buber, *Tales of the Hasidim: The Early Masters* (New York: Schocken, 1975), preface and introduction.

17. For Horedezky's view, see *Ha-Hasidut ve-ha-Hasidim*, 2nd ed. (Tel Aviv: n.p., 1943), and the abridged English version, *Leaders of Hasidism* (London: Hasefer Agency for Literature, 1928).

18. Most trenchantly, Ada Rapoport-Albert disputes Horedezky's contention that Hasidism provided Jewish women with religious opportunities previously unavailable. See "On Women in Hasidism: S. A. Horodecky and The Maid of Ludmir Tradition," in *Jewish History: Essays in Honour of Chimen Abramsky*, ed. Ada Rapoport-Albert and Steven J. Zipperstein (London: Peter Halban, 1988). Nehemiah Polen has, however, argued that, while offering a necessary corrective, Rapoport-Albert takes things too far. See "Miriam's Dance: Radical Egalitarianism in Hasidic Thought," *Modern Judaism* 12 (1992): 1–21. In distinguishing different currents within Hasidism, Naftali Loewenthal has recently suggested that the Habad movement, from the outset but increasingly in the twentieth century, established a full-fledged spiritual role for women in Hasidism. See his "Women and the Dialectic of Spirituality in Hasidism," in *Within Hasidic Circles: Studies in Hasidism in Memory of Mordecai Wilensky*, ed. Immanuel Etkes et al. (Jerusalem: Bialik Institute, 1999), 7–65.

19. David Roskies, for instance, sees the Yiddish text of Rebbe Nachman of Breslov's bilingual *Sippurey Mayses* as specifically directed toward women: "Bilingual texts were always aimed at a differentiated Jewish audience. Because Hebrew remained the language of the learned Jewish male, the Hebrew record of Nachman's stories, parables, and dreams was more complete and reliable than the Yiddish original. The Yiddish was for proste mentsn, the simple folk, especially women." *A Bridge of Longing: The Lost Art of Yiddish Storytelling* (Cambridge: Harvard University Press, 1995), 30. *Sippurey Mayses* was first published in 1815, virtually at the same time as *Shivhe Habescht*. Roskies's reference to

"proste mentsn" is taken from Rabbi Noson's Yiddish preface to the *Sippurey Mayses*. In an influential study of the relation between Yiddish and Hebrew writing in the nineteenth century, originally published in 1973 but reissued in 1996, Dan Miron believes that writing in Yiddish was directed toward women: "True, Yiddish literature never occupied a high position in the cultural hierarchy of traditional Ashkenazic Jewry. It always addressed itself to the unlearned, particularly to women." He goes on to link Hasidic tales to this tradition of earlier Yiddish literature: to this tradition "was added toward the end of the eighteenth century and at the beginning of the nineteenth the immensely popular literature of hasidic legend and hagiography, which was also written (in part) in Yiddish." *A Traveler Disguised: A Study in the Rise of Modern Yiddish Fiction in the Nineteenth Century* (New York: Schocken, 1973), 2.

20. The first printing of the first collection of Hasidic tales—*Shivhe HaBescht* (In Praise of the Baal Shem Tov)—was in Hebrew (in 1814), but three Yiddish editions of the tales were soon published (between 1815 and 1817). See Murray Jay Rosman, *Founder of Hasidism: In Quest of the Historical Ba'al Shem Tov* (Berkeley: University of California Press, 1996), for a list of earliest editions. Yiddish editions thereafter appeared throughout the nineteenth century.

21. For a broader assessment of this controversy, see Iris Parush, "The Politics of Literacy: Women and Foreign Languages in Jewish Society of Nineteenth-Century Eastern Europe," *Modern Judaism* 15 (1995): 183–206; Shaul Stampfer, "Gender Differentiation and Education of the Jewish Woman in Nineteenth-Century Eastern Europe," *Polin* 7 (1992): 63–87; Miron, *A Traveler Disguised;* and Roskies, *Bridge of Longing.* As the titles of their articles indicate, Parush and Stampfer emphasize the nineteenth and early twentieth centuries; they nonetheless address issues relevant to those of Eliach. Stampfer brings numerous examples to show the gender divide between men and women in terms of reading and study in Hebrew and Yiddish. He argues, however, that the linguistic divide did not necessarily translate into an inferior position for women's study of tradition. Parush too emphasizes the gender divide between Hebrew and Yiddish and, contra Stampfer, believes that the divide operated (and was designed to operate) to restrict women's engagement with tradition. But her concerns lie in broader view of the significance of languages for Jewish women and modern Judaism.

22. *Hasidic Tales*, xxii.

23. Ibid., 23–24.

24. The response of women during the Holocaust, as well as women's postwar writing about the Holocaust, has received significant attention in recent years. For a foundational study see Madeline Heineman, *Gender and Destiny: Women Writers and the Holocaust* (New York: Greenwood, 1986). For a range of writing, narrative and analytical, that addresses response both during and after, see *Different Voices: Women and the Holocaust,* ed. Carol Rittner and John

Roth (New York: Paragon, 1993). Most recently, see Judith Tydor Baumel, *Double Jeopardy: Women and the Holocaust* (Portland: Vallentine Mitchell, 1998); Brana Gurewitsch, *Mothers, Sisters, Resisters: Oral Histories of Women Who Survived the Holocaust* (Tuscaloosa: University of Alabama Press, 1998); and S. Lillian Kremer, *Women's Holocaust Writing: Memory and Imagination* (Lincoln: University of Nebraska Press, 1999). This literature can be viewed in the context of women's response to crisis and catastrophe in Jewish history. For a focus on women's special initiative, see Shlomo Noble, "The Jewish Woman in Medieval Martyrology," in *Studies in Jewish Bibliography, History and Literature in Honor of I. Edw. Kiev,* ed. Charles Berlin (New York: Ktav 1971), 347–55; and Ivan Marcus, "From Politics to Martyrdom: Shifting Paradigms in the Hebrew Narratives of the 1096 Crusade Riots," *Prooftexts: A Journal of Jewish Literary History* 2 (1982): 40–52. Finally, see David Roskies's brief comments on the paucity of material detailing Jewish women's responses to catastrophe in *Against the Apocalypse: Responses to Catastrophe in Modern Jewish Culture* (Cambridge: Harvard University Press, 1984) and in *The Literature of Destruction* (Philadelphia: Jewish Publication Society, 1989). One can find in this literature intermittent but suggestive references to the role of languages in relation to women. See also above, note 18.

25. *Hasidic Tales,* xxii.

26. Eliach has said that she made an initial agreement with the Bluzhover rebbe, the dominating figure in *Hasidic Tales,* that her male graduate students would conduct the interviews with him, during which time Eliach would be in attendance, listening. At an early meeting, however, Eliach had an opportunity to demonstrate facility in traditional texts, and her facility prompted the rebbe to change his mind and permit her to conduct the interviews herself. I am indebted to Nehemiah Polen for his initial reference to this incident, and to Yaffa Eliach for recounting it in detail in a personal communication (July 3, 2000).

27. Eliach's task of chronicling the independent role of traditional women is evident as well in her massive study, *There Once Was a World: A Nine-Hundred-Year Chronicle of the Shtetl of Eishyshok* (Boston: Little, Brown, 1998).

28. An exception is Jerome Mintz, *Legends of the Hasidim: An Introduction to Hasidic Culture and Oral Tradition in the New World* (Chicago: University of Chicago Press, 1968). Styled as an anthropological study, the interview for Mintz is fieldwork. Although Eliach implicitly shares some of Mintz's anthropological strategies and clientele, she is involved in a different form of cultural mediation. In her foreword to *Hasidic Tales,* Eliach traces her antecedents (I believe correctly) to Buber, Peretz, Kafka, and Agnon—literary (and, in the case of Buber, philosophical) figures who collected Hasidic tales and rewrote them for non-Hasidic, often secular, audiences. Among the vast commentary on such projects, Sander Gilman's remarks on Aron Marcus, Buber, Czech writer Jiri Langer, and Kafka come closest to paralleling my own approach. See *Jewish*

Self-Hatred: Anti-Semitism and the Hidden Language of the Jew (Baltimore: Johns Hopkins University Press, 1986), 271–86. David Jacobson terms such projects "neo-Hasidic" (he is not the first to do so); the issues that inform his discussion under this rubric, however, feel distant from those most crucial for considering Eliach's collection. See *Modern Midrash: The Retelling of Traditional Jewish Narratives by Twentieth-Century Hebrew Writers* (Albany: SUNY Press, 1987), especially chapter 1, "Neo-Hasidic Tales: Micha Yosef Berdyczewski and Y. L. Peretz."

29. James Young, *Writing and Rewriting the Holocaust: Narrative and the Consequences of Interpretation* (Bloomington: University of Indiana Press, 1988), 40–43. Young comments on *Hasidic Tales* in the chapter entitled "From Witness to Legend: Tales of the Holocaust." Regrettably, he presumes *Hasidic Tales*, because it often features Hasidic Jews, to recuperate a traditionally conservative theological agenda—"justifying the ways of divine providence"—and he interprets the tales accordingly (he actually refers only to a single tale, the first in the collection). While some tales can be read in this way, however, many (including those I focus on in this essay) can be seen to challenge such a view. Young's subtext here, I would argue, is that "legend," because unconcerned with the events themselves, bolsters "divine providence," a view that does not confront the cruelest dimensions of the Holocaust. Hence, Young's model leaves little room for the genre of interview to play a fundamentally constitutive role.

30. To be sure, interviews are among the earliest postwar written responses. I refer below to what is perhaps the greatest of these projects, that of David Boder. But the 1970s appear pivotal, due in part, to be sure, to the maturing of the field of oral history, but also to the intensifying dissatisfaction with models of description and explanation of the Holocaust based almost exclusively on Nazi documents. I develop this briefly in the body of this essay.

31. *Center for Holocaust Studies Newsletter* 3 (1991): 3.

32. Eliach also clearly articulates this polemical agenda on behalf of the victims in the "Discussion" section that follows her 1980 lecture, "Jewish Tradition in the Life of the Concentration Camp Inmate," in *The Nazi Concentration Camps: Proceedings of the Fourth Yad Vashem International Historical Conference, Jerusalem, January, 1980*, ed. Y. Gutman and A. Saf (Jerusalem: Yad Vashem, 1984), esp. 243–47.

33. Daniel Jonah Goldhagen, "The Paradigm Challenged: Victim Testimony, Critical Evidence, and New Perspectives in the Study of the Holocaust," *Tikkun* 13 (1998): 40–47. Goldhagen persuasively, if briefly, contrasts Holocaust historiography with that of the Soviet gulag. Goldhagen's list of historians includes Martin Broszat, Eberhard Jackel, Hans Mommsen, Raul Hilberg, Christopher Browning, and Istvan Deak. In contrast, H. G. Adler, Israel Gutman, and Hermann Langbein draw heavily on survivor accounts. Although Goldhagen does not refer to Saul Friedlander, Friedlander's recent work, attempting to integrate his own perspective as a survivor with critical history of

the Holocaust, would seem both symptom and revision of the trend Goldhagen takes to task. See *Nazi Germany and the Jews*, vol. 1, *The Years of Persecution, 1933–1939* (New York: HarperCollins, 1997), particularly Friedlander's polemical comments on pp. 2 and 5.

34. The archive at Yale has nourished interpretations by a number of important scholars. Geoffrey Hartman, long associated with the Yale Video Archive, reflects on the contributions of oral history in *The Longest Shadow* (Bloomington: Indiana University Press, 1997). In *Holocaust Testimonies: The Ruins of Memory* (New Haven: Yale University Press, 1991), Lawrence Langer bases his analysis on material from this archive as well. See also Shoshana Felman and Dori Laub, *Testimony: Crises of Witnessing in Literature, Psychoanalysis, and History* (New York: Routledge, 1992), where material from the archives gives rise to reflections pedagogic and psychoanalytic. This said, the success of the oral history endeavor has also bequeathed its own set of problems. Dominick LaCapra, for instance, can refer to "testimony" and problematically assume that what is meant is videotaped interviews of survivor accounts. While these accounts rightly come under the rubric of testimony, they do not exhaust the category; written memoirs and, of course, personal oral communication antedate video accounts and constitute a major source of Holocaust testimony. That a scholar as thoughtful and industrious as LaCapra could inadvertently make such an assumption suggests the potential extent of the problem. See Dominick LaCapra, *History and Memory after Auschwitz* (Ithaca: Cornell University Press, 1998), 10–11. For a more extended critique of these issues, see my essay "The Specter of Eloquence: Reading the Survivor's Voice," in *Celebrating Elie Wiesel: Stories, Essays, Reflections,* ed. Alan Rosen (Notre Dame: University of Notre Dame Press, 1998), 41–56.

35. David Boder, "Topical Autobiographies of Displaced People Recorded Verbatim in Displaced Persons Camps, with a Psychological and Anthropological Analysis" (Chicago: David Boder, 1950–57), 3161. The sixteen volumes were mimeographed and put on microfilm but never published. In 1949 Boder published a one-volume abridgment, *I Did Not Interview the Dead* (Urbana: University of Illinois Press, 1949). His introduction to this volume served as a basis for his remarks in the addenda to "Topical Autobiographies" and elaborates on the issue of language and languages:

> I endeavored to keep the material as near to the text of the original narratives as the most elementary rules of grammar would permit. I kept in mind that most of the displaced persons had spent their time of imprisonment in camps among inmates of divergent tongues and dialects. For years they had been deprived of all reading matter (even prayer books), of religious services, of radios, and often of opportunities to talk with others in their own tongue. It is no wonder that their

language habits show evidence of trauma. Moreover, the emotional states aroused by the recollection of episodes of such unparalleled stress definitely contribute to the peculiar verbal structure and the discrepancies in time and place found on occasion in the narratives. Words describing the emotional range in the voices of the narrators, and their gestures at the time of speaking, have been italicized and enclosed in parentheses. Editorial explanations are enclosed in brackets. (xiii–xiv)

A second abridgment of Boder's interviews has recently been published under the title *Fresh Wounds: Early Narratives of Holocaust Survival,* ed. Donald L. Niewyk (Chapel Hill: University of North Carolina Press, 1998). In the light of Boder's comments and the overall thrust of his project, it is regrettable that Niewyk has chosen to filter out what does not conform to standard English—what Boder referred to as the "peculiar verbal structure." For Niewyk's comments on his editorial decisions regarding language, see p. 6.

The seventy interviews of Boder's "Topical Autobiographies" are now accessible on the World Wide Web (http://voices.iit.edu/), sponsored by the Illinois Institute of Technology, Boder's former employer. While the site indicates that at some point in the future it hopes to make available the aural interviews in the original languages, it too presents exclusively the English transcripts. The tapes in the original languages are available at the Library of Congress and in the archive of the United States Holocaust Memorial Museum.

36. "Topical Autobiographies," 3160.

37. Ibid.

38. Wirth-Nesher develops this evocative notion in commenting on Henry Roth's use of English in *Call It Sleep.* See "Between Mother Tongue and Native Language: Multilingualism in Henry Roth's *Call It Sleep,*" *Prooftexts: A Journal of Jewish Literary History* 10 (1990): 297–312. Whereas Wirth-Nesher invokes this notion to refer to a presence that never was, I draw on it to commemorate a phenomenon that once existed. That said, the experience is similar.

39. Primo Levi, *The Drowned and the Saved,* trans. Raymond Rosenthal (New York: Vintage, 1989), 88–104. "We immediately realized, from our very first contacts with the contemptuous men with the black patches [the SS], that knowing or not knowing German was a watershed. Those who understood them and answered in an articulate manner could establish the semblance of a human relationship. To those who did not understand them the black men [again, the SS] reacted in a manner that astonished and frightened us; . . . whoever did not understand or speak German was barbarian by definition; if he insisted on expressing himself in his own language—indeed, his nonlanguage— he must be beaten into silence and put back in his place, pulling, carrying, and pushing, because he was not a Mensch, not a human being" (91–92).

40. This is the same Bronia referred to in the tale "The Vision of the Red Stars." She is featured in a number of tales and cited regularly by Eliach as a interviewee. She appears both under the name Koczicki and, having later remarried (to Rabbi Israel Spira), under the name Bronia Spira.

41. *Hasidic Tales,* 26. Lenore Weitzman has recently discussed the crucial role of language in "passing" during the Holocaust. See "Living on the Aryan Side in Poland: Gender, Passing, and the Nature of Resistance," in *Women in the Holocaust,* ed. Dalia Ofer and Lenore J. Weitzman (New Haven: Yale University Press, 1998), 187–222, esp. 211–12. Facility, accent, and passive knowledge of a language—particularly here German and Polish—were salient factors. Weitzman's premises regarding the facility with languages of Polish Jewry are, however, impressionistic. A more detailed and rigorous account can be found in Chone Shmeruk, "Hebrew-Yiddish-Polish: A Trilingual Jewish Culture," in *The Jews of Poland between Two World Wars,* ed. Yisrael Gutman et al. (Hanover, N.H.: University Press of New England, 1989).

42. *Hasidic Tales,* 31.

43. For scholarship and reflection on the German language and the Holocaust, see Victor Klemperer, *LTI: Notizbuch eines Philologen* (Berlin: Aufbau Verlag, 1947); Nachman Blumental, "On the Nazi Vocabulary," *Yad Vashem Studies* 1 (1957): 49–66; George Steiner, "The Hollow Miracle," in *Language and Silence: Essays on Language, Literature, and the Inhuman* (New York: Atheneum, 1977); Shoshana Felman, "Poetry and Testimony: Paul Celan, or the Accidenting of Aesthetics," in Felman and Laub, *Testimony,* 25–42; and Sara Horowitz, "The Night Side of Speech," in *Voicing the Void: Muteness and Memory in Holocaust Fiction* (Albany: State University of New York Press, 1997).

44. *Hasidic Tales,* 117.

45. Parush ("Politics of Literacy"), Stampfer ("Gender Differentiation"), and Shmeruk ("Hebrew-Yiddish-Polish") all address, with various emphases, the intersection between language and acculturation in the different strata of nineteenth- and twentieth-century Eastern European Jewish society.

46. *Hasidic Tales,* 195.

47. The Hebrew reads: "lakachti etchem echad me'ihr v'sh'naim m'mishpacha," and continues, "v'heveti etchem tzion" [and I will bring you to Zion, that is, Israel] (Jeremiah 3:14). The verse in its entirety, then, prophesies a comprehensive redemption of all Jews, including transporting them to Israel. Traditional commentaries emphasize that "one of a city, and two of a family" implies that at the time of redemption God will not leave any one—no matter how few or how remote may be the place where they reside—behind. Seen against this tradition of interpretation focusing on comprehensive redemption of every member of the Jewish people, the rebbe's use of this verse to dramatize the tragic plight of Holocaust survivors is that much more pointed.

48. Historically, however, it is questionable whether the statue was ever geared to the "masses." As John Higham has observed, however, the poem

could come into prominence only when the politics of immigration were receptive. Only when immigration was no longer in "significant numbers" were the connotations Lazarus assigned it brought to the foreground. In Higham's words, "So long as millions of immigrants entered 'the golden door,' the Statue of Liberty was unresponsive to them; it served other purposes. After the immigrant ships no longer passed under the New Colossus in significant numbers, it enshrined the immigrant experience as a transcendental national memory." "The Transformation of the Statue of Liberty," in *Send These to Me: Jews and Other Immigrants in Urban America* (New York: Atheneum, 1975).

49. According to Marc Shell, for America to cultivate a "foreign" language is not something new but rather integral to its polyglot history: "Since 1750, we have seen, there had been a dialogue about whether there should be only one official language and which language that should be: English or one of the 'foreign,' that is, non-English languages, whether ancient or modern. That dialogue, barely recognizable, was sometimes expressed in the form of literary debates about whether the American language itself was not essentially a 'foreign'—that is, non-English—language" ("Babel in America," 112). To make English the language that is foreign thus builds on, as well as recasts, this debate.

50. Mary Louise Pratt, "Comparative Literature and Global Citizenship," in *Comparative Literature in the Age of Multiculturalism*, ed. Charles Bernheimer (Baltimore: Johns Hopkins University Press, 1995), 64.

51. That the words at issue are Lazarus's makes the issues of opacity and translation apposite, for Lazarus was known for her gift for languages (she was fluent in French, German, and Italian, and, according to her friend Sophia Hawthorne, perhaps adept in Greek and Latin as well) and for her accomplishments in translating these languages. Moreover, the postwar moment appeared ripe for circumventing the opacity of the poem. For just as, according to Eliach's rendering, the GI was translating for the Bluzhover rebbe the words (or some words) of Lazarus's poem "The New Colossus" into Yiddish, so was I. L. Beilin celebrating Lazarus and "The New Colossus" in his Yiddish monograph, *Dos Lebn fun Ema Lazarus* (The Life of Emma Lazarus), published in New York in 1946. According to Beilin, Lazarus has herself rewritten the message of the statue: "she has given [to the statue] the possibility of a deeper content than the sculptor has ever seen to give" (37, translation mine).

52. *Hasidic Tales*, 206.

53. According to Eliach, her interviewees would also be moved by this mimetic impulse and would quote in the original language. In contrast to Tula, however, who narrates traumatic events mimetically but keeps ironic distance, invoking the original language moved the speaker "totally into the past" (personal communication, July 2000). Noting a special way that this impulse played itself out, Gurewitsch emphasizes that her interviewees would "always" mime the persecutor's German commands in the original German (personal communication, November 1999).

54. In elaborating the multilingualism of Polish Jewry, Shmeruk quotes a memoir that comments on what qualified as a foreign language: "Father, who went only to heder, since there was no money for the yeshivah, knew five languages: Hebrew, Yiddish, German, Polish, and Ukrainian, although he apparently could not write Ukrainian. No one thought of this as anything extraordinary. I would even venture that no one even noticed. 'True' foreign languages were French and English. If you had asked my father before World War I, he would certainly have answered that he knew no foreign language" ("Hebrew-Yiddish-Polish," 289; my emphasis). Shmeruk cites Roman Zimand, "Gatunek: Podroz," *Kultura* 11 (1983): 24. He notes that in the interwar period one could no longer assume that most Jews could speak five languages but rather three (Hebrew, Yiddish, Polish). But if Zimand is correct, one might infer that the peripheral status of English remained the same.

55. *Hasidic Tales*, 206–7. To be sure, dreaming of bread is not unique to this story but is poignantly common in contemporary as well as postwar accounts of the Holocaust. What is special to this story is the way the dream is played out many years later and, most interesting to me, the link to languages and storytelling.

56. Born in Tomaszow, in southeastern Poland, Lerman was a partisan fighter from 1942 until the end of the war. Having settled after the war in the United States, Lerman has been an important figure in efforts to memorialize the Holocaust, particularly in his association with the United States Holocaust Council (of which he served as chair, 1993–2000) and the United States Holocaust Memorial Museum. Even given his prominence, his interruption of the commemoration was likely viewed as provocative.

57. *Hasidic Tales*, 212.

58. Ibid.

59. Ibid., 213.

60. For an excellent survey of the images of English associated with commerce, see Richard Bailey, *Images of English: A Cultural History of the Language* (Ann Arbor: University of Michigan Press, 1991). To know that such associations go back centuries does not, however, take the sting out of the Cracovian's caustic expression, "the language of dollars." See also Gerry Knowles, *A Cultural History of the English Language* (London: Arnold, 1997); and Dick Leith, *A Social History of English*, 2nd ed. (London: Routledge, 1997).

61. See, for example, Wirth-Nesher, "The Languages of Memory," in Werner Sollars's *Multilingual America* (New York: New York University Press, 1998): 313–26.; and Rosen, "The Language of Survival."

3

A Pedagogy of Trauma (or a Crisis of Cynicism)

Teaching, Writing, and the Holocaust

JANET ALSUP

"Looking back at the experience of that class, I therefore think that my job as a teacher, paradoxical as it may sound, was that of creating in the class the highest state of crisis that it could withstand, without 'driving the students crazy'—without compromising the students' bounds."[1] In this excerpt from "Education and Crisis; or, the Vicissitudes of Teaching," Shoshana Felman refers to a class she taught at Yale called "Literature and Testimony." In her essay she describes how her students responded emotionally to class reading and discussion of Holocaust and other testimonial texts. Felman's students were shocked and saddened by what they read and heard, and it was clear that the class affected them in ways Felman had not expected. Students told her how they were having dreams about the course; they called her at all hours to talk about what they were thinking; and they took advantage of class time she provided to "work through" their very visceral response by talking to their peers.

In another essay, Felman calls such a response "secondary witnessing," or experiencing trauma not as a firsthand survivor but through the words and retellings of a survivor.[2] The students' trauma was filtered through time and space, as well as through the text they were reading, but Felman insists that it was trauma nonetheless. Felman claims that her students experienced such trauma secondarily, in a way that Dori Laub describes as "participating in the reliving and reexperiencing of the event" by, for example, listening to survivor testimony.[3]

After reading Felman's essay, I began to wonder about the ethical implications of traumatizing students. Even if we do so out of a desire to have them understand a pivotal historical event, how can we justify forcing our students into crisis? If we want students to "never forget" the event (as the often-repeated imperative commands), then they must have an unforgettable (or perhaps, in Blanchot's terms, immemorable) experience, an experience that does not allow them to view the texts as they would any other course assignment—as a "knowledge." Perhaps there is an inherent connection between effective Holocaust pedagogy and traumatic experience. Felman asks herself similar questions: Is there a relation between crisis and the very enterprise of education? Is there a relation between trauma and pedagogy? Can trauma instruct pedagogy, and can pedagogy shed light on trauma? Can the process of testimony—that of bearing witness to a crisis or a trauma—be made use of in a classroom situation?[4] Felman's answer is, in part, that effective teaching only takes place through a crisis, and if it does not encounter such a crisis (or trauma) the class may not have been fully successful. In other words, she values trauma as a component of pedagogy. But how does a teacher create a classroom crisis that facilitates deep thinking and feeling but that does not "drive the students crazy" as Felman warns?

With current rhetoric and writing theory placing such value on a classroom that recognizes the difficulties—both political and ethical— of writing a knowledge that suppresses violence, discomfort, and uncertainty, it seems that Holocaust texts and representations would most effectively trouble many of the assumptions contemporary pedagogy seeks to interrogate. Consequently, in the fall of 1998, I co-taught a class that had the complexity of Holocaust representation as its unifying theme. The class, called "Writing the Holocaust," was a second writing course for many sophomores and juniors. It was organized around a series of Holocaust texts that took the students though various genres: history, memoir, fiction (short story and novel), poetry, film, graphic novel, and the museum as text. It asked students to answer questions about memory, history, genre, and language in representing the Holocaust, as well as to grapple with questions of accuracy, effectiveness, and purpose.

While we did not see the goal of the course as the production of trauma, we did focus the class on questions that were inherently troubling, thereby making easy answers impossible and, consequently, the course potentially frustrating. The class was founded on the idea that a comprehensive account of the Holocaust in any medium is, if not impossible, then pretty close to it. There can be different representations, but each will inherently fail. We addressed these issues in the class in part through Blanchot's definition of the disaster as "what escapes the very possibility of experience—it is the limit of writing. Which does not mean that the disaster, as the force of writing, is excluded from it, is beyond the pale of writing."[5] On one hand this attempted communication about the Holocaust must fail because the disaster can never be fully spoken. However, ironically, it is only through this attempt that the disaster can be realized. During this communicative act, such as writing, the speaker makes present the event in more complex, perhaps personally vexing, ways. So the writing might not succeed, but the reader nonetheless experiences a sense of the limit of writing and knowledge.

In planning the course, we worried about how students would confront the emotionally draining memoirs, novels, and films; we worried that our students might respond as Felman's did—with sadness, horror, and emotional overload. It was a crisis we thought we were prepared for, so we created space in the course plan for students to work through these difficulties in writing and with small- and large-group discussion. What I do not think we realized at the beginning of the course was that the trauma students would encounter would be different from what we expected and, in many ways, more complex. Our students would not only reach emotional crises; they would reach intellectual and pragmatic ones as well. Students would not just have trouble reading and "dealing with" the texts; they would have trouble negotiating the impossibility of Holocaust representation with their attempts to represent their understanding of it in writing—to speak the unspeakable, in other words. They would also have trouble thinking about what they had learned in a way that made the knowledge seem "useful," and they would be frustrated by feelings of guilty helplessness. Our students, undergraduates a few years younger than Felman's graduate students, sometimes seemed jaded from secondary school exposure to the Holocaust and the "politically correct" response they felt they were compelled to have. Many of them responded to our course theme with tired resignation: "Here we go again." They felt like they had heard all of this before, and they did not know what they could do about something that happened thirty years before they were born. So they sometimes refused to respond at all, choosing a quiet apathy, or they responded in unexpected, rebellious ways.

I will argue in this essay that even if our students' responses were not the ones we expected, and even if it has taken me several years to begin to understand them, they reflect a type of secondary trauma, a sort of crisis resulting from student experience with the class and its subject. I call this crisis a crisis in cynicism, and it is exemplified by the experiences of one student, whom I will call Steve. I believe that this crisis is directly related to how the Holocaust will be remembered as it becomes more chronologically distant, and hence abstract, to those learning about it. As the event becomes more "historical" to our students, it runs the risk of becoming less "real." Therefore, students become more likely to respond to the event with cynicism, resulting either in passive acceptance of what they see as the teacher's agenda or in rebellion against this perceived authority. Because such cynicism seems to be related to the process of remembering, it is likely to be felt in many or most classes that address the Holocaust; consequently, teachers should explore ways to address such a cynical response when it occurs. In order to begin such a pedagogical conversation, I will tell the story of Steve and his crisis of cynicism.

Steve seemed to respond with passive acceptance when he wrote the first two essays for our course. However, for the third and final essay students chose their own topics, and they were asked to post topic ideas on the course's electronic listserv. Our hope was that students would not only choose a genre or issue of particular interest to them but would synthesize their semester-long study of Holocaust theory and texts in a way that was also personally meaningful. Students posted many possibilities for final paper topics, ranging from writing about historical representation in terms of other genocides to reading and analyzing survivor memoirs we had not read in class. But Steve did what we never expected: he proposed writing a paper denying that the Holocaust occurred.

The student who proposed the denial essay was a white, Protestant, middle-class college sophomore, outspoken and confident, who typically sat in the back row. His hair was cut very short (at first we feared like a "skinhead"—however, this was later proven not to be the case) and his build was athletic. Despite his habit of staking out the back corner of the room, he seemed genuinely interested in the issues the class confronted.

Steve had dutifully written the first two papers about history and memory (paper 1) and the effectiveness of film as a Holocaust genre (paper 2). He had been thinking about the issues of representation and its impossibility, and he had been reevaluating his prior definitions of history and memory. Overall, he had been doing exactly what we hoped students would, so we assumed he was learning.

But Steve also came to our class knowing from past experiences in school that he was supposed to be shocked and dismayed by the tragedy. He also assumed that teachers have an "agenda" when they teach about anything, the Holocaust included. He quickly hypothesized that he was supposed to have the kind of response Felman's students had and which I described at the beginning of this essay: more or less "traditional" trauma. This is not to say that Steve was not shocked and dismayed sometimes in our class or that all of his responses were insincere. Perhaps he felt emotional trauma at times. However, his response to the third paper assignment is evidence that something else was going on with Steve, something that was not quite pretending for the sake of the teacher or a result of a true emotional response, something that Felman never addressed. Here are Steve's ideas for the third paper, as he posted them on the class listserv:

1. Explain the benefits of studying the Holocaust.
2. Argue a paper in support of the position that the Holocaust did not happen.
3. Write about how the Holocaust still directly affects us today.
4. Why do you believe that the Holocaust did happen?
5. Is there any objectivity when studying the Holocaust? If no, speculate on why there isn't.

   I would like to personally dare anyone to write a paper on my possible topic #2. I believe if a student can write a well supported paper in support of Holocaust denial, then that student has achieved a level of objectivity that makes my topic five moot. (Course listserv, November 1998)

Steve's posted topics, regardless of how interested he was in any of them, seem sarcastic and cynical. He hits every possible topic that questions the ideology on which the course was based; he proposes deconstructing the reasons for studying the event, asking whether or not it actually occurred, and, in a shocking but perhaps most intelligent move, turns the tables on us by asking about historical objectivity. Of course, we as co-teachers had been encouraging arguments all semester over the question of objectivity, over whether history can completely and accurately represent the event. Steve took these questions to their cynical extremes: if there is no objectivity, then how can we disregard *any* possibility, including denial?

Steve's post had serious repercussions in the class. As co-teachers we were angry, shocked, and defensive on both personal and professional levels. Consequently, we decided almost immediately, in a kind of gut-level, instinctive way, to rule out the "denial" topic. The words were too explosive, too potentially harmful. Judith Butler writes, "Language has its own agency. . . . Speech does not merely reflect a relation of social domination; speech enacts domination, becoming the vehicle through which that social structure is reinstated."[6] So even if talk is only talk, it nonetheless has a direct, material effect on individuals. Butler and bell hooks argue that speech *is* action,[7] that it has material and ethical implications that can be as powerful as physical actions. Consequently, certain students in the class, including Jewish students, responded to Steve's post with horror and disbelief; we could only imagine how peers might respond to an entire essay in a peer review group. On the other hand, ruling out the topic also had negative effects on classroom community and seemed for a time to poison the classroom atmosphere as students took sides with either Steve or the instructors. And Steve was angry because, as he saw it, his academic freedom had been impinged upon. Needless to say, the class listserv was quite active. It was definitely a crisis—a crisis of ethics, identity, and pedagogy.

I have thought a great deal about Steve's proposal. Perhaps the frustration on which the class was based just finally got to him; perhaps he was trying to get attention and see what kind of reaction he would get. Maybe he really thought it would be an interesting paper, even though he said (and I believed him) that he was not a Holocaust denier. Maybe his past school experiences with the Holocaust had led him to impatience with the "agenda" his teachers clearly held and seemed, to him, to force onto the class. Regardless of the exact reasons for his posting, Steve broached the topic that as teachers we had hoped would not be raised: denial. We had considered asking students to read some material written by deniers as a way of deconstructing and delegitimizing their arguments, but we decided the risk for student misunderstanding was too great. (We did not even want the stuff in circulation.) And then Steve put the issue right out there, with one short e-mail message.

Perhaps Steve was what Peter Sloterdijk calls "cynical" or a victim of "enlightened false consciousness."[8] He was clearly very aware of the circulations of power and ideology, so in that sense he considered himself enlightened. He thought he understood the motivations of his instructors and the types of papers they wanted him to write. In his first two class papers he followed these ideological constraints as he saw them; he followed the "rules" and wrote what he thought was expected of him. But when the third paper was assigned and he was given freedom to choose his topic, his cynicism became visible, and he felt he could no longer "play the game" while still engaging in critical, and personally satisfying, thinking and writing. The temptation was too great to show his instructors that he was quite knowledgeable about their agenda and was ready to rebel against it. So he proposed questions for writing that shook the very foundation of the class: write about why one would even study the Holocaust, explore whether or not the Holocaust really happened, and so forth. Steve posted on the class listserv, obviously a very public forum, some rather explosive ideas. He must have been well aware that one of his co-teachers and several students in the class were Jewish; he was aware that others were supportive of the theory and ideology on which the course rested. And to make matters even more complex, Steve later told us that he really had no intention of writing a paper that denied the Holocaust and that he certainly believed the Holocaust had happened. He just thought it would be interesting to make the proposal. So questions remain: Why did Steve choose to post these paper ideas when he knew how others might react? What benefit did he see resulting from this action?

We may never be able to answer these questions definitively, but I want to explore two possibilities. In a recent essay, Stephanie Foote writes, "The national news has recently discovered a new kind of criminal—the young, aggrieved, middle class white male."[9] She explores why white, male students are sometimes resentful of critical, politicized pedagogies that seem to turn them into the metaphorical enemy. Of course, ultimately Foote sees this phenomenon as yet another reason to implement such pedagogies, but only after anticipating possible student rebellion and thinking about effective ways to respond as the teacher. A parallel argument contends that as a result of feeling helpless and angry in the face of societal guilt, white men choose to "turn the tables" and use this supposed victimhood to claim for themselves a new kind of minority status, one that gives them permission to speak out, to rebel. Steve may have believed that while engaging in harsh critique of the Nazi "whiteness," we were, by association, singling out white, non-Jewish men of European heritage with the same critique.

Amy Lee writes that teachers and students "need to recognize that power is linked to discourse, to one's ability to speak a self publicly," and she sees, after Foucault, the indissoluble connections between discourse and the disciplinary power that results.[10] To illustrate her case, she tells the story of one of her students who wrote an essay about how homosexuals make bad parents and hence should not be allowed to adopt children. This student knew that his topic was outside of the bounds of accepted discourse, but he chose to write it anyway. Acting outside this normalized discourse had the potential of marginalizing the student writer from his classmates and his teacher. However, this student also knew that his topic was accepted in the wider "dominant" discourse of the heterosexual community. Consequently, he felt empowered to make his claims, despite the risk of censorship in the class. Similar to Steve, this student was on the margins of the class discourse community. However, both he and Steve were aware of a larger discourse community that might be more accepting. Steve, a white American, may well have been reacting to the designation of the Holocaust as a sacred topic, unavailable to critique. It was not relevant to Steve that he did not actually believe that the Holocaust did not happen; he still was upset by the implicit ban on the discussion. Even though Lee's student actually claimed to believe that homosexuals were bad parents, and Steve said that he did not believe in Holocaust denial, they seem to have engaged in similar intellectual moves. Both seem to have rejected the dominant ideology of their college class; both rebelled against their carefully honed cynicism, which allowed them to be successful in school up to this point; and both found new status as a kind of majority turned minority, well-educated white male turned into marginalized rebel.

But there is a second possible cause for Steve's posting: a crisis of helplessness in the face of the course content. Perhaps Steve had experienced his own "disaster" (in Blanchot's terms); he had reached the point of personal trauma, a limit to knowledge, and was looking for a way out. His proposal was a way of throwing up his hands and saying, "Well, if there's nothing I can do, then what about this?" Because he could not find his way out, because he could not find a way to move from the limit of knowledge to a practical, ethical "here's what I can do" response to the immense pain and suffering of the Holocaust's victims, he decided to rebel against the dominant ideology of shock and sadness by giving us, the teachers, what he knew we least wanted. Perhaps Steve, consciously or not, decided that if we were not going to provide him with a way to cope with the trauma our pedagogy produced, he would opt to resist our pedagogy and the ideology that sustained it.

Of course, it is also possible that Steve was simply naive and blithely unaware of the possible implications of his post prior to sending it. However, according to Slavoj Zizek, naïveté can be one outward manifestation that cynicism takes. To the outside viewer, and sometimes even to the subject him- or herself, naïveté may be how a subject's actions are understood; however, Zizek argues that despite perceptions, what appears to be naïveté is often grounded in and built upon cynicism. "Cynical reason is no longer naïve," he writes, "but is a paradox of an enlightened false consciousness: one knows the falsehood very well, one is well aware of a particular interest hidden behind an ideological universality, but still one does not renounce it."[11] So what appears to be naïveté is sometimes an expression of cynicism. The subject succumbs to the dominant ideology of the institution (that is, school) and is seemingly ignorant of the ideological construction within which he acts. But the truth is that he *is* aware of this ideological construction and chooses either to obey its dictums or rebel against them. When he obeys he appears simply naive; when he rebels he can appear both naive and bent on self-destruction.

In the case of Steve, therefore, his supposed naïveté might actually exist in conjunction with a sense of cynicism—he may understand the classroom ideology (or the larger ideology of how the modern, "civilized" world understand the events of the Holocaust) and even accept it; however, this acceptance may be, at least in part, built upon a cynical view of all school- or institutionally sanctioned knowledge. He "accepts" such knowledge (at least on one level) because he thinks he must do so in order to be successful in the institution. So while Steve's proposal of the denial topic could demonstrate a naive misunderstanding of the ideology of the university, it may also demonstrate an ideological cynicism masked by a veil of naive thinking and response. It is hard to believe that after fourteen or fifteen years of schooling Steve did not understand the ideology of the institution of "school"—therefore, it becomes easier to believe that even if he was naive about the effect his posting would have, it was based at least in part on a cynical response to ideological knowledge. He is, consciously or unconsciously, trying to rebel against an ideology he knows well and has perhaps grown tired of accepting unquestioningly.

But if these possibilities for Steve's posting are even close to accurate, they leave me with even more questions than when I began. Did the way we set up our class precipitate Steve's crisis? Could we have more effectively responded to his post? How might we have structured the class to prevent Steve's feelings of defensiveness or frustration? Is the kind of crisis Steve endured at all the same as the trauma Felman describes in her essay? Was his crisis ultimately a pedagogically worthwhile or productive experience, or did it simply reinforce his cynicism? We could have allowed Steve to write the paper he proposed; we could have spoken to him individually about the post before rejecting his proposal; we could have used his response as an opportunity to explore issues of ideology, ethics, and avoidance; we could have encouraged him to engage in some pragmatic or political action that might work against cynicism. Maybe some answers are available in looking closely at Steve's final writing for our course. His portfolio introduction, written at the conclusion of the semester, gives a clue to his feelings about the course and its material:

> Is human suffering at the hands of other humans over? Of course not, nor will it ever be. So what is to be done? Many people come to this point and become paralyzed with the frustration of not being able to find a way to do anything about it. But by examining past atrocities, you can find ways to translate Jews and Germans into humans hurting humans. You can translate Black slaves and White slave masters into humans hurting humans. And the hope is, for me, that you can translate yourself into one of those humans, and make the decision not to hurt another. (December 1997)

It is easy to substitute "I" for "Many people" in Steve's writing and understand this paragraph as a description of both the trauma he experienced in the course and how he attempted to resolve it by finding in it some broader relevance. In Blanchot's language, Steve describes the "disaster" and a realization that reading and writing about the Holocaust produced a crisis in how he interacts with other human beings. (It is unclear, for example, whether he "substitutes" himself for a victim or a perpetrator.) Steve may have been attempting to negotiate the conflict between a cynical acceptance of a so-called politically correct ideology and his own feelings of frustration and helplessness.

As I said at the beginning of this essay, we never thought this particular kind of crisis, this intellectual crisis exemplified by Steve, would occur. So although we were prepared to help students work through difficult and often shockingly gruesome texts, we were not prepared to deal with Steve's cynicism or his troubled relation to knowledge. And Steve was not the only student to react in such a way. There were others who supported his writing topic proposal in less vocal ways, just as there were students who had emotional crises like Felman describes, although perhaps less severe. However, Steve's experience exemplifies the kind of crisis we least expected, and the type of trauma that perhaps taught us the most about teaching a pedagogy of trauma.

In many ways, our class and Felman's had similar goals. We both wanted to expose students to the Holocaust (and in Felman's case, other historical and literary testimonies) in a way that would teach them something about writing, reading, and humanity. But out students' responses showed us that we may have accomplished something different. Of course, I have here used one student as the focal point of this essay, even though I could have discussed many other students whose responses were somewhat different. Nevertheless, an important difference between our class and Felman's is the age of our respective students. As I mentioned earlier, Felman's class was filled with graduate students, while ours were undergraduates, a few as young as freshmen. I hinted earlier that Steve's crisis could have been linked to his frustration in failing to find some sense of relevance in reading and writing about the Holocaust. He seemed to be rebelling against a cynical acceptance of the classroom ideology of liberal intellectualism. My point is that the issue of relevance might be magnified in undergraduate (and even high school) classrooms because of the age of the students and their increasing chronological distance from the event of the Holocaust and hence any feeling of connection with it.

For a long time, goals for representing (and teaching) the Holocaust have been twofold: so that it would never happen again and so that readers would never forget the victims. Those goals need not disappear with younger students, but they may have to be modified as the Holocaust becomes a fetish or a commodity and becomes woven into the fabric of twenty-first-century American culture. Kali Tal claims that such "commodification" is essential to any historical event if it is to be remembered by society. She writes: "However unpopular, I consider it imperative to reduce the Holocaust from 'holy object' to 'something which happened in history' if we are to understand, for example, exactly what George Bush meant when he called Saddam Hussein 'another Hitler' and why this naming seemed to serve as a justification for going to war against Iraq."[12]

Tal claims that if we as a culture do not allow the Holocaust as event to become a part of our cultural "myth" or cultural fabric, then it will disappear and will not be remembered. This integration is already starting to occur: in recent years, more and more films and novels have appeared with Holocaust-era settings and Holocaust-inspired characters. These texts are not always historically accurate; sometimes they are fictional, sometimes they are comic, sometimes they just "use" the concept of "Nazi" or "concentration camp" as a convenient metaphor or premise.

Many Holocaust scholars (not to mention survivors and their children) find such commodification and "mythologization" of the Holocaust offensive and dangerous. With the release and subsequent controversy over Holocaust "memoirs" that turned out to be at least in part fictional (for example, Wilkomirski's *Fragments* [1996] and Hirsch's *Hearing a Different Drummer* [2000]), some have feared that if the Holocaust becomes just another cultural narrative it will be easier for deniers to spread and support their claims. Although these are reasonable fears, I agree with Tal that to some extent the event will inevitably become commodified, will have to become a kind of cultural metaphor, in order for it to be remembered at all. I think Steve's crisis in our class is an example of the dynamic of cultural memory and commodification, of what happens when a memory is understood cynically. Perhaps the course should have encouraged students to make comparisons between the Holocaust and other, more contemporary "genocides" (such as those in Rwanda, Afghanistan, Cambodia, or the Balkans). Though such a comparison should not be seen to encourage a ranking of horror in which some genocides are seen as "worse" or "better" than others, such a discussion might help students to see a larger relevance, a theme that they could take from the class and play out in their contemporary circumstances.

An example of such a discussion is one that occurred at Purdue University in 2001 during its annual conference on the Holocaust. In addition to historical and scholarly discussions, participants created locally significant plans of action for battling prejudice against the community's growing Latino community and the recent increase in racist graffiti on public buildings. Instead of encouraging such conversations, we often insist on seeing the Holocaust as a sacred, completely unique event, a view that I am not completely unsympathetic to. However, the question is, does this point of view work for our students? How does it encourage a pedagogy of trauma that nonetheless comes with no guarantee against a cynical backlash like Steve's?

These questions are important for Holocaust education. I believe that in the end, Steve's crisis resulted in his ability to discover ways in which the limit of knowledge about the event is relevant to his circumstances. He was able to do this at least in part because of the cynical stance he and so many other students take into all their classes, especially on those topics about which they think the institution has predetermined what students' responses should be. Ironically, his rebellious response to our classroom ideology resulted in real, albeit unplanned, learning. Yet how many other students in the class stayed firmly planted in their cynicism and never thought about the event or their reading and writing in new ways? How many of them never experienced any kind of trauma or crisis at all, and hence did not learn much from the course?

A cynical stance to memory and history poses a unique challenge for Holocaust education. Such a stance may become more common in our classrooms as students become more historically distant (and hence emotionally and psychologically distant) from the event. A culture, such as that of which our students are a part, will inevitably "commodify" or "mythologize" a historical event in order to make it part of cultural memory. However, *how* an event is commodified or mythologized (for example, whether it is fetishized and misrepresented or remembered with accuracy and emotional/intellectual depth) is something that can be determined, to some extent, by educators. Teachers can structure classroom experiences in ways that decrease the likelihood of unexamined cynical responses and increase intellectually and emotionally sincere ones. One way this might be done is to revisit the concept of witnessing and rethink the way witnessing—or to be more specific, secondary witnessing—can be experienced in the classroom.

Felman's conception of secondary witnessing, described at the beginning of this essay, involves a reexperiencing of the event through reading or viewing Holocaust texts. Such reexperiencing will hypothetically enable the student to experience the event emotionally. Only after this emotional experience can real intellectual understanding follow, in part because central to understanding the event intellectually is understanding the impossibility of its being fully understood, a realization that has an emotional (or visceral) component. However, Steve's experience in our class suggests that encouraging secondary witnessing in the classroom is a more complex process than at first it might appear. If we view the reading or viewing of memoirs, novels, histories, and films as one "layer" of Holocaust education, another layer may very well be responding to these texts, such as writing or talking about them. My co-teacher and I provided for these layers of experience in our class. However, I have come to see that there is another layer that is equally important if we are to teach students about the Holocaust. This final pedagogical layer involves an awareness of and sensitivity to students' past educational and personal experiences with the event as well as their ideological stance toward education, especially education that has implied or stated ethical implications. I believe the concept of secondary witnessing is a useful one when considering effective Holocaust education, and I think an education of trauma can have powerful, even life-changing effects on students. However, without a consideration of the student's ideological stance upon entering such a classroom, without an understanding and even an expectation of a cynical, jaded, or rebellious response, appropriate pedagogical modifications will not be made, and such trauma or witnessing is less likely to occur.

Steve was able to experience his own type of secondary witnessing because he interrogated his cynical response and publicly rebelled against the perceived classroom imperative to "feel." However, I do not think Steve's ability to seek his own meaning in the class was the norm; my instincts tell me that most students when feeling such cynicism were probably content to either "play the game" for the course grade they wanted or simply not participate. If we recognize the possibility for such student responses and anticipate their occurrence, we can change how we plan and teach courses about the Holocaust. For example, we might structure more overt discussion about the relevance of Holocaust education and why it is important to our culture to "never forget." We might encourage students to go out into their communities and take action that extends their classroom experience. We might talk to them openly about their feelings of cynicism and helplessness when they confront the topic and how these feelings are normal as a society attempts to bring a historical event into the web of cultural memory. I believe such pedagogical practices—practices that take into consideration not only the Holocaust as event but also the ideological stance of students— can bring the concept of secondary witnessing into the twenty-first-century classroom, a classroom of intellectually cynical, but exceedingly smart, young adults.

Notes

1. Shoshana Felman, "Education and Crisis; or, the Vicissitudes of Teaching," in Shoshana Feldman and Dori Laub, *Testimony: Crises of Witnessing in Literature, Psychoanalysis, and History* (New York: Routledge, 1992), 53.

2. Shoshana Felman, "In an Era of Testimony: Claude Lanzmann's Shoah," *Yale French Studies* 79 (1991): 39–81.

3. Felman and Laub, *Testimony,* 76.

4. Felman, "Education and Crisis," 1.

5. Maurice Blanchot, *The Writing of the Disaster,* trans. Ann Smock (Lincoln: University of Nebraska Press, 1995), 7.

6. Judith Butler, *Excitable Speech: A Politics of the Performative* (New York: Routledge, 1997), 18.

7. See bell hooks, *Talking Back: Thinking Feminist, Thinking Black* (Boston; South End Press, 1989).

8. Peter Sloterdijk, *Critique of Cynical Reason* (Minneapolis: University of Minnesota Press, 1987).

9. Stephanie Foote, "The Conditions of Ethical Teaching," *Concerns: A Publication of the Women's Caucus for the Modern Language Association* 27, nos. 1–2 (2000): 59–73.

10. Amy Lee. *Composing Critical Pedagogies: Teaching Writing as Revision* (Urbana, Ill.: NCTE, 2000), 168.

11. Slavoj Zizek, *The Sublime Object of Ideology* (London: Verso, 1989), 29.

12. Kali Tal, *Worlds of Hurt: Reading the Literatures of Trauma* (New York: Cambridge University Press, 1996), 8.

4

The "Erotics of Auschwitz"

Coming of Age in The Painted Bird and Sophie's Choice

SHARON OSTER

What does it mean to come of age within the context of the Holocaust? To write a coming-of-age novel, a *Bildungsroman*, is to write the narrative of an authentic developing self in a particular social milieu with all its components: educational and cultural, as the German term implies, but also emotional, psychological, and, of course, sexual. Given both literary and moral imperatives to represent the Holocaust authentically— that is, in tenable and proportionate terms in accord with historical truths—and the generic imperative to represent the maturing self authentically, a grave conflict presents itself to the writer of such a work. The dictates of history, as Alvin Rosenfeld has pointed out, tell us that "one of the characteristics of Holocaust writings at their most authentic is that they are peculiarly and predominantly sexless. This is doubtless one reason," he goes on, "why latter-day authors who have had no direct, firsthand experience of the camps have such a hard time writing about them: the contemporary imagination, inflamed as it is by hyped-up sexual fantasies, can hardly understand an order of experience where eros is so deprived and the sexual drive so stunted."[1] And yet this is what two controversial, contentiously labeled "Holocaust novels,"

Jerzy Kosinski's *The Painted Bird* (1965) and William Styron's *Sophie's Choice* (1976), manage to achieve.[2] The dictates of the *Bildungsroman* demand that the protagonist assimilate experience as he (in both cases here) undergoes social and sexual maturation, an impossible task in the experience of the Holocaust. These competing plots—the individual and the historical—thus get entangled: the horrors of the Holocaust distort the *Bildungsroman* formula as the experience of the Holocaust gets sexualized. These entangled plots, moreover, converge upon, and are authenticated at the expense of, wounded female bodies. Both authors betray their struggle to achieve narrative authenticity by deploying a sexualized aesthetics of violence, resembling what Rosenfeld calls an "erotics of Auschwitz."[3]

What is interesting about Rosenfeld's comment is that he applies this expression to *Sophie's Choice* but not to *The Painted Bird*. Many critics, in fact, have been particularly harsh on Styron for the sexualized experiences of his protagonist, Stingo, "in the unimaginable reaches of Brooklyn, an ineffective and horny Calvinist among all these Jews" (39)—as inappropriate in what purports to be a book about the Holocaust. Perhaps because Sophie, both concentration camp survivor and the primary object of Stingo's insatiable lust, is such a significant character, Styron's eroticization and violent use of her is extremely obvious and not uncharacteristic of his writing. In her recent study *Holocaust Fiction* (2000), Sue Vice casually notes with reference to a particular plot detail that, "as is often the case with his borrowings [from testimonial sources], Styron sexualizes" it.[4] More pointedly, Rosenfeld asks: "what . . . does [Stingo's] mighty erotic struggle have to do with Auschwitz? By and large, nothing at all."[5] And perhaps most caustically, Joan Smith claims, "Here we have the secret of the novel's popularity: the juxtaposition of sex and the Holocaust has been dressed up as art, thus sanctioning its passage from the back room to the shelves reserved for the literary."[6] Smith concludes that female sexuality in *Sophie's Choice* "has nothing to do with real women but exists to legitimize masculine sexual fantasies which are violent, vicious and ultimately lethal."[7] Given this overwhelming response to Styron, the burning question remains: why, given the extremely sexually violent scenes depicted throughout *The Painted Bird*, as I will illustrate, are the same charges not leveled at Kosinski?

True, many critics of Kosinski's novel have expressed uneasiness with its graphic depictions and grotesqueness. Rosenfeld comments that "the level of deviance is so high and so constant in Kosinski, in fact, as to appear almost gratuitous, leading readers to question whether *The Painted Bird* is a terrifying and obscene book or a book about the terrors and obscenities of the Nazi period."[8] While Rosenfeld believes it to be the latter, Paul Lilly is more skeptical about Kosinski's personal motives, noting that "the writer's words seek to make victims of his readers in order to ensure escape from his own sense of powerlessness."[9] In effect, for Lilly, Kosinski reproduces linguistically the violence his protagonist undergoes physically and emotionally, taking revenge on his readers.[10] Yet even as critics address the sexual promiscuity and experimentality of characters in Kosinski's other novels, not to mention in his own life, no one seems willing to address the sexual deviance, violence, and misogyny in *The Painted Bird* as in any way inappropriate.

Even with the controversial origins of Kosinski's novel, he still has a more authentic connection to the Holocaust than does Styron, lending *The Painted Bird* the aura of a memoir. Yet both novels transgress generic boundaries. Vice points out the "generic hybridity" of *The Painted Bird*, as "fictional autobiography" yet also *Kunstlerroman* which, like *Sophie's Choice*, chronicles the development of an artist and his emerging artistic voice. Here, too, her failure to address the role of sexuality in such a development is conspicuous. Whereas Styron's Stingo tells us (incessantly) that he longs for sexual gratification, for Kosinski's boy-narrator, though he also loses his virginity, his desire emerges vicariously in acts of voyeurism, through fantasy, and more obliquely in his desire for dominance and power.[11] That this boy learns his position of gendered sexual power, of male prowess, through what he witnesses is undeniable, culminating as it does in fantasies of Nazi power. He may be a victim, but at least he is not a female, raped victim. To avoid questions of sexuality and sexual violence in Kosinski's novel any more than in Styron's is effectively to misread it altogether.

Critical debates continue to rage over who is authorized to write Holocaust novels, how we distinguish a legitimate Holocaust novel from an illegitimate one, and, particularly when the doors of fiction are opened, what ethical implications result from fictionalizing the Holocaust. In these debates, which have culminated most recently in the uproar over Binjamin Wilkomirski's *Fragments*, even Holocaust "testimonies" are subject to questions of legitimacy, authenticity, and truth-value, given the troubled relationships among trauma, memory, history, and its representation.[12] Fiction, by definition "imaginative," "fanciful," even "deceitful," seems free from history and ought not to pose these problems. Yet the reverse is true for Holocaust fiction. Holocaust narratives like *Sophie's Choice* and *The Painted Bird* disrupt generic categories, blur the line between truth and fantasy, and deform traditional literary forms. "Holocaust fictions are scandalous," states Vice bluntly in the opening line of her book; "that is, they invariably provoke controversy by inspiring repulsion and acclaim in equal measure."[13] No matter which side of the debate one chooses, it is impossible to read such novels extricated from the historical, ethical, and epistemological implications they raise about the Holocaust.

The relationships between fact and fiction, history and imagination, and author and narrator therefore make biography an unusually significant aspect of Holocaust literary criticism. If, in fact, one's representations of the Holocaust are *not* based in real lived experience, are *not* testimonies, but rather (true to the rules of fiction) are *fabrications* of one's own imagination—subjective, idiosyncratic, perhaps rhetorical—the author seems automatically suspect of deception, of representation in bad faith, or of exploiting the incontrovertible suffering of others for literary gain. Discussing *Sophie's Choice* under the chapter heading "Exploiting Atrocity," for example, Rosenfeld sees Styron's novel as a "fanciful" account of the Holocaust, which inaccurately represents it as a universalized manifestation of "absolute evil" rather than one resulting from "particular crimes against particular people."[14] Many critics have leveled similar charges against Styron.[15] The suggestion is that an "outsider" like Styron risks offending Holocaust victims and survivors to cash in on the symbolic capital of the Shoah; as a cluster of events of world-shattering pain and destruction, it becomes the ineffable placeholder for incontrovertible truth. Because their very fictionality risks profaning the hard, cold, yet sacred truth of the Holocaust, Holocaust novels thus become limit cases for "faithful" fiction, and their authors' intentions are subjected to extreme scrutiny.

From this suspicious perspective, we might read each novel's explorations of sexuality and sexual violence as enabled by their having been set within the context of a subject as taboo as the Holocaust. As Smith quips, "why stop at one taboo when you can break another?"[16] To represent the Holocaust requires taking an ethical stand: to be or not to be true to the memories of its victims. Fictional representations of the Holocaust cannot avoid this ethical engagement with history. And yet to fictionalize also means to risk "naturalizing" the Holocaust, a problem that, for Saul Friedlander, is perhaps greater than that of ideological appropriation, because it can lead to forgetting "the horror behind the words."[17] Paradoxically, fictional accounts must render the horrific ordinary, for in order to create this fictional world in the first place, one must reproduce a realm where horror defines reality and thus constitutes a fundamental aspect of quotidian life, for all its incomprehensibility.

Once the doors are then open to this realm "beyond good and evil," however, an author can abuse this poetic freedom, indulging in representations that in any other context would constitute a generic or ethical transgression. This is poetry after the Holocaust, after all. Perhaps we unfairly expect too much of such writers, expecting the work of one artist to perform the labor of many and carry the weight of history, too. Is the discomfort such a novel produces (by virtue of its subject matter) excusable only on the grounds that the author "really" experienced what he represents? And if so, are we willing to accept such "uncomfortable" subjects as sexual deviance and sexual violence along the way? When dealing with the representation of sexual transgression within a Holocaust novel, we must ask: does it engage the moral questions posed by representing the Holocaust, or does such representation involve an ethical transgression all its own? Put more simply, does the Holocaust become an alibi for gratuitous sexual exploration, masking what would otherwise be conceived as pornography?[18]

As Kosinski and Styron, a Polish survivor and an American observer, both create aesthetic portrayals of the horrific inhumanity of this historical event in their respective novels, their representations of evil become cathected through a variety of sexual obsessions and neuroses that may reflect more about each author than about the historical event being addressed.[19] Yet both (despite Kosinski's Polish national origin) also produce what can be considered distinctly American narratives, inflected by the confessional tradition of the Puritans, the epic *Bildungsroman* of the nineteenth century, and the embrace of psychoanalytical and sexual exploration popularized in the 1960s and 1970s, the latter permanently altering what is acceptable in American literature.[20] Although both authors confront the difficulties of breaking the shroud of silence hitherto surrounding the Holocaust with rather different narrative techniques, each creates a narrator whose self-conscious and disturbingly voyeuristic "witnessing" and subsequent reporting relies on, must be justified by, his authorial authenticity—his *having been there* in some capacity. Kosinski's first-person narrator, a young gypsy boy who survives the abuse and torture of rural peasants during the occupation, was taken for quite some time to be Kosinski himself as a child in Poland, just as Styron's narrator Stingo, a fledgling, frustrated, southern white writer in New York, has been revealed as a double of Styron by Styron himself.[21] Both authors' choice to blur the distinction between narrator and author suggests a slippery attempt to establish narrative authenticity, a continuity between fiction and biography that retains the freedom of poetic license.

While Kosinski eventually insisted that what was taken as his "testimony"—given his survivor status as "insider"—is only fiction, Styron as Stingo tries to overcome his position as "outsider" in two ways: first, by employing an analogy between the Holocaust and American slavery—the latter with which both character and author have a more intimate connection—and importing the arguments of well-known historians to back his comparison; and second, by adopting Sophie's story—the testimony of the "true" survivor—as his own. Such rhetorical strategies register on the levels of both content and form. Though he constantly refers to history in the text, Kosinski ultimately attempts to deny its role in his pursuit of pure aesthetic integrity and poetic freedom. This results in an existential, self-contained, hermetically sealed text that wavers between the picaresque and the mythical, as scholars have pointed out.[22] Conversely, Styron's absolute reliance upon the historical fact of the Holocaust (as well as of American slavery) yields a realistic, semi-autobiographical novel that, often drawing on unacknowledged sources, is by turns permeated by historiographical discourse, Holocaust memoir, and flashes of the "testimonial" revelation of his heroine, Sophie.[23]

Lusting after Sophie, Stingo spies longingly on Nathan's violent, sexual treatment of her, then goes on to sleep with Sophie himself before he can truly claim her story for his own. Stingo fulfills the prerequisites for narrative authenticity and sexual fantasy simultaneously. Kosinski's boy, always at a relatively safe, convenient vantage point for spying, describes the violent murder and abuse between peasants, but he focuses especially on the violent rapes of several women, incidents of incest and bestiality, and all in such detail that he becomes suspect of enjoying an almost titillating, self-indulgent fascination. Here is where Kosinski's drive toward authenticity, which is achieved not through subjective reflection or emotional interiority but through the representation of bodies in pain, crosses over into a kind of narrative sadomasochism.[24] Thus, whereas Kosinski denies recourse to the "pure" historical facts of his experience, and Styron has no firsthand experience of the Holocaust to turn to, both authors fill their gaps of authenticity with female bodies, which, as they undergo violations both violent and sexual, provide access to, and illustration of, certain unspeakable truths about the Holocaust.

Whether such violence is "real" or not, "true" or not, it is its excessive representation with which I am concerned. Such excessiveness may be said to signal the very problem of authentic representation at hand: its eroticized quality is symptomatic of an author struggling to make real (what is for him) the historical imaginary. Because such suffering cannot otherwise be authenticated by each author's own life experience, both substitute other bodies in pain to produce what Elaine Scarry has identified as the fundamental condition of pure materiality.[25] The "corruption" of these two novels thus occurs not on the level of historical referentiality but rather through the symbolic displacement of that history onto some other object of desire. Why else, we are compelled to ask, deploy such violent, sexual aesthetics? The desire to illustrate the "truth," however, gets overtaken by the desire to "look" at one's illustrations. My aim here is to examine the unsettling nature of the sexualized aesthetics of authenticity in these two coming-of-age novels, and how we become implicated in this pleasure of looking.

It is my claim that the historical authenticity of the Holocaust, on the one hand, and the epistemological authenticity of the sexually violated body, on the other, dialectically substantiate one another, mutually authorizing each writer's exploration of both taboo subjects at once. In these novels, where the reader is asked to identify with the narrator/witness, commingled representations of the maturing sexual self and of the Holocaust mutually distort one another, destabilizing the border between authentic violence and titillating gratuitousness, between "witnessing" and plain old voyeurism.

The Aesthetics of Masochism

If Kosinski achieved narrative authority by letting his fiction pass for authentic testimony, Styron conversely deploys narrative authority, both of his protagonist, Stingo, and of various additional voices of academic authority, to effect a voice of authenticity. Since Stingo narrates throughout, and effectively comes of age as a hero ought to, we are led to ask of Styron, "Why Sophie?" Why does Sophie's and not Stingo's choice secure the title of the novel? A controversial novel written by a southern Protestant white man whose autobiographical protagonist lusts after and tells the story of a Holocaust survivor, a Polish Catholic woman whose father may have been an arch-anti-Semite, *Sophie's Choice* has raised considerable controversy. On the one hand, George Steiner and Elie Wiesel condemn this book for Styron's "outsider" status. In *Language and Silence* (1982), Steiner calls for a kind of sacred silence around the Holocaust and makes the ethical claim that "those of us who have not survived have *no right* to forgive the unforgivable."[26] He implies that to represent the Holocaust in order to understand it is to forgive its perpetrators, and if you are not a survivor you *should not* do this. Wiesel's point is more epistemological: an oft-quoted authority on this subject, Wiesel has argued of Auschwitz that "only those who lived it in their flesh and in their minds can possibly transform their experience into knowledge. Others, despite their best intentions, can never do so."[27] Essentially for Wiesel, if you have not lived it, you simply *cannot* represent it. The "Holocaust novel" must be authenticated by experience before it can even be read as valid. This argument is compelling enough, but it seems to sneak the ethical "ought not" in through the back door of the epistemological "cannot."[28]

On the other hand, in defense of Styron's novel, Richard Rubenstein argues that Styron "is not Elie Wiesel and could not have written an eye-witness memoir of what actually took place at Auschwitz as did Wiesel. Styron is a Southern Protestant who has written a *Bildungsroman* . . . [he] did not experience the Holocaust at first hand and he chose not to write about it as if he had."[29] Though Styron's writing may offend some Jews, or make them feel uncomfortable, Rubenstein goes on, critics misunderstand Styron if they think he was trying to write a representative Holocaust novel. Rather, *Sophie's Choice* needs to be read in its own terms.[30] In his own defense in 1997, Styron invoked the words of Hannah Arendt, who told him, "An artist creates his own authenticity; what matters is imaginative conviction and boldness, a passion to invade alien territory and render an account of one's discoveries."[31] Arendt warned Styron that he would probably receive flak, as he did, for "poaching on the turf" of Jewish writers. Yet Styron also recalls how the idea that he should avoid the subject altogether never came up in his discussion with Arendt, who flatly rejected Steiner's call for silence, especially when Styron noted that the demand for silence was often coming the loudest from those who were busy scribbling books about Auschwitz. . . . Certainly the subject required almost unprecedented caution and sensitivity, and respect verging on reverence; but to make Auschwitz, in the literary sense, sacrosanct and beyond reach of words was a pietism I had to reject, if only because it made no sense to me that this monumental human cataclysm should remain buried and lost to memory. Why should writers be denied the chance to illuminate these horrors for future generations?[32]

Some might call this Styron's literary arrogance or even violence; others might agree with him. Yet perhaps only in the last decade, when thousands of authentic voices of the Holocaust have, indeed, been able to speak for themselves, it is interesting that Styron still feels compelled to invoke the voice of such a famous Jewish philosopher of the Holocaust as Arendt. Perhaps he cannot really "create his own authenticity" without her authoritative validation.

Whereas Styron, the writer, can rely upon the support of Arendt, an "insider," within the novel, Stingo, the writer, gains authentic access to the Holocaust through Sophie. Once the reader penetrates the rather thickly padded frame story of Stingo the sexually frustrated, virginal, fledgling writer in New York, Sophie clearly emerges as the significant figure in the text, but as object rather than subject—her story becomes Stingo's central narrative, as he retells it within the context of his own personal experiences. Though Sophie's role eventually emerges also as a literary one, Stingo's fascination with her is sexual from start to finish. Alvin Rosenfeld aptly points out in his review of the novel that "*Sophie's Choice* is not an historical novel and, despite its fascination with Auschwitz, is at bottom not even primarily 'about' the Holocaust," but rather belongs to the *Kunstlerroman* tradition, dealing instead with the maturity of the young artist.[33] He goes on to say that Sophie serves Stingo as any female muse does the aspiring writer, that eventually she helps to bring about both Stingo's literary and sexual maturity (the two areas, Rosenfeld notes, in which Stingo must compete with the more virile, Jewish Nathan). That he competes with Nathan at all illustrates the extent to which Stingo regards Sophie as both sexual and intellectual property.

Stingo's gradual subsumption of Sophie's voice begins near the opening of the novel's fourth chapter, when Sophie's hitherto Polish dialect disappears within Stingo's fluent secondhand account of her now unfolding story. Stingo decides to complete Sophie's wish "to write about Auschwitz" (496), an act he later describes as a sort of last gift to the now dead woman. In the last chapter of the novel Stingo resurrects from his older notes the line "Someday I will understand Auschwitz," but he edits his own notes to what they *should* have said, mainly, "*Someday I will write about Sophie's life and death, and thereby help demonstrate how absolute evil is never extinguished from the world.* Auschwitz itself remains inexplicable" (560). Here the text announces its own moment of genesis, the untold last testament (and now defining narrative) of a woman who took her own life. Sophie's death alone authenticates Stingo's "obligation" to write her story. Presented in three versions, like the Gospels, Sophie's story is subject to the reader's interpretation, such that the role of the actual author (Stingo) recedes into the shadows. Questions of truth and accuracy loom large throughout this text as Sophie continually revises her story, each time admitting prior lies and revealing a less sympathetic attitude toward Jews on the part of her family, and a less victimized portrait of herself. In fact, we learn that she makes many choices along her path, not just the one with which Stingo's narrative reaches its climax and which earns the novel's title.

More important, then, is Stingo's concluding comment above that his narrative will demonstrate the fact that absolute evil will always exist in the world: this and his undying libido are the shaping forces of Sophie's story. The resignation to evil in these lines echoes the very attitude with which Stingo begins his own narrative, when he reveals that his sole source of income is that derived from the sale by his great-grandfather of a slave boy, Artiste. The slave's name suggests a doubling of Stingo—how one artist dies so that another can flourish, a doubling that echoes Stingo's earlier account of the guilt he feels over having survived Okinawa, while the son of a coworker, Eddie Farrell, died there. Stingo imagines his life to be deeply related to Eddie's: "nothing ever pierced me so deeply as Farrell's brief, desolating story of his son Eddie, who seemed to me immolated on the earth of Okinawa that I might live—and write" (26). Hearing Farrell's story evokes in Stingo the kind of survivor guilt that he will later learn plagues Sophie. Though he may also feel guilt over taking the proceeds from the sale of Artiste, however, it certainly does not stop him from actually taking it. In fact, if anything it makes his taking the money necessary—now he *must* write. Now both Stingo's life and his desire to be a writer seem somehow fateful, necessary, sanctified as a true calling by the deaths of Billy Farrell, Artiste, and, we find, Sophie. Hence Stingo's moral conflict: how to justify his complicity with the system of slavery and his "survival" of war on two accounts, especially as he lives off the economic proceeds of the former and the literary proceeds of the latter. Stingo's writing is completely tied up in redeeming this, perhaps disproportionate, guilt. Like Sophie, we will learn, Stingo feels helpless before universal forces of evil: "For these many years afterward, as accusations from black people became more cranky and insistent that as a writer—a lying writer at that—I had turned to my own profit and advantage the miseries of slavery, I succumbed to a kind of masochistic resignation, and thinking of Artiste, said to myself: What the hell, once a racist exploiter always a racist exploiter" (34). In other words, profit and success inherently and unavoidably involve exploitation on some level—individual responsibility for changing this does not enter into this equation. Since the speaker is Stingo now looking back—that is, the Stingo post-Sophie—why should we believe that the Stingo who writes Sophie's story is any less of a racist exploiter, now of Sophie's life story, her miseries, and those of the victims of Auschwitz? Does his self-conscious admission of guilt absolve him of responsibility for either of these exploits?

Stingo's "masochistic resignation" is closely linked to that which Sophie herself displays throughout her narrative; unlike Stingo, however, Sophie takes the real punishment for her guilt. Repeatedly she is sexually and emotionally abused: a victim first of her evil father, then of her lover Kasik, of Rudolph Höss, of Höss's lesbian housemaid, of a digital rapist on a New York subway, among others, and then finally of Nathan, her consistently violent and abusive lover. Sophie resigns herself masochistically to Nathan's violence to assuage her immense guilt, which actually long preceded her "choice," before even going to Auschwitz, stemming from the realization of her complicity with her father's anti-Semitic politics. Narrating Sophie's punishment makes Stingo a kind of "witness"; it authenticates his narrative, his guilt, and his mission as a writer.

Yet Stingo also gets to enjoy her pleasure, or the pleasure which looking at her yields: her "achingly desirable, harmoniously proportioned Elberta peach of a derrière," her "young female body all creamy bare, with plump breasts that had perky brown nipples, a smoothly rounded belly with a frank eyewink of a bellybutton, and (be still my heart, I remember thinking) a nicely symmetrical triangle of honey-hued pubic hair" (209, 389). Because Sophie's narrative is filtered through Stingo's desires such as expressed here, when he says to her,

"You *know* you weren't a collaborator. . . . You know you were just a *victim*," we have trouble verifying Sophie's role (497). It changes with different accounts of her story, particularly when after Nathan beats her she admits having hated the Jews all along. At that moment she begins to attribute Nathan's brutality to his Jewishness, his trying to buy her love "like all Jews." She declares how "It's really true, in the end they are all exactly alike *sous la peau*, under the skin," everything until now has been lies, and that she really hates all those dirty Jews (383–84). Stingo merely writes off her comments to anguish and then chimes in himself, calling Morris Fink a "fucking little hebe" and a "money-mad, money-greedy Jewish bastard" after falsely accusing Morris of robbing him. The narrator's possibly ironic comment which concludes this section, calling Sophie and himself "two anti-Semites, on a summer outing," does not counteract the effect of the above epithets just because Stingo is self-conscious about them. Stingo's interpretation again reflects his resignation to "absolute evil," his inevitable complicity with it, as though his guilt somehow makes him its victim, too.

Both Sophie and Stingo have contributed to and survived systems of racial oppression at the expense of others' lives: Stingo's family owned slaves, and he now lives off of the sale of Artiste. Sophie's father is figured as the original Polish Hitler, and, as Nathan cruelly reminds her, she came to "breathe the clear Polish air while the multitudes at Auschwitz *choked slowly on the gas*" (227). Nathan accuses her of having hidden behind Poland's anti-Semitism for protection while others who could not do so died, a notion that proves true according to Sophie's confession of having tried to use her father's anti-Semitic pamphlet to win favor from Höss. They may both suffer from survivor guilt, yet Styron's alignment between Stingo and Sophie is inherently uneven— particularly as Sophie undergoes such brutality. Sophie is cruelly punished, but Stingo only suffers vicariously. Yet Styron wants to portray them both as perpetrators and *also victims* of these horrendous systems of oppression and cruelty—those victims who are often overlooked, as Styron basically says himself.[34] For this to work, Sophie's suffering must authenticate Stingo's, and as Stingo recounts it, redeem Stingo's guilt if not her own.

What is most troubling is just how much this literary and spiritual appropriation is tied up with Stingo's sexual desire for Sophie, how her punishment and sexual appeal become intertwined in what Rosenfeld calls "a new and singularly perverse type of sex object . . . the desirability of the Mutilated Woman."[35] When Stingo finds Sophie after overhearing for the first time a violent fight between her and Nathan, he observes the following:

> She stretched out her hand. . . . As she did so I saw for the first time the number tattooed on the suntanned, lightly freckled skin of her forearm—a purple number of at least five digits. . . . To the melting love in my stomach was added a sudden ache, and with an involuntary motion that was quite inexplicable . . . I gently grasped her wrist, looking more closely at the tattoo. Even at that instant I knew my curiosity might be offensive, but I couldn't help myself. (54)

By now we already know that Stingo has learned how his childhood love, Maria Hunt, had taken her life only a few weeks before, and only a few blocks from him in New York. He at first broods over "whether [he] might not have been able to save her, to prevent her from taking such a terrible course" (47). But his mourning quickly turns to sexual fantasy: "my departed Maria was standing before me, with the abandon of a strumpet stripping down to the flesh. . . . Naked, peach-ripe, chestnut hair flowing across her creamy breasts, she approached me where I lay stiff as a dagger . . . 'Oh Stingo, fuck me'" (47–48). Joan Smith attributes this fantasy of the dead girl to the book's "triumphant, all-conquering necrophilia" (we are reminded here that by the time this narrative is written, Sophie is dead, too).[36] It is *this* fantasy that Sophie and Nathan interrupt, first with their "fucking" and then with their violent fighting. Stingo's "offensive curiosity" about Sophie's tattoo, then, arises on the heels of an aborted fantasy, at the point of an autoerotic *coitus interruptus*.

Perhaps feeling that he can save *this* victimized woman, unlike Maria, that he can "take over this flaxen Polish treasure where Nathan, the thankless swine, had left off" (53), Stingo makes Sophie his new object of conquest, a purpose for his writerly mission. Given that Stingo realizes the offensiveness of his curiosity about her tattoo, however, one would think he would exhibit a bit more reverence, or respect, in his description of her. Instead we get this:

> As she went slowly up the stairs I took a good look at her body in its clinging silk summer dress. While it was a beautiful body, with all the right prominences, curves, continuities and symmetries, there was

something a little strange about it—nothing visibly missing and not so much deficient as reassembled. And that was precisely *it*, I could see. The odd quality proclaimed itself through the skin. It possessed the sickish plasticity (at the back of her arms it was especially noticeable) of one who has suffered severe emaciation and whose flesh is even now in the last stages of being restored. Also, I felt that underneath that healthy suntan there lingered the sallowness of a body now wholly rescued from a terrible crisis. But none of these at all diminished a kind of wonderfully negligent sexuality having to do at that moment, at least, with the casual way her pelvis moved and with her truly sumptuous rear end. Despite famine, her behind was as perfectly formed as some fantastic prize-winning pear; it vibrated with magical eloquence, and from this angle it so stirred my depths that I mentally pledged to the Presbyterian orphanages of Virginia a quarter of my future earnings as a writer in exchange for that bare ass's brief lodging—thirty seconds would do— within the compass of my cupped, supplicant palms. Old Stingo . . . there must be some perversity in this dorsal fixation. (55)

Perhaps so. For Rosenfeld, this perversion grows out of Styron's southern upbringing, an "irrepressible and emphatically regional fascination with the elaborate interconnections among race, sex, and death."[37] Indeed, traces of the Holocaust emerge here almost gothically, visually as a kind of palimpsest on Sophie's skin. That Stingo becomes aroused in spite of this, perhaps by this, suggests how quickly he can make that horror disappear. Almost in a kind of defense mechanism, Stingo transforms witnessing into the more palatable experience of desirous looking: before he can register her pain (perhaps because he cannot), it gets converted into his pleasure. Sophie's body is literally "damaged goods," there for the taking, visually and verbally; her reality authenticates Stingo's as her own simultaneously gets erased.

On account of Stingo's vocation as hungry writer and status as a young virgin, we may excuse him. After all, he arrives in Brooklyn hoping to fill what he realizes is "the large hollowness I carried within me . . . unacquainted with love and all but a stranger to death" (27). But it is Styron's choice to create such a protagonist, for whom Sophie will fill that void, with her body and with her story—her life and her death. Moreover, she serves Styron as well: Stingo plainly states, "I have thought that it might be possible to make a stab at understanding Auschwitz by trying to understand Sophie" (237). Such a statement assumes that Sophie bears a clear synecdochic relationship to Auschwitz,

as Styron tries to force Sophie to represent an entire nation and experience. Sophie has become the catalyst not only for Stingo's sexual and
literary maturity but for his spiritual maturity as well, and not just for
Stingo, but for anyone trying to understand Auschwitz. Sophie enables
Styron to claim authenticity for himself as a writer, where historically, in
relation to the Holocaust, there is none.

The Aesthetics of Sadism

Though Kosinski's first fictional work in English has raised critical hairs
since its publication in 1965, the credibility of the novel never quite recovered from the "Great Kosinski Scandal," as one critic has called it.[38]
In a June 1982 *Village Voice* article, Geoffrey Stokes and Eliot Fremont-
Smith not only doubted the autobiographical nature of Kosinski's work
but essentially accused Kosinski of lying and even of passing off others'
writing as his own.[39] Since then, much controversy has centered on the
authenticity of the "testimony" presented in *The Painted Bird:* did Kosinski, a Polish survivor, émigré, and eventual celebrity, actually experience all the horror and violence that he recounts in this novel? Is he the
"boy" wandering through war-ravaged Eastern European villages, repeatedly abused? For if not, how can representing such violence be justified? Kosinski never claimed that *The Painted Bird* was 100 percent
truth, but he never denied it either. The novel was first taken by critics
to be autobiographical, lauded by the very authority who condemned
Styron, Elie Wiesel. In the *Times Book Review,* Wiesel wrote of the book,
"Written with deep sincerity and sensitivity, this poignant account tran-
scends confession." Later, after Kosinski's suicide in 1991, Wiesel said,
"I thought it was fiction, and when he told me it was autobiography I
tore up my review and wrote one a thousand times better."[40] Wiesel's
authority authenticated this text with his stamp of approval.

According to biographer James Park Sloane, Kosinski's apparent
survivor status, charisma, and magnetic sex appeal launched Kosinski
into the American public eye, and into some of the most fashionable
New York circles: he dined with the Oscar de la Rentas, played polo with
the Dominican playboy Porfirio Rubirosa, hobnobbed with actors Shir-
ley MacLaine and Peter Sellers (the stars of the adaptation of his third
novel, *Being There*), appeared on Johnny Carson, and was even cast a role
in Warren Beatty's film *Reds.* He also became known for frequenting and

making fashionable certain New York S/M clubs and for seducing women wherever he went.[41] Until his death, Kosinski was both a celebrity and a symbolic figure in the American media imagination; as Sloane put it, "Always lurking beneath the surface of his public persona was the sense that he was a man who had been through unimaginable horrors, who had been to Hell and had returned to tell about it."[42] Which is why, when the *Village Voice* attacked Kosinski, it came as such a shock to the literary world. Moreover, when Polish journalist Joanna Siedlecka published her exposé of Kosinski, entitled in translation "The Ugly Black Bird," she argued to the world that the gruesome experiences Kosinski depicts in his novel were pure fabrications, that contrary to the tortures his protagonist undergoes and witnesses in rural, peasant Poland, his family lived in relative bourgeois comfort during the war years, even when in hiding.[43] Apparently Kosinski had a long history of personal lies, exaggeration, and self-fashioning, but Siedlecka exposed him as having betrayed those Poles who helped his family, Poland, and thereby history.

Kosinski responded with no remorse about his writing. He defended his aesthetic principles, closely aligned with his existentialist life philosophy: above all, in life and in art, the highest priority is "the incident." In his words, "an incident is simply a moment of life's drama of which we are aware as it takes place. . . . To bypass that moment, to dilute it in the gray everydayness, is to waste the most precious ingredient of living: the awareness of being alive."[44] Wary of the anesthetizing, and therefore dangerous, effects of popular culture, Kosinski believed it is the artist's job to intensify our awareness of such moments, to provoke, and to "cast spells" upon the reader.[45] The purpose of fiction, Kosinski felt, is "to engage the reader in a drama that is much more condensed and crystallized than the drama of our daily existence" and above all "to evoke a concrete dramatic response: to accept the artist's vision or to reject it." Given this, Kosinski stays true to his intention not to impose a moral on the reader but rather "to generate a moral judgment" in him or her.[46] In exercising what Cynthia Ozick calls "the rights of fiction," Kosinski uses narrative rhetorically to shock his reader, to defamiliarize reality in order to obtain a truth perhaps truer than history, if we only allow ourselves to see it.[47] In the attempt to reproduce the experience of horror, however, such rhetoric can slip into a fetishization of the very violence Kosinski tries to combat.

The debate over the "truth-value" of *The Painted Bird*, over whether or not the scenes in the novel actually occurred, may be well worn and inconclusive, but it raises the important question: can the depiction of trauma ever escape the perception that it is confessional or testimonial on some level? Friedlander insists that "the extermination of the Jews of Europe is as accessible to both representation and interpretation as any other historical event." Yet given this "most radical form of genocide encountered in history," he also makes clear that "some claim to 'truth' appears particularly imperative . . . there are limits to representation *which should not be but can easily be transgressed*."[48] It seems Kosinski transgresses such limits, but not in obvious ways. Although Kosinski was taken by the American public as a kind of spokesperson for his generation of Holocaust survivors, he claims in his afterword to *The Painted Bird* that he saw himself "solely as a storyteller," that "facts about [his] life should not be used to test the book's authenticity, any more than they should be used to encourage readers to read *The Painted Bird*" (xiii–xiv). Yet even if this novel is not to be taken as strict autobiography, its setting and plot approximate, if not the exact events of Kosinski's life, then those of one who lived through the Holocaust, as he himself did. If only for this reason, its protagonist does beg a comparison with Kosinski.

As framed by an anonymous third-person narrator—with a particular bias—the novel opens with a long, italicized preface. This preface introduces the first-person "testimony" to come, set, we are told, in "the first weeks of World War II, in the fall of 1939," when "a six-year-old boy from a large city in Eastern Europe was sent . . . to the shelter of a distant village" (3). The boy is not, like Kosinski, explicitly named a Jew; rather, he "differed ethnically" from those around him and "was considered a Gypsy or Jewish stray" by the villagers (4). The boy himself does little more than advance these suspicions later in his narrative, leaving the question of his ethnicity open-ended. The speaker, however, tells us how this boy, "olive-skinned, dark-haired, and black-eyed," contrasted with the villagers around him, who were "isolated and inbred, were fair-skinned with blond hair and blue or gray eyes" (3). Describing the villagers as "inbred," "backward," "ignorant," and "brutal," the speaker clearly establishes himself as superior to them, aligning himself rather with the educated boy who is about to descend backward into what seems like a pre-"civilized" place, untouched by time. While this placement of the "primitive" within modernity succeeds as a critique of Western progress, such a juxtaposition creates a keen narrative tension between reality and myth. Given Kosinski's claims to creating a "mythic domain, in the timeless fictive present, unrestrained by geography or history" (xiii), that he places this mystical setting right within the heart of present-day Eastern Europe creates an analogue between this "primi-tive" "heart of darkness" and the "civilized," advanced culture of the Nazis just beyond its perimeter. Though his point succeeds—Nazi evil is a form of human evil—he assumes his reader's knowledge of history and geography as a prerequisite for understanding a narrative that tries to surpass both.

As the novel proper begins, in the form of the boy's first-person ac-count, the boy achieves a distance from those around him first and fore-most structurally, by the nature of his dual position as observer and narrator. That he is a child makes him less suspect of tampering with the "facts" for a didactic purpose. Rather, the young boy's impression-ability and lack of fully formed subjectivity contribute to the sense that his impressions are immediate and accurate, as if his innocent eyes are a window onto the world. The narrator's use of terse, matter-of-fact commentary helps to maintain an unquestioning tone of voice through-out. This lends a veneer of objectivity perhaps less believable in an adult narrator, as well as the freedom from internal reflection, merely to mirror.

There is subjective mediation, however. At times the boy's descrip-tions are highly poeticized, such that the child's perspective is rendered in adult terms. This blurring of narrative perspective allows this narra-tor more freedom in terms of what he can actually tell. By adopting the child persona, the adult writer need no longer repress those elements otherwise too sexually explicit, violent, or vulgar to be morally and so-cially acceptable as subjects. For instance, the narrator's great preoccu-pation, even disgust, with the physical, often the physically grotesque, seems appropriate for a six-year-old boy confronting perhaps for the first time that which is radically "other." In a wonderfully imagistic pas-sage about his first guardian, Marta, the narrator proceeds to describe her "withered body," "long scraggy neck," "the bubbly saliva dripping from her lips," and the "countless corns, bunions, and the ingrown toe-nails on [her] gnarled feet" (5). Such description, while suggesting the depth of this rural hell, becomes excessive, even misogynistic. Formally, what from a child's eye is grotesque and horrifying *because* of its other-ness is not viewed by the adult writer as a temporary perspective shaped by age or lack of experience and then revised, but is instead endorsed, elaborated, and embellished with poetic language.[49] In attempting to render "truthfully" the boy's perspective, the writer departs from the naive gaze of the boy and slips into a spell of poetic effusion at the expense of the boy's first female guardian.

Naturally, in a first-person narrative the protagonist must remain alive and, if his insider testimony is to be taken with any authority, fairly well intact. Yet this seems a structural alibi for the boy's voyeurism. For example, when the boy observes the heinous murder of Lekh's lover, Stupid Ludmila, he remains miraculously hidden, near enough to discern every detail, yet far enough to be safe from harm. Ludmila, however, doesn't seem to die for no reason; before she is gang-raped by the farmers, then tortured and beaten to death by their wives, she sexually assaults the boy. When Lekh could not be found, the boy describes how Ludmila, drunk, chased him into a field, "threatened me with a belt and commanded me to take off my pants." He goes on: "she drew my face closer to her and ordered me to lie down between her thighs. I tried to free myself but she whipped me with the belt. My screams attracted the other shepherds" (53). Almost like a scene from an S/M porn film, this scene turns from kinky to utterly horrific, particularly as the boy (now suddenly ignored) portrays Ludmila as complicit:

> Stupid Ludmila noticed the approaching group of peasants and spread her legs wider. The men came over slowly, staring at her body.
> Without a word they surrounded her. Two of them immediately began to let down their pants. . . . A tall shepherd mounted the woman while she writhed below him, howling at his every move. The man struck openhanded blows at her breasts, leaned over and bit her nipples and kneaded her belly. When he finished and rose, another man took his place. Stupid Ludmila moaned and shuddered, drawing the man to her with her arms and legs. The other men crouched nearby, looking on, snickering and jesting. (53–54)

Do we really need to know that the shepherd "bit her nipples"? Such erotic details transform this metaphor for the horrors of the Holocaust into the stuff of an orgiastic sideshow. If this were not excessive enough, the boy goes on to describe the wives' violent, clearly jealous, responses to their husbands' "lover":

> The women held Stupid Ludmila down flat against the grass. They sat on her hands and legs and began beating her with the rakes, ripping her skin with their fingernails, tearing out her hair, spitting into her face. . . .

Stupid Ludmila lay bleeding. Blue bruises appeared on her tormented body. She groaned loudly, arched her back, trembled, vainly trying to free herself. One of the women now approached, holding a corked bottle of brownish-black manure. To the accompaniment of raucous laughter and loud encouragements from the others, she kneeled between Ludmila's legs and rammed the entire bottle inside her abused, assaulted slit, while she began to howl and moan like a beast. The other women looked on calmly. Suddenly with all her strength one of them kicked the bottom of the bottle sticking out of Stupid Ludmila's groin. There was the muffled noise of glass shattering inside. Now all the women began to kick Ludmila; the blood spurted round their boots and calves. When the last woman had finished kicking, Ludmila was dead. (54–55)

Could the boy have embellished this scene in his memory? Does he come to understand this heinous rape and murder as Ludmila's punishment for how she tried to humiliate him? Sex and violence are inextricable here, as understood and retold by the boy. Though the boy sees Lekh sob over his lover's dead body at the scene's conclusion, the boy leaves without comment. The narrator, as witness, assumes Ludmila's suffering as his own, as Ludmila is denied any voice other than her groaning in pain; her only agency comes from her ability, if you will, to fuck and to suffer. These two attributes become conflated in her death scene as she "groaned loudly, arched her back," and "trembled," as if climaxing in orgasm. Her murder is explicitly gendered, then eroticized as she is assaulted "to the accompaniment of raucous laughter and loud encouragements" by the village women, in a kind of primitive, ecstatic orgy. Ludmila's sexually violent death serves as a sacrificial subterfuge through which the boy undergoes a critical rite of sexual initiation, simultaneously traumatized and unharmed, both subject and object of such violence.

Because it is seldom the boy himself who undergoes the worst acts of violence, if his constant suffering is to be conveyed nevertheless, his textual existence must not permit him a moment's respite. During another sexually violent episode, this time involving a young "Jewess," the boy's perspectival identification is again troubling. The injured girl was found after having fallen from the floor of a passing train (on its way, presumably, to a concentration camp), and Rainbow, a local farmer, widower, and believer in "heavenly signs" like this one, took her home, adjacent to where the boy is staying (103). Like the boy, she had "thick eyebrows and very black eyes" as well as "long, glossy black hair," suggesting the (stereo)typical racial features of an Eastern European Jew (102). Yet in spite of their similarity in look, the boy continues to refer to her as "the Jewess" to insist on his ethnic difference from her.

Awakened by "noises and cries from [Rainbow's] barn" that night, to secure his vantage point, this time the boy "found a knothole through which [he] could see what was happening." As the scene progresses, Rainbow proceeds violently to rip off the girl's dress amid her helpless shrieks; she tries to escape, but he "kneeled on her long hair and held her face between his knees." Eyeing the girl now fully naked, the narrator remarks, "The light of the oil lamp threw shadows on her flesh." The scene becomes completely erotic, and we become the voyeurs: "Rainbow sat at the girl's side and stroked her body with his big hands. . . . Slowly Rainbow took off his knee boots and breeches, leaving on only a rough shirt. He straddled the prostrate girl and moved his hands gently over her shoulders, breasts, and belly" while she "moaned and whined" (104). Given the boy's visual, almost cinematic gaze, we are directed to identify with Rainbow, to feel the charge of his cruel power and her helplessness, when we remember that he is sexually assaulting an already traumatized, lost victim of Nazi persecution. It all seems so wrong, and yet desire propels us to keep reading to see if the unthinkable will occur. Referring to this scene, Lilly notes how Rainbow's "power over the girl is analogous to the now grown narrator's power over his readers, us."[50]

The scene then takes a cruel, perverse turn when Rainbow finally "with one brutal push opened her legs and fell on her with a thud." We realize she may be just a small girl in tremendous pain as this man forces himself upon her: "the girl arched her body, screamed, and kept opening and closing her fingers as though trying to grasp something" (104). Cruelty then turns to absurdity as Rainbow actually gets stuck inside the frail girl's body. Watching the two screaming, spitting, swearing, the narrator remarks: "I had often seen the same thing happen to dogs. Sometimes when they coupled violently, starved for release, they could not break loose again. They struggled with the painful tie, turning more and more away from each other, finally joined only at their rear ends. They seemed to be one body with two heads, and two tails growing in the same place. From man's friend they became nature's freak. They howled, yelped, and shook all over" (105). Nothing could be more detached than to compare this scene to that of desperate, sex-starved dogs. Rainbow begins to beat the wretched object of his sexual desire and violence "until he was exhausted," she who had, according to him, "sucked him in and wouldn't let go of him" (107). Even the critique of Rainbow's ignorance and superstition of Jewish vampirism loses its critical force when the protagonist counters it with nothing less than the most stereotypical ideas of peasant bestiality and, furthermore, fails to recognize his own complicity as the front-row member of the audience. Like the boy, we yearn to find out what happens as help arrives: "I could see nothing; I only heard the girl's last piercing shriek" (106).

Though Lilly at least addresses the sexual violence in the above scene, he fails to link it to Kosinski's narrative voice in other texts, which in his view is "limited by what it sees, a kind of eyeball, although certainly not a transparent one. Kosinski's fictive eyeball looks through a keyhole, as it were, seeing but not being seen."[51] In effect, Kosinski's voice is that of the literary voyeur who, when narrating scenes like that above, must enjoy a perverse pleasure.[52] That the boy was haunted by "strange dreams" (107) following this episode suggests how deeply it affected him. Yet how? What is the content of these dreams? Does he dream of raping or being raped? We are never told. As in many of these more disturbing scenes, it is as though the acts of witnessing and narrating are enough—that witnessing justifies the telling without qualification, self-reflection, or even moral judgment. The pain and/or pleasure taken in its retelling is left ambiguous.

Ultimately, we see the boy identify with the "true" oppressors outright when he has his first encounter with a German officer. In contrast to the basic revulsion he felt toward the peasants, his reaction is one of admiration. He claims never to have seen such a "striking uniform" before, with its "proud peak of the cap" and the "bold sign of the swastika" on the sleeve (112). While it is quite normal that those who are oppressed identify with their oppressors, and this display of Nazi aesthetics is unsurprising, this depiction nevertheless reflects the narrator's continual preoccupation with visual impressions. If the boy is to maintain his status above and apart from the villagers, his only other choices for models of identification remain the Jews—who, as the example of the "Jewess" suggests, are feminine, weak victims, rapable and reducible to animals—or the German officers. Clearly the latter is the more compelling choice:

> The instant I saw him I could not tear my gaze from him. His entire person seemed to have something utterly superhuman about it. . . . In a world of men with harrowed faces, with smashed eyes, bloody, bruised

and disfigured limbs, among the fetid, broken human bodies, he seemed an example of neat perfection that could not be sullied: the smooth, polished skin of his face, the bright golden hair showing under his peaked cap, his pure metal eyes. Every movement of his body seemed propelled by some tremendous internal force. The granite sound of his language was ideally suited to order the death of inferior, forlorn creatures. I was stung by a twinge of envy I had never experienced before, and I admired the glittering death's-head and crossbones that embellished his tall cap. I thought how good it would be to have such a gleaming and hairless skull instead of my Gypsy face which was feared and disliked by decent people. . . . In the presence of his resplendent being, armed in all the symbols of might and majesty, I was genuinely ashamed of my appearance. I had nothing against his killing me. (113–14)

It is possible that we are meant to pity the narrator's sincere jealousy of the officer, revealing as it does the paradoxical self-hatred and shame that can accompany victimization. Yet that would require our distance from him, and until this point we are given no reason to create such distance. Rather, the boy's unifying perspective is all that holds this episodic, barbaric, and otherwise chaotic narrative together. To distance ourselves from him would be readerly suicide.

In contrast to the boy's stereotypical portraits of the villagers as superstitious, backward, and barbaric, this passage suggests not only his individual desire for the officer's opulence but also a welcome *aesthetic* relief from the "bloody, bruised and disfigured limbs" and the "fetid, broken human bodies" among whom the boy has lived. Rather, fascinated both by the aesthetic "symbols of might and majesty" on the Nazi uniform and by the officer's stereotypical Aryan features—his "bright golden hair," "pure metal eyes," and "superhuman" quality—the boy is almost disappointed when he is taken into the protective custody of a priest, whose "cassock was a miserable thing in comparison with the uniform adorned by the death's-head, crossbones, and lightning bolts" (114). In contrast to its grotesque underbelly, reserved for the peasants, here Kosinski exhibits what Susan Sontag has dubbed "fascinating fascism": a "utopian aesthetics" of "physical perfection" that "implies an ideal eroticism: sexuality converted into the magnetism of leaders and the joy of followers."[53]

The boy's desire to identify with Nazi power is later confirmed during his first sexual experience with Ewka. Since an earlier traumatic experience has rendered him mute by this point, the boy's means of communication are completely restricted to visual signs, isolating him even further within the scope of his own gaze. Yet his traumas thus far have not squelched his sexual appetite, and may in fact have aroused it. Although he first describes Ewka somewhat plainly as "tall and blond and thin with breasts like unripe pears and hips that allowed her to squeeze easily between the staves of a fence" (144), as the two engage in vividly rendered sexual exploration, Ewka turns out to be the ideal lover. She demanded little from him and taught him everything as she "tried to make [him] become a man" (147). During his nights with Ewka, his dreams waver between the Aryan ideal and the grotesque:

> I forgot my fate of a Gypsy mute destined for fire. . . . In my dreams I turned into a tall, handsome man, fair-skinned, blue-eyed, with hair like pale autumn leaves. I became a German officer in a tight, black uniform. Or I turned into a birdcatcher, familiar with all the secret paths of the woods and marshes.
>
> In these dreams my artful hands induced wild passions in the village girls, turning them into wanton Ludmilas who chased me through flowery glades. . . . There was another kind of dream, bringing me a different kind of vision. Ewka's attempt to make a grown man of me succeeded instantly. One part of my body grew rapidly into a monstrous shaft of incredible size, while the rest remained unchanged. I became a hideous freak; I was locked in a cage and people watched me through the bars, laughing excitedly. (147)

The first fantasy is to become the hunter, not the hunted. Whether he becomes the German officer or Lekh, the birdcatcher, at least he is the subject of power, not its object; no longer a "painted bird"—the outsider marked for destruction, feminized and raped like Stupid Ludmila, or the "Jewess" and other Nazi victims.[54] That he dreams this in the context of his first sexual relationship emphasizes what he has learned: the power to victimize, to control the fate of others, is intimately tied to his burgeoning masculinity and sexuality.

In a curious reversal of the gaze, in his nightmare the boy becomes the object of others' power, the "hideous freak" constituted by their consuming voyeurism. Yet it does not render him impotent; on the contrary, even when a caged animal, he imagines himself as well endowed as a porn star.[55] His sexuality here is distorted, grotesque, and shameful, foreshadowing how his affair will end: he eventually spies on Ewka only to see her copulate with a goat. The boy's rite of passage into manhood is accompanied by a severe nihilistic turn. He tells us that "the time of passivity was over" and resigns himself to join the forces of the "Evil Ones" (154). Seizing the power of these forces means becoming the hunter, the persecutor, the rapist. Marking his move into manhood, the desire for such sadistic power explains the detached, cruel tone of all we have been reading thus far.[56]

The boy finally attains the opportunity to identify with the Evil Ones during the final raid of the Kalmuks. When they appear in the village, he compares their appearance to his own:

> They all had black oily hair which glistened in the sun. Almost blue-black, it was even darker than mine, as were also their eyes and their swarthy skins. They had large white teeth, high cheekbones, and wide faces that looked swollen.
>
> For a moment, as I looked at them, I felt great pride and satisfaction. After all, these proud horsemen were black-haired, black-eyed, and dark-skinned. They differed from the people of the village as night from day. The arrival of these dark Kalmuks drove the fair-haired village people almost insane with fear. (176)

Having racially identified with these men, the narrator then proceeds to watch from his hiding place in the bushes, with a cold eye, as the drunk, renegade soldiers savagely mutilate and rape dozens of peasant men, women, and children. Furthermore, the rapes are vividly described in all their variations: on horseback, from behind, with a woman sandwiched between two soldiers on a horse, with whips, of children who are then tossed away, with horses, until the whole scene turns into a macabre circus of sexual violence.

The narrator claims to be "overwhelmed with dread and disgust" at this spectacle, yet he cannot look away, not if the novel is to be written. Yet his choice to render it in full detail remains both excessive and brutal. The boy cynically believes himself fated to remain in league with men such as these because of his racial features: "I was black. My hair and eyes were as black as these Kalmuks'. Evidently I belonged with them in another world. There could be no mercy for such as me. A dreadful fate had sentenced me to have black hair and eyes in common with this horde of savages" (178–79). The boy's nihilistic conclusion (based solely upon his physical appearance) reflects his internalization of the logic of Nazi persecution—he is resigned to evil. Then, as if to intensify his own punishment, he continues to indulge in describing their violence as evidence of *his* cruel, sealed fate rather than that of those actually suffering physical mutilation. Once again, the narrator becomes the cathexis of victimization—in his identification with the murderers he becomes one of them, at once cruel victor and helpless victim, sadist and masochist. This is the crime of this scene: the loss of the humanist subject. The *Bildungsroman* has become inverted. Rosenfeld explains that to understand this "literary paradigm" of Holocaust literature, "we must understand the revisionary and essentially antithetical nature of so much of Holocaust writing, which not only mimics and parodies but finally refutes and rejects its direct literary antecedents. The *Bildungsroman* . . . is one of these." In such cases where it is employed, "one sees not only a reversal of a familiar literary pattern but also a repudiation of the philosophical basis on which it rests."[57]

Perhaps it is scenes like those above—gratuitous in their sexual violence—that caused critics to question if such things *actually happened* to Kosinski. For if they did not actually occur, what other reasons could he have for depicting such scenes in detail? In response to the claim that the novel exploits the horrors of war to "satisfy [his] own peculiar imagination," Kosinski argues:

> In point of fact, almost none of those who chose to view the book as a historical novel bothered to refer to actual source materials. Personal accounts of survivors and official War documents were either unknown by or irrelevant to my critics. None seemed to have taken the time to read the easily available testimony, such as that of a nineteen-year-old survivor describing the punishment meted out to an Eastern European village that had sheltered an enemy of the Reich. (xxi)

To justify his violent depictions, Kosinski ultimately needs recourse to the actual horrors of a *specific* time and place—Eastern Europe under German occupation during World War II—for his narrative to be compelling. Although Kosinski perhaps wanted his readership to ignore the facts of his own life as authenticators of the novel, he claims to have relied on the testimony of others, suggesting that perhaps his novel could not have stood on its own without this recourse to "reality." We might call *The Painted Bird* an anti-*Bildungsroman* in that its protagonist resists integration at every turn. This tension is resolved, however, by

Kosinski's subsequent position in the American media, both as he who has looked into the face of a universal evil and as the particular native informant whose unique life experience proffers him a certain "sacred" celebrity status—Kosinski the survivor, the authentic confessor/writer in Calvinist, capitalist America, who like the boy in the final pages of the novel can thus say, "speech was now mine" (234). As Sloane notes, writing *The Painted Bird* thus "was a task that could be done with freedom in America . . . because the facts upon which the story was based existed far away in time and place, and on the far side of what seemed increasingly an impenetrable wall."[58] And it is precisely in America, after all, with its long literary tradition of Puritan confessions of authentic experience, that Kosinski found such great success.

Conclusion: The Erotics of Reading Auschwitz

In a recent discussion of so-called Holocaust novels—in particular, of *Sophie's Choice*—Cynthia Ozick argues, "the rights of fiction are not the rights of history."[59] She contends that to call novels such as Styron's, about Auschwitz, "historical novels" is oxymoronic, since fiction operates chiefly in the realm of imagination, while "history is rooted in document and archive."[60] Her attempt to separate radically the fields of fiction and history—fields whose integrity and circumscription have long been under the scrutiny of historiographers and discourse theorists alike—reflects the general anxiety that, as the last generation of Holocaust survivors dwindles away, the historical reality of the Holocaust will be swept under the rug of authorial fabrication and personal ideology. *Sophie's Choice*, Ozick argues, not only does not accord with the facts of history (in which most Holocaust victims were Jews) but even distorts them through Styron's ideological focus on the "exceptional case" of Sophie, a Catholic Polish woman. Sophie must therefore be read as a product of Styron's particular imagination; less a character than a polemical, ideological choice lest "in the name of the autonomous rights of fiction . . . anomaly sweeps away memory; anomaly displaces history."[61]

Ozick's point is well taken: perhaps we should not call *Sophie's Choice* a "Holocaust novel," because we cannot expect fiction to bend to history's rules. But if so, then we cannot call *The Painted Bird* a "Holocaust novel" either; it, too, operates according to its own rules, apparently violating different rules of history. In the face of neo-Nazi revisionist history,

Ozick's concern makes perfect sense, but imposing such constraints upon Holocaust novels means restricting poetic license, that principle which defines fiction as such. I believe Ozick would acknowledge that history, fiction, and testimony are all bound to the same medium of representation, language—in all its potential corruptibility. Yet to claim, as Ozick does, that the camera ought then to be privileged over the word in its ability to resist the corruption of truth is not the answer either, for it renders us unable effectively to read both Holocaust fiction *and* testimony, and to distinguish the two.

Rather, and here I agree with her, "if there is any answer at all to this argument . . . it must lie in the novelist's intention." When a novel claims to be "directed consciously toward history," she goes on, "that the divide between history and the imagination is being purposefully bridged . . . then the argument for fictional autonomy collapses, and the rights of history can begin to urge their own force."[62] In other words, you can't have it both ways: you can't maintain historical authenticity and exercise fictional autonomy, not, at any rate, if you plan to "touch on the destruction of six million souls, and on the extirpation of their millennial civilization in Europe."[63]

Sophie's Choice and *The Painted Bird* try to have it both ways. In both novels, the historical reality of the Holocaust is taken for granted (whether each author experienced it directly or not), and on that basis the author is liberated to explore the otherwise taboo subject of sexuality against a backdrop of truth. Representing the Holocaust becomes an alibi for gratuitous sexual exploration, without providing adequate justification for why. In a paradoxical move at once brilliant and troubling, by simply referring to the undeniable truth of the Holocaust in all its materiality, each author thereby authenticates his freedom from history altogether to explore the realm of the imagination. The violence used to illustrate the horrors of the Holocaust, moreover, gets intertwined with sexual titillation: violated female bodies become the ultimate symbolic loci of "the banality of evil." Furthermore, since such violence may be a "truth" of the Holocaust, we are compelled to keep reading, to keep watching. It is somehow our "duty" to be vicariously abused as these victims actually were, since to question the veracity of these representations would be implicitly to question the actuality of the Shoah.

In both novels, we are limited to the perspective of male narrators, protagonists who hold the dual position of witness (for Kosinski's boy, firsthand; for Stingo, secondhand) to traumatic sexual violence and thus its vicarious victim. By virtue of their voyeuristic perspectives, their status as witness gets mingled with their role as agent of desire. Through their eyes we are directed to watch violence enacted upon others, and thus we retain the power of the voyeur. They manage to diffuse their pleasure through suffering, and therefore as readers identifying with their first-person perspectives, so do we. *The Painted Bird* may be an embellished narrative, *truthful* if not true. Its excessive sexual violence may be a sign of Kosinski's overcompensation in establishing that truthfulness. It may even have paved the way for Styron's novel, one that so explicitly infuses Holocaust representations with desire. Yet we cannot dismiss these extreme literary cases on these grounds, "true" or not.

Rather, we must recognize a different kind of truth they reveal, that there is an extremely disturbing element of pleasure—the close twin of its opposite, pain—involved in the experience of reading certain Holocaust narratives. This may be what produces in many readers (including myself) a sense of "uneasiness" described by Saul Friedlander, a feeling one gets when an interpretation or representation of the Holocaust is somehow wrong.[64] Perhaps this discomfort (in some readers so severe as to result in desensitization or sheer doubt)[65] prevents us from understanding our own pleasure, the uncontrollable pleasure of looking, the satisfaction of a curiosity, from a voyeuristic distance, as if at a horrible literary car crash. Our impulse to judge the truth-value of these works strictly in terms of history safeguards us from this disturbing possibility. This way, if certain events didn't "really happen," then we don't have to deal with them, their moral implications, or the feelings they produce. If they did "really happen," it becomes morally difficult to read their representations critically. Because *we* are not able, perhaps not ready, perhaps not willing, to get beyond history, our reading of these novels is limited.

Notes

1. Alvin Rosenfeld, *A Double Dying: Reflections on Holocaust Literature* (Bloomington: Indiana University Press, 1980), 164.

2. Jerzy Kosinski, *The Painted Bird*, 2nd ed. (New York: Grove Press, 1976); William Styron, *Sophie's Choice* (New York: Vintage, 1992). All subsequent references will be to these editions, and page numbers will be cited parenthetically in the text.

3. Rosenfeld, *A Double Dying*, 164.

4. Sue Vice, *Holocaust Fiction* (London: Routledge, 2000), 124. In addition to providing an excellent review of the criticism of these and other Holocaust novels, Vice's goal is not to read Holocaust fiction in competition with Holocaust testimony, but on its own literary terms: "to construct a typology of Holocaust fiction" rather than "to consign the genre as a whole to the status of a failed supplement." She aims to construct a typology that is "not concerned with prescriptive 'rules' . . . but with a description of actual fictive practice" (8). I take her position as a point of departure from which to argue specifically how descriptions of eroticized violence function in these novels.

5. Rosenfeld, *A Double Dying*, 164.

6. Joan Smith, "Holocaust Girls," *Misogynies* (New York: Fawcett Columbine, 1989), 106–19, 108.

7. Ibid., 118.

8. Rosenfeld, *A Double Dying*, 76.

9. Paul Lilly, *Words in Search of Victims: The Achievement of Jerzy Kosinski* (Kent, Ohio: Kent State University Press, 1988), 18.

10. In his afterword to *The Painted Bird*, written in 1976 in response to the novel's initial controversy, Kosinski names as his purpose in writing the novel "to examine 'this new language' of brutality and its consequent new counter-language of anguish and despair." Here he claims to be citing the writing of "a Jewish concentration camp inmate shortly before his death in the gas chamber" (xii).

11. It is worth pointing out here the links among voyeurism, pleasure, and power: in her widely critiqued essay "Visual Pleasure and Narrative Cinema," Laura Mulvey has linked "scopophilia," or the "pleasure in looking," to the cinematic gaze and patriarchal culture. Referring to Freud's *Three Essays on Sexuality*, Mulvey notes how Freud associated scopophilia with "taking other people as objects [and] subjecting them to a controlling and curious gaze." This can develop into a "perversion, producing obsessive voyeurs and Peeping Toms whose only sexual satisfaction can come from watching, in an active controlling sense, an objectified other" (434). Mulvey identifies two types of "looking" enacted by the male looker upon the female object: "fetishistic scopophilia," which "can exist outside linear time as the erotic instinct is focused on the look alone," and "voyeurism," which "has associations with sadism" (438). *Feminisms: An Anthology of Literary Theory and Criticism*, ed. Robyn R. Warhol and Diane Price Herndl (New Brunswick: Rutgers University Press, 1993), 432–42.

12. In his "Witness and Testimony in the *Fragments* Controversy" (chapter 9 in this volume), Michael Bernard-Donals suggests that testimony is not the representation of history, but rather that such narration acts formally to rend history, to disrupt it, much in the same way that, initially, the traumatic event did for the witness. The act of presenting testimony, then, is to present and

thereby reproduce the *experience* of trauma—not to reproduce in some positivist, mimetic way actual events, or content, but the affect of trauma. Redirecting these questions to fiction, we see that the way Bernard-Donals suggests we read testimony is essentially the way we always read fiction, works that act in self-conscious, mediated ways to produce that very same affect. In fiction, then, it cannot be enough to disrupt the formal mechanisms of representation; rather, beyond this, an author must convey clearly to his or her reader how to read such disruptions: authentically or rhetorically. Is the fictional text a naive attempt to remember and communicate a trauma (no matter how unsuccessful, logically speaking, the resulting text is), or is it a staged performance of just such an attempt? I contend that the mediation of the text is a key factor in determining what we as readers can reasonably expect from a Holocaust narrative, and where the ethics of reading it lie.

13. Vice, *Holocaust Fiction*, 1. In terms of how the Holocaust disturbs literary form, she points out, for example, how the plot of any Holocaust novel cannot allow for such literary staples as suspense, the battle over good versus evil, or choice of ending, since the outcome is already known (2–3).

14. Rosenfeld, *A Double Dying*, 159.

15. Irving Howe describes Styron's novel as a "sentimental 'universalizing' of the Holocaust." "Writing and the Holocaust," in *Writing and the Holocaust*, ed. Berel Lang (New York: Holmes & Meier, 1988), 175–99, 183; For a more recent and most forceful objection to Styron's use of the "exception," Sophie, to define the historical rule, see Cynthia Ozick, "The Rights of History and the Rights of Imagination," *Commentary* 107, no. 3 (1999): 22–27. See my discussion of Ozick's argument below.

16. Smith, *Misogynies*, 107.

17. Saul Friedlander, ed. and intro., *Probing the Limits of Representation: Nazism and the Final Solution* (Cambridge: Harvard University Press, 1992), 18, 1.

18. Smith asks a similar question of *Sophie's Choice:* "could it be that what [Styron] is really doing in telling Sophie's story is using tragic events as a vehicle for sexual fantasies which would otherwise be condemned as belonging on the unacceptable side of the boundary between literature and porn?" *Misogynies*, 112.

19. I would like to thank Eric Sundquist for suggesting this idea to me, for conducting the engaging seminar out of which this essay developed, and for his generous feedback on an early draft.

20. To cite two egregious examples, one need only think of Philip Roth's *Portnoy's Complaint* (1967) and of Erica Jong's *Fear of Flying* (1973), which gave birth to "the zipless fuck."

21. Styron told several interviewers that Stingo was based on himself, a nickname for himself, and that the novel was partly autobiographical. See Michael West, "An Interview with William Styron," *Island*, 6 February 1977, 46–63; Hilary Mills, "Creators on Creating: William Styron," *Saturday Review*

7 (September 1980): 46–50; and Michel Braudau, "Why I Wrote Sophie's Choice," *L'Express*, 28 February 1981, 76; all reprinted in *Conversations with William Styron*, ed. James L. W. West III (Jackson: University Press of Mississippi, 1985).

22. Sara Horowitz calls *The Painted Bird* "a grotesque turn of the picaresque" in *Voicing the Void* (Albany: SUNY Press, 1997), 71; Vice also calls it a picaresque novel, citing Geoffrey Green, "The Nightmarish Quest of Jerzy Kosinski," in *The Anxious Subject: Nightmares and Daymares in Literature and Film*, ed. Moshe Lazar (Malibu: Undena, 1983), 51–87. However, she also sees it as having an "ambiguous generic identity," sharing characteristics of an "historicized allegory," a "fictionalized autobiography," and "*Kunstlerroman*, one specifically about learning to write the trauma of the Holocaust" (*Holocaust Fiction*, 89, 82, 83). Kosinski himself created a new generic category for his novel, "autofiction," which James Park Sloane describes as "a sort of modified autobiography in which much emphasis is placed upon standing outside one's experience and writing about it in unfamiliar language; its deeper rationale is that all remembered human experience is, in one sense, fiction. . . . It is, more nearly, an argument that *there is no such thing as truth*—a powerfully nihilistic concept, but a highly interesting one." *Jerzy Kosinski: A Biography* (New York: Dutton, 1996), 217.

23. *Sophie's Choice* is most commonly read as a *Kunstlerroman*, a novel of an artist's maturation. However, Cynthia Ozick calls it a "richly literary *Bildungsroman*" ("The Rights of History," 25); James E. Young calls it a "documentary fiction" ("Holocaust Documentary Fiction: The Novelist as Eyewitness," in *Writing and the Holocaust*, ed. Berel Lang [New York: Holmes & Meyer, 1988], 200–215, 201); for Vice it seems at first an autobiographical novel, later a "comic Kunstlerroman," and when dealing with Auschwitz, "faction" (*Holocaust Fiction*, 118); Rosenfeld says it is, by turns, a "parody of the Southern novel," "the American Jewish novel," "the novel of Sexual Initiation," and "the novel of the Holocaust" ("The Holocaust According to William Styron," *Midstream* 25 [December 1979]: 46).

24. Lilly makes a similar point concerning how the boy is transformed "from passive victim to active inflictor of pain." *Words in Search of Victims*, 30.

25. Elaine Scarry, *The Body in Pain: The Making and Unmaking of the World* (New York: Oxford University Press, 1985). In her compelling argument, Scarry locates moments of creation and destruction of the world in the body in pain, as it provides the materiality that substantiates these moments for knowledge. Revealing the dual nature of pain—as something that can be neither denied nor confirmed—Scarry artfully reformulates the Cartesian *cogito*, such that "to have pain is to have certainty; to hear about pain is to have doubt" (13).

26. George Steiner, *Language and Silence* (New York: Atheneum, 1982), 163.

27. Quoted in William Styron, "A Wheel of Evil Comes Full Circle: The Making of *Sophie's Choice*," *Sewanee Review* 105 (Summer 1997): 395–400, 399.

28. One analogy, of course, is the slave narrative, authenticated by the framing of a white editor who testifies to the authenticity of the narrative itself. Since such a convention was constituted in response to the racism of the postbellum world, it is no longer an option today. Instead we have the critic, whose approval or rejection can serve a similar function.

29. Richard L. Rubenstein, "The South Encounters the Holocaust: William Styron's *Sophie's Choice*," *Michigan Quarterly Review* 20, no. 4 (1981): 425–42, 440.

30. Ibid., 441.

31. Styron, "Wheel of Evil," 397.

32. Ibid.

33. Rosenfeld, "The Holocaust," 43.

34. In his essay "Hell Reconsidered," Styron defends against the preconception that Auschwitz was "a place where Jews were exterminated by the millions in gas chambers—simply this and nothing more" (98), which is incomplete in that it fails to acknowledge "the vast number of gentiles who partook in the same perdition visited upon the Jews" (101). By invoking critics and historians such as George Steiner, Stanley Elkins, and Richard Rubenstein, Styron includes himself in the interpretive historiographical tradition that sees the Holocaust as somehow a continuation of slavery, or at least that the comparison between the two phenomena is fruitful. In *This Quiet Dust* (New York: Random House, 1981), 95–105.

35. Rosenfeld, "The Holocaust," 47.

36. Smith, *Misogynies*, 114.

37. Rosenfeld, "The Holocaust," 47.

38. Stephen Schiff, "The Kosinski Conundrum," *Vanity Fair*, June 1988, 114–19, 166–70, reprinted in *Critical Essays on Jerzy Kosinski*, ed. Barbara Tepa Lupack (New York: G. K. Hall, 1998), 223.

39. Geoffrey Stokes and Eliot Fremont-Smith, "Jerzy Kosinski's Tainted Words," *Village Voice*, June 22, 1982, 41–43.

40. Cited in James Park Sloane, "Kosinski's War," *New Yorker*, October 10, 1994, 46.

41. Ibid., 47.

42. Ibid.

43. Ibid., 48.

44. Interview with Gail Sheehy, "The Psychological Novelist as Portable Man," *Psychology Today*, December 1977, 52, 55–56, 126, 128, 130, reprinted in Lupack, *Critical Essays*, 121.

45. Ibid., 121.

46. Ibid., 124.

47. Ozick, "The Rights of History," 23.

48. Friedlander, *Probing the Limits*, 1, 2.

49. Vice calls this a Bakhtinian "double-voicedness," a blend of the free indirect discourse of the more mature boy in retrospect, and the *"faux-naif* narration" of the younger one. My question is: where is Kosinski's voice? *Holocaust Fiction*, 82, 85.

50. Lilly, *Words in Search of Victims*, 22.

51. Ibid., 3.

52. Referring to Kosinski's brief experience in the 1950s as a photographer, Sloane comments on Kosinski's scopophilic penchant: "The inability to look away, followed by fascination, then identification, was a harbinger of Kosinski's future response to the grotesque." *Jerzy Kosinski*, 72.

53. Susan Sontag, "Fascinating Fascism," in *A Susan Sontag Reader*, ed. Elizabeth Hardwick (New York: Farrar, Straus, Giroux, 1982), 305–25, 317. In pornographic culture, Sontag argues, "the SS has become a referent of sexual adventurism. Much of the imagery of far-out sex has been placed under the sign of Nazism" (323).

54. Sontag also argues the connection between political and sexual power: "Like Nietzsche and Wagner, Hitler regarded leadership as sexual mastery of the 'feminine' masses, as rape." Ibid., 323.

55. Sloane makes much of Kosinski's sexuality, recording from friends' reports of his activity and well-known prowess as a graduate student in Warsaw: "Like each of his close friends, Krauze was immediately and greatly impressed by Kosinski's talent for seduction. Indeed, seduction, as Kosinski practiced it, was a veritable art form; Krauze is not the only acquaintance of that period who remembers Kosinski as having the ability to pick up a woman 'between tram stops.'" Sloane goes on, "Kosinski's sexual appetite seemed limitless, as did his openness to experimentation and desire to test boundaries." *Jerzy Kosinski*, 86, 87.

56. This attitude may have autobiographical origins, as Sloane notes, "in the eyes of adults who knew him, the boy simply had a mean streak. . . . A witness to so much violence, while he himself was compelled to self-restraint, Kosinski now bore within him seeds of the imaginative revenge dramas he would one day create." *Jerzy Kosinski*, 58.

57. Rosenfeld, *A Double Dying*, 29. Rosenfeld refers here to Lawrence Langer, who argues about Elie Wiesel's *Night* that it "illustrates with unmitigated horror this reversal of the *Bildungsroman* formula." Langer, *The Holocaust and the Literary Imagination* (New Haven: Yale University Press, 1975), 84.

58. Sloane, *Jerzy Kosinski*, 190.

59. Ozick, "The Rights of History." In addition to *Sophie's Choice*, Ozick discusses German writer Bernard Schlink's 1998 novel *The Reader*, which I do not address here.

60. Ibid., 23. In a recent interview, Ozick rejected the idea of writing Holocaust fiction altogether as inappropriate, given the wealth of testimony in

print, while admitting, however, that she continues to do so herself: "I don't agree with the sentiment 'write what you know.' That recommends circumscription. I think one should write what one doesn't know. . . . All the same, I'm against writing Holocaust fiction: that is, imagining those atrocities." Katie Bolick, "The Many Faces of Cynthia Ozick," *Atlantic Online*, May 15, 1997, http:// www.theatlantic.com/unbound/factfict/ozick.htm.

61. Ibid., 27.

62. Ibid.

63. Ibid., 25.

64. Friedlander, *Probing the Limits*, 2.

65. Such doubt was the case for many first-year UCLA undergraduate students with whom I recently read this novel.

5

Maus and the Epistemology of Witness

RICHARD GLEJZER

> If forgetfulness precedes memory or perhaps founds it, or has
> no connection with it at all, then to forget is not simply a weak-
> ness, a failing, an absence or void (the starting point of a recol-
> lection but a starting point which, like an anticipatory shade,
> would obscure remembrance in its very possibility, restoring the
> memorable to its fragility and memory to the loss of memory).
> No, forgetfulness would be not emptiness, but neither negative
> nor positive: the passive demand that neither welcomes nor
> withdraws the past, but designating there what has never taken
> place.
>
> Maurice Blanchot, *The Writing of the Disaster*

> Memory is something that goes round in circles. However, it's
> made up of messages, it's a succession of little signs of plus or
> minus, which file in one after the other and go round and round
> like the little electric lights on the Place de l'Opera that go on
> and off.
>
> Jacques Lacan, *The Seminar of Jacques Lacan, Book II: The Psychoses,*
> *1955–1956*

Art Spiegelman concludes his two-volume *Maus* with an instance of
embedded memory, where he recollects a moment of his father's recollection. The final page depicts Vladek telling the story of his reunion
with his wife, Anja, after being separated for over a year upon their arrival at Auschwitz. Vladek's story ends with an uncharacteristically

brief description of the reunion: "It was such a moment that everybody around was crying together with us. More I don't need to tell you. We were both very happy, and lived happy, happy ever after."[1] However, everything that precedes this conclusion speaks of a very different ending to Vladek's story—the death of their first son, Richieu, Anja's suicide decades later, Vladek's tumultuous relationship with his second wife, Mala. Similarly, the very last caption after Vladek's story is done depicts an equally complex scene. Vladek, having concluded his "survivor's tale," rolls over in bed and says to Artie: "So . . . Let's stop, please, your tape recorder . . . I'm tired from talking, Richieu, and it's enough stories for now . . ." (2:136). Like the immediately preceding rendering of the "happy ever after" of Vladek's story, this other memory, Artie's memory of his father's words to him, where his father addresses him as his other son, the one who did not survive the Holocaust, speaks to an object of memory that addresses something beyond the more commonly referential aspects of testimony. Although these two concluding moments are both in some ways counterfactual—we have seen throughout *Maus* that Vladek and Anja did not live "happy ever after" and that Richieu was poisoned to prevent capture, both moments do offer up something true, something of the forgetfulness of which Blanchot speaks and Lacan's plus or minus of memory's circulation. The moment of reunion in Vladek's story does premise a "happy ever after," as does the survival of Richieu in Vladek's parting from Artie. This final moment of reunion, a reunion that leads to the survival of Richieu as well as a "happy every after" with Anja, never happened, and thus it cannot be remembered except as something forgotten, something that intrudes at the ending of *Maus* as a minus that is present, as something missing that can only be accounted for counterfactually. But it is this counterfactual conclusion that ultimately grounds the act of witnessing in this text, where the epistemology of testimony breaks down in favor of a more particular knowledge effected in witnessing. Throughout *Maus*, Spiegelman points toward the way witnessing is constituted by memory and the necessarily conflicting epistemologies that result from memory's re-constitution, its re-membering of an impossible link between seeing and knowing.

This is not to say that memory itself is "unreliable" or that it is "reliable" or even something in between. Rather, following Spiegelman's conclusion to *Maus*, I would like to consider such questions on a structural rather than a merely formal plane, where we can consider the ways in which the structure of memory informs or imbues remembering with what Blanchot calls forgetfulness and what Lacan describes as the oscillation of plus or minus, moments within testimony that attempt to speak what a subject remembers. But what, then, is this "what" of remembering? What exactly does a subject re-member when testifying? What is it that *Maus* points us toward as the object of memory as it is expressed within testimony? How we address these questions sets the stakes for what we are to do with all Holocaust testimony, how we are to grapple with and, in the end, value the words that survivors speak.

In the first essay in this volume, James Young articulates memory as something ultimately residing in Spiegelman himself, as something to be traced not only in *Maus* but also in the ways in which Spiegelman himself speaks about *Maus,* how he comments on his text and its inadequacies. Young's examination of the "commix" form of *Maus* illuminates the ways in which he sees the text as a kind of "working through," where the very form of the text offers a trace of Spiegelman's own relationship with what he remembers as a second-generation survivor: "Spiegelman reproduces his hand's movement in scale—its shakiness, the thickness of his drawing pencil line, the limits of miniaturization— all to put a cap on detail and fine line and so keep the pictures underdetermined. This would be the equivalent of the historian's voice—not as it interrupts the narrative, however, but as it constitutes it." And it is in Spiegelman's role as historian that Young defines the object of memory here as ultimately referential, all the while acknowledging that such a referent cannot be signified in the story itself. Young acknowledges that the real of Vladek's memory is ultimately beyond our ability to recall. Young concludes, however, that the object of Spiegelman's *Maus* then becomes the very telling of the story, its coming into being: although the object of Vladek's memory cannot be regained, we can know something of its telling, of its constitution.

In the second volume of *Maus,* Vladek says something similar when discussing his own relationship to his memories of Auschwitz: "All such things of the war, I tried to put out from my mind once for all . . . until you rebuild me all this from your questions" (2:98). For Young, and to some extent for Dominick LaCapra's reading as well, *Maus* most importantly sheds light on how we "rebuild" memories, how we "work through" in the very construction of testimony. LaCapra takes this one step further in that his own investigation of the generic dialogue—the text's "hybridity"—that produces *Maus* offers a kind of "working through" that other texts may not. LaCapra concludes: "Indeed the very images in *Maus* may be seen not as imaginative representations of the unrepresentable but as condensed and at times disconcerting mnemonic devices that help to recall events one might prefer to forget, and the complex relations between image and word, father and son, mother and son, history and art serve as reminders of the difficulties and variable functions of memory-work that is addressed to extreme experience and limit-events."[2] Like Young, LaCapra argues for a focus on the "memory-work" itself, that the work of memory can have a referential security in ways that the traumatic object of memory cannot. Similarly, Young begins his analysis by grappling with Saul Friedlander's concern that this problem of memory may in fact lead us to nothing more than keeping "watch over absent meaning." This "absent meaning" is problematic to the notions of memory that both Young and LaCapra point toward, both worrying about what it might mean to focus on such meaning, what a focus on absent meaning might do to the very real meaning that resides in historical referent to testimony, even if such a referent is the telling itself. However, I do not see these two forms of meaning as being at odds. In fact, following Blanchot, we can trace the underside to the memory that both LaCapra and Young prioritize, the forgetfulness that is bound to memory. Or, put in terms of Lacan's understanding, memory necessarily posits both plus and minus, where the signifier not only represents the subject but also invokes the demand for another signifier, something that leaves a definitive trace within the story that is not simply what cannot be known. In this sense, one cannot examine memory without forgetfulness, cannot invoke a plus without its corresponding minus. In doing so we lose the trace of witnessing that founds memory, that serves as the very ground to testimony.

The difficulty of distinguishing forgetfulness from memory rests on how a given subject situates some traumatic kernel within a narrative that attempts to resolve the kernel in time while also leaving such trauma outside such temporal articulations. Put another way, the problem with attempting to know something about the object of a given testimony is that the past is itself an atemporal signifier pasted onto a temporal rendering, where a given speaker is not subject to something in the past as much as to its rendering in the present. Both LaCapra and Young focus on this last part, the act of testifying. Another way of reading *Maus* is not as a text that records a recording but rather as a text about the temporal distortion of trauma. Spiegelman does not do this by simply overlapping images and words, though this is certainly part of its power. Rather, what gives *Maus* its tension involves the way in which Spiegelman himself confronts the very possibilities of bearing witness to something he did not in fact see, of coming to some recognition and knowledge of an experience that not only occupies a position radically other from his own history but also fixes him particularly and traumatically.

Spiegelman's story of the Holocaust is clearly his father's story: Vladek Spiegelman's tale, as represented by his son, has the same stretched texture as the narratives of Primo Levi, Elie Wiesel, and Charlotte Delbo. But unlike these other witness accounts, we have the presence of an-other, of one who was not physically present at the camps, one who had yet to be born while the Final Solution was under way. This position of another—of Artie Spiegelman—changes the very nature of the narrative itself. Rather than relating a content of the event, a historical narrative, *Maus* presents us with a testimony about testimony. In doing this, Spiegelman points not toward the specific historical evidence of the event of the Holocaust but instead situates the event itself in the very act of testifying. By placing one act of testifying in another, Spiegelman lays bare the traumatic point of contact between them, the point of impasse that is more than just the transmission of Vladek's or Artie's story. Spiegelman opens up the very moment of memory's constitution, a moment that precedes the testimony that forms the substance of his text. This moment of witness, where testimony has yet to be written, marks what Blanchot terms the "utter burn" of the disaster, a moment that is atemporal but which has very real temporal effects. Put another way, Spiegelman's *Maus* presents us with the relation between event and knowledge, between seeing and understanding, exposing the trauma that functions as a locus of force.

Spiegelman's construction of this opening between what Artie wants to know, what he hopes to see in his father's words, and the narrative that his father offers presents us with a frame for asking how we see something and how we in turn speak about—recognize and understand—what we saw. Such renderings are inherently difficult when it comes to representing knowledge or experiences not our own, where what we can see rests in what others saw. In addition, there is a temporal dimension to this act of witnessing and testifying that cannot be thought of solely in terms of a linear causality. As Lacan explains in his "Logical Time and the Assertion of Anticipated Certainty," a moment of seeing posits a moment of recognition, followed by a moment of concluding. But such a chain necessarily works retroactively as well, where the moment of seeing is only the moment of seeing insofar as recognition points back to it, which in turn is an effect of the moment of concluding. "But to discern in the temporal modulation the very function by which each of these moments, in its passage to the sequential one, is reabsorbed therein, the last moment which absorbs them remaining, would be to restore their real succession and truly understand their genesis in the logical movement."[3] The subjective question present in such a moment of seeing offers a way of considering witnessing as temporally and logically disassociated from testimony, since to speak about what one saw is to presume the I that both sees and speaks. This disjunction between the time of seeing and the time of concluding offers us the crucial ontological distinction between witnessing and testifying.

Two differing implications result from distinguishing witnessing from testimony or seeing from knowing. Following Shoshana Felman, we might posit that an event itself (an act of seeing) is visible from a given representation (the result of concluding), so that the moment of concluding and the moment of seeing are the same in terms of content.[4] Or we might say that the event itself is so radically particular that there is no way to access the moment of seeing within any particular act of testimony—Jean Baudrillard's theory of simulation.[5] These two distinct positions on how we might define the relation between trauma qua moment of seeing and testimony qua moment of understanding or concluding present us with two different interpretive poles that are formalistically oppositional. Spiegelman, however, traces a different epistemology of trauma, one neither driven by a given content of experience as Felman's position nor so dismissive of the effects of seeing as Baudrillard's. Spiegelman instead presents us with a notion of seeing that is not a content, not a knowledge that we hope to transmit as a whole. The moment that Spiegelman's narrative invokes is one that is discernible within a testimony without being reducible to a given testimony—it is the forgetfulness that precedes memory. Put another way, Spiegelman offers us an examination of the very real rupture between the act of seeing and the act of knowing, while showing that this rupture persists within any given testimony.

Maus spends much of its focus not on Vladek's memories of Poland and Auschwitz or Artie's memories of his childhood, though both of these are of course very prominent, but rather on the interaction between Artie and his father or Artie and the story he is telling. Even when we are following Vladek's narrative or Artie's own telling of his past, the narrative frame is always very much in focus. In this we see Artie's relation to the narrative that he is both removed from yet implicated by: as the survivor of survivors, he is both subject to the events of his parents' experiences and yet removed from them. This being inside the experience, inside the testimony, yet seemingly not a witness to the object of the testimony creates a temporal tension in the way that Artie approaches the narrative he is seeking. On the surface, Artie only seems interested in the story, in the historical "facts" that Vladek can supply. More importantly, Artie expects to find something there, or rather expects to see something in the content of his father's story—some object that he might make answer his own demand. The tension rests in Artie's preoccupation with testimony: on the one hand this preoccupation shields him from seeing, while on the other it offers up a testimony to something to which he does in fact bear witness.

We see this clearly in the way Artie is pulled by Vladek's story, that the story is what compels him to talk with his father. Chapter 1 of *Maus* opens with Artie's first meeting with Vladek in two years. From that moment of meeting, the text takes only a page to move right into Vladek's recalling Poland with Artie recording his fathers words on a small pad. Similarly, chapter 3 opens with the image of Artie in a trench coat with a briefcase, saying, "I visited my father more often in order to get more information about his past" (1:43). This preoccupation with the content of Vladek's narrative is central to all of the first volume of *Maus*. But while Artie is clearly preoccupied with the content of his father's story, the text as a whole problematizes this preoccupation. Before we even get to chapter 1, the text includes a brief childhood exchange between Artie and his father, where the complex relationship between father and son sets up the entire later exchanges between them:

> VLADEK: Why do you cry, Artie?
> ARTIE: I-I fell, and my friends skated away w-without me.
> VLADEK: Friends? Your friends? . . . If you lock them together in a room with no food for a week . . . Then you could see what it is, friends. (1:6)

This binding of the survivor testimony with Artie's own childhood traumas and experiences undermines the more purely historical content focus that Artie takes to Vladek's testimony.

This complex intersection between Vladek's past as a camp survivor, Artie's relationship to Vladek, and the telling of the story erupts continuously throughout the first volume of *Maus* in particular. Following the introductory focus on Artie's interest in Vladek's story that begins chapter 3, the scene shifts to the dinner table:

> VLADEK: So finish at least what's on your plate!
> ARTIE: Okay . . . Okay. [new scene] Y'know, Mala, when I was little, if I didn't eat everything Mom served, pop and I would argue 'til I ran to my room crying.
> MALA: You should know it's impossible to argue with your father.
> ARTIE: . . . Mom would offer to cook something I liked better, but pop just wanted to *leave* the leftover food around until I ate it. (1:43)

Vladek's insistence that Artie clean off his plate leads in turn to a conflict with Mala. This is a particularly painful and telling moment for the figure of Artie. In searching for "the story," he must pass through his father's present, a present that veils the supposed object of his gaze: to see something of the Holocaust, Artie must negotiate his own relationship with his father, his own very real memories. This moment ties together Artie's own past ("finish at least what's on your plate") with the memories of his mother ("Mom would offer to cook something I liked better"), with his father's experiences as a Holocaust survivor (he says later, "Yes! So it has to be. Always you must eat all what is on your plate"), and with the current conflicts in the Spiegelman family (between Vladek and his son, between Vladek and Mala, and over Artie's position within their marriage). This very specific moment of the text offers the kernel that *Maus* as a whole is constantly trying to address. There is certainly something traumatic that binds these layers together, something we might call the Holocaust (following Felman), but also something radically particular to these figures (following Baudrillard). The way the frame of the narrative holds these layers together—the way the text does not prioritize Vladek's story over the telling of the story—presents us with the relationship between testimony and witnessing, where testimony refers to some-thing that is distinct from it, an act of witnessing that leaves its real traces in the narrative of those who experience it. In these layered moments in *Maus*, Spiegelman presents us with both the inadequacies of testimony as a record of witnessing and the way a testimony carries the moment forward, revealing that there is a palpable effect of the moment of seeing that runs through any attempt to speak. Even as the text itself occupies a point of conclusion, a point that orients the subject as an effect of some moment of seeing, it here portrays the temporally real moment of understanding, a moment that is less a point in time than it is an extension between two signifying points within narration.

We see this bound yet sliding enactment of narration most noticeably in the scenes where Artie questions Vladek about Anja's diary, a theme that holds much of the first volume together and which also recurs at crucial points in the second volume. Vladek mentions Anja's keeping a diary as part of his relating their life in Poland. After Vladek describes the hanging of black marketeers in the Jewish quarter of Sosnowiecz (Vladek makes the distinction that it was not yet an official ghetto), Artie asks what his mother was doing while Vladek was working the black market:

> ARTIE: What was Anja doing at this time?
> VLADEK: Housework . . . and knitting . . . reading . . . and she was writing always in her diary.
> ARTIE: I used to see Polish notebooks around the house as a kid. Were those her diaries?
> VLADEK: Yes, and also no. [change frame] Her diaries didn't survive from the war. What you saw she wrote after. Her whole story from the start.
> ARTIE: Ohmigod! Where are they? I need those for this book. (1:85)

The movement from wanting to know his mother's experience to the act of testimony rests in how Anja's diaries as signifiers situate this conversation. As in the earlier scene, this conversation places Vladek's testimony against Artie's questioning, which in turn intersects with Artie's own memories of his mother ("I used to see Polish notebooks around the house as a kid"). At the point where there is a possible recognition about his mother, Artie's need not to see something of her or even to say something about what he sees forces him to move to a secondary testimony, another moment of temporal tension: "Where are they? I need those for this book." Even in their absence, Anja's diaries persist in this testimony; they signify a missing moment that strings together something of the event that is Artie's stated object but which Artie misses even in his constant pursuit. The force of his persistence increases as the diaries take on a potentially tangible form.

When Vladek still cannot remember the location of the diaries, Artie's search brings him to Mala. Interestingly, Mala instead offers corroboration for Vladek's account of life in Sosnowiecz, citing the selection of her mother in particular: "In the stadium? Yes . . . they got my mother then" (1:92). In the midst of her testimony, Artie breaks off the conversation to look for his mother's diaries, disregarding the very real "content" that he so eagerly seems to be after. In looking through Vladek's cluttered den, Mala remarks about Vladek: "He's more attached to things than people!" (1:93). The next caption shows both Artie and Mala giving up the search:

> MALA: I really don't know how long I can take him. I really don't.
> ARTIE: I better be getting home. I'll look for those diaries next time.

This aversion to the conflict between Mala and Vladek is typical for Artie; he works very hard to focus on one strand of testimony, his father's story, even as he keeps encountering possible moments of witnessing concerning his mother that he refuses to recognize. However, this refusal is itself undermined by the absence of the text that Artie has endowed with the ability to answer all questions, all inadequacies: the absent diary of his mother.

This misrecognition surrounding the diary's place in his search comes up yet again when Artie and Vladek are talking about an early comic of Artie's that detailed his own experience with Anja's suicide. In the midst of this discussion, another conflict between Mala and Vladek erupts, followed by Vladek's attempt to bring Artie into his relationship with Mala:

> VLADEK: You see what I have with her? Always, whatever I do is
>   no good.
> ARTIE: Did you find Mom's diary?
> VLADEK: So far this didn't show up. I looked, but I can't find.
> ARTIE: I've *got* to have that! (1:105)

As in the earlier moment with Mala, Artie shifts the conversation away from the present onto the material of the testimony. Artie's last line ("I've *got* to have that!") emphasizes the value of the content of the diary over any given act of seeing. In other words, at this point in the text, Artie works at not seeing by emphasizing knowing or understanding. However, although he tries to conclude, to remain in the realm of testimony so as not to see, something of bearing witness remains to prevent his elision of knowing and seeing.

There still is a dimension of the event—of the "utter burn"—that remains even in this desire to have an understanding. It is significant that the testimony he is most after is that of his mother, Anja. We see the intersection between the searched-for testimony and the inadvertent seeing or witnessing in the final pages of the first volume of *Maus*, where Artie finally learns the fate of his mother's diaries. In the act of telling how he and Anja were separated as they entered Auschwitz, Vladek reflects on their possible fates:

> VLADEK: Anja and I went each in a different direction, and we couldn't know if ever we'll see each other alive again.
> ARTIE: This is where Mom's diaries will be especially useful. They'll give me some idea of what she went through while you were apart.
> VLADEK: I can tell you . . . she went through the same what me: terrible. (158)

At this point Artie pushes Vladek to look again for the diaries, and Vladek then tells Artie what happened to them:

> VLADEK: These notebooks, and other really nice things of mother . . . one time I had a very bad day . . . and all of these things I destroyed.
> ARTIE: You What?
> VLADEK: After Anja died I had to make an order with everything . . . these papers had too many memories. So I burned them.
> ARTIE: You burned them? [next caption] Christ! You save tons of worthless shit, and you . . .
> VLADEK: Yes it's a shame! For years they were laying there and nobody even looked in.
> ARTIE: Did you ever read any of them? . . . can you remember what she wrote?
> VLADEK: No. I looked in, but I don't remember . . . only I know that she said, "I wish my son, when he grows up, he will be interested by this." (1:158–59)

The first volume then ends with Artie leaving his father's house uttering "Murderer." This exchange, like the dinner conflict of chapter 3, offers the same competing levels of testimony. In this case, Artie hears Vladek's story, he knows what Vladek says. However, he does not see what Vladek sees. But he does see some-thing, some-thing particular. This is the most crucial example of a moment when the testimony of the survivor—Vladek's testimony—offers only testimony; it does not give Artie the possibility of witnessing what Vladek saw. More importantly, this moment does show a moment of seeing on Artie's part, the first such moment in the narrative of *Maus*. At this moment, Artie sees some-thing about his past and recognizes it. His final assertion ("Murderer") marks this recognition in a way much different from his comic "Prisoner from a Hell Planet," which serves as the center of the text as it deals with his own story surrounding the death of his mother.

At the end, Artie walks away and the possible testimony on Anja is foreclosed—he will never know what she wanted him to know—there is no memory that will cover over this moment of forgetfulness. She is forever lost. This is the traumatic kernel that this text cannot put into words but cannot help but speak. It is the moment in *Maus* where the impossibility of testimony speaks over the very real testimony of Vladek or even of Artie's remembrances of his youth.

The diaries come up for the last time late in the second volume, where Vladek shares a package with Artie:

> VLADEK: But before I forget—I put here a box what you'll be happy to see. . . . I thought I lost it, but you see how I saved.
> ARTIE: Mom's diaries?!
> VLADEK: No, no! On those it's no more to speak. Those it's gone, Finished! (2:113)

What Vladek hands over to Artie instead is a collection of photographs of Anja's family, stills that were the only things that survived the war. Over the next three pages, Vladek recalls the fate of each member of Anja's family, concluding: "Anja's parents, the grandparents, her big sister Tosha, little Bibi, and our Richieu . . . All what is left, it's the photos" (2:115). Artie then asks about Vladek's family, for which there are no prewar photos: "So only my little brother, Pinek, came out from the war alive . . . from the rest of my family, it's nothing left, not even a snapshot" (2:116). This discussion over the photos mirrors the loss of the diary, situates the same point of forgetfulness within the fabric of both Vladek's and Artie's stories. This is an effect of the very fabric of Spiegelman's text, the form by which it subjectifies the temporal movement between seeing and knowing, a forgetfulness that is the effect of memory. Spiegelman's text shows us this presence of forgetfulness as the very moment of seeing, as that which testimony impossibly tries to retrieve even as its goal is its erasure.

What such an erasure points toward is not the inability of history to be remembered, though this may also be true. Rather, Spiegelman's text shows a certain meconnaisance, a radical falsity of knowledge as a means of grounding or stabilizing the place from which a witness sees or speaks. To access being through knowledge is to replace being with knowledge, is to reduce the moment of seeing, the moment of ontological impasse, to a coherence that denies some traumatic kernel. Even as Artie consistently speaks of memory as an answer to being, the trauma that is both cause and object of his gaze eludes such reduction. The same holds true for Vladek's recollection of his reunion with Anja in the second volume of *Maus:* the only means of eluding trauma is to posit it as forgetfulness, but the rest of the story refuses to be mis-taken, and thus even moments of closure, "happy ever after," serve to substantiate such radically absent signs. In this sense, *Maus* teaches us that in the face of testimony—of the demand for knowledge as enough to bear the weight of seeing—the originary trauma of seeing insists, a trauma whose subject has yet to be found.

Notes

1. Art Spiegelman, *Maus: A Survivor's Tale*, 2 vols. (New York: Pantheon, 1986, 1991), 2:136. Hereafter cited parenthetically in the text.

2. Dominick LaCapra, *History and Memory after Auschwitz* (Ithaca: Cornell University Press, 1998), 179.

3. Jacques Lacan, "Logical Time and the Assertion of Anticipated Certainty," trans. Bruce Fink, *Newsletter of the Freudian Field* 2 (Fall 1988): 10.

4. See Shoshana Felman, "Education and Crisis; or, the Vicissitudes of Teaching," in Shoshana Felman and Dori Laub, *Testimony: Crises of Witnessing in Literature, Psychoanalysis, and History* (New York: Routledge, 1992), 1–56.

5. See Jean Baudrillard, "The Precession of Simulacra," in *Simulacra and Simulation*, trans. Shiela Faria Glaser (Ann Arbor: University of Michigan Press, 1994), 1–42.

2

Memory, Authenticity, and the "Jewish Question"

6

Promiscuous Reading

The Problem of Identification and Anne Frank's Diary

SUSAN DAVID BERNSTEIN

A few years ago when I was teaching Anne Frank's *The Diary of a Young Girl*, one student in my class related the following: "My roommate went to Poland this last month and stayed with her boyfriend's family. While discussing their plans, she said she wanted to visit a concentration camp. This topic then diverged into a discussion of Anne Frank. Their family, native to Poland, had never heard of Anne Frank and said she was a creation of America and their involvement in the war. *The Diary* there is not the popular reading requirement it is here." This disbelief, of a piece with more vociferous voices of Holocaust deniers, curdles in contrast to so many readers who not only know of Frank's life and her violent death but also feel as if they actually know her. Cara Wilson, who auditioned unsuccessfully for the role of Anne Frank in the 1956 Twentieth-Century Fox film adaptation, wrote to Otto Frank that his daughter's diary "spoke to me and my dilemmas, my anxieties, my secret passions. She felt the way I did . . . I *identified so strongly* with this eloquent girl of my own age, that I now think *I sort of became her in my own mind*."[1]

Wilson's assertion, representative of countless others, brings to the forefront the limits and liabilities of reading and teaching the Holocaust through identification. American multicultural and identity studies have repeatedly brought this dynamic into sharp relief as students study, teachers teach, and scholars write across boundaries of gender, sexuality, class, race, ethnicity, religion, and nation and across historical divisions. I am interested in exploring Frank's diary as well as its various adaptations and appropriations as a way to gain purchase on a persistent pedagogical motif, especially in Holocaust studies, that courts reading through cross-identification.[2]

What kind of witnessing does reading through identification promote? Put differently, is it possible to convert a historically distant bystander into an engaged witness by focusing on identification? How does identification correlate with sympathy, empathy, and understanding? In what follows, I will explore different facets of identificatory reading primarily but not exclusively around Anne Frank. By "reading" I mean studying as a way to understand that which challenges comprehension, like the Shoah and other large-scale programs of human atrocity. Nevertheless, the question of what I call promiscuous identification, or reading without vigilance to the process of negotiating simulated realities of text-based rather than experience-based knowledge, applies more generally to the enterprise of analyzing textuality of any sort.

I offer another vignette from the classroom, this time in the context of a course on the Victorian novel. After an energetic discussion during which some students explained their vehement dislike for a particular character depicted as the perpetrator of various crimes, I posed a question: "How do you read an account of a crime in a novel or a crime story on television differently than a news report of an actual crime or current event of human violence?" Several students replied that in fictional versions, the event seems more real because there is access to the thoughts and feelings of the characters, something that supposedly objective newspaper reporting elides. While I had expected someone to recognize a discursive distinction between a story largely based on actual occurrences in the world and a story primarily about invented people and events, I too realized that the slippage between invention and fact is a complicated matter. But this conversation brought to the forefront the power of imaginative discourse as a tool to promote identifications, whether sympathetic, antagonistic, or some other affective engagement. No doubt reading printed texts, whether labeled fiction or otherwise, has been shaped by contemporary media of immersion, including film, television, and most recently the Internet.[3]

In a sense, reel knowledge has displaced real knowledge, a kind of "unreality-effect" or the "derealization of ordinary life" as a consequence of the hyperstimulation of visually saturated media. The inversion of this "unreality-effect"—but clearly an offshoot of its pervasiveness in our culture—is what I would call the realization of extraordinary lives, as young people in particular are encouraged by teachers and writers to assume the roles of Holocaust sufferers and victimizers. What is the source of this impulse to identify, to attempt through reading, role-playing, and film viewing to try on the most horrific episodes of history? We talk about narrative pleasure, plunging into the thrilling grip of a captivating plot. Reading also capitalizes on character pleasure—the sense of intimate knowledge of someone who is a textual construction, sometimes with a real-world historical counterpart, sometimes not. Readers routinely pursue these textual pleasures. What about generic distinctions between fictive and autobiographical textual representations? What is at stake in sympathetic identification with Anne Frank through her diaries or Jane Eyre in the fictional autobiography that bears her name?

I would like to explore this process of reading through identification in relation to Anne Frank's witnessing the trauma of the Holocaust through her diary; I would also like to consider how disrupting identification through a recognition of incommensurable difference also opens up spaces for seeing and knowing, a kind of knowledge that is paradoxically rooted in a recognition of the reader as necessarily an impossible or partial witness to a recondite testimony. This humanist impulse behind the cross-identificatory practice of reading through putting oneself in the place of the other has obvious ethical intentions. Teaching horror through identification is also about teaching empathy, compassion, and history. The United States Holocaust Memorial Museum has framed its teaching of Hitler's Final Solution precisely through this mode of reading by issuing each visitor an "identification card" that "tells the story of a real person who lived during the Holocaust."[4] In this way, the museum-goer is interpolated into the position of witness and would-be victim, not unlike what occurs in the board game *Gestapo: A Learning Experience about the Holocaust*, developed by an American rabbi a few decades ago.[5] Called "experiential learning," these strategies aim to simulate some sense of what it may have been like to live as a European

Jew during the Shoah.[6] How does one account for the assorted starting points of knowledge and identity in approaching such identificatory exercises? How might we accentuate the division between sufferer-witness and secondhand viewing, between remembering lived experience and imagining even what is unimaginable?

Identification is a directional conundrum in which imagining oneself as the other blurs into assimilating the other into one's own place. In *Identification Papers* (1995), Diana Fuss calculates a distinction between identity, as a public persona, and identification, as an internal psychical process on which self-recognition and identity depend. In one sense, identification encompasses the oscillations between difference and similitude running through self/other relations. In effect, then, identification operates as a kind of bypass through the other, a detour that in turn secures one's own identity, a provisional substitute for an other than cannot be known.[7] Thus, in Fuss's formulation, only through the position of an unknowable other is the formation of a sense of self possible. In the psychical landscape of American culture, Anne Frank appears to be a very compelling other—at least if we judge from the wide range of literary texts where speakers confess an identification with Frank. We might understand these assertions of identification as a strategy of plumbing the other in order to shore up one's own identity by virtue of *not* being a Holocaust victim, like the thrill of fully awakening from an overwhelming nightmare.

Frank's diary also offers a study of identification formation inasmuch as her entries are replete with the teenage struggles of sorting out the boundaries of her identity in relation to the impinging others in the close annex and the large-scale othering of Jews in Nazi-ridden Europe. No wonder the process of identification is particularly fraught in Frank's writing, and no wonder that identification with Frank is particularly acute for Americans whose geographical distance from the Holocaust lends an accent to European Jewish otherness.

Reading *The Diary of a Young Girl* is necessarily entangled in the many instances of identification that have propelled Anne Frank's identity into a peculiarly American sacred icon of the Holocaust. Thus Eleanor Roosevelt's introduction to the first American edition in 1952 spotlights the diary's coverage of "the crucial years from thirteen to fifteen in which change is so swift and so difficult for every young girl." Roosevelt's omissions clear the path of identification from potential obstacles, details of jarring otherness. Anne Frank is not referred to as

Jewish—indeed, the word does not appear at all. Instead, the horrors of still too recent difference, in the decade following the Holocaust, dissolve into resemblance as Roosevelt concludes: "her diary tells us much about ourselves and about our own children. . . . I felt how close we all are to Anne's experience, how very much involved we are in her short life and in the entire world."[8] What is at stake in encouraging readers to identify with, in this case, Anne Frank's "experience"? Can this act of identification with a sufferer-witness of trauma begin to approach this "experience," and is this what we seek by encouraging such identificatory reading practices?

Besides Roosevelt's celebration of Frank's diary that "tells us much about ourselves," Meyer Levin's 1952 book review in the *New York Times* launches Anne Frank much like a treasured tourist who "goes on living" in spite of the genocide that ended her life at fifteen: "From Holland to France, to Italy, Spain. . . . And now she comes to America. Surely she will be widely loved, for this wise and wonderful young girl brings back a poignant delight in the infinite human spirit."[9] From this profile as universal healer of an unspeakable American crisis of post-Holocaust guilt, the iconic *Diary of a Young Girl* then became a touchstone publication for the commercial category of young adult literature in the 1970s and 1980s, as well as a regular feature on middle-school curricula. With scores of stage and screen adaptations, what can only be called the Anne Frank industry now encompasses an online site where one can purchase postcards, posters, books, and videos. Perhaps the most salient example of all-too-fluid identifications is encoded in the title, *I Am Anne Frank*, of a 1996 New York musical performance whose creator, Enid Futterman, remarks, "The first time I read her diary, I identified strongly with Anne, because I too was a dark-haired, slightly built, fourteen-year-old Jewish girl, trying to become a woman and a writer. I did not then understand that the difference between us was greater than the difference between the horror of Belsen and the shelter of Brooklyn. Perhaps the real difference between us was just the opposite: Anne Frank did not think or write like a victim."[10]

When I assign this book in a course on gender and autobiography, my students' relationship to Anne Frank has already been well established earlier in their education, often in classes in middle school or junior high school, sometimes in Jewish religious studies classrooms affiliated with a synagogue or temple. In many cases, women reported first receiving *The Diary of a Young Girl* along with their first diary from mothers, aunts, or grandmothers. The coupling of Frank's record of trauma with blank pages to be filled inaugurates the diary as a genre of disaster, as a space where one can remember the mundane as a way to forget horrific events that exceed familiar frames for understanding. I recall from my own childhood how the "Secret Annex" of 1940s Amsterdam merged in my reading with bomb shelters of 1960s United States, as visions of menacing Communists and a potential nuclear holocaust offered a contemporary anchor for the Holocaust. Do we want to promote the mingling of different kinds of trauma willy-nilly, and if not, how can we sharpen that zone between different orders of disaster, some lived, others imagined so that—we hope—they will never be lived?

Reading through identification is a process that undergirds our textual engagements. For identification is a complex way of enacting a relationship between ourselves beyond scenes of reading and those selves fashioned out of language looping back to our apprehension of worlds beyond the text. For Hélène Cixous, reading by identification is a matter of imaginary self-expansion where a reader occupies, as it were, the fantasized horizon of another's represented landscape.[11] For Elin Diamond, such reading by identification is "distinctly imperialistic and narcissistic: I lose nothing—there is no loss of self—rather I appropriate you, amplifying my 'I' into an authoritative 'we.'"[12] Given the psychical dimensions of identification that Fuss delineates, both loss and risk are encrypted in this process, a crucial consequence to which I will return. But with regard to a more superficial construction of identification that Diamond assails, I would like to call this unreflective assimilation of the read subject into an untroubled unitary reading self "promiscuous identification." Put another way, promiscuous identification highlights a correspondence between textual and historical subjects that champions an uncomplicated resemblance, one that displaces a vexed and more productive non-resemblance, a rift also inherent in acts of witnessing trauma, even by those who witness themselves as victims of horror. For my purposes, "promiscuous" accents crossing borders in this process of reading without due notice, without heeding distinctions between the "I" that reads and the autobiographical "I" that is consumed in the act of reading. I propose "dissonant" identification to chart the contingencies and liabilities of an engaged reading. For it is crucial that such analysis not compromise a keen sense of engagement, a concept that has replaced "relevance" as a keystone in pedagogically ensuring that students experience their education as something that matters in their lives.

Although promiscuous reading often encompasses gratification by increasing the reader's sense of plenitude of self, other aspects of this reading habit occasion discomfort and pain. For, as Diamond observes, identification can also function as assimilation, but in the other direction: "To identify is apparently not only to incorporate but to be incorporated. To be radically destabilized."[13] This rendezvous with alterity echoes the paradoxical nature of identification as the psychical play that Fuss demarcates between self and other, between relation and estrangement, and between knowing and not knowing. Identification is not a benign or neutral enterprise. Whether a matter of direction or degree, in this version of identification symbolic rendezvous veers into nightmare. My childhood terrors were prompted by such excess of identification on first reading Frank's diary, as I kept late-night sentinels for the return of Hitler, not an uncommon fantasy among Jewish American girls identifying with Frank in the early 1960s when Adolf Eichmann was apprehended in Argentina. Cynthia Ozick warns that "the young who are encouraged to embrace the diary cannot always be expected to feel the difference between the mimicry and the threat."[14] In other words, to what extent would it be useful to push this erasure of difference, to propel oneself through reading into Frank's horrific history? Cathy Caruth reminds us of the ethical dimensions of identification where "history, like trauma, is never simply one's own, that history is precisely the way we are implicated in each other's traumas."[15] Yet how does one navigate such gyrations of possible and evanescent mutuality in the classroom?

In her account of teaching testimonies of Holocaust survivors, Shoshana Felman capitalizes on this kind of self-identification, both her own and her students'. Whereas Felman renders herself a teacher-witness "to the shock communicated by the subject matter," her students become second-degree witnesses.[16] It may well be harrowing to apprehend testimonies of the Shoah, but does this insulated reception even warrant the term "witnessing"? For Felman pursues in the classroom what she terms "life-testimony," which extends beyond the individual private life into "a point of conflation between text and life." This conflation—this identification—is, observes Felman, "a textual testimony which *can penetrate us like an actual life.*"[17] Like the disturbing version of identification Cixous and Diamond discern, consuming testimony functions for Felman as uneasy implosion. In a sense, Felman's interdisciplinary graduate course titled "Literature and Testimony" amplifies identification so that real-world distinctions between Yale graduate students in the 1980s and survivors of the Holocaust devolve into a psychoanalytic occasion about memory and trauma. What gets effaced or displaced in this imbrication of reading and "actual life"? What possible forms of apprehending historic events of crisis open up through this mode of identification?

The Discourse of Sympathetic Identification

Before exploring the question of identification in relation to Frank's diary and to the Holocaust, I offer an abbreviated history of the discourse of sympathetic identification. Fuss points out that the nineteenth-century philosophical concept of "sympathy" is the ancestor of the Freudian scientific notion of identification.[18] A social historian of nineteenth-century culture, Raymond Williams, uses the concept of "structure of feeling" to attend to both elements, a mingling of sympathetic observation with imaginative identification.[19] We might analyze deployments of sympathetic identification through two axes: the representational value of images of sympathizers and of sufferer-victims and the consequential significance, the human impact on those readers or viewers who are prompted to identify with those who have suffered.[20]

In his 1871 *The Descent of Man,* Charles Darwin locates sympathy historically as a recent and Western moral acquisition, something not experienced by ancient Roman gladiators or by gauchos of the pampas or African "savages except toward their pets." Sympathy, then, is the dividing line between humans and other animals, and between so-called advanced civilizations, whether modern-day or Western, and those considered outside the pale. For Darwin, sympathy functions as the benchmark for humanity: "This virtue, one of the noblest with which man is endowed, seems to arise incidentally from our sympathies becoming more tender and more widely diffused, until they are extended to all sentient beings."[21] Darwin ranks as more evolved those who can sympathize beyond themselves and their immediate kind; sympathy traverses "an artificial barrier" separating nations and races, despite the contradiction that this capacity to sympathize does not transcend social and political barriers of race, place, and time.

Adam Smith's 1761 *Theory of Moral Sentiments* offers an anatomy of sympathy that recognizes the necessary distance sympathizing entails as suffering works as a spectacle remotely viewed: "Mankind, though naturally sympathetic, [can] never conceive, for what has befallen another, that degree of passion which naturally animates the person principally concerned."[22] For Smith, this sympathetic distance is a crucial facet inasmuch as it underscores that identification can only be momentary and partial. Likewise, Raymond Williams invokes the term "negative identification" to underscore the inevitable gap that structures historical imagination, the hiatus between the immediacy of the present, one's active enthrallment with the moment, and the distant suffering of another social group of a bygone era: "the present is accurately and powerfully seen, but its real relations, to past and future, are inaccessible."[23]

Christopher Castiglia expands upon Smith's assessment of sympathetic distance by acknowledging that "if one expresses an emotion too extreme or a suffering too unusual, the audience will be unable to identify and will experience no sympathy."[24] Smith's comment recalls distinctions between sympathy and empathy. On the one hand, sympathy is by definition only an approximation, an emotional simile built on a scaffold of comparison and difference, while empathy seeks to simulate through imaginative identification the position of the sufferer, to understand this position by trying on the emotions imagined to accompany an experience. On the other hand, sympathy entails mutuality and reciprocity; one sympathizes with those with the capacity to return this affective affiliation. The idea of empathy, however, recognizes that imaginatively entering into the another's experience is necessarily one-sided and limited. One can sympathize with someone else who shares sufficient resemblance to experience the sympathizer's own emotional reality, whereas empathy implies division and difference between subject and object. Holding onto such gaps lodged within the meanings of sympathy and empathy pertains to my idea of a dissonant and vigilant practice of identification to forestall the liabilities of promiscuous identification.

In a similar vein, Geoffrey Hartman admonishes against texts (particularly the visually saturated media of television, film, and the Internet) that promote overidentification with sufferer-victims, an imaginative encounter that might result in retreat and detachment through "compassion fatigue" or even a diffused anxiety or "secondary traumatization" that ironically displaces the historical specificity of the events one is studying through emotional engagement. Hartman wisely acknowledges that many readers or viewers would be unable to manage the welter of feelings triggered through identification with those who experience trauma that profoundly demands forgetting or mastery.[25]

Sympathetic identification also involves questions of power and agency where appropriating, assimilating, and ventriloquizing the emotional experiences of the sufferer become the purview of the imaginative sympathizer. Drawing on Foucault's theory of power, Castiglia conceptualizes "sympathetic discipline" as a kind of surveillant measure that would naturalize social hierarchies through "spectatorial normalization," as if radical differences between sympathizers and African American sufferers of slavery or European Jewish sufferers of the Holocaust could be bridged through enlightened emotion. Castiglia is particularly interested in technologies of sympathy as he seeks to understand occasions of identification as politically nuanced and historically situated acts. For instance, the rhetoric of antebellum abolitionist William Lloyd Garrison enacts a narrative of transcendence whereby black suffering is assimilated into white interiority, a symbolic constituent for emotional depth. In effect, such sympathetic identification functions as affective sameness whereby political and social difference devolves into merely "the product and sign of individual affect," as Castiglia maintains.[26] Rey Chow assigns such cross-identifications with an imperializing impulse where "fantasy idealizations" of others "enact imaginary usurpations."[27]

Thus far I have brought together different theoretical inflections for honoring the varied and crucial obstacles to identification such as Williams's "negative identification" for the necessary limits of imaginatively stepping in someone else's historical shoes. Likewise, Teresa de Lauretis invokes "disidentification" as a disruptive space created by hybrid conglomerations of identity that never align completely. Rather than seeing the limits of identification as a deficit or not seeing the limits at all, disidentification valorizes or privileges the impossible coincidence or fit between sympathizer and sufferer. At the same time, disidentification also captures a sense of what exceeds any attempt to identify in the first place by heeding the ineffable lodged at the heart of conveying trauma.[28] Doris Sommers's work on *testimonios* underscores this process of thwarted identification: "The testimonial 'I' does not invite us to identify with it. We are too different, and there is no pretense here of universal or essential human experience."[29]

Fictions of Identification

For the most part, the various fictions of identification with Anne Frank have been directed at young readers. While we would expect adult readers to be responsible for monitoring their own complex responses to texts that encourage such identification, with young readers the matter of accountability is more fraught, and young audiences—the YA (young adult) market—are the target of much of the Anne Frank and Holocaust education industry that capitalizes on identificatory practices. Cherie Bennett and Jeff Gottesfeld's *Anne Frank and Me* (2001) tells the story of an American teenager, Nicole Burns, who readily believes Holocaust deniers on the Internet, as the authors draw an analogy between the political dangers of ignorance and denial. When Nicole's class visits an exhibit on Anne Frank, she and her classmates are assigned identities of Jewish teenagers in Europe during the Holocaust, a simulation exercise designed to make this sordid chapter in recent human history more accessible and thus less forgettable or deniable. Suddenly hit by an automobile, Nicole is catapulted from 1990s suburbia to 1942 Paris as she now inhabits the Jewish identity assigned to her in class. Fuss maintains that identification "invokes phantoms," that it involves "the very possibility of communing with the dead," and this is precisely what *Anne Frank and Me* plays out.[30] In this role, Nicole encounters on a train from Paris to Auschwitz a rather upbeat Anne Frank who professes her faith in God, details that contradict what biographical material remains of Frank and her post-hiding life. One liability of promiscuous identification, then, is this conflation of fact and fiction to the extent that what little can be known is sacrificed to sheer invention, but without regarding the complexities of such imaginative speculations.

Like Hannah Stern in Jane Yolen's 1988 *The Devil's Arithmetic*, Nicole undergoes a conversion experience from a cynical teen to a believer and Holocaust witness through this simulation-induced dream journey into the bloody jaws of unspeakable horrors including the gas chambers. The authors acknowledge their debt to Yolen's novel by having Nicole's class watch an adaptation of *The Devil's Arithmetic*. This interpolative gesture is part and parcel of the rhetoric of promiscuous identification where boundaries are recklessly traversed. Yolen's novel is framed by a Passover seder, the ritual retelling and remembering of the suffering of Jews in Egypt and the Exodus; this reenactment of the Pesach through narrative and through embodiment, like ingesting symbolic material foods such as matzo, signifies a modest and ritualized simulation exercise in order to build a bridge from the present to the very remote past and to link generations across time and space. After her journey into the Holocaust, instead of turning away whenever her Aunt Eva (a survivor) talks about concentration camps, now Hannah says, "I remember. Oh,

I remember." But what are we to make of Hannah's initial refusal to remember, her adolescent exasperation or boredom with her ancestors'
tales of traumas from another time, and how are we to read now her
born-again reverence for this history of horrors? Might there be psychical and ethical costs of making excessively imaginable to children what
by definition contradicts the conceivable, an event far more proximate
in time than biblical history?[31]

Both of these stories propelling contemporary American girls back
into the Holocaust have also existed as dramatic performances on stage
or television, media that encourage promiscuous identification even
more insistently than books. The recent Disney film *Anne Frank: The
Whole Story* (2001) claims "to present the entirety of Anne's life" by virtue
of portraying her arrest, deportation, starvation, and death. That Michael Eisner, the head of the Walt Disney Company, refers repeatedly
to his subject "Anne" by first name only in his brief onscreen introduction indicates a linguistic intimacy given Frank's status as the focal point
of identification for Jewish children sufferers of the Shoah.[32] Eisner goes
on to claim that these "intense" scenes that show Frank's physical degradation and death at Belsen are also part of this "whole story" that "offers some valuable lessons about courage, humanity, and the bonds of
family." Is this the redeeming element in dramatizing Frank's last
months alive? Are young viewers who have been encouraged to identify
with Frank through her diary and its manifold appropriations now
given more visual effects to also imagine her deplorable demise in a concentration camp?

Wary of the "unreality-effect" generated by our visually saturated
culture, Hartman instead recommends that "minimal visibility" can
open up mental spaces that promote more effective seeing, listening,
and intimate understanding.[33] Ironically, while the Disney film purports
to tell Frank's "whole story," a required caveat periodically reminds the
viewer: "The film does not use the words that Anne used in her diary to
express her feelings." In this way linguistic identification is undercut at
the same time that promiscuous viewing is courted through converting
into visual images experiences that by definition defied such facile witnessing across time and space from the couch in front of the television
set in 2001.

Time travel as a technique to encourage identification with a history
of human atrocities also features in Octavia Butler's 1979 *Kindred*, the
story of a young African American woman named Dana setting up

house in California in 1976 with her white husband. She begins to shut-
tle mysteriously back and forth between her present life and the world of
her antebellum ancestors, her slaveholding great-great-grandfather
who will eventually rape the slave woman who becomes Dana's great-
great-grandmother. The novel is replete with plantation brutalities and
the emotional hurricane that engulfs the time-tossed Dana, whose narration often inhabits the edge between viewing from outside and within
the past: "I had seen people beaten on television and in the movies. I
had seen the too red-hot substitute streaked across their backs and
heard their well-rehearsed screams. But I hadn't lain nearby and
smelled their sweat or heard them pleading and praying, shamed before
their families and themselves."[34] In a sense, *Kindred* privileges experiential knowledge over text-based knowledge, though of course this lesson
is inevitably text-bound to its readers. Where Dana is transported
through time to acquire experience-drawn knowledge, her reading
knowledge of "every possible degradation" takes her to a different time
and place:

> I read books about slavery, fiction and nonfiction. I read everything I
> had in the house that was even distantly related to the subject—even
> *Gone With the Wind*, or part of it. But its version of happy darkies in ten-
> der loving bondage was more than I could stand. Then, somehow, I got
> caught up in one of Kevin's World War II books—a book of excerpts
> from the recollections of concentration camp survivors. Stories of beat-
> ings, starvation, filth, disease, torture, every possible degradation. As
> though the Germans had been trying to do in only a few years what the
> Americans had worked at for nearly two hundred.[35]

The passage implies that Dana's identification with Holocaust sufferers
facilitates her realizing the history of American slavery victimage, exem-
plifying Fuss's idea that identification, a matter of relation, works by
way of a "detour through the other that defines a self."[36] Dana returns
finally to her historical present with a scar on her face and an ampu-
tated arm, "solid evidence," concludes her husband, "that those people
existed."[37]

In Emily Prager's 1991 novel *Eve's Tattoo*, such embodied evidence
is purchased in a store where New Yorker Eve Flick gets a tattoo on
her arm to mimic the concentration camp number branded on a German woman whose photograph Eve has found. By assimilating this

identification number into her skin like a costume, Eve remodels her
identity. Comparing the tattoo to an MIA bracelet, Eve tells the face in
the faded photo: "Immortality for you, Eva. You're coming with me
into the twenty-first century." In naming the unidentified woman after
herself, Eve packages her identity as a recycled other while she also ap-
propriates an identity for this Holocaust other through herself. So lead
the tangled paths of identification into tautologically correlated identities. To defend her tattoo, Eve tells a friend: "The people who lived
through the Third Reich will all be dead. And when the people who
experienced an event are no longer walking the planet, it's as if that
event never existed at all. There'll be books and museums and monu-
ments, but things move so fast now, the only difference between fantasy and history is living people. I'm going to keep Eva alive. She'll go
on living, here, with me."[38] That "living people" must validate,
through presence, past events and the people who lived these events
implicates identification as the foundation of historical knowledge.
Nevertheless, the identity prompted by the worn photograph lives
"through" and not "with" Eve by virtue of this act of appropriation.
Eve's logic suggests that only by inhabiting the identities of those who
have died, as she does through the stories she constructs around her
tattoo, can history be distinguished from fantasy. Yet her remodeled
identity as Eva conflates fantasy with the reality of a photograph along-
side her knowledge of the Third Reich. In a way Eve Flick exemplifies
what Hartman diagnoses as "memory envy" as a psychic consequence
of the excesses of sympathetic identification where one desires "strong
memories" that carry cultural capital as historically valuable.[39]

Through Eve's flexible fabrication of herself as Eva the Holocaust
survivor, the nuances of identification emerge. As a pedagogical model,
Eve contours her tattoo narrative to resonate with the degree of identification each interlocutor can sustain: "Look, people will ask me about the
tattoo and I'm going to tell them tales, based on facts from my reading,
tales specially chosen for them, so they can identify, so they can learn."[40]
The key to learning, Eve claims, is through identification, but not everyone follows the same path in this process. When she encounters an old
man with a tattooed number on his arm, Eve falters in her mission to
teach through identification, and she confesses shame for her stunt to
someone she considers to be the genuine article, an authentic survivor.
Now a celebrated transvestite of Yiddish theater, Jacob tells Eve he
managed to stay alive in Nazi Europe through assuming identities, first

as an Aryan girl in training for the Lebensborn program, then as a hard-working Jewish boy. Strategic performance of Identification in this instance means salvation.

Dissonant Identifications

This example from *Eve's Tattoo* offers possibilities for foregrounding a distinction between promiscuous and dissonant versions of identification, the first gliding across textual, historical, and psychic borders without due notice, the second enacting a kind of stammering around the edges of readers, textual subjects, and historical beings. What are some ways of teaching this dissonant identification around reading Frank's diary? How might it be possible to complicate the process of identification as double-sided, where assimilating a textual subject into a reading self also strains against points of resemblance? In other words, how might we enact a politics of identification, as historically and culturally contingent, as inevitably partial and divided, in teaching trauma?[41] In exploring the possibilities of dissonant identifications, I take up the editing history of Frank's diary as well as how Frank's use of dialogic address positions the reader as both distant and intimate, a rhetorical construction that allows Frank to relay the conditions of trauma that also defy communication.

Delineating the editing history of *The Diary of a Young Girl* foregrounds the complex production of a commodity that gets mythologized into the seeming immediacy and intimacy of the diary form. It is well known that Otto Frank first edited his daughter's diary for public consumption by eliminating 30 percent of the entire text, including some passages on sexuality and unflattering remarks on her annex inmates, now victims of the Holocaust. Less well known is that Frank herself began editing her diary, an action in which we see her reshaping her entries into a construction she imagines for public eyes. The 1986 Critical Edition of the diary published by the Dutch Department of War Documentation establishes three versions: version A as the unedited diary, to date never published intact and by itself; version B as Frank's own edited version, begun four months before her arrest; and version C, drawn from both A and B, as Otto Frank's editing, the text translated into fifty-five languages. With the understandable impulse to distance his daughter's text from the Shoah that stole her life, Otto Frank expressed his desire for the published diary to accentuate what he termed "Anne's idealism and spirit," that is, to create an image of a girl struggling with mundane adolescent problems rather than the crisis of her identity as a Jew in Nazi-occupied Amsterdam. Thus the more familiar version C deletes explorations of religious faith, a specific reference to Yom Kippur, to ensure that Anne Frank is not rendered too Jewish.

Frank herself began rewriting her diary upon hearing a 1944 London broadcast calling for eyewitness accounts, such as letters and diaries, of the suffering of the Dutch under German occupation.[42] Frank's revisions consisted of omitting passages and adding others from memory, a kind of "testimony" where the partial memories of present and past mingle as Frank also continued with the ongoing diary she had begun in 1942. The Critical Edition, translated into English in 1989, graphically displays these three versions as horizontal sediments on each page, an archaeological arrangement that dislodges the assumption that the commonly known version of the diary (Otto Frank's edition at the bottom of each page) is unexpurgated full disclosure. That a stand-alone publication of version A (the unedited diary) does not exist signifies the impossibility of unmediated testimony, pushing against the veneer of intimacy the diary genre might promise. At the same time, the triangulated edition gives visual form to competing notions of constructing traumatic history and of voicing consciousness within contexts that seek to stifle that very consciousness. This format also bespeaks the patterns of deferral implicated in representing memories of crisis, divided between variant available records and the unthinkable horror that eludes representable knowledge.

In teaching Frank's diary, I focus on such issues of production, foregrounding through pages from the Critical Edition the complexities of these imbricated versions. I then turn to Frank's dialogic structure of address to the blank space of writing she names "Kitty." This rhetorical strategy offers a model for this conflictual mode of identification that entwines assimilation with expropriation. Frank's dialogic structure of address that routinely frames entries with "Dear Kitty" and "Yours, Anne" poses both the possibility and impossibility of identification. On the one hand, this address, along with the confiding tones that inflect what Frank imparts, signifies Frank's desire for an audience, not a detached other but an intimate friend. On the other hand, Frank constructs Kitty as outside the reality of Frank's own experience, as a naive listener who must be informed about the atrocity of war, the barely imaginable terrors of the programmatic annihilation of European Jews.

After about a year, Frank tells her interlocutor: "Since you've never been through a war, Kitty, and since you know very little about life in hiding, in spite of my letters, let me tell you, just for fun, what we each want to do first when we're able to go outside again."[43] This telling "just for fun" jars against historical contingency, the unfolding of the chain of catastrophic events once Frank and her family do "go outside again." A dissonance of identification emerges between the future that Frank and her blank space of "Kitty" cannot know and the outcome of Frank's murder at Belsen, which the reader, standing in for Kitty, cannot forget.

Frank explicitly poses the limits of crossing this divide between self and other on which identification depends as she claims the insurmountable difference between hearing a testimony and living the trauma of the Holocaust that eludes as it haunts the language of description. Take this address to Kitty: "Although I tell you a great deal about our lives, you still know very little about us. How frightened women are during air raids; last Sunday, for instance, when 350 British planes dropped 550 tons of bombs on Ijmuiden, so that the houses trembled like blades of grass in the wind. Or how many epidemics are raging here. You know nothing of these matters, and it would take me all day to describe everything down to the last detail."[44] Caruth contends that the act of testimony is a paradox: it brings to mind what has been forgotten, some unfathomable horror that exceeded available knowledge in the first place and thus confounds remembering. The dissonant identification highlighted by the addressor/addressee dichotomy of Anne/Kitty also signifies a structure for the porous memory of testimony.

Rachel Brenner observes how the construction of Kitty as "ignorant addressee" works as a literary device to promote the story's accessibility where "the complete unawareness of the addressee . . . de-intensifies the teller's emotional involvement with her tale."[45] This managed "emotional involvement" might also explain Frank's making-strange herself as a Jew, an identity too vexed to inhabit even in the act of testifying to a life in hiding because of that very identity. The following passage manifests this discordant identification: "Our thoughts are subject to as little change as we are. They're like a merry-go-round, turning from the Jews to food, from food to politics. By the way, speaking of Jews, I saw two yesterday when I was peeking through the curtains. I felt as though I were gazing at one of the Seven Wonders of the World. It gave me such a funny feeling, as if I'd denounced them to the authorities and was now spying on their misfortune."[46] Frank's remove here from "the Jews" of "misfortune" and her alignment instead with informants recalls

W. E. B. DuBois's concept of "double consciousness," which he defines in *The Souls of Black Folk* as "this sense of always looking at one's self through the eyes of others, of measuring one's soul by the tape of a world that looks on in amused contempt and pity."[47] Frank's uncanny feeling of seeing Jews as if "gazing at one of the Seven Wonders of the World" exposes liabilities of identification as the horizon of self-estrangement. For Frank to identify as a Jew also means to imagine her own incalculable destruction based on a heinous politics of identification.

In teaching Frank's diary, then, I repeatedly direct the class to such problems of reading and writing through identification as we sort through the incommensurability of selves involved in the act of testimony: between experience and its telling, between remembering and forgetting, and between who writes and who reads, between what we imagine and what we cannot know. The electronic discussion list for the class provided a space for mediating and meditating upon these gaps; one posting showcases the dilemmas of reading through identification:

> We must not forget that it is to Kitty that she writes and not to us. Therefore we must be distanced from the experience on a basic principle of morality. We must not delve into her private thoughts . . . and turn those thoughts into our own. . . . In the attempt to turn Anne Frank into a symbol of resistance to apathy, the person she is in reality is lost. . . . She has gone from our world and if we are to use her memory we must offer respect for her decision to pour her thoughts toward a book. We must not attempt to locate ourselves in the story with the notion of turning her into us for we cannot.

This reader suggests that honoring the memory of Frank resides in resisting promiscuous identification, refusing to colonize for oneself ideas of Frank gleaned from the words of her diary. Yet it is also difficult to resist one's own private Anne Frank, a peculiarly psychological mirror for Jewish American girls in particular. Here it might be useful to invoke again Fuss's distinction between identity as a public persona, that is, a social construction to be formulated, scrutinized, dismantled, and identification as an elusive and recondite psychical phenomenon, the engine of self-recognition. In reading through identification, how do we misrecognize the life we are imagining in our attempts to sound the edges of our own? Dissonant identification captures the value of affective engagement as a strategy for approaching, for self-consciously apprehending, traumatic knowledge. At the same time, this dissonance reminds us of the impossibility of sympathetic identification, since the nature of witnessing trauma unsettles the fantasy of authentic mutuality.

Notes

1. Quoted in Cynthia Ozick, "Who Owns Anne Frank?" *New Yorker*, October 6, 1997, 79; emphasis added.

2. Diana Fuss poses this question: "Is a program of fostering identifications across culturally constructed lines of race, ethnicity, class, gender, sexuality, religion, or citizenship a viable political strategy?" *Identification Papers* (New York: Routledge, 1995), 8.

3. See Jerome McGann's *Radiant Textuality: Literature after the World Wide Web* (New York: Palgrave, 2001), especially for his discussion of the Ivanhoe game, an electronic, Web-based learning tool that capitalizes on reading through the pleasures of breaking boundaries between past and present readers as well as between readers and characters.

4. Although it was the regular practice of handing out these identification cards as visitors entered the museum, more recently these cards have become an option only upon request, as the complexities of identification in this context have come under scrutiny.

5. Rabbi Raymond A. Zwerin, Audrey Friedman Marcus, and Leonard Kramish, *Gestapo: A Learning Experience about the Holocaust* (Denver: Alternatives in Religious Education, 1976).

6. One of the most widely used classroom activities of this genre is the "brown-eyed/blue-eyed simulation" exercise developed by Jane Eliot. Social psychologists have noted the significant impact of role-playing on people's understanding of circumstances outside their own experience. See Ron Jones, *No Substitute for Madness: A Teacher, His Kids, and the Lessons of Real Life* (Covelo, Calif.: Island Press, 1981), for a description of his simulation of the appeal of Nazism.

7. Fuss, *Identification Papers*, 2–3.

8. Eleanor Roosevelt, introduction to *Anne Frank: The Diary of a Young Girl* (New York: Doubleday, 1966), xiv.

9. Meyer Levin, "The Child behind the Secret Door," *New York Times Book Review* (15 June 1952): 1–2.

10. Enid Futterman, "My Journey with Anne Frank," February 3, 2000, http://www.musicalheaven.com/i/i_am_anne_frank.html.

11. Hélène Cixous and Catherine Clément, *The Newly Born Woman*, trans. Betsy Wing (Minneapolis: University of Minnesota Press, 1986), 148.

12. Elin Diamond, "The Violence of 'We': Politicizing Identification," in *Critical Theory and Performance*, ed. Janelle G. Reinelt and Joseph R. Roach (Ann Arbor: University of Michigan Press, 1992), 390–98, 392.

13. Ibid., 391.

14. Ozick, "Who Owns Anne Frank," 79.

15. Cathy Caruth, *Unclaimed Experience: Trauma, Narrative, and History* (Baltimore: Johns Hopkins University Press, 1995), 24.

16. Shoshana Felman and Dori Laub, *Testimony: Crises of Witnessing in Literature, Psychoanalysis, and History* (New York: Routledge, 1992), 18.

17. Ibid., 2.

18. Fuss, *Identification Papers*, 4.

19. Raymond Williams, *Culture and Society, 1780–1950* (New York: Harper and Row, 1966), 88.

20. For further discussion of these two vectors of assumptions related to Holocaust simulations, see Simone Schweber, "Simulating Survival," *Curriculum Inquiry* (forthcoming).

21. Charles Darwin, *The Descent of Man, and Selection in Relation to Sex* (Princeton: Princeton University Press, 1981), 101.

22. See Christopher Castiglia's discussion of Smith on sympathy in his essay on sympathetic identification and American abolitionists, "Abolition's Racial Interiors and the Making of White Civic Depth," *American Literary History* 14, no. 1 (2002): 32–59.

23. Raymond Williams, *The Country and the City* (New York: Oxford University Press, 1973), 78.

24. Castiglia, "Abolition's Racial Interiors," 36–37.

25. Geoffrey Hartman, "Tele-Suffering and Testimony in the Dot Com Era," in *Visual Culture and the Holocaust*, ed. Barbie Zelizer (New Brunswick: Rutgers University Press, 2001), 111–24, 119.

26. Castiglia, "Abolition's Racial Interiors," 41. On the politics of affect in imaginative discourses such as the novel, see Nancy Armstrong, *Desire and Domestic Fiction: A Political History of the Novel* (New York: Oxford University Press, 1987); and Ann Cvetkovich, *Mixed Feelings: Feminism, Mass Culture, and Victorian Sensationalism* (New Brunswick: Rutgers University Press, 1992).

27. Rey Chow, *Writing Diaspora: Tactics of Intervention in Contemporary Cultural Studies* (Bloomington: Indiana University Press, 1993), 53.

28. For a discussion of de Lauretis's concept of "disidentification," see Sidonie Smith, *De/Colonizing the Subject: The Politics of Gender in Women's Autobiography*, ed. Sidonie Smith and Julia Watson (Minneapolis: University of Minnesota Press, 1992), 110–11.

29. Doris Sommers, "'Not Just a Personal Story': Women's *Testimonios* and the Plural Self," in *Life/Lines*, ed. Bella Brodzki and Celeste Schenck (Ithaca: Cornell University Press, 1988), 108.

30. Fuss, *Identification Papers*, 1.

31. A novel for young readers about the Holocaust that resists the kind of promiscuous identification evident in both *The Devil's Arithmetic* and *Anne Frank and Me* is Lois Lowry's *Number the Stars* (1989). Inspired by the legend of King Christian X of Denmark's wearing a yellow star badge in solidarity with Jewish Danish citizens, Lowry tells the story of Annemarie Johansen, whose family helps spirit her Jewish friend and family safely out of Denmark as Nazis occupy Copenhagen. See Lowry's afterword for her discussion of her choreography of fact, fiction, and truth. Cherie Bennett and Jeff Gottesfeld, *Anne Frank and Me* (New York: Putnam, 2000); Jane Yolen, *The Devil's Arithmetic* (New York: Viking, 1988); and Lois Lowry, *Number the Stars* (Boston: Houghton Mifflin, 1989).

32. Eisner makes this comment: "Anne Frank has come to symbolize the millions of children who were murdered or uprooted by Hitler's armies. . . . The film goes beyond Anne's famous diary to present the entirety of her life. We've tried to accurately depict the conditions she faced and as a result tomorrow's conclusion contains scenes that may be too intense for some children." The Disney adaptation was first aired on ABC in May 2001.

33. Hartman, "Tele-Suffering and Testimony," 118.

34. Octavia E. Butler, *Kindred* (Boston: Beacon Press, 1979), 36.

35. Ibid., 116–17.

36. Fuss, *Identification Papers*, 2.

37. Butler, *Kindred*, 264.

38. Emily Prager, *Eve's Tattoo* (New York: Vintage, 1991), 11.

39. Hartman, "Tele-Suffering and Testimony," 122. Hartman cites Binjamin Wilkormirski's *Fragments* as a recent textual symptom of "memory envy."

40. Prager, *Eve's Tattoo*, 12.

41. Fuss asks a related question: "Is a program of fostering identifications across culturally constructed lines of race, ethnicity, class, gender, sexuality, religion, or citizenship a viable political strategy?" (*Identification Papers*, 8).

42. Holocaust deniers have seized upon Frank's deliberate editing of her diary with a view toward publication as evidence that her journal is a contrived rather than an authentic story. Such politically motivated readings would posit a historical truth as univocal, fixed, and objective, yet such concepts have been interrogated by an array of theorists in recent years.

43. Anne Frank, *The Diary of a Young Girl*, the Definitive Edition, ed. Otto H. Frank and Mirjam Pressler, trans. Susan Massotty (New York: Doubleday, 1991), 115 (July 23, 1943).

44. Ibid., 244 (March 29, 1944).

45. Rachel Brenner, "Writing Herself against History: Anne Frank's Self-Portrait as a Young Artist," *Modern Judaism* 16 (1996): 123.

46. Frank, *Diary*, 80 (December 13, 1942).

47. W. E. B. DuBois, *The Souls of Black Folk* (New York: Penguin, 1996), 30.

7

Humboldt's Gift and
Jewish American Self-Fashioning
"After Auschwitz"

ELIZABETH JANE BELLAMY

In his 1978 comments on the proceedings of the International Sympo-
sium on Saul Bellow, Tony Tanner sees Bellow's protagonists as aware of
the problems of history, but he argues that these problems "do not functionally enter his fiction."[1] Tanner's cogent claim should resonate with
any ongoing effort to assess Bellow's novels within the historical framework of the Holocaust. To be sure, in four of Bellow's novels the subject
of the Holocaust is manifest. In the 1940s, early in his career, Bellow
wrote the brooding novels *Dangling Man* and *The Victim*, both explicitly
conceived in the shadow of genocide and the death camps. Much later in
his career is the 1989 novella *The Bellarosa Connection*, which is about
Broadway producer Billy Rose's helping Harry Fonstein escape from the
Nazis. And, of course, situated prominently between these novels is the
widely read *Mr. Sammler's Planet* (1970), one of Bellow's "signature" novels
from the decade that established him as among this country's most brilliant novelists. But the survivor-refugee Sammler — a Polish Jew in the
eyes of the Nazis, but scrupulously cultivating Britishness — often strikes
the reader as oddly more absorbed in the medieval mysticism of Meister
Eckhart or with utopian futures on the moon than with shouldering the

oppressive weight of history. In short, the character of Sammler, conceived some thirty years ago, is a key reminder that, in Bellow, there is no unified construct of "the Jew," let alone a Jew definitively shaped by Holocaust catastrophe. As any number of Bellow scholars have argued over the years, Judaism is both central to Bellow's characters and unpredictably refracted by the multiplicity and instability of their Jewish identity. In the final analysis, one could argue that the Holocaust is much more defining of the work of, say, Singer, Ozick, and Spiegelman, and that Bellow, when read in the light of Tanner's claim that the problems of history "do not functionally enter his fiction," cannot always fit comfortably in the category of "Jewish-American Holocaust literature."[2]

Rather than directly attempting to insert selected novels of Bellow's into a Holocaust framework, it may be more productive to read them with and against the grain of the temporal and psychic space of Adorno's "after Auschwitz," conceived in 1949 as a means of designating the temporally discontinuous structure of trauma in the aftermath of the Holocaust.[3] As a radical problematizing of memory, Adorno's "after Auschwitz" can be provisionally defined as an obscure psychic threshold of repression, disavowal, denegation, or foreclosure—all psychic defenses against a working through of the unspeakable horrors of the Holocaust that nevertheless cannot seal off these horrors entirely. The temporal frame of Adorno's "after Auschwitz" emphasizes that there can be no incremental, progressive working through of the implications of trauma. If we always come "after" the event, argues Adorno, we are also always "too early" to grasp it. In such a scheme there can be no working through of Auschwitz, only an eruptive "acting out" where the return of the repressed horrors of the Holocaust nevertheless fail to induce a salutary consciousness of the trauma.[4] Thus, Adorno suggests in his later essay "What Does Coming to Terms with the Past Mean?" that a remembrance and "making sense" of the Holocaust are as much psychoanalytic as political imperatives.[5] For Adorno, the temporal frame of "after Auschwitz," particularly in Germany, enacts a psychoanalytic and cultural allegory of an extended melancholia that refuses to allow for a genuine mourning.

I contend that it is worthwhile to reassess selected Bellow novels in the light of the difficult-to-trace psychic displacements of "after Auschwitz." Novels such as *Mr. Sammler's Planet* and *The Bellarosa Connection* explicitly engage the Holocaust. But to what extent can certain other

Bellow novels be read as being not so much "about" Auschwitz as about
the more elusive space of "after Auschwitz" — and all the psychic complexities this temporal frame entails? Adorno's essay "What Does Coming to Terms with the Past Mean?" was published in Germany in 1977,
just one year before Tanner's resonant claim, made in the smaller arena
of Saul Bellow studies, that the problems of history "do not functionally
enter [Bellow's] fiction." To forge this temporal juxtaposition paves the
way for further speculation about why it can yield richer interpretations
to insert Bellow within the framework of "after Auschwitz." Bellow first
acceded to literary superstardom during the decade from the early 1960s
to the early 1970s. At the same time, we should bear in mind that the term
"Holocaust" did not assume common currency until the 1960s (a vivid
reminder that, for many, the Holocaust was, in effect, an encrypted
trauma without referent) and that the discipline of Holocaust historiography, so vital to the process of working through the Holocaust in a context of meticulous historical accuracy, did not become fully constituted
until sometime in the mid-1970s. The first major wave of Bellow's literary
acclaim, then, overlaps intriguingly with the first wave of "after Auschwitz," during which time writing a novel such as *The Bellarosa Connection*,
with its thorough engagement with the Holocaust, might scarcely have
seemed possible. To echo Tanner, history may not *functionally* enter into
Bellow's fiction, but it is nevertheless worth examining the extent to
which it enters through the "back door" of the vexed permutations of
cultural memory "after Auschwitz."

This essay offers some scattered speculations on what it would mean
to read Bellow under the temporal sign of "after Auschwitz," focusing
primarily on *Humboldt's Gift* (1973), a novel in which the Holocaust is
scarcely alluded to and yet is oddly implicated in the poet Von Humboldt Fleisher's tragic demise. I am interested in tracing what can be referred to as a kind of latent "Holocaust-effect" in the novel, such that although *Humboldt's Gift* has nothing to do with the Holocaust, it may, at
certain key moments, have much to do with the temporal frame of
"after Auschwitz."

Reading Bellow "after Auschwitz," however, does present some
stubborn and unpromising methodological obstacles that must be
frankly addressed. First is the difficulty of historicizing Bellow's Jewish
American protagonists within Adorno's predominantly European context. Given the historical context of Adorno's theorizing of the melancholic frame of "after Auschwitz" — that is, the distinctly European

aftermath of Hitler's Final Solution for German and Eastern European Jewry—Bellow's Jewish American (or often Jewish Canadian American) protagonists do not readily fit Adorno's schema. To further expand on this disjunction, I would like, before focusing on *Humboldt's Gift,* first to glance at *Herzog* (1961), a novel that catapulted Bellow to literary fame. In this novel we gain a sense of just how elusive it can be to insert Bellow within the historical frame of "after Auschwitz."

In *Herzog,* to be sure, there are scattered moments when Bellow's preeminently "suffering" protagonist becomes animated about the Holocaust. We can be reminded, for example, of Herzog's exchange, as tense as it is comic, with his despised, Calvinist psychiatrist, the "Nordic Anglo-Celtic" Dr. Edvig. Angered by Edvig's "Protestant Freudianism" and his underinformed fascination with the bizarrely dramatic conversion of Herzog's wife, Madeleine, to Christianity, Herzog is moved to remind his therapist of the legacies of Christian brutality: "From a Jewish standpoint, you know, this hasn't been one of your best periods."[6] At another point, recalling one of his lecture tours in Europe, Herzog, in a jarringly vivid reminiscence, remarks that he "thought he scented blood in Poland" (37). But in the larger scheme of the novel, Herzog, reinforcing Tanner's claim, is not inclined to dwell on the oppressive weight of large-scale catastrophe. Alarmed that he has endangered his little daughter, June, in a car accident and overwrought at being arrested for possession of his father's ancient revolver, Herzog sits in the back of a police car, distracting himself from his misery by compulsively engaging in a silent conversation with an imaginary interlocutor who seeks to instruct him in reality's harshness: "History is the history of cruelty, not love, as soft men think" (353). But Herzog, despite his earlier conviction that "he scented blood in Poland," refuses to be chided: he is thoroughly content to be one of the "soft men" who believe in the power of love over cruelty. At the novel's conclusion, Herzog, far from the "madding crowd" and recuperating in his dilapidated farmhouse in the isolation of the Berkshires, muses to himself: "We must get it out of our heads that this is a doomed time. . . . We love apocalypse too much. . . . Excuse me, no. I've had all the monstrosity I want" (388–87).

Admittedly, Herzog's musings are unpromising terrain for literary analysis "after Auschwitz." For Herzog, the best therapy for personal "monstrosities" is not necessarily a revisitation of the apocalypse of a decimated European Jewry but rather a reimmersion in family memories. Herzog's preferred mode of mourning "after Auschwitz" is the mnemonic path of an inherited family sentiment (which he often refers to wryly as "potato love"), shaped less by the horrors of Nazi Germany than by his parents' emigration from czarist Russia to Montreal, Canada. Shamelessly recalling his uncontrollable weeping at his father's funeral, Herzog, with a lyricism as comic as it is buoyant, admits: "I am infected by the Old World with feelings like Love—Filial Emotion. Old stuporous dreams" (342). Thus the novel includes a long section on Herzog's Montreal childhood remembrances, how he was pampered as a child, how his Aunt Zipporah cursed her bootlegging brother in Yiddish—remembrances that represent the triumph of strong family bonds over nihilism. "Infected by the Old World," Herzog inherits his own family's yearning for a seamless *Yiddishkeit*, the old Europe of the shtetl. Herzog's "trauma," if it can be called that, is not the trauma of refugee experience or survivor guilt but rather a poignant conflict between, on the one hand, a desire to assimilate and embrace the New World and, on the other, an increasingly urgent need to preserve his family's Old World Jewish heritage. For Herzog, then, it is the potential waning of family memory and the threat of losing the richly textured immediacy of immigrant experience that most justify the imperative to "never forget."[7]

The hyperactive and often comic contours of Herzog's family memories resurface in Charlie Citrine, the protagonist of *Humboldt's Gift*, who also luxuriates in family ancestry as an escape from what Tanner calls "the problems of history." The novel abounds with such childhood reminiscences as Citrine's trips to Chicago's Russian Bath with his father, or his mother's "sing[ing] trembly Russian songs."[8] Of his attachment to his family while growing up, Citrine admits, "Oh, I loved them all terribly, abnormally" (70). The fecundity of Citrine's family memories is in stark contrast to the mnemic impoverishment of his beloved and absurdly wealthy brother Ulick, who "had forgotten or tried to forget the past" (235). Ulick, whose shopping centers and condominiums are transforming the topography of southeast Texas, is thoroughly preoccupied with an aggressive pursuit of capital, a pursuit that, as he frequently boasts, crowds out any indulgence in family memory: "And you know I can't remember a thing, not even the way Mama looked. . . . Our grandfather was one of ten guys in the Jewish Pale who knew the Babylonian Talmud by heart. . . . I don't even know what it is" (236). Although of his own photographic memory Citrine wryly concedes that "There are clinical experts who think that such completeness of memory is a hysterical symptom" (374), he is impervious to Ulick's "pathologizing" of hyper-memory: "My own belief was that without memory existence was metaphysically injured, damaged" (236). For both Herzog and Citrine, then, memory-as-(comic-)neurosis offers a salutary, protective transcendence of history's traumas—and a prime example of Tanner's contention that the problems of history "do not functionally enter [Bellow's] fiction."

Despite Herzog's and Citrine's many personal defeats, the comic-sentimental contours of their "symptomatic" family memories (with their roots not in Nazi Germany but in czarist Russia) give these protagonists a plenitudinousness that resists the melancholic frame of "after Auschwitz." Moreover, the comic-sentimental contours of their cultural memory present us with a second and far greater difficulty in reading Bellow under the sign of "after Auschwitz," that is, the challenge of integrating the peculiarly elusive quality of his comedic voice with Adorno's "high" theoretical seriousness. One reason why, to re-echo Tanner, the problems of history "do not functionally enter his fiction" may be because in Bellow, as Sarah Blacher Cohen argues, there is never "a total capitulation to despair."[9] Interestingly, critics who have analyzed Bellow's humor in detail tend to discuss it in terms of antinomies, such as Elaine B. Safer's observation that Bellow's humor encompasses both "the mythological and the mundane," or Cohen's observation that his humor is a strange combination of "philosophical obscurity and gutter clarity."[10] Safer and Cohen are sensitive to Bellow's startling, indeed disorienting, tonal oppositions that stubbornly resist any comfortable synthesis. The point I wish to emphasize here is that the odd tensions generated by Bellow's humor, resiliently avoiding a "total capitulation to despair," tend to crowd out larger historical concerns—such as the melancholic frame of Adorno's "after Auschwitz."

As we have seen, for Citrine, as for Herzog, the cornerstone of cultural memory is czarist Russia, such that in *Humboldt's Gift*, references to the Holocaust are only occasional and widely scattered. And when such references do occur, they tend to be uttered in a spirit of what can best be characterized as comic kitsch. As we have seen, Ulick boasts that he is immune to family nostalgia. But perhaps more to the point for the difficulties of assessing Ulick within the framework of "after Auschwitz" is his impatient directive to his brother not to chat with his Ukrainian gardener: "He was a concentration-camp guard and still insanely anti-Semitic" (239). In this context, we can also be reminded of

Citrine's longtime friend George Swiebel and his admiration for Charlie's sleek, silver Mercedes: "Murder Jews and make machines, that's what those Germans really know how to do" (33). How can we properly read Ulick's and Swiebel's remarks "after Auschwitz"—reducing, as they do, any gesture toward Holocaust piety to mere comic shtick? In *Humboldt's Gift* the Holocaust is relegated to the novel's shadows, re-emerging only infrequently as oddly desacralizing moments of manic-comic paranoia in the post-Holocaust. Adorno conceived of the psychic space of "after Auschwitz" as an overdetermined terrain of repression, disavowal, and foreclosure—a battleground between the conflicting impulses of "acting out" and "working through." But in *Humboldt's Gift*, it is as if, "after Auschwitz," Ulick and Swiebel consciously seek to *contain* the horrors of the Holocaust within the parameters of comedic "bad taste" and, in Swiebel's case, a kitschy Germanophobia. Neither repressing the past nor making a sincere attempt, echoing Adorno, to "come to terms with the past," Ulick's and Swiebel's "joke-y" indulgences are virtual parodies of what Adorno sought to preserve as the highly *affective* space of "after Auschwitz."

All of which is to say that the agility and suppleness of Bellow's comic imagination seem stubbornly incommensurate with Adorno's "high" theoretical seriousness, threatening to subvert any attempt to read *Humboldt's Gift*—or, for that matter, any other Bellow novel—under the sign of "after Auschwitz." But the psychic complexities of the tragic poet Von Humboldt Fleisher—usefully, if somewhat bluntly, described by Richard Stern as "the largest second banana in Bellow's fiction"—offer more promising possibilities for reading the odd tensions of Bellow's comedy through the lens of "after Auschwitz."[11] By way of a tentative approach to Humboldt's complexities in the post-Holocaust, I begin by juxtaposing two passages in the novel. At one point, Citrine confesses that he has "snoozed through many a crisis (while millions died)" (104), whereas Humboldt, the genius poet and Citrine's longtime friend, claims, on the other hand, that "history was a nightmare during which he was trying to get a good night's rest" (3). Once again, Citrine, snoozing "after Auschwitz," perfectly illustrates Tanner's contention that the problems of history "do not functionally enter [Bellow's] fiction." But Humboldt's enigmatic claim that he is "trying to get a good night's rest" from history's nightmare presents an intriguing challenge to Tanner, enticing the reader to trace the ways that Humboldt's tragic demise, the novel's major subplot, can productively be read "after Auschwitz."

In 1984, Bellow eerily described *Humboldt's Gift* thus: "it's a broad comedy and the theme is death."[12] *Humboldt's Gift* as death-comedy presents a paradox that deserves a careful unpacking. The tragicomic contradictions of the wrongheaded Humboldt, the brilliant, nationally acclaimed poet who nevertheless hurtles toward an ignominious death in a shabby flophouse, doomed to enact the clichéd "Agony of the American Artist" (like Humboldt's own poet-heroes Edgar Allan Poe, Hart Crane, Randall Jarrell, John Berryman, and other members of America's Dead Poets Society), are aptly summarized by Daniel Fuchs in a series of questions: "Is he a genius? a disaster? a martyr? a con man? all of these things? Should he be viewed with sympathy? contempt? both? And, whatever the answer, from what point of view can such discriminations be made?"[13] One point of view from which such discriminations could be made is to read Humboldt's spectacular demise against the grain of Adorno's "after Auschwitz" in order to better understand, which is not to say "solve," the complex, contradictory ways in which Humboldt is at once tragic martyr and comic schlemiel.

Humboldt, author of the once highly acclaimed *Harlequin Ballads*, is one of the most celebrated poets of his generation. (One is reminded that his real-life prototype, Bellow's friend Delmore Schwartz, was praised by the likes of T. S. Eliot, Ezra Pound, Allen Tate, John Crowe Ransom, Wallace Stevens, and William Carlos Williams.) But as a second-generation child of Jewish immigrants, Humboldt also suffers intense cultural anxieties about assimilation. Thus, one psychic cost of his yearning to become the new T. S. Eliot (about whom he relished gossiping) is his dark brooding about how he is perceived as a Jew by, in Citrine's phrasing, "fastidious goy critics on guard for the Protestant Establishment and the Genteel Tradition" (10). To be sure, Humboldt's often comic anxieties about his Jewishness do not constitute a major thread in the overall fabric of the novel. But they do reach an intriguing crisis point in 1952 when he joins the faculty of Princeton University. Because *Humboldt's Gift* is such a sprawling, episodic novel, it may seem inadvisable to focus on one self-contained subplot. But as Fuchs observes, the novel's Princeton episode is the oldest episode in Bellow's writing of the manuscript and thus an episode key to the novel's very conception. Thus I offer a close reading of this episode as a particularly resonant site where Humboldt's contradictions constellate "after Auschwitz."[14] The Princeton campus of the 1950s is far removed geographically (though not temporally) from the events of the Holocaust;

but if *Humboldt's Gift* is indeed a comedy with a "death-theme," this paradox, as I will argue, can be fully nuanced only under the temporal sign
of "after Auschwitz." As will eventually become clearer, Humboldt's
anxieties about his Jewish identity, escalating in pastoral Princeton,
intersect with the aftermath of the Holocaust in particularly tragic ways.
To be sure, "ambivalences about Jewishness" can threaten to become
an overworked, tired rubric, but under the sign of "after Auschwitz,"
Humboldt's anxieties can be revisited with renewed energy.

As we have seen, "after Auschwitz" is an overdetermined terrain of
psychic displacements; and finding a point of entry into this terrain's
"trace-effects" is not a simple task. In order to trace the labyrinthine
process of interpreting Humboldt "after Auschwitz," I suggest that we
first ponder the special intensity of 1952 as a pivotal year in his life. For
Humboldt, 1952 is a much-anticipated year of spiritual renewal, an opportunity to end his nearly decade-long slide into paranoia, clinical depression, addiction to amphetamines and gin, dried-up inspiration, and
dwindling finances. In 1952, Humboldt accepts a year's replacement appointment at Princeton, in the process managing to persuade the department chair, Ricketts, to cobble together another visiting lectureship
for his old friend Citrine.[15] So 1952 holds out the promise of a happy, if
exilic, reunion year for their intense literary friendship, as well as a base
for Humboldt's exuberant fantasies about an Adlai Stevenson victory in
the upcoming presidential elections, and about the possibility of his own
imminent move from Princeton to Washington: "He was going to be
the Goethe of the new government and build Weimar in Washington"
(26).[16] But in the wake of the urbane Stevenson's defeat by Eisenhower,
there would be no "Goethe in Washington"—only an increasingly paranoid, depressed, and fading poetic genius staving off his seemingly inevitable decline as, in Citrine's succinct, metrocentric description, "a
professor of English in the boondocks" (116).

For the turbulent Humboldt, however, Princeton at least represents
academic respectability and equilibrium. As he tells Citrine, "I have to
get the enchantment back. . . . I have to locate myself" (124). But at this
point we should pause to consider the extent to which Bellow depicts
Humboldt's seemingly benign acceptance of a year's visiting lectureship
at Princeton as nothing less than a highly fraught tragic flaw. Consistently throughout Bellow's long career, in interviews, in lectures, and in
his fiction (perhaps most recently in *The Dean's December*), Bellow has expressed open contempt for the university as destructive of literary genius,
prompting Ben Siegel to observe, "Certainly no other subject stirs in

him equal rancor and resentment."[17] Humboldt's need to "locate himself" at Princeton is, in effect, a need to surround himself with what Bellow has repeatedly denounced as mere professional custodians of culture. For Bellow, the prospect of a poet-genius lost amidst the dreary, uninspired ranks of a professoriat "in charge of masterpieces"—or, expressed far less delicately in a 1971 essay, the ranks of "brutal profs and bad-tempered ivy-league sodomites"—is a chilling scenario.[18] In short, Bellow's resentment toward the university is the point at which his celebrated comedic tone begins to break down. And if we bear in mind that the already vulnerable Humboldt's faculty appointment is a precarious, one-year non-tenure-track line, then one wonders if Bellow is not urging his readers to feel the same kind of tragic pity and fear for Humboldt's arrival at Princeton that readers of *King Lear* feel for Shakespeare's aged king, turned away by his daughters and descending into madness on the stormy heath.

Contextualizing Humboldt's Princeton sojourn within a tragic framework is further justified if we turn momentarily from Bellow's despised university to a brief meditation on the centrality of the city in Bellow's fiction. Though often depicted in his novels as a deteriorating city with foul smells, Bellow's Chicago, as is obvious to all of Bellow's readers, is as energizing as it is vulgar—a city central to the experiences and reminiscences of a number of his characters, including, perhaps most notably, Herzog and Citrine. And as Molly Stark Wieting has observed, "The cities are, of course, among Bellow's most brilliant creations."[19] The point I wish to emphasize here is that in *Humboldt's Gift*, the city may be nothing less than Bellow's *necessary* condition for literary inspiration.

For Bellow, not having a Chicago—a "city of one's own"—may be the quintessential tragic condition, lending an ominous resonance to Citrine's impatience whenever Humboldt "ran down the city. The city was lousy" (16). What merits close scrutiny, then, is Humboldt's curious disinclination to "locate himself" in a city (not even his native Upper West Side), that is, his decision to spend a precarious year as, to echo Citrine, "a professor of English in the boondocks," where it is almost tragically scripted that this once prominent literary intellectual and once adored Greenwich Village salon personality will languish unappreciated.

The novel's Princeton episode centers on Humboldt's miserably failed stratagem for gaining a permanent tenured appointment.[20] "Madly gloomy" following Eisenhower's defeat of his beloved Adlai

Stevenson, and his "art dwindl[ing] while his frenzy increased" (116), Humboldt trades creative inspiration for manic scheming to attain "academic respectability." His scheming is primarily designed to torment the pretentious Martin Sewell, whom he has replaced for the year. The mellower Citrine displays, at the most, a mild, comic contempt for Sewell, who is in Damascus on a Fulbright: "Paul of Tarsus woke up on the road to Damascus but Sewell of Princeton would sleep even deeper there" (32). But the paranoid Humboldt, always prone, in Citrine's phrase, to "keen Jewish terrors" (30), thoroughly despises Sewell, who he is convinced is anti-Semitic. Though no admirer of the effete Sewell, Citrine has learned to become wary of his beloved friend's paranoid frenzies: "Sewell an anti-Semite? Nonsense. It suited Humboldt to hoke that up" (126). But punishing Sewell persists as the focus of Humboldt's acting out of what escalates into a complex love-hate relationship with Princeton and his conviction that the faculty is covertly anti-Semitic: he schemes (in Sewell's own office, no less) to be awarded an endowed chair in modern literature so that, as he tells Citrine, Sewell "will come back and find that the old twerps who wouldn't give him the time of day have made me full professor" (121).[21]

Always lurking just beneath the surface of Humboldt's fabled charm and erudition are intense cultural anxieties about assimilation; and his lifelong self-fashioning as the new T. S. Eliot reaches a tragicomic climax at Princeton, whose elitism releases the full force of a once-latent Jewish self-loathing. In Humboldt's attempt to convince the hesitant Citrine that Sewell is a mighty adversary who deserves to be outwitted, his darkest anxieties about his Jewishness become readily and self-destructively activated: "In Princeton you and I are Moe and Joe, a Yid Vaudeville act. We're a joke—Abie Kabibble and Company. Unthinkable as members of the Princeton community" (120). And thus a central paradox in his obsessive desire to remain at Princeton lies tragicomically exposed. Seduced by Princeton's elitism yet tormented by the specter of its covert anti-Semitism, Humboldt is convinced that he and Citrine are being condescended to by goyish professors patrolling the borders of Princeton "good taste." Poised on the verge of assimilation into the Ivy League, Humboldt—the very paradigm of what Citrine calls "the culture Jew" (152), who abandons a more *heimisch* Greenwich Village to seek membership at elite, Protestant Princeton—nevertheless indulges in lurid fears that he and Citrine, in the end, can only be perceived as performing a "yid vulgarity" and self-mockery for the Princeton professoriat (120). Even as he schemes to become Princeton's new Sewell (a Sewell whom he despises), Humboldt, revered author of *Harlequin Ballads,* entertains the possibility that he has himself become a harlequin court jester, a Vaudeville performer — or, in his inimitable phrasing, "a Yiddisher mouse in these great Christian houses" (120). And thus, once again, the reader is left with the difficult task of sifting through the odd tensions of Bellow's comic tone. To echo Fuchs, is Humboldt a genius? a disaster? a martyr? a con man? At Princeton, is he T. S. Eliot — or is he Abie Kabibble?[22]

With Humboldt's impossible contradictions, we are beginning to draw closer to why the novel's Princeton episode can be most productively explicated under the sign of "after Auschwitz." His insistence on spending a precarious year at Princeton — or, put another way, his refusal to revive his waning literary inspiration in "a city of his own" — is complicated further by the fact that he had the option of spending that same year of 1952 being wined and dined in Berlin at the invitation of Germany, seeking to honor Humboldt with a lectureship at Berlin's Free University. When he informs Citrine of this invitation, his friend is enthusiastic. Knowing that the manic-depressive Humboldt's professional and financial options are declining, and convinced that Princeton's effect on him can only be corrosive, Citrine believes that the Berlin invitation, not the entrapments of Princeton, could be restorative for the fading poet's career: to be celebrated as the Great American Poet abroad strikes Citrine as an opportunity for a new lease on life. "That sounds grand," he encourages Humboldt, without the irony characteristic of so many of their exchanges. But the turbulent Humboldt tells Citrine that he has already refused the invitation without hesitation.[23] The first reason he offers Citrine for this hasty dismissal of the Berlin invitation constitutes vintage Bellow humor — specifically, the manic-comic paranoia that, as we have seen earlier, is so resistant to interpretation "after Auschwitz": "'I don't feel quite ready,' said Humboldt. He was afraid that he would be kidnapped by former Nazis" (32). Like George Swiebel's admiration for Citrine's silver Mercedes, Humboldt's refusal to go to Germany is expressed in a zany display of kitschy, postwar Germanophobia, that is, a comic manifestation of what Citrine, earlier in the novel, had referred to as Humboldt's "keen Jewish terrors."

Humboldt's second stated reason for not going to Berlin is seemingly tossed in as a mere afterthought. Though doubtful that it was ever

Bellow's intention, it is nevertheless this second reason that can strike
the reader as far more resonant "after Auschwitz": "If I spent a year in
Germany, I'd be thinking of one thing only. For twelve months, I'd be a
Jew and nothing else. I can't afford to give an entire year to that"
(50–51). Of this refusal, Citrine offers his readers the following commentary: "Humboldt didn't want to go to Germany, a country where no
one could follow his conversation" (51). Citrine does not elaborate further, and the matter of Humboldt's refusal of the Berlin invitation drops
out of the narrative. But for the reader attuned to the complex psychic
space of "after Auschwitz," Humboldt's second reason for his refusal offers a rich enigma that demands further unpacking: among other
things, this refusal could be read as illustrating the odd psychic displacements that characterize the overdetermined framework of "after
Auschwitz." The process of unpacking this refusal can begin with the
psychic displacements that, as we have seen, characterize Humboldt's
anxieties about his Jewishness—and with the strong suspicion that
Humboldt derives no small pleasure from imagining he is perceived as
a mere "Yiddisher mouse" at Princeton. Humboldt's disinterest in Germany signals the possibility that, in choosing instead to join the Princeton faculty, he was anticipating the perverse satisfaction he would enjoy
while performing the dual role of Von Humboldt Fleisher, revered
poet, and Von Humboldt Fleisher, Vaudeville comic, reveling in a
Princeton gentility itself conflicted about whom they have invited in
their midst.

We are now at the core of how it can be productive to interpret
Humboldt's refusal of the Berlin invitation under the sign of "after
Auschwitz." To be sure, preoccupied with becoming the new T. S.
Eliot, Humboldt would not have embraced any perception of himself as
a Jew "after Auschwitz"; nor has a remembrance of Nazi genocide in
any way shaped his cultural imaginary or influenced his trajectory as a
poet. But one of the lessons of the temporal space of "after Auschwitz"
is that the horrors of the Holocaust can never be entirely sealed off. And
thus, in this pivotal year of 1952, Humboldt seems uncannily attuned—
however unconsciously—to an oppressive cloud of German postwar
guilt.[24] When Citrine claims that no one in Berlin would be able to follow Humboldt's conversation, he seems to be hinting at far more than
simply the language problems of those living abroad. (Although Humboldt speaks no German, the Germans would undoubtedly have spoken
good English.) It is as if Citrine, picking up on Humboldt's insistence

that for a year in Berlin "I'd be a Jew and nothing else," recognizes that Humboldt suspects he has been invited to Berlin less as a famous poet than as a famous *Jewish* poet: "after Auschwitz," the Free University may be seeking not so much a T. S. Eliot as a prominent "culture Jew" whose mere presence on the faculty will be salutary for Germans.

In this year of 1952, Humboldt demonstrates no manifest consciousness of Holocaust trauma. Nevertheless, when he tells Citrine he "can't afford to give an entire year" to the Free University, Humboldt in effect may be signaling that he has no intention of enacting a seamless allegory of "Jewishness" for contrite, liberal German gentiles eager, in the temporal space of "after Auschwitz," to find ways to alleviate their guilt about the Final Solution. For Humboldt, the choice between a year at Princeton (and its covert anti-Semitism of the 1950s) or Berlin's Free University (seeking atonement for Germany's anti-Semitic sins, and eager to begin the process of working through Germany's "unmasterable past") is both a choice *and* no choice at all: Humboldt *has* to accept the appointment at Princeton, where he prefers to cultivate the energizing, if precarious, instabilities of Jewish American identity—the sometimes resourceful, sometimes enervating liminal "double consciousness" that comes of being both an American insider and a Jewish outsider. And the reader is left wondering if on some level Humboldt knows that this double consciousness simply will not "translate" from America to Berlin. Throughout his career, Humboldt has actually thrived as much as he has suffered in the interstices of the American literary scene's veiled anti-Semitism. Having at one time attained star status in the American intellectual marketplace, he is judged by his literary followers as an assimilated American success: he has been judged to be "in good taste" by the culture club of—to quote Citrine—"fastidious goy critics on guard for the Protestant Establishment and the Genteel Tradition." But in the highly concentrated elitism of Princeton, as we have seen, Humboldt also indulges fears that he is "a Yiddisher mouse in a great Christian house," enjoying, however self-destructively, his melodrama of Jewish self-loathing. In such a scheme, it is not being kidnapped by Berlin's "former Nazis" that he fears; rather, he is more likely averse to being bored by the city's benevolent philo-Semites.

What recent historiography has portrayed as a West German democracy seeking "normalization" in the post-Holocaust is tantamount, in Humboldt's elliptical phrasing, to "a country where no one could follow his conversation." What Bellow never makes clear can be placed in sharper focus: the reader can reasonably infer that "after Auschwitz," Humboldt's intensely personal desire to "act out" his double conscious-ness cuts an oblique angle through the heavy sincerity of Germany's collective, national effort at working through its brutal past. At Prince-ton, as Citrine earlier observed, it suits Humboldt to "hoke up" anti-Semitism among the professoriat. And Humboldt knows that his "keen Jewish terrors," the neurotic but fertile substrate for acting out his com-plex melodrama of self-loathing, will not "play" in Berlin, solemnly pre-occupied with, as Jürgen Habermas has phrased it, "mov[ing] beyond the horizons of its own life-history"—or, more specifically, striving to confront "the images of that unloading ramp at Auschwitz."[25] It is de-cidedly not the morbidly traumatized liberal German Gentile that Humboldt seeks to interact with for a year; rather, it is the insufferably plenitudinous Sewells of Princeton "on guard for the Protestant Estab-lishment." And thus Humboldt's desire lies not with Berlin's newly cul-tivated philo-Semitism but with genteel Princeton anti-Semitism—not an overt, racially based anti-Semitism that threatens to culminate in genocide but rather a more subtle anti-Semitism that Humboldt can subvert as he plays with his Jewishness. In effect, Humboldt pins the Jewish "star" on himself—not in Germany but in America, where it is easier to be himself *while not being himself* than in a country where "[f]or twelve months, I'd be a Jew and nothing else."[26] For Humboldt, even a possible continued descent into Lear-like madness at Princeton seems a far more desirable alternative than obligingly performing "Jewishness" for a Berlin intelligentsia grappling with the oppressive weight of Ger-man modernity's "Jewish question."

In the temporal space of Adorno's "after Auschwitz," Humboldt re-jects Berlin and thus remains a poet without a city. Time and again throughout *Humboldt's Gift*, we are informed that Humboldt himself adores European high modernism—Yeats, Rilke, Goethe, Proust, Bal-zac, and Joyce—all celebrating exile as yielding intellectual freedom and creative power. And these high modernist celebrations of exile al-most always mean that the writer "is not at home" in a European city (such as Joyce's Dublin). But Humboldt, the lover of European high modernism, has, ironically, never been to Europe—preferring to be "not at home" not in Berlin but in the Princeton countryside. And thus does he remain the poet-genius without a city. Not only will there be no "Weimar in Washington": there will also be no Humboldt renaissance in post-Weimar—and post-Holocaust—Berlin.

Humboldt's rejection of the Berlin invitation seems insignificant enough at the time, but the fact is that in its wake, Humboldt's tragic decline is swift. As we have seen, much of the discomforting comic tension of the Princeton episode centers on Humboldt's manic scheming to secure a permanent appointment at Princeton. But although his scheming is comic, Citrine observes an ominous "look of peril [that] grew around his mouth." Humboldt, knowing that he will be forced off the Princeton faculty when Sewell returns from *his* own chosen international city of Damascus, schemes to be awarded a permanent endowed chair in modern poetry. The department chair, Ricketts, who claims to be supportive of Humboldt, declares that he is unable to fund such an appointment, but this setback merely fuels Humboldt's appetite for further strategizing. Humboldt gets in touch with an old acquaintance, Wilmoore Longstaff, head of the Belisha Foundation, who enthusiastically agrees to endow the professorship, a maneuver deeply satisfying to Humboldt. (As Citrine observes, in Humboldt's mind, "Ricketts was outgeneraled.") But the Belisha Foundation's trustees reject Longstaff's proposed budget, along with the funding for Humboldt's chair. Following this chain of events, the tragic momentum of Humboldt's decline is unstoppable. Ricketts and Princeton "win" the game, Humboldt resigns from the faculty, and shortly thereafter he tries to run his wife down "on a back road in New Jersey" (136). He is eventually taken off in a straitjacket to Bellevue and later dies of a heart attack in a flophouse. And thus does Humboldt hover inconclusively between sensitive poet and pathetic victim crushed by society.

As if the task of interpreting Humboldt's decline "after Auschwitz" were not complicated enough, it should not go unnoticed that, in the light of Humboldt's Berlin aversions, Bellow has embedded an odd irony within the manifest "Germanness" of Humboldt's name, weirdly echoing that of the nineteenth-century German philologist and educational theorist Wilhelm von Humboldt. Humboldt's name encrypts an additional proleptic irony in that the major university in Berlin before World War II was the Humboldt University—the Free University having been established in West Berlin after the war to fill an educational vacuum. It is almost as if the Free University *intimately hails* Humboldt to join its ranks and help it usher in a new era "after Auschwitz." But the poet without a city refuses to listen to the echoes of his own name in Berlin. And thus does Humboldt, despite his refusal to enact "Jewishness" for Germans, ironically become a Jew "by fate," every bit as much as the European Jews Freud or Benjamin or Celan—or the Adorno who defined the parameters of Humboldt's own fateful and overdetermined temporal frame of "after Auschwitz."

Even as West German democracy, in its effort to become "normalized," seeks a "working through," so also does Humboldt "act out" his own anxieties as a kind of personal counter-response to that "working through." Improbably enough, then, Humboldt's ill-fated decision to remain at Princeton can be directly inserted into the larger space of "after Auschwitz"; and, in the final analysis, *pace* Tanner, the problems of history *do* "enter" *Humboldt's Gift.* The Berlin invitation is the seemingly "everyday" moment at which Humboldt's anxieties, intimately rooted within the history of Jewish American assimilation, confront the extreme historical event of the Holocaust, the point at which his localized story of poetic failure intersects with the psychic aftermath of large-scale catastrophe. *Humboldt's Gift* is far removed from the events of the Holocaust. And yet, the psychic displacements that characterize the temporal space of "after Auschwitz" can be detected within the interstices of Fuchs's questions about Humboldt's contradictions: is he a genius? a disaster? a martyr? a con man? What is finally at stake here is no salutary consciousness of the Holocaust itself but rather an eruptive narrative where personal trauma intersects with the aftermath of historical catastrophe. Humboldt's comically framed but, in the end, self-destructive decision to reject the Free University and remain at Princeton can be seen, "after Auschwitz," as a kind of arresting *point de capiton* for Bellow's otherwise agile and unlocatable comic voice: it is the point at which the "broad comedy" of *Humboldt's Gift* becomes transformed into Humboldt's "death-theme." Over the years, Adorno's most oft-cited and now clichéd observation has been that after Auschwitz, it is no longer possible to write poems. The melancholia of this observation resonates in *Humboldt's Gift* where, "after Auschwitz," Humboldt too can write no more poetry.

I conclude by offering some scattered theoretical speculations on the value of performing such a close reading of the Princeton episode of *Humboldt's Gift.* Anything less than a close reading fails to reveal the complexities of Humboldt's disavowals and psychic displacements "after Auschwitz"; and my close reading has succeeded, I hope, in identifying *Humboldt's Gift* as a compelling test case for current debates about the limits of representing the Holocaust. A close reading offers up the Princeton episode as a kind of Kantian "sublime" for Bellow's novel: Humboldt rejects the Free University's invitation not because of any "consciousness" as such of the catastrophe of history that had recently transpired in Germany; rather, the Holocaust as that which cannot be represented in the novel is what, in no small way, ironically impels his ruinous experience at Princeton. Writing within the temporal frame of "after Auschwitz," Jean-François Lyotard has argued, "The silence that surrounds the phrase 'Auschwitz was the extermination camp' is not a state of mind, it is a sign that something remains to be phrased which is not, something which is to be determined."[27] Within the narrative framework of *Humboldt's Gift*, Auschwitz remains to be "phrased" by the academics of the Free University—and certainly remains to be phrased by Humboldt, who, though readily articulating his manic-comic dread of "be[ing] a Jew and nothing else" in a country struggling to name the unnameable, also serves to illustrate Lyotard's contention that Auschwitz "is a sign that remains to be phrased" in the novel.

In the final analysis, I contend that we cannot fully understand Bellow's more recent works, such as *The Bellarosa Connection*, that are manifestly about Auschwitz until we first understand his crucial earlier "after Auschwitz" phase—a phase offering no direct confrontation of the facts of the Holocaust, and certainly no integrated discourse of the voices of perpetrators and victims, but rather an excess beyond representation. The unrepresentability of trauma "after Auschwitz" lends an additional rich texture to the novel's tragic Princeton core. At Princeton, Humboldt enacts no "mourning work," and the reader is left to bear witness to a breakdown of the knowledge of catastrophe.

Notes

1. Tony Tanner, afterword to *Saul Bellow and His Work*, ed. Edmond Schraepen (Brussels: Free University of Brussels, 1978), 131.

2. For comprehensive attempts to place Bellow within the framework of the Holocaust, see S. Lillian Kremer, *Witness through the Imagination: Jewish-American Holocaust Literature* (Detroit: Wayne State University Press, 1989); Regine Rosenthal, "Memory and the Holocaust: *Mr. Sammler's Planet* and *The Bellarosa Connection*," in *Saul Bellow at Seventy-Five: A Collection of Critical Essays*, ed. Gerhard Bach (Tübingen: Gunter Narr Verlag, 1991), 81–92; and Alan Berger, "Remembering and Forgetting: The Holocaust and Jewish-American Culture in Saul Bellow's *The Bellarosa Connection*," in *Small Planets: Saul Bellow as Short Fiction Writer*, ed. Gloria Cronin and Gerhard Bach (East Lansing: Michigan State University Press, 2000), 315–28.

3. The temporal frame of "after Auschwitz" was first established in Adorno's chapter "After Auschwitz" in his *Negative Dialectics*, trans. E. B. Ashton (New York: Continuum, 1973).

4. The last decade or so has experienced a burgeoning interest in assessing the psychic complexities of "after Auschwitz." A brief sampling of the bibliography includes Eric Santner, *Stranded Objects: Mourning, Memory, and Film in Postwar Germany* (Ithaca: Cornell University Press, 1990); Dominick LaCapra, *Representing the Holocaust: History, Theory, Trauma* (Ithaca: Cornell University Press, 1994); Andreas Huyssen, *Twilight Memories: Marking Time in a Culture of Amnesia* (New York: Routledge, 1995); Geoffrey Hartman, *The Longest Shadow: In the Aftermath of the Holocaust* (Bloomington: Indiana University Press, 1996); Cathy Caruth, *Unclaimed Experience* (Baltimore: Johns Hopkins University Press, 1996); and Michael Rothberg, *Traumatic Realism: The Demands of Holocaust Representation* (Minneapolis: University of Minnesota Press, 2000).

5. Adorno, "What Does Coming to Terms with the Past Mean?," trans. Timothy Bahti and Geoffrey Hartman, in *Bitburg in Moral and Political Perspective*, ed. Geoffrey Hartman (Bloomington: Indiana University Press, 1986), 22–31. The basis for the translation is the text in Adorno's *Gesammelte Schriften*, vol. 10, pt. 2 (Frankfurt am Main: Suhrkamp Verlag, 1977), 555–72.

6. Saul Bellow, *Herzog* (New York: Fawcett Crest, 1961), 71. All further references to *Herzog* are taken from this edition, hereafter cited parenthetically in the text.

7. For a pathbreaking study of the concept of "post-memory" as a means of thinking about memory and the generations born after the Holocaust, see Marianne Hirsch, *Family Frames: Photography, Narrative, and Postmemory* (Cambridge: Harvard University Press, 1997).

8. Saul Bellow, *Humboldt's Gift* (New York: Avon Books, 1973), hereafter cited parenthetically in the text.

9. Sarah Blacher Cohen, *Saul Bellow's Enigmatic Laughter* (Urbana: University of Illinois Press, 1974), 4.

10. Elaine B. Safer, "Degrees of Comic Irony in *A Theft* and *A Bellarosa Connection*," in Cronin and Bach, *Small Planets*, 298; Cohen, *Bellow's Enigmatic Laughter*, 19.

11. Richard G. Stern, "Bellow's Gift," *New York Times Magazine*, November 21, 1976, 46.

12. Pierre Dommergues, "An Interview with Saul Bellow," *Delta* (Montpellier, France) 19 (1984): 17.

13. Daniel Fuchs, *Saul Bellow: Vision and Revision* (Durham, N.C.: Duke University Press, 1984), 264.

14. Fuchs writes that the episode's roots go as far back as *Herzog* (ibid., 274).

15. It bears mention that Bellow himself taught at Princeton in 1952.

16. Here Bellow seems to be playing off the irony of the fact that Hitler dogmatically maintained that the Weimar Republic was de facto ruled by the Jews.

17. Ben Siegel, "Saul Bellow and the University as Villain," in *Saul Bellow in the 1980s: A Collection of Critical Essays*, ed. Gloria L. Cronin and L. H. Goldman (East Lansing: Michigan State University Press, 1989), 137.

18. Bellow, "The University as Villain," *Nation*, November 30, 1957, 362 (quoted in Siegel, "Bellow and the University," 154); Bellow, "Culture Now: Some Animadversions, Some Laughs," *Modern Occasions* 1 (Winter 1971): 162 (quoted in Siegel, "Bellow and the University," 140).

19. Molly Stark Wieting, "The Symbolic Function of the Pastoral in Saul Bellow's Novels," in Cronin and Goldman, *Bellow in the 1980s*, 81.

20. Humboldt's prototype, Delmore Schwartz, himself was obsessed with tenure. In his journal he once wrote morbidly: "I shall get tenure in the grave" (quoted in James Atlas, *Delmore Schwartz: The Life of an American Poet* [New York: Avon Books, 1977], 253).

21. Atlas writes that Delmore Schwartz, often claiming that he had suffered as a Jew during his years on the Harvard faculty, was always aware of "the antipathy to Jews that persisted in the English Departments of Ivy League universities well into the forties" (ibid., 153). Schwartz, looking for teaching opportunities beyond Harvard, once wrote to Princeton's R. P. Blackmur around 1946, "you might do worse than importing one of the children of Israel from Cambridge, Massachusetts, an importation you once mentioned frequently and then ceased to mention" (quoted in ibid., 246).

22. In this context, it is worthwhile noting that Atlas describes Delmore Schwartz as himself a natural mime: "His comic gift drew inspiration from the Borscht circuit, American vaudeville, and the polemical style of a Russian intellectual" (ibid., 51). Interestingly, writer Dwight MacDonald, remembering the young Schwartz of twenty-four, describes him as "an intellectual equivalent of the Borscht Circuit *tummler*, or stirrer-upper . . . [his voice] running up and down the scale of sarcasm, invective, desperate rationality, gasping ridicule" (interview with F. W. Dupee, 1974; quoted in ibid., 94–95).

23. Delmore Schwartz similarly turned down an offer to teach at the American University in Salzburg. Interestingly, Schwartz hated to travel, and in a 1974 interview with Elizabeth Pollet he confessed, "How could I go to Europe when I can't even shave at home?" (quoted in ibid., 116).

24. One of the first and most ambitious efforts at "psychoanalyzing" the German national character *(Volkstümlichkeit)* was Alexander and Margarete Mitscherlich's groundbreaking *The Inability to Mourn: Principles of Collective Behavior* (1967; New York: Grove Press, 1975), a thorough study of the extent to which postwar German society of the 1950s struggled to confront and work through its Nazi past. Their book provides compelling arguments that the psychic processes of mourning and melancholia are not just interior and private but also inherently cultural, social, and political in their ramifications. A precursor of the Mitscherlich book is Karl Jaspers's 1947 *Die Schuldfrage: Von der politischen Haftung Deutschlands* (Munich: Piper, 1987), the first attempt to analyze German postwar guilt.

25. Jürgen Habermas, *The New Conservatism: Cultural Criticism and the Historians' Debate,* ed. and trans. Shierry Weber Nicholsen, intro. Richard Wolin (Cambridge: MIT Press, 1989), 229–30.

26. My play on words with the "Jewish star" has been inspired by a brilliant paper, "Bad Taste, Catskills Humor, and the Jewish Star," given by David Suchoff at the 1998 Modern Language Association Convention in San Francisco.

27. Jean-François Lyotard, *The Differend: Phrases in Dispute,* trans. George Van Den Abbeele (Minneapolis: University of Minnesota Press, 1988), 57.

8

Mormon Literature and
the Irreducible Other

Writing the Unspeakable in Holocaust Literature

REINHOLD HILL

In *The Differend: Phrases in Dispute,* Jean François Lyotard enters the discourse between Holocaust deniers and Holocaust scholars and argues that the opposing views of the two cannot presently be reconciled. Lyotard argues that although the deniers employ the language of scholars, their goals are not scholarly, and scholarly debate cannot resolve the disputes that exist between the agendas of deniers and scholars. While Lyotard examines what he calls "the differend" in the light of the debate between Holocaust deniers and Holocaust scholars, the differend provides a useful starting point for an examination of competing worldviews, what Lyotard expresses in terms of "phrase regimens," or language usage. In this essay I explore the representation of one marginalized group (Jews, Judaism, and the Jewish Holocaust) by another (Mormons) and argue that Mormon representations of Jewish life and experience (especially the experience of the Holocaust) are often flawed because Mormon authors do not recognize the competing values of the groups and thus create a differend that cannot be resolved. Through the examination of Margaret Young's *House Without Walls* and Eugene England's "Summer Solstice," I explore the possibility of resolving the differend through an application of Maurice Blanchot's *The Writing of the Disaster.* (Lyotard allows for the possibility of resolving the differend, and thereby the impasse, in a future where the referents become absolute, but such a future is removed from normative reality and exists only outside "logical space.")[1]

In order to fully explore the difficulties inherent in Mormon representations of the Holocaust, it is necessary to explore Mormon theology regarding Jews and Judaism. Mormons view themselves as God's chosen people, but unlike most other members of Christian faiths, they do not regard themselves as the successors to God's covenant with Israel. In Mormon theology, the Abrahamic covenant is alive, and Mormons hold divine birthright through their ritual adoption into the covenant. Certainly, Mormonism views itself as "a new and everlasting covenant," but it is not one that replaces God's original covenant with his chosen people, the Jews. Joseph Smith, founder of the Church of Jesus Christ of Latter-day Saints, taught through the *Book of Mormon* that the Jews were God's chosen people and that anti-Semitic attitudes were antithetical to God's teachings: "O ye Gentiles, have ye remembered the Jews, mine ancient covenant people? Nay; but ye have cursed them, and have hated them, and have not sought to recover them. But behold, I will return all things upon your own heads; for I the Lord have not forgotten my people."[2]

According to Steven Epperson, *The Book of Mormon* "is for all its christocentrism peculiarly pitched toward the realization of God's covenant with Israel. Israel's covenant dominates the text the way a 'main theme' presides through the exposition, development, and recapitulation of a sonata."[3] Epperson argues that Smith was unique among religious leaders of the nineteenth century because he did not actively seek to proselytize or convert Jews.[4] Indeed, Smith was critical of such efforts among the Christian denominations, as the above passage attests.[5]

Smith's feelings about Jews and Judaism, however, were not without their contradictions. In order to more fully understand the Bible and other ancient scripture, Smith sought to learn Hebrew and other ancient languages. Joshua Seixas, son of Rabbi Gershom Medes Seixas, a prominent Jewish leader, was hired to teach Smith Hebrew in Kirtland, Ohio.[6] Epperson cites Moshe Davis to suggest that this period of interaction between Smith and Seixas was of crucial importance to the development of early Mormon theologies.[7] Nonetheless, the friendly encounter between Smith and Seixas aroused in Smith "an inclusive, conversionist impulse."[8] Seixas did not embrace Smith's "restored" gospel, and their interactions brought Smith to write that he had met a "peculiar people" who practiced "true piety [and] real religion."[9] Epperson concludes: "For a man who claimed that he was told by divine revelation that 'all the sects . . . were an abomination' in the sight of the Lord, such adjectives as 'true' and 'real' for another religious community were hardly trivial."[10]

The same ambiguity that brought Smith to seek to convert Seixas to Mormonism continues to influence contemporary Mormonism. Lawrence Wright claims that "the number of Mormons throughout the world may soon equal that of the Jews, and indeed, many see a parallel between the two faiths."[11] To illustrate similarities between Mormons and Jews, Wright quotes Harold Bloom, who writes that "Mormons have repeated in a deep sense the pattern of Jews—they are a religion that has become a people."[12] Wright points out that, like the Jews, Mormons have an exodus and have "forged their early identity as a scorned people."[13] It should come as no surprise that when non-Mormon writers conflate Mormon and Jewish experience, Mormons themselves will do so also. Nonetheless, Wright is quick to point out that, "Unlike the Jews, the Mormons are a missionary people,"[14] thus illustrating one important difference between the worldviews of Mormons and Jews. Mormons are apt to disregard such differences in their conflation of identities, which leads to the differend between the phrase regimens of Mormons and Jews explored below.

Margaret Young's novel *House Without Walls* is difficult to categorize: it is part romance, part Holocaust fiction, part religious didacticism.[15] The story opens with the protagonist, Sarah Sinahson, returning home to Hamburg after her experience in the Bergen-Belsen concentration camp.[16] Sarah, who is a Jewish convert to Mormonism, is stunned that her house still exists among the rubble in Hamburg, and her memory is taken back to the blessing two Mormon missionaries left on the house years earlier. Everyone in Sarah's family is dead, but upon seeing her home she thinks back on a different time and place and remembers her conversion to Mormonism.

Young is honest about the motivations of many young converts when she describes Sarah's crush on a handsome Mormon boy, Hans, but the novel describes much more than an attachment to Mormonism because of romantic fancy. Sarah is possibly saved by her Mormon connections when her father insists that she go to a local Mormon family for

shelter. Sarah is housed for a time in a forest cottage, but when her ben-
efactors are killed in a bomb raid, she is forced to fend for herself, is captured by the Nazis, and is sent to Bergen-Belsen.[17]

Sarah does not return to Mormonism after her experience in the
camps. Instead, she marries Abraham, a rabbi from her prewar community in Hamburg, so that she can emigrate to the United States with
him. Once in the United States, Sarah begins a new, Jewish life with
Abraham. They have a son, Isaac, and the final two-thirds of the novel
revolve around Isaac's relationship with the daughter of Sarah's prewar
Mormon boyfriend. Isaac is drawn to Mormonism, converts, and returns to Germany as a Mormon missionary. Young attempts to further
complicate the plot by having Sarah and Abraham visit Isaac in Germany during the Munich Olympics.

For all of the novel's emphasis on Mormon Christ-centered values of
salvation, it portrays a surprisingly vibrant picture of Jewish culture.
When Young explores Abraham's life before the Holocaust, the reader
is given a clear sense of Jewish tradition:

> Abraham Cohen was the fourth in a family line of rabbis. It was the
> Jewish custom that every firstborn male child should belong to God.
> The father paid a token sum for his son's release to his care.
>
> Abraham was the firstborn of his father's family. Though the elder
> Rabbi Cohen, Samuel, had fulfilled the requirements of the Law in
> buying his boy back, Abraham understood throughout his life that he
> was expected to become a servant of God, a scholar of Judaism, a rabbi.
> He fulfilled the expectations magnificently. He not only learned the
> writings of past scholars and prophets—the *nauvey*—but loved them.[18]

Young respects Jewish tradition and life, and she attempts to instill in
her reader an appreciation of this tradition through her detailed rendering of Jewish custom and tradition. Jewish ritual, tradition, and ceremony are drawn with obvious reverence, and her pictures provide min-
ute descriptions that incorporate a liberal smattering of Hebrew words
and phrases to lend an authentic feel to her text:

> Simon and an acquaintance of Rabbi Silverstein assisted with the
> child's circumcision. The wine was slipped into the eight-day-old
> infant's mouth, and the rite of Brith Milah was performed: the child
> was put under the covenant of his fathers and circumcised as a token of

his identity. For had not God said, "My covenant shall be in your flesh for an everlasting covenant"?

The child, whom Abraham symbolically named Isaac, cried vigorously as the ritual was performed. Abraham took him in his arms and whispered, "*Shah, shah*," and the cries quieted to whispers. "Oh this will be a good boy," Abraham prophesied to all present—and to the world. (100)

God's covenant with Judaism, which Mormons, unlike many other Christians, believe continues still, is emphasized throughout Young's discussion of Jewish life and tradition. We are shown Abraham teaching his son the significance of Hanukkah, the meaning of the festival, and its application to modern life. The description Young gives the Passover is particularly infused with emotion in the light of the description she has given the Holocaust:

Sarah cleaned the house for a week in preparation for Passover. The night before the Pesach feast, she hid bread crumbs behind the closet door, on a chair. Then ten-year-old Isaac found and collected the crumbs. In the morning, the crumbs were burnt. Passover began.

On the Seder plate were bitter herbs, recalling the bitterness of slavery; a roasted bone, symbol of the lamb sacrifice; apples, wine, nuts and cinnamon, representing the mortar the ancient Israelites slaved to make for the Egyptians; parsley dipped in salt water, for the greenness of spring and the tears of the Hebrew slaves; a whole egg, symbol of the newness of life; three pieces of matzoth for the three ancient divisions among the Israelites. A cup was reserved for Elijah, the invited but invisible guest. Abraham's chair was cushioned as a reminder that the Jews were now free to sit or lean as they chose.

Isaac squirmed in his chair, eyes glowing. Abraham nodded to him.

"What makes this night different from all other nights?" the child asked, and Isaac and Abraham spoke the ritual conversation. The family recited the plagues of God on the Egyptians and remembered the passing over of the Angel of Death. (114)

On a personal, visceral level, Young's descriptions draw in the reader. A Mormon audience will be drawn to the story because it appeals to the faithful: the faithful Mormon reader is introduced to another religious culture that is similar, that has a rich religious tradition, and which Mormon theology embraces as a chosen, covenant community.

But this is also the problem with the story and with the novel as a whole: the picture drawn by Young is a *Mormon picture* of a Jewish experience. Thus the novel is trapped in a peculiar Mormon worldview that cannot reasonably represent the experience of the Holocaust in any terms except those that relate to Mormon ideals of redemption. That is, the novel presents a picture of the Holocaust and life after the Holocaust that demonstrates Mormon values that emphasize redemption through a literal savior in the person of Jesus Christ.

In the world Young creates through her novel, if Sarah will not return to Mormonism (though clearly her heart is drawn in this direction), then God will take Isaac. Isaac's loss occurs when he is married to his Mormon girlfriend, Elsa, in a Mormon temple ceremony. Although Abraham was not comfortable with Isaac's decision to serve a Mormon mission or to marry this Mormon girl in a ceremony in which he cannot participate, at the novel's conclusion Abraham sounds a note of reconciliation that conforms to a Mormon worldview when he compares the temple destroyed in Jerusalem to the Mormon temple in Salt Lake City: "My son, if this were a Jewish wedding, you would crush a glass in remembrance of the destruction of our temple. For you, perhaps you don't remember the destruction of your temple, since this one is—since it has been restored to you. I think maybe there is good in this. Maybe it is good to remember that in his own time, in his own way, God restores whatever man destroys. Therein is your hope. And mine" (222). In this passage we find the differend. In some forms of Judaism, especially the Judaism portrayed by Young, one would expect the father to be distraught because he is losing his son who is marrying outside God's covenant, while for the Mormon reader it is clear that Abraham cannot attend his son's wedding because he is not Mormon, and only worthy, practicing Mormons may enter Mormon temples. Young has done a good job of establishing Abraham's identity as a more or less orthodox Jew, but the Jewish view is lost in Young's telling because she is unaware of the incommensurable phrase regimens between Mormonism and Judaism that cause her portrayal to break down. Perhaps more importantly for this discussion, Abraham speaks of God's redemption as an action by God rather than a result of human action. The gulf between the views of redemption—in this case, redemption brought about by God's intervention versus redemption as a result of human endeavor—results in a differend, incommensurable under the phrase regimen employed by Young. The implications of Young's ending are clear: Mormonism, particularly the restoration tendencies of Mormonism, provides hope for redemption through God's literal redemption. In Young's conception, much of the lesson of the Holocaust must be glossed over because the Holocaust does not yield such a redemption.

Nonetheless, the portrait Young paints is as accurate as any can be that attempts to address and reconcile the differend between the belief systems of Mormons and Jews. Young's novel is further problematized by her husband's preface to the book. In his introduction, Bruce Young discusses the Mormon doctrine of posthumous temple work, which allows those who did not receive Mormon ordinances in this life to receive them in the next. According to Young, "the names of some of those killed in the Holocaust, the Nazi destruction of the Jews, have been placed in files at the Provo Temple," and he and his spouse have done Mormon temple work in their behalf: "There was something terribly anonymous in their persecution and murder. They were treated not as individuals but as nameless members of a despised race. Temple work, we have felt, somehow reverses that process. Those who were destroyed en masse are redeemed one by one. Those deprived of names and voices are given names and voices again. We think of them as individuals, one at a time" (xiv). Jewish reaction to the practice of posthumous baptism for victims of the Holocaust was understandably negative. Ernest Michel, chairman of the World Gathering of Holocaust Survivors, led the protest against the Mormon practice after learning that his parents, victims of Auschwitz, were posthumously baptized into a Christian faith.[19] According to the Associated Press, the Mormons who posthumously baptized the Holocaust victims did so because they were motivated by "love and compassion" after visiting Holocaust memorials. They did not realize that what they did might be offensive. There is clearly a differend in the language used by the Mormons motivated by "compassion" and the language of the relatives of the Holocaust victims. Church leaders have agreed to remove the names of Holocaust victims who do not have Mormon relatives from the church's genealogical index, which will effectively halt temple baptisms of the victims. Nonetheless, in Mormonism there is no exaltation (God's highest reward for the faithful) for the non-Mormon. All the righteous, if they are to receive this reward, must undergo conversion to Mormonism and receive all Mormon ordinances.

Louis Zucker, the first Jewish professor at the University of Utah, writes: "Mormons, I think, are in the habit of magnifying similarities between Judaism and Mormonism and etherealizing the differences into shadow. We should have a clearer and truer knowledge of each other."[20] Nonetheless, the differend, as presented by Lyotard, is not resolvable between the Mormon and Jewish genres of discourse, because although the possibility of phrasing the differend exists, it is not practical to do so when the goals of the genres of discourse are not the same.[21] Young focuses on supernatural intervention in Sarah's life (symbolized, for example, by the survival of her childhood home). Her genre is a genre of salvation, which focuses on God's intervention to bring about the end of sin. Salvation is a result of the work of God, his interest and intervention in human affairs. Jewish representations of the Holocaust, however, are more likely to be written in the genre of redemption, specifically contemporary Jewish conceptions of redemption, which focus on human action in bringing about an end to sin.

The differend between Mormon conceptions of salvation and contemporary Jewish conceptions of redemption complicates any meaningful dialogue between Mormons and Jews because such dialogue is restricted by the inability to resolve the differend between the genres of discourse. In the case of Holocaust literature, the vexing question is one of ultimate responsibility for both the Holocaust and life after the Holocaust.

Zucker examines the differend between Mormon salvation and Jewish redemption in his discussion of Mormon interpretations of the Old Testament in relation to Jewish understanding: "There simply is no meeting ground between the Mormon line of argument and the Pharisaic or Rabbinic development of Scripture in the Talmud. The one speaks of Salvation in the next world; the other speaks of Halachah, the way, ethical conduct in human relations. The knowledgeable Jew is also aware of over 2000 years of Jewish experience and thought, of challenge and response, after the Old Testament."[22] The otherworldliness of Mormon interpretation contrasts with the this-worldly emphasis of Jewish interpretation. The regimens provided by the different focus in worldviews challenge assumptions of salvation and redemption that cause difficulties for Mormon writers attempting to incorporate the Jewish Other into their texts.

Beyond the obvious generic difference, there is a clear contrast between Young's fictional novel and Eugene England's personal essay "Summer Solstice." The picture England draws is strikingly different from Young's. England's essay is set in Idaho on his ninth birthday. He realized, after seeing Claude Lanzmann's account of the Holocaust, *Shoah*, that his ninth birthday coincided with the beginning of the Nazi liquidation of the Warsaw ghetto. Drawing from several sources, including Lucy Dawidowicz's *The War against the Jews*, England creates parallel worlds, the world of a nine-year-old Mormon boy in Idaho and that of a nine-year-old Jewish boy in the Warsaw ghetto. Instead of focusing on aspects of religion or culture, England focuses on experience. He remembers helping his father on the farm that day, playing with his friends, and rushing to the movies. He describes his despair when he learns that the price of seeing a movie has increased and that he does not have enough to go to the movie. Then he contrasts these experiences with the experiences of the children of the Jewish orphanage on the day of the liquidation of the Warsaw ghetto:

> By four o'clock in the afternoon, about when I, eight time zones away, had run the morning's first load of wheat out of the pit and turned off the elevator, six thousand people were being loaded into forty cattle cars, packed so tight they could only stand. After a journey of fifteen hours, without water or toilets, they were put onto a siding with other trains at the small town of Treblinka. Twenty cars at a time were disconnected and pushed to a small locomotive the four miles to the camp. Suddenly the car doors were opened and a variety of guards, Ukranian, Latvian, German, began pushing them out of the cars, beating them with whips and clubs, and screaming, "Get out, get out. Hurry. Leave the baggage. Get undressed! You're to be disinfected."[23]

England repeatedly contrasts his experience as a nine-year-old boy in Idaho with the experiences of the Jews in the Warsaw ghetto. Instead of minimizing the differences, England magnifies them. One way of reading England's approach to portraying the Holocaust is to examine Maurice Blanchot's assertion that "Reading is anguish, and this is because any text, however important, or amusing, or interesting it may be (and the more engaging it seems to be), is empty — at bottom it doesn't exist; you have to cross an abyss, and if you don't jump, you do not comprehend."[24] England seems to force the reader to attempt to jump into the abyss and begin the process of trying to comprehend. The gap between experiences elicits the desire to grasp and to comprehend, even if such comprehension is elusive. Where Young draws a picture that emphasizes similarity in experience, England maximizes differences, even emphasizing the incommensurable difference between Mormon and Jewish experience. As England evokes historical figure and personal experience, the reader seeks to reconcile his or her experiences with the experiences of the Other, but England does not allow such reconciliation to occur.

England describes, as Dawidowicz does, the leader of the orphanage, who ensures that the children have clean clothing and fresh water for their journey. Korczak, the leader of the orphanage, takes one of the children, England's imagined Julek, by the hand and escorts the children to the train station. Korczak is given the opportunity to leave the children, but he does not. Again at Treblinka he is encouraged to leave the children, but he refuses. England takes the reader inside the gas chamber and describes the horrific annihilation of the ghetto:

> At this point the record ends. . . . I feel I must try to speak for them, to imagine a voice for at least one, and so have chosen nine-year-old Julek to take us all the way into that chamber. . . .
>
> *Then the door opened and they pushed us inside one big room. Some fell down but the doctor still held my hand. He tried to keep us standing against the wall, but when they closed the doors everyone began crying and pushing back to get out the door.*
>
> *Then I heard a loud engine start up at the back. . . . The doctor yelled at us to stand still and breath quietly and soon it would end. . . . We fought each other to climb up and get air. . . . I could feel the doctor under me, and he pushed me up and held me until there was no breath to breathe.*[25]

England feels obligated to write the story, to provide a voice for the voiceless. As Bernard-Donals and Glejzer say of Lyotard in this volume, the sublime "involves an obligation to utterance rather than an insistence upon silence." But how does one reconcile the obligation with the impossibility of utterance? As Blanchot has written, "There is no reaching the disaster. Out of reach is he whom it threatens, whether from afar or close up, it is impossible to say: the infiniteness of the threat has in some way broken every limit."[26] Blanchot provides a partial answer when he argues that it is a human desire to push the limits of writing: "The human movement is the one that goes right to the limit. Still, it is possible that as soon as we write, and however little we write (the little is only too much), we know we are approaching the limit—the perilous threshold—the chance of being turned back."[27] The threat of "being turned back" follows Blanchot's assertion that

"The disaster, unexperienced. It is what escapes the very possibility of experience—it is the limit of writing. This must be repeated: the disaster de-scribes. Which does not mean that the disaster, as the force of writing, is excluded from it, is beyond the pale of writing or extratextual."[28] It is not in the gas chamber, however, that England evokes the disaster.

At the end of his personal essay, England returns the reader to Idaho and the normalcy of his life as a nine-year-old boy: "As I awoke in the dark on August 7, 1942, about the time Julek Jacobowicz died, I realized my father was standing by the bed, his hand on my shoulder. 'We need to get going,' he said quietly. 'Your grandpa wants to go with us today, so let's help with his chores.' We ate and got down to Grandpa's by 5, in time for Dad to milk the last big black and white Holstein."[29] The contrast at this point of the essay could not be more striking: England's return to the juxtaposition of his experience with what has just occurred to Julek evokes both the written and extratextual moment that cannot be written and is unexperienced. England implies rightly that his experience as a nine-year-old, indeed the experiences of all who have not experienced the disaster, makes it impossible to grasp the disaster, the events that are the Shoah. Instead of taking the traditional Mormon approach to understanding Judaism and the Jewish experience by focusing on perceived religious similarities, England chooses to maximize the difference of the experiences, thus providing the reader an opportunity to glimpse the extratextual disaster.

Margaret Young's book is trapped in a Mormon conception of Jewish life. The difficulty of representing an Other—in this case the Jewish Holocaust experience—and the self is not unique to Mormon popular literature or criticism. Trinh Minh-Ha has written that the conversation about the Other is essentially a conversation about the self: "'Them' [the Other] always stands on the other side of the hill, naked and speechless . . . 'them' is only admitted among 'us,' the discussing subjects, when accompanied or introduced by an 'us.'"[30] Lyotard further argues that "the blindness is in putting yourself in the place of the other, in saying *I* in his or her place, in neutralizing his or her transcendence."[31] Young uses a Mormon Jew to explore the Holocaust, but in so doing she loses the Otherness of the Holocaust experience. The Other in Young's novel is actually one of "us" (that is, one of her intended Mormon audience), and we are left with an incomplete picture of the experience of the Other, both because we have not confronted the

Other and because the entire genre of the novel, the genre of salvation, conflicts with the genre of redemption that is characteristic of much Jewish Holocaust literature. We are left with the neutralized experience of the "*I.*"

England's personal essay does not evoke the disaster through the thick description of the experience of the gas chamber, but rather in the return to the normalcy of his experience in stark contrast to the experience of the selection, transport, and gas chamber. As Bernard-Donals and Glejzer argue regarding the sublime, "it is the elusiveness, and the horror in the face of that elusiveness, of the attempt to match the infinite sense data of our lifeworlds to the capacity of reason which would hope to bring some kind of pattern or unity to it." In the case of England's personal essay, there is no possibility of reconciling the destruction of the gas chamber with England's experience on his ninth birthday. It is in the stark contrast of the experience and the unexperienced that England offers a moment that might provide, in Bernard-Donals and Glejzer's words, "the excessive, perhaps traumatic effect" that allows both the possibility and the risk of redemption.

Notes

1. Jean-François Lyotard, *The Differend: Phrases in Dispute*, trans. Georges Van Ben Abbeele (Minneapolis: University of Minnesota Press, 1988), 53–58.
2. *The Book of Mormon: Another Testament of Jesus Christ* (Salt Lake City: The Church of Jesus Christ of Latter-day Saints, 1989), 2 Nephi 29:5, 1–10.
3. Steven Epperson, *Mormons and Jews: Early Mormon Theologies of Israel* (Salt Lake City: Signature Books, 1992), 34.
4. Ibid., 37.
5. Ibid., 37, 52.
6. Ibid., 80–82.
7. Ibid., 85.
8. Ibid., 88.
9. Qtd. in ibid., 89.
10. Ibid.
11. Lawrence Wright, "Lives of the Saints," *New Yorker,* January 21, 2002, 40.
12. Harold Bloom, *The American Religion* (New York: Simon and Schuster, 1992), quoted in Wright, "Lives of the Saints," 40–42.
13. Wright, "Lives of the Saints," 42.
14. Ibid.

15. While there are several texts by Mormon authors that deal with the Holocaust indirectly, I have selected Young's and England's texts because they deal with the Holocaust most directly, and in strikingly different ways.

16. Young's selection of Hamburg for the setting of her novel is significant on several levels. First, it is the scene of the most written about Mormon experience of World War II. Helmuth Huebner, a Mormon youth in one of the Hamburg congregations, became one of the youngest anti-Nazi activists to be executed. For a complete account of the Huebner group and their activities see Blair R. Holmes and Alan F. Keele, *When Truth Was Treason* (Urbana: University of Illinois Press, 1995). For an examination of the less-than-positive aspects of Mormonism favored by the Third Reich see Ernst Helmreich, *The German Churches under Hitler* (Detroit: Wayne State University Press, 1979), 404–6.

17. Douglas Tobler, "The Jews, the Mormons, and the Holocaust," *Journal of Mormon History* 18 (1992): 87–88, reports several incidents of Mormons helping Jewish friends and acquaintances which undoubtedly have influenced the accounts in Young's novel.

18. Margaret Young, *House Without Walls* (Salt Lake City: Desert Book, 1991), 11, hereafter cited parenthetically in the text.

19. Associated Press, "Mormons, Jews Sign Agreement on Baptized Holocaust Victims," May 5, 1995, http://www.jewishgen.org/infofiles/ldsagree.txt.

20. Louis Zucker, "A Jew in Zion," *Sunstone* 6 (September–October 1981): 41.

21. Lyotard, *The Differend*, 129.

22. Zucker, "A Jew in Zion," 43.

23. Eugene England, "Summer Solstice," *Sewanee Review* 103, no. 1 (1995): 51.

24. Maurice Blanchot, *The Writing of the Disaster*, trans. Ann Smock (Lincoln: University of Nebraska Press, 1995), 10.

25. England, "Summer Solstice," 55–57, italics in the original.

26. Blanchot, *Writing of the Disaster*, 1.

27. Ibid., 8.

28. Ibid., 7.

29. England, "Summer Solstice," 57.

30. Trinh T. Minh-Ha, *Woman, Native, Other: Writing Postcoloniality and Feminism* (Bloomington: Indiana University Press, 1989), 65–67.

31. Lyotard, *The Differend*, 109.

9

Beyond the Question of Authenticity

Witness and Testimony in the Fragments *Controversy*

MICHAEL BERNARD-DONALS

Then the Lord said to Moses: "Write this in a document as a memory, and read it aloud to Joshua: I will utterly erase [blot out] the memory of Amalek from under heaven!"

Exodus 17:14

It is upon losing what we have to say that we speak—upon an imminent and immemorial disaster. . . . We speak suggesting that something not being said is speaking: the loss of what we were to say; weeping when tears have long since gone dry.

Maurice Blanchot, The Writing of the Disaster

Dominick LaCapra has written extensively on what he calls the "exceptionally vexed" relationship between history and memory after Auschwitz: history and memory cannot be conflated, and in resisting this conflation we trouble the relation between witness and testimony, as well as the relation among what happened, what we recognize as occurrences, and what we can say about those occurrences.[1] "Memory is both more and less than history, and vice versa," he says;[2] "with respect to trauma, memory is always secondary since what occurs is not integrated into experience or directly remembered."[3] Cathy Caruth goes even further: "the victim of [trauma] was never fully conscious during the [event] itself,"[4] and so any testimony of the event will bear at best an oblique relation with it, since we can only say what we know as experience. Though we live in what Shoshana Felman aptly calls an era of testimony, testimony's relation to the events of history—to what the witness saw—has become a tenuous one.[5] We cannot view testimony as a window on the past; at its most extreme—in memories of trauma— testimony marks the absence of events, since they did not register on, let alone become integrated into, the victim's consciousness. A testimony may be effective, and it may allow a reader to glimpse a trauma (though perhaps not the one that purportedly lies at the testimony's source), but it alone does not provide evidence of that event.

It is this vexed relation of memory, witness, and testimony that I want to examine through the lens of Binjamin Wilkomirski's *Fragments*,[6] a "memoir" whose main character survived the Holocaust as a child. The book was originally published in Germany in 1995; by 1996 it had been translated into a dozen languages and had become an international sensation, in part because it was a lucid, excruciating tale that registered upon—traumatized—its readers.[7] In late 1998, Daniel Ganzfried, whose investigation of Wilkomirski appeared in the Swiss weekly *Weltwoche*,[8] shocked those who had lauded the book: he found documents to suggest that Binjamin Wilkomirski was a fabrication of a Swissborn clarinet maker named Bruno Doesseker, that Doesseker had never been to a concentration camp "except as a tourist," and that if *Fragments* is a memoir, it comprised other people's memories.

It seems clear now that the events depicted in *Fragments* and the events of the author's life as found in the historical record do not coincide. But for many the matter is not settled: even for some of the its detractors, *Fragments* stands as a powerful testimony to events that are unavailable to those who were not there and that are available as open wounds to those who were. Israel Gutman, a survivor with serious doubts about the historical veracity of the book, says nonetheless that "Wilkomirski has written a story which he has experienced deeply, that's for sure."[9] If LaCapra is right, and the traumatic occurrence is not "integrated into experience or directly remembered," then testimonies involve both a remembering and a forgetting—the suppression of the event and its articulation as narrative; a blotting out and a writing down—and the authentication of testimonies of events like the

Shoah becomes difficult at best, at least in part because corroborating
testimonies and other evidence have been lost. I want to suggest in
this essay that our ability to establish the authenticity of the Wilkomirski memoir on historical grounds is complicated by its ability to
compel readers to "see" the events about which the author writes,
though he may not have experienced them at all. This characteristic
seems to fly in the face of history: the veracity or coherence of eyewitness testimony—the testimony's ability to render or represent a series
of events in plausible or verifiable terms—is one of the pillars on which
the historical reality or truth of events rests. But it suggests that a testimony's authority, the extent to which we might say that the speaker or
writer provides an opportunity for the reader to witness an event, is
relatively autonomous from history; it suggests that there is a marked
difference between history as what happens to people (the events that
lie beyond or behind historical accounts) and history as what we know
about what happened (and for which there is evidence); and it suggests
(*pace* Lyotard) that to write what happened we need to be attentive to
and find ways to express "what is not presentable under the rules of
knowledge" or of history.[10]

The central question is how a memoir like *Fragments* can at once be
a false testimony and still produce an effect on readers that induces
them to witness. To answer this question, I will consider three problems inherent in the structure of memory, particularly traumatic memory, as it has been developed in the work of Cathy Caruth, Shoshana
Felman, and others over the last ten years or so.[11] The first is testimony's relative autonomy, or independence, from history. If it is true
that the traumatic incident is repressed at the moment of occurrence or
deformed during testimony, then testimony cannot easily be elided
with the act of witnessing. But if so, we also need to consider—as a second, correlative problem—whether utterances or texts that are not tied
directly to the historical events that are purportedly their object (like
Fragments, but also like, say, *Life Is Beautiful*) should be considered testimonies. Third, we need to consider how testimonies—as relatively autonomous from the events—shape a witnessing in the reader or viewer
and whether this "transference" of trauma takes place at the level of
content or of structure. Finally, I consider at the end of this essay the
risks involved in a theory of trauma and testimony that sees them as resulting from what I take to be an inescapable relation of memory and
forgetting.

L'Affaire Wilkomirski and the Status of the Text

In early 1994, Eva Koralnik, a literary agent in Zurich, received a copy of the Wilkomirski manuscript through the mail; it made such an impression upon her, and upon editors at the press she sent it to, Suhrkamp Verlag in Frankfurt, that it was sold in six months and in production by February 1995. The story was presented as a memoir told from the perspective of a child who, at the beginning of an ordeal that "escap[ed] the laws of logic,"[12] was presumably no more than four or five years old. The story takes place in the years between the German occupation of the Baltic countries and the immediate aftermath of the war through the early 1950s, and it alternates between two main narrative strands: the author's experiences in two camps (Majdanek and an unnamed camp that was identified later as Auschwitz) and his later life in orphanages immediately after the war. In the afterword the author writes that he had at that time "received a new identity, another name, another date and place of birth," but that none of it has to do "with either the history of this century or my personal history."[13] The book seemed to attest to the radical disjunction between history and memory, between the fragmentary but indelible images of a past the author could not shake and the historical circumstances into which those images were fit.

It was the disjunction between Wilkomirski's memory and the historical record that most bothered Daniel Ganzfried, an Israeli-born Swiss writer and author of a novel based on his father's experiences as an Auschwitz survivor. Ganzfried began an investigation that would, he hoped, uncover the author's true identity and past. He found that *Fragments* was written by Bruno Doesseker, a clarinet maker whose adoption papers record his birth in early 1941 to Yvonne Grosjean, an unmarried woman who was herself, along with her brother, separated from impoverished parents.[14] Bruno was placed with foster parents, Kurt and Martha Doesseker, in 1945 and was adopted by them legally in late 1957. Until then, the boy's father paid toward the cost of his son's care. In 1981 Bruno Doesseker inherited a small sum from the modest estate of Yvonne Grosjean, whom he calls his "so-called natural mother."[15] The writer's house is full of archival material about the events that composed the Final Solution and its aftermath, including oral testimonies, films, photographs, and historical accounts. Ganzfried was convinced that this archive forms the core of the Wilkomirski

memoir and that inconsistencies in the account—for example, a female camp warden would not have worn a formal uniform out on patrol in the Polish countryside, as Wilkomirski "remembers" one
doing—are the result of the autodidact's scattershot approach to a history of the Holocaust. (Doesseker claims that the research helped to
place into context the flashes of memory that result from a child's
perspective on events and that it offered "the calming 'possibility' of
finding 'the historical center' of [my] own past.")[16] Ganzfried asked
Doesseker whether he was circumcised, a "natural question to ask of a
Jewish man," to which he answered yes. Doesseker's former girlfriends, however, said that he was not. Ganzfried claims that no child
so young could have survived not just one camp but two, and this
claim has been bolstered by Raul Hilberg, who believes it all but impossible for a child to have been hidden for three years. And yet Israel
Gutman, a survivor of Majdanek, though he was not at the camp
while Wilkomirski claims to have been there, says that an extraordinary few children survived: "Look . . . we know that during the Holocaust extraordinary things happened, which did not correspond to the
general rules. . . . I don't know whether one should look at everything
[Wilkomirski] said under a microscope."[17] Ganzfried is especially wary
that Doesseker is far too emotional about the stories he tells and the
responses he gets from readers of his work: "He cries a lot—and always at the right moment," Ganzfried says, and Lappin and Gourevitch report that they were equally taken aback by his behavior. Doesseker's current companion, Verena Piller, and a psychiatrist with whom
he has traveled and spoken at conferences, Elitsur Bernstein, both say
that his emotional condition and physical infirmities are consistent
with those of a man who has suffered a severe trauma or set of traumatic experiences.[18] Lappin suggests that as a child Bruno Doesseker
constantly tinkered with the story of his origins—a friend recalls that
"he used to say that his adoptive parents wanted him as a medical experiment," and a couple says he told them in the 1960s that "he had
been in the Warsaw ghetto and was saved from the Holocaust by a
Swiss nanny"[19]—as a way of dealing with the trauma of a forcible separation from his mother, Yvonne Grosjean. Lappin found that Doesseker's mother was separated from her parents as a *verdingkind* ("earn-
ing child") under a seventeenth-century system of child welfare, not
abolished until the 1950s, in which poor or unmarried parents sent
their children away to work for other families in exchange for food

and shelter. "Beatings and sexual abuse were often part of their childhood"; Bruno may have been separated from his mother under similar circumstances.[20]

The most straightforward interpretation of these contradictions is that *Fragments* is a fabrication, a hoax, or a delusion. But regardless of whether or not a traumatic kernel lies at the heart of the book, *Fragments* may well function as a vehicle for witnessing even though it does not qualify as a testimony. And this raises an interesting question: can fiction serve effectively as a vehicle for memory? One warrant for an affirmative answer can be found in a rhetorical tradition that pays attention to what resides behind the language of a discourse rather than in the speaker's integrity or the degree to which the discourse can be squared with a state of affairs. The extent to which a discourse has authority depends on its ability to move an audience to "see" an issue or an event that exceeds language's ability to narrate it. A text's authority originates in its ability to indicate (though perhaps not produce) knowledge of what lies beyond what can be logically understood, beyond what "makes sense."[21] But cannot a testimony about the Shoah, regardless of its ability to make sense, be called into question if we impeach the character or the veracity of the speaker?

To tell a certain truth, any testimony of the Holocaust would have to agree with or at least corroborate a good deal of other eyewitness testimony. It would have to represent an internally coherent reality to which other witnesses have testified.[22] Yet Holocaust testimony is often extrinsically incredible (the events to which the witness testifies seem impossible, unreal) and intrinsically incoherent (exhibiting gaps, silences, and disjunctions). It is also true that potentially corroborating eyewitnesses and other documentary evidence have been destroyed. The relation between truth as content and what lies beyond truth—what might be called, in psychoanalytic terms, the real—is the matter at issue in the debate, late in Plato's *Phaedrus,* on the value of writing. Ammon charges that writing is not a drug for memory, but for reminding:[23] writing cannot bring the object of knowledge to the reader, though writing does remind the reader of it (making it "truly written on the soul").[24] In fact, the conundrum is whether writing or rhetoric produces truth or an image of truth, and most readers of the *Phaedrus* suggest that the best it can do is the latter. Writing, and ideally rhetoric, can, however, indicate what lies at the source of language (at its point of origin) something to which language does not provide unfettered access.

Jean-François Lyotard, in *The Differend*, makes a similar point: particularly in the case of limit events like Adorno's "Auschwitz," it is not enough for an eyewitness to testify to the reality of an event to give the event authenticity or establish its veracity. "Reality is not a matter of the absolute eyewitness, but a matter of the future."[25] To project an occurrence into the reader's or viewer's future, "it is necessary to be able to name and show referents that do not falsify the accepted definitions" and also to name the event in different instances so that it "obey[s] heterogenous regimens and/or genres."[26] Literary language (fiction) qualifies as such a projection; to qualify as testimony, literature must be mapped onto "the signification that learning establishes"—the tapestry of historical evidence, other testimonies that verify and corroborate the witness's—while it "lends an ear to what is not presentable under the rules of knowledge."[27] Yet Lyotard is unclear about the relation of what this kind of language allows the reader to see to the historical events at its heart. Whether readers of testimonial accounts see the horror of Auschwitz cannot be answered easily; whether what they see is historical and meets the demands of "accepted definitions" is less difficult if there are other accounts whose historical details match it. *Life Is Beautiful* may allow readers to catch a glimpse of events beyond what the film can represent, but it is not historically accurate unless it meets not just an indicative criterion but also an intrinsic or extrinsic one. The same is true of *Fragments:* it may function as testimony, but what the reader sees may not match what is in the narrative, let alone what Bruno Doesseker saw.

Witness and Testimony

In 1997, two interviews were conducted with a Holocaust survivor, Mary R., who lives in Saint Louis and acts as a docent in that city's Holocaust museum. In part Mary's job is to testify to the events that she witnessed during her childhood in Lodz and later in the women's barracks in Auschwitz. Her interview makes clear that she is accustomed to narrating the events of the Holocaust as she was connected to them. But the testimony she provides is an imperfect vehicle that fails to contain what she saw. As she puts it, her work at the museum is not easy because what she says day after day "may be similar, [but] it's not learned by heart stuff; after all I can only tell my particular story, I can't tell you anything else."[28] In fact, her particular story of the events to which she bears witness *is* something else, something other than the testimony she provides. Whatever she manages to get across can only pale in comparison to the horrors of watching her mother die in the ghetto or of four years in DP camps. But Mary cannot recall those experiences, because as she witnessed them she did not conceptualize them *as* experiences.

As they make their way through the Saint Louis museum during their first meeting, the interviewer points to a railway car and asks about Mary's transport from Lodz.

> INTERVIEWER: You were there with your mother and father?
> MARY R.: Just my father. My mother died in the ghetto.
> I: Of starvation?
> M: [hesitation] She became sick. [Hesitation] And that combination, I guess. . . . [Silence]
> I: Was she living with you?
> M: Oh, of course, we were in that one little room together, but she had hepatitis and she had pneumonia, there weren't enough medications, she was a fragile person. [Silence]
> I: How was taking care of her?
> M: Very difficult. I don't even like to think about it. In all, eleven million civilian people killed in the concentration camps and otherwise by Germans. Out of that were six million Jewish people, and out of that were a million and a half children.[29]

The silences and hesitations that appear throughout this section of Mary R.'s interview mark spaces in which the experience of her mother's death cannot be narrated but nevertheless haunt her. Caruth would say that the gaps mark a separation between the survivor's witnessing of the traumatic occurrence before it is processed as experience and its return as a departure in the narrative of the testimony. The mother's death returns in the context of the deaths of eleven million during the Shoah—the particular act of witnessing becomes embedded in another, more generalizable and historically understood event that can (though problematically) be conceptualized at the universal level. "Very difficult. I don't even like to think about it. In all eleven million civilian people killed." The witnessing makes itself apparent only in the gap between the particular event and the conceptual, historical narrative of the Shoah, and the testimony is so troubled by the traumatic occurrence that it falls apart before our eyes. The witness makes available an absence that so disrupts her present that presence and absence become inseparable, so much so that Mary R.'s language becomes submerged by her gestures, and while she cannot describe the death of her mother in the ghetto, the interviewer may see something else in the rupture of her testimony: "eleven million . . . six million . . . a million and a half."

Caruth's point in "Unclaimed Experience" is that history and trauma bear an indissoluble connection with each other. We consider history that which can be preserved as a memory and written, but the event that serves as the object of history, that which happens, is erased or blotted out. Maurice Blanchot's argument about the "immemorial" nature of the disaster suggests that once an experience occurs, it is forever lost; at this point—"upon losing what we have to say,"[30] the point of forgetfulness—writing begins. Forgetfulness is the source of memory. The "victim of [trauma] was never fully conscious during the [event] itself: the person gets away, Freud says, 'apparently unharmed.'"[31] The witness saw, but only saw, the traumatic deed or circumstance; the circumstance was never fully known—and hence could not be remembered—and what follows is a profusion of language. In survivor testimonies like Mary R.'s we read the displacement of the trauma—the historical event, lost to memory—by the language of the testimony, the sometimes broken, sometimes contradictory stories of the camps, or of hiding, or of the aftermath. But it is a language disrupted by that event, a language of repetition, in which the event is narrated over and over again but in wording that may not be clearly associated with the event.

Wilkomirski's book is composed of such language. It is not a narrative that reconciles two lives and languages so much as it is a series of tableaux in which one set of experiences, of orphanages, homes, and schools, is connected to another set, of the camps. In the first part of a typical pair of images, the young Binjamin is hiding near a pile of corpses when one of them—a woman's—begins to move. Binjamin watches in horror as its belly bulges and writhes and a rat emerges, slick and blood-covered. He wonders what this birth scene suggests of his own origins. Then: "Many years later, I went with my wife for the birth of our first son. . . . The first thing that slowly became visible was the half-round of the baby's head. As a first-time father, I didn't know how much dark hair a newborn baby can have. I wasn't ready for this little half-head of hair. All I could do was stand still and stare at it, once again, and like an echo from before, I heard the ringing and crackling noise in my chest."[32]

In Langer's terms (following Charlotte Delbo's), two irreconcilable selves, or narrative memories, do battle here for control over the story and over the writer's ability to understand the relation between images that—if we take him at his word—indicated memories separated by thirty years.[33] The two selves "interact and intersect continually" throughout the narrative of *Fragments*.[34] But neither the witness nor the viewer or reader of the testimony can glean any history—any knowledge of what happened—from the passage above. Between the horrible memory of the corpse that Binjamin cannot seem to shake and the image of his son's birth, into which that memory intrudes unbidden, is something unavailable to knowledge. Whatever it is, either in the narrative of *Fragments* or in Mary R.'s testimony of her mother's death, it cannot be presented as a narrative. Whatever it is, it is seen but not recognized by Bruno Doesseker and—in different terms, but seen nonetheless—by the witness to the text: the reader. But whatever it is, it is lost "to what we were to say."[35]

What cannot be placed into the narrative—what the boy Doesseker saw that became coded in the language of the Holocaust and that makes its way to the surface of the text as Binjamin Wilkomirski's memory—has a place of sorts in testimony. "There are no feelings left. . . . I'm just an eye, taking in what it sees, giving nothing back."[36] The moment of witness is here: in losing what he has to say, he begins his testimony, a testimony that refers to what was blotted out as much as to what was fixed as a memory. Here, in the no-place of the narrative, is the gaping wound, the trauma experienced by the writer (who may or may not be the boy Binjamin; we may never know) and witnessed only in terms of the absence of Doesseker's own place in the historical circumstances he narrates. In Langer's terms, the self caught up in the time of the killing wins the battle over the present.

Testimonial narratives do not disclose history; instead, they disclose—where the narrative most clearly shows its seams—the effect of events upon witnesses. As a memoir, *Fragments* functions in the same way: its language does not easily follow the general rules of historical narratives—"very difficult. I don't even like to think about it. In all eleven million civilian people killed"—and by itself it does not give us a way to adjudicate the competing claims of Bruno Doesseker and Daniel Ganzfried. As for the narrative itself, and its depiction of events that support it, its gaps cannot be said simply to represent inaccuracies; rather—as Caruth suggests, speaking of Freud—they represent and "preserve history precisely within this gap in his text."[37] Each encounter with memory repeats the initial trauma, but by other means—narrative means—which are constantly interrupted by a gap of memory and of experience.

Secondhand Witnessing

This does not mean that *Fragments* cannot be disproved as an inaccurate account of the events it purports to narrate (as testimonies, written memoirs, or fictions can be). It means that the book's significance, whatever it is, cannot be attributed to the worth of *Fragments* as history but rather must be connected to events unrecorded (or unwritable) as history (or, as a reader of a draft of this essay aptly put it, apart from history). Shoshana Felman goes further, suggesting that the effectiveness of a work may be the result, not of any correspondence between what it represents and the object of representation, but of a kind of transference. The effect of testimony, in Doesseker's case coded in the language of the Shoah and structured by a language that displaces the reader's sense of the normal (or of history), opens a moment in which the reader of the testimony becomes a secondhand witness, seeing not the experience described but something that stands beyond or before it, not history but history's real.[38]

Felman's understanding of trauma parallels Caruth's: as in Freud's case of an accident from which the victim apparently escaped, the traumatic event remains unknown. What follows in the absence of the event's name but in the full awareness that something horrible has taken place is a compulsive speaking "in advance of the control of consciousness, [in which] testimony is delivered in 'breathless gasps.'" It is a "*precocious testimony* . . . that speak[s] beyond its means," that testifies to an event "whose origin cannot be precisely located but whose repercussions, in their very uncontrollable and unanticipated nature, still continue to evolve even in the very process of testimony."[39] One of the problems inherent in the historical testimony of the event of the Shoah, then, is that—as critics like James Young and Saul Friedlander have warned—the memory of the event (particularly the traumatic one) evolves in the telling, and its language is uncontrollable and cannot be anticipated. Pursued by the obligation to speak, the witness is not necessarily pursued by the obligation to provide a historically accurate accounting of the event, because the event as such has disappeared.

What complicates matters is that, for Felman, the trauma that pursues the witness also pursues witnesses to the witnessing. In her seminar at Yale, students experienced what she calls a "crisis" of witnessing, in which—after reading poetry and narratives of witness, and after viewing several videotaped testimonies from the Fortunoff Archive—they became profoundly ill at ease with what they were seeing and broke into an "endless and relentless talking." The accident—the disaster—"had *passed through* the class."[40] The trace or abyss of the event that made itself evident in the "stuttering" of the texts—their silences, their incommensurabilities, their figural displacements—produced anxiety in Felman's students. The Wilkomirski book, marked by stutters, breaks, and impossible juxtapositions of images, relies, like all written and oral testimonies, on metonymic substitutions, in which a term is displaced by another resembling and presumably associated with it by the text containing them. For Hayden White, the importance of metonymy is that the extrinsic relation—the order of reality outside the discursive context in which these terms may be related—allows the reader to understand more clearly the aspects of the reality that the metonymic figure is meant to distinguish.[41] But this focus needs to be paired with another, critical dimension of the nature of displacement: the distance between the effect of metonymy or of metaphor and its (absent) cause. Metonymy, as a contiguous chain of signification, a word-to-word exchange, presumes a context in which terms make sense, and the displacement of one term by another defers understanding (or closure of the historical hermeneutic). But metonymy also forces a disjunction between a term and its substitute: by not allowing a reader outside the chain of signification (because metonymy presumes the context inside which the substitution takes place), the displacement potentially disrupts that context. In Françoise Meltzer's terms, "in spite of its apparent difference of meaning in each case, each signifier in this chain has in fact the same meaning as the one before it: the lack which spells desire,"[42] forcing the reader to pay attention not to that which appears familiar—the different aspects of the same—but to the impossible relation between all the attributes of the object or event and the singular, palpable sense of the object or event itself.

In a different context, Friedlander connects the repetitiousness of metonymy, which reduces the object of discourse to something inanimate, and the uncanny. Through repetition "we are confronted with [an uncertainty brought on by the representation] of human beings of the most ordinary kind approaching the state of automata by eliminating any feelings of humanness and of moral sense. . . . Our sense of *Unheim-lichkeit* is indeed triggered by this deep uncertainty as to the 'true nature'" of the referent of the narrative itself.[43] Wilkomirski's narrative is a catalog of metonymy: German soldiers are referred to as "the gray uniform," "the black uniform," "bull-neck," and their Swiss counterparts, civilians, as "fat faces, strong arms, terrible hands." The writer refers to himself as "skin" or "the voice." These repetitions become a sign that what was once homely or familiar to us is actually made up of the shards of its attributes, but these attributes cannot possibly be the sum total of the homely or familiar. This does not mean that the point of origin of the metonymic chain—history as what happened to Doesseker—is identical in the writer and the reader. The disruptive capacity and displacement of metonymy are here related to the reader's experience, but they are not comparable, let alone interchangeable. Whatever originated the writing—whatever brought Doesseker to write *Fragments*—is lost to memory and is only available in the historical record; what readers see through the anxiety, the *Unheimlichkeit*, resulting from the repetitive language of the book is likewise lost when they try to regularize it as knowledge. The best we can say is that the moments are related structurally; their homology is lost.

Felman argues that the uncertainty brought on by a repetition of figure or image in combinations—like the uncanny—defies our capacity to link them or provide a context that makes sense of them. What remains is the resulting talk—the testimony of the secondhand witness—and the need to work through the resulting chaos with a narrative that orders the precocious and puts it in its proper place.[44] One of Felman's students, "caught between two contradictory wishes at once, to speak or not to speak," says, "I can only stammer," and turns, as a result, to literature, and "read[s] as if for life."[45] Clearly the crisis that passed through the class and the irretrievable event—the initial trauma—are not commensurate events. To say that the events of the Shoah that form the kernel of Mary R.'s testimony and the crisis of witnessing are the same is absurd. But structurally, they are intimately related: in both cases the language of testimony is a locus of witnessing, marking both the loss of the event and the cause of writing.

Philip Gourevitch reports that while he was interviewing Bruno Doesseker for his *New Yorker* essay, he read an essay on memory by Alan Baddeley. Baddeley reports that memories can be "coded" differently depending upon the context in which one does the remembering.[46]

Gourevitch goes on to suggest, as Lappin did earlier, that Doesseker's attempts to address the forgotten events of his own life with a narrative were biased by the reaction he received as he "encoded" them with the context of the Holocaust. As the public reception of the Holocaust changed gradually from shameful taboo to hallowed icon, the reaction to the stories Doesseker told about his own experiences as a "survivor" changed as well. "When [Doesseker] said 'nightmare' and [the reaction] came back 'Holocaust,' he could both resist and creep up on the possibility, in a hypnotic, semiconscious manner, which not only seemed like memory but felt like it, too. . . . Wilkomirski [said], 'By the time I started my historical research I slowly got used to the idea that a part of my memory is in a part of Auschwitz.'"[47] Whatever Doesseker's motives, it is no surprise that, if his aim was to produce a document through which readers would experience the shock, if not the traumatic instance, of the horrors of the Shoah, then his research (which involved looking at photographs of the camps and of the destruction of Jewish central Europe) would have provided a vocabulary of the *Unheimlichkeit* with which to do so. And if Doesseker himself was shocked, if not traumatized, by what he read and saw in his research, then it is perfectly plausible that he would have experienced an uncanniness similar to that which Felman's students did. The relentless need to bridge the abyss of memory brought on by the recurrence of trauma as it impinges upon one's ability to write or to speak may be filled with images and language one has already come upon. If Elena Lappin is right, and Bruno Doesseker was forcibly separated from his mother and had experiences that he still cannot name and which have had a hold on his imagination since then, we should not be surprised that he testifies to those experiences through the language of the most significant horror of the twentieth century, whose effect on individuals and on a culture is unspeakable and altogether unknowable and which may well take the place of and (mis)name the events to which he does not have access. As Lappin has said, "Wilkomirski often refers to his memories as being film-like. They are, I believe, more than that: they are, I believe, derived from films. . . . I cannot believe that *Fragments* is anything other than fiction. And yet, . . . anguish like [his] seemed impossible to fabricate."[48] Whether the events and the story bear any direct relation to one another is—given what we know about the dynamic relation between forgetfulness and memory—an open question.

Conclusion

I want to conclude by indicating a few ethical implications of the preceding discussion of testimony, implications that trouble some of the assumptions we hold about Holocaust remembrance that are associated with injunctions such as *never forget* and *never again*. If a witness's participation in the events of history—particularly traumatic events—is irrecuperable except through the fragmented and troubled narratives that fail to contain those events, then the connection between the events and the resulting testimony is more tenuous than we would like to think. These narratives may well serve as evidence of the events composing the day-to-day litany of destruction; and the historical circumstances concerning witnesses' accounts—some of which were found buried amid the rubble of ghettos, some of which are corroborated detail by detail in other accounts—may confirm their status as evidence. But when corroborating historical circumstances—witnesses, documents, place-names recollected—cannot be recovered, the best we can do is to rely on the effect of the document itself. Hayden White would argue that testimony's status as evidence depends in part upon its effect, and that effect—produced metonymically by design or by circumstance—is, in the case of *Fragments*, a profoundly disturbing one.

But this case puts a great deal of pressure on the relation between the effects of a testimony and its source. Such a conclusion is disturbing—Wilkomirski may be a liar, after all; no one would say the same of Mary R.—and it is all the more profoundly so if it leads, as Philip Blom has suggested, to an erosion of "the very ground on which remembrance can be built"[49] or results in "a new revisionism that no longer attacks the truth of the Holocaust but only individual claims of survival."[50] Blom is right to be concerned, if he means that to undermine the authority of the writer of a Holocaust testimony, and to prove that the writer was never there and did not see what he claims to have seen, is to eliminate one piece of evidence supporting arguments that the atrocities of the Shoah occurred. Taken together, eyewitness accounts, documentary evidence, trial transcripts, and diaries form the tapestry of suffering that we have inherited as the narrative of the Holocaust. But as accounts of horrible events that are inaccessible to the memories of the tellers, such testimonies by those who survived and by those who merely claim to have done so or who have merely read survivors' accounts function similarly and have similar effects: they indicate an event as it occurs before anyone's ability to speak of it, not so much in their accordance with the facts of history (facts that are accessible only through narrative) but in the way they disrupt the narrative of history and force the reader, or the interviewer, to see something horrible, perhaps a trace of the traumatic event. These effects are only available one witness, one reader, at a time. In the case of the Wilkomirski "memoir," we may well be able to undermine the authority of the writer if we take him to be trying to establish a narrative of the circumstances of the Holocaust that will settle the matter, either of history or of biography. The converse is also true: a lack of credibility seems to throw open to question the veracity of testimonies of other survivors. But to say this is not to lessen the disastrous effect of the testimony or the testimony's ability to indicate something about the nature of the event, though that disaster may not be the historical object we take to be coequal with the narrative's content. Lappin suggests that the author of *Fragments* may have suffered some shocking accident in his separation from his mother or in the years when he lived in orphanages and foster care or in the care of adoptive parents. The uncanny effect of the book's metonymic language indicates that any such event is inaccessible not only to its readers but to the author as well.

This is a troubling place to be left, given the stakes. I am reminded of how high they are this year by my eight-year-old's question about the armed police officer stationed outside the door of our synagogue as we entered to recite the Kol Nidre, by the violence in Jerusalem, and by the cries of "death to Jews" that have been heard coming from the mouths of stone-throwing men in Ramallah, from those of demonstrators here in the United States. As some have said of the Wilkomirski affair, to suggest that false testimony may nonetheless be an effective instrument through which we may bear witness to the Shoah is to provide Holocaust deniers with one more way to doubt all testimonial evidence about what happened in Europe between 1933 and 1945. So to conclude that there is, in the Wilkomirski "fraud," a traumatic kernel that may be connected somehow to the horrors inflicted on the victims of the Final Solution would seem to fly in the face not only of good taste but of human decency as well. Our jobs, as teachers and as righteous people, should be to honor the memories of the dead and to ensure that we recognize the destroyer Amalek in whatever guise he might return (Hitler, czar, anti-Semite, demagogue) and blot him from memory; in short (though this may not be the same thing), to destroy him.

And yet this is precisely the problem: how do we do this? Let me re-call two stories. The first is that of Amalek found in the portion of the Torah in Exodus called Beshallach. In this story, the Jews, who have left Egypt and seen the pharaoh's army destroyed by the hand of God, begin to complain: they don't know where they're going, they're hun-gry, and they're beginning to grow impatient with Moses. To make matters worse, their flank is attacked by the Amalekites, who pick off the elderly, the young, and the weak. At the end of the portion, the Amalek-ites are defeated, and the Lord says to Moses: "'Inscribe this in a docu-ment as a memorial, and read it aloud to Joshua: I will utterly blot out the memory of Amalek from under heaven.' . . . The Lord will be at war with Amalek throughout the ages."[51] On a traditional reading, this pas-sage is understood to be God's imperative to the Israelites that they should always bear in mind what Amalek did to them so that with God's help they can blot him out in whatever incarnation and in whatever age. But the language of the passage is not quite so clear; in fact, it in-scribes an ambivalent relation between memory and forgetfulness. In the command to Moses to inscribe as a memory in writing and then blot out the memory of Amalek, the same root—to remember—is used both to command memory, writing, and its blotting out. The Torah scholar Kornelis Houtman notes in his commentary that the Hebrew for "blot out" means literally to erase, to unwrite. So what is commanded is to re-member to unremember, to create and inscribe a memory that at the same time blots out or unwrites what lies at the core of the memory it-self. This is the point Caruth makes about the relation of traumatic memory to testimony: the event itself is blotted out, making testimony's relation to the event troubled at best and tenuous at worst. So Amalek does not stand as a warning to be ever vigilant to recognize Amalek again; this injunction warns about the impossibility of such recognition.

The second story was told to me several years ago by Sydney Ber-nard, my father-in-law. As an infantryman during World War II, he was shipped to Europe quite late, and along with his outfit he slowly traveled through the ruins of western Europe toward Germany. He was out on patrol in little village when he came across a couple who imme-diately identified him as Jewish (he never said how) and explained to him that they, too, were Jewish and had remained alive by hiding from the Germans. My father-in-law panicked, turned, and tried to get away as quickly as he could. He finished the story by saying that he was mor-tified by his behavior and that he would not have recalled the incident had I not asked him about the film *Schindler's List*. His response to that couple, not unlike the responses of many Americans—and particularly American Jews—to the Holocaust, was simply avoidance. On finishing the story Syd told me he was bothered that many people believe that, through watching *Schindler's List*, they understood what the Holocaust was like. That response is the polar opposite of avoidance: give the event a name or a face—make it recognizable (assign it to the fictional genre of noir, horror, or suspense; give it a bittersweet ending)—and cover over the horror of the event which we would rather not confront. And yet in this strategy, as in avoidance, we can never confront the abyss of the events because it is filled in with a knowledge—with what we already know. We will know Amalek when we see him coming because we have so thoroughly coded horror (or anti-Semitism, or trauma) as "Holocaust." Both forms of avoidance rest upon prior knowledge: the first keeps what one knows unchallenged by refusing to encounter the different; the second refuses the different by masking it with the familiar. The horror (what was seen but is not contained by language or knowledge) remains disruptive and leaves a mark, as it did with my father-in-law.

At the heart of any memory is a forgetting, the loss of the original event and that loss's destructive force on any subsequent testimony; this is all the more true of traumatic memory. This loss complicates the project of recuperating the fact of the Holocaust through the memories of those who were there, and it lies at the center of the problem of testimonies that may not bear witness to the Shoah but provide evidence of some other trauma. This is why Wilkomirski's "memoir" is so problematic: there may be a traumatic kernel wrapped inside the narrative of destruction, but it is one to which neither we nor the writer has access. That the elusiveness of this kernel should give succor to the deniers is a terrible result, but it is an unavoidable one. So instead of trying to avoid this problem, we should recognize it and in so doing find other, perhaps firmer ground on which to take issue with the deniers' lies. It is the void at the heart of memory that makes the tasks of writing and speaking about the Shoah at once so urgent and so fraught. It means that while we desperately wish to anticipate the next Amalek so we can blot him out, we will likely be mistaken and be outflanked by the actual disaster. But it also means that our writing indicates aspects of our language and of our being that are both much less and a great deal more than what we would readily acknowledge.

Common sense tells us that testimony undoubtedly bears some causal relation with the events it depicts, and when accounts of those events diverge, we generally think that at least one of the testimonies is erroneous, flawed, or patently false. But if much of the contemporary work on trauma is right and the horrible events witnessed by the survivor never registered consciously, instead producing a void in memory that triggers a torrent of language whose "precocity" we cannot predict, then testimony may also (or may instead) bear a relation to another event, one to which even the witness may not have access. Such an event is not distinct from history, if we think of history as what happened, but the event lies outside, or precedes, history if like Louis Mink we think of history as what is "*there* with a determinateness beyond and over against [the historian's or witness's] partial reconstructions."[52] As in the testimony of Mary R., whose response to a question about her mother's death in the ghetto is a rote answer about the number of children who died at the hands of the Nazis, what was seen and what one can say both originate in historical events; the effect of the seen, however, gets in the way of the fabric of testimony, leaving the witness to find some other language to stand in the breach. Witness is a moment of forgetting, a moment of seeing without knowing that indelibly marks the source of history as an abyss. It is a moment of the disaster; and that moment, the moment of forgetting, demands that the memory be inscribed, though it is a memory—a testimony—whose historical circumstances and whose discursive control are simply not available to subsequent witnesses. And what we experience as readers of such testimonies is just as susceptible to rewriting, and to misrecognition, as the memories of Bruno Doesseker or of Mary R., and as soon as we testify to the event and work through it in such a way that we find a name for it, we inevitably misname it. Such a conclusion doesn't seem preferable to the alternative, which is that testimonies proven false can be banished from what one writer has called the "Holocaust archive" so as not to taint what remains.[53] But it is a conclusion we have to contend with given the structure of memory, witness, and testimony that has been laid out over the last several years. If nothing else, it requires us to recast our thinking about testimony's relation to witness and to history so we are on guard against the "new revisionism" that Harvey Peskin is justly concerned with. Blanchot is right: the disaster ruins everything—writing, memory, the certainty of knowledge. But if it also forestalls turning the Shoah into a certainty to be filed (or argued) away or made sacred and untouchable, perhaps this kind of "ruin"—though it does not give us access to its historical correlative—is preferable, for it provides access to the complexity of witness itself.

Notes

1. See Dominick LaCapra, *Representing the Holocaust: History, Theory, Trauma* (Ithaca: Cornell University Press, 1994), 205–23; and LaCapra, *History and Memory after Auschwitz* (Ithaca: Cornell University Press, 1998), 180–210.

2. LaCapra, *History and Memory*, 20.

3. Ibid., 21.

4. Cathy Caruth, "Unclaimed Experience: Trauma and the Possibility of History." *Yale French Studies* 79 (1991): 187.

5. Shoshana Felman, "Education and Crisis; or, the Vicissitudes of Teaching," in *Trauma*, ed. Cathy Caruth (Baltimore: Johns Hopkins University Press, 1995), 16–17.

6. Binjamin Wilkomirski, *Fragments: Memories of a Wartime Childhood*, trans. Carol Brown Janeway (New York: Schocken, 1996).

7. *Fragments* is one of a number of Holocaust representations written by those born during or immediately after the war. To mention only two, Art Spiegelman's *Maus* (in two volumes [New York: Pantheon, 1986, 1991]) and Bernhard Schlink's *The Reader* (trans. Carol Brown Janeway [New York: Vintage, 1998]) do not attempt to render (only) the events of the Shoah but (also) to critically examine the vexed relation of history, memory, and text (which in the case of Spiegelman is partly pictorial and in the case of Schlink is largely discursive). *Fragments*, it seems to me, occupies a curious place in the literature of the post-Holocaust generation because of the book's broad claims for historical authenticity and because (unlike Spiegelman or Schlink) the author's purpose seems to be primarily to testify to a witnessing. For these reasons I am unwilling to extend the claims I make here to other second-generation Holocaust texts.

8. Daniel Ganzfried, "Die geliehene Holocaust-Biographie," *Weltwoche*, August 27, 1998, http://www.weltwoche.ch/3598/35.98.wahrodernicht.html.

9. Elena Lappin, "The Man with Two Heads," *Granta* 66 (Summer 1999): 61.

10. Jean-François Lyotard, *The Differend: Phrases in Dispute*, trans. Georges Van den Abbeele (Minneapolis: University of Minnesota Press, 1988), 57.

11. See Caruth, "Unclaimed Experience"; Felman, "Education and Crisis"; and Michael Bernard-Donals and Richard Glejzer, "Between Witness and Testimony," *College Literature* 27, no. 2 (2000): 1–20.

12. Wilkomirski, *Fragments*, 4.

13. Ibid., 154.

14. See Ganzfried, "Die geliehene Holocaust-Biographie." Two essays on the Wilkomirski affair appeared in English during the summer of 1999: Philip Gourevitch's "The Memory Thief" (*New Yorker*, June 14, 1999, 48–68) and Elena Lappin's "The Man with Two Heads." The historian Stefan Mächler published *Der Fall Wilkomirski* (Zurich: Pendo, 2000), which exhaustively reviews the research and establishes definitively that *Fragments* is not historically verifiable. I rely primarily on the two English-language sources because they were the most widely available in the United States prior to the English translation of Mächler's book. (See Stefan Maechler, *The Wilkomirski Affair*, trans. John E. Woods [New York: Schocken, 2001].)

15. Lappin, "The Man with Two Heads," 26.

16. Gourevitch, "The Memory Thief," 56–57.

17. Lappin, "The Man with Two Heads," 46.

18. Maechler, *The Wilkomirski Affair*, 84–91; Lappin, "The Man with Two Heads," 40–44.

19. Lappin, "The Man with Two Heads," 59.

20. Ibid., 63. See Rudolf Braun's *Industrialization and Everyday Life*, trans. Sarah Hanbury Tenison (Cambridge: Cambridge University Press, 1990), for details on child welfare in Switzerland during its transition to industrialism from the 1660s through the twentieth century, particularly 154–60. Mächler's book does not take up the question of Bruno Doesseker's welfare status.

21. See Lawrence Rosenfeld's "The Practical Celebration of Epideictic," in *American Rhetoric: Context and Criticism*, ed. Thomas W. Benson (Carbondale: Southern Illinois University Press, 1989), 221–66; and Rosenfeld, "Central Park and the Celebration of Civic Virtue," in *Rhetoric in Transition: Studies in the Nature and Uses of Rhetoric*, ed. Eugene E. White (University Park: Penn State University Press, 1980), 131–56; see also Dale Sullivan's "Kairos and the Rhetoric of Belief," *Quarterly Journal of Speech* 78 (August 1992): 317–32.

22. See Martin Jay, "Of Plots, Witnesses, and Judgments," in *Probing the Limits of Representation: Nazism and the "Final Solution,"* ed. Saul Friedlander (Cambridge: Harvard University Press, 1992), 97–107; and Carlo Ginzburg, "Just One Witness," in Friedlander, *Probing the Limits of Representation*, 82–96.

23. Plato, *Phaedrus*, ed. and trans. James H. Nicholls (Ithaca: Cornell University Press, 1998), 275a.

24. Ibid., 278a.

25. Lyotard, *The Differend*, 53.

26. Ibid., 55.

27. Ibid., 57.

28. Lucy Stanovick, interview with Mary R., St. Louis, Missouri, March–April 1997, 2.

29. Ibid., 1–2.

30. Maurice Blanchot, *The Writing of the Disaster*, trans. Ann Smock (Lincoln: University of Nebraska Press, 1996), 21.

31. Caruth, "Unclaimed Experience," 187.

32. Wilkomirski, *Fragments*, 88.

33. Lawrence Langer, *Holocaust Testimonies: The Ruins of Memory* (New Haven: Yale University Press, 1991), 47.

34. Ibid., 7.

35. Blanchot, *Writing of the Disaster*, 21.

36. Wilkomirski, *Fragments*, 87.

37. Caruth, "Unclaimed Experience," 190.

38. Quoted in Ginzburg, "Just One Witness," 86.

39. Felman, "Education and Crisis," 29–30.

40. Ibid., 52.

41. See Hayden White, *Metahistory: The Historical Imagination in Nineteenth-Century Europe* (Baltimore: Johns Hopkins University Press, 1978), 34–36.

42. Françoise Meltzer, "Unconscious," in *Critical Terms for Literary Study*, ed. Frank Lentricchia and Thomas McLaughlin (Chicago: University of Chicago Press, 1995), 160.

43. Saul Friedlander, "The 'Final Solution': On the Unease in Historical Interpretation," in *Lessons and Legacies: The Meaning of the Holocaust in a Changing World*, ed. Peter Hayes (Evanston: Northwestern University Press, 1991), 30.

44. See Felman, "Education and Crisis," 54–57; LaCapra, *Representing the Holocaust*, 205–23.

45. Felman, "Education and Crisis," 58.

46. Gourevitch, "The Memory Thief," 66.

47. Ibid.

48. Lappin, "The Man with Two Heads," 61.

49. Philip Blom, "In a Country . . . ," *The Independent* (London), September 30, 1998, features, 1.

50. Harvey Peskin, "Holocaust Denial: A Sequel," *Nation*, April 19, 1998, 34.

51. Jewish Publication Society, *The JPS Torah Commentary: Exodus* (Philadelphia: Jewish Publication Society, 1991), 96.

52. Louis Mink, *Historical Understanding* (Ithaca: Cornell University Press, 1987), 93.

53. Daniel Listoe, "Witnessing in the 'Virtual Archive': The Future Form of the Holocaust Past," Midwest Modern Language Association, Marriott City Center, Minneapolis, November 5, 1999.

3

The Ethical Imperative

10

Maurice Blanchot
Fighting Spirit

GEOFFREY HARTMAN

The problem caused by writers who helped to create a murderous climate that contributed to the Holocaust is verbal as well as moral: can the abused words be restored to a kind of innocence or neutrality? "No word tinged from on high," Adorno wrote, not even a theological one, can be justified, untransformed, after Auschwitz.[1] Sublime yet rabid utterances, motivated by a self-styled Christian or post-Christian "spiritual revolution," had justified persecution and genocide. Difficult as the transformation is that Adorno calls for, to keep silent because of skepticism or despair is not a way out. The silences of speech always occur within the context of speech and, like a joker, remain part of the pack.

I have described Blanchot's dilemma too. He began his career before the war as a contributor to extreme right-wing journals. These articles were often characterized by a crude, as if visceral, anti-Semitism, but more significantly by what Charles Maurras distinguished as *antisemitisme de raison*, supposedly not a blind but a reasoned hatred, in reality a mixture of age-long Christian contempt, ignorant clichés about the Jews, and political opportunism. (The claim of rationality, in fact, helped hatred to turn deliberate and systematic.) In 1938 Blanchot gave up much of his political journalism—until a brief return (during his *re-trait littéraire*) between 1958 and 1969—and sometime after that his atti-tude toward Judaism underwent a marked change.[2]

Blanchot has remained silent about his early journalism. Given the complexities of the ideological picture in the 1930s, even a sustained memoir might falsify the past. It is tempting, though, to link his retreat (into literary theory) or refusal (of a certain kind of politics)[3] to an in-creasingly exigent style that seems devised to dismantle fascism's *mot d'ordre*, its decisionist use of language. The refusal refers to Blanchot's re-jection of the return of de Gaulle; but it leads me to wonder whether something like it also occurred in 1938. His article "Le refus," published first in 1958, begins: "At a certain moment, faced with public events, we know we must refuse." This seems to differ radically from the prototype of the "great refusal" (a refusal of death, that is, of death as unredeem-able) Blanchot ascribes to Hegel's systematic quest for permanence and totality, and which must be reaffirmed although we know it to be an il-lusion.[4] By refusing a certain kind of political action, fixated on the "now" and verging on apocalyptic or heroic expectation—on hope in a future brought into being by terror, by an absolute disruption—Blanchot could be said to refuse this violently redemptive refusal of human limits.[5] The question persists, however: why is Blanchot's new style accompa-nied by referential vagueness and impersonal drift? Does the author oc-clude uncomfortable facts? Or is his reticence the result of a deeper understanding of acts of writing that are not journalistically engaged and so challenge the parade of a firm and consistent personal identity?[6]

Blanchot as literary critic develops an impersonality theory as radi-cal as Mallarmé's. He sharpens the paradox whereby the self produced by the work also disappears into it: the author, he claims, has no more of an independent existence than an actor does, "that ephemeral personal-ity who is born and dies every evening, having exposed himself exces-sively to view, killed by spectacle."[7] The recession of the self, rather than self-fashioning, receives major emphasis; in accord with what Martin Jay has characterized as "down-cast eyes" in modern French thought, Blanchot asserts that "to speak is not to see" and that the writer has no secrets, no intimacy to espy.[8]

There is no way to reconcile those two obligations, which elicit differ-ent idioms that cannot both be contained by thought. Ethics, says Blan-chot, falls into contradiction or goes mad. And though one of these id-ioms is post-Hegelian—that is, historical, dialectical, and expressionistic, prefigurative of total secular fulfillment—it is, surprisingly, the other, which takes passivity to be a task, that gradually but surely dominates Blanchot's postwar writing.

Indeed, the very concept of agency disappears behind a "disaster," which is the subject of *L'Écriture du desastre* (1980). Blanchot never gives a precise historical location to the disaster, the story of which—not of the disaster itself but of the suffering entailed by it (and it is just possible that Blanchot is using an astrophysical analogy, the disaster being that of an exploded star whose shock waves are the sole signs of its prior existence)—is closely associated with the "detour of writing" and literary space. Literary space defines a negation to the second power: a rupture with a politics of rupture, including the worldly power of words *(puissance)* and their mimetic ability *(pouvoir)* to create their own world. This negation of a negation, far from inducing a dialectical and progressive gain, undoes words as instruments of ego or will.[9] Blanchot's earlier break with a journalistic politics that was proposing a revolution superseding 1789 and Republican France may be connected with his turn to the strange temporality of literary space.

This temporality is often depicted as a past aligned with the *pâtir* in "passion" and "patience," and with *pas* as ambiguously a step (forward) and a sign of the negative. The negative phrasing so pervasive in Blanchot always retards an *élan vital*, particularly a prophetic or futuristic *pas au-delà*. His method of *entre-dire* (a curious, self-disrupted, back-and-forth of anonymous voices or narrators) is checked by an *arrêt qui interdit* or "death sentence" (to cite the title of his earliest novel) whose effect is to confute promissory speech. Levinas writes that there is no philosophy without death; for Blanchot, there is no writing without death. Yet as a writer, how can he desire rather than ward off an interruption he describes as if it were literally a dying, "the heart ceasing to beat, the eternal, pulsing drive to talk arrested?"[10]

A sense of the mortal rather than the culpable informs all of Blanchot's work. This *memento mori*, however, is not allowed to be a springboard: there is no "let the dead bury the dead" but rather a sense of revenance, of uncanny and unpredictable repetitions (he gives a more vivid impression of this ghostly repetition in his fiction). Even if the past has a presence called history, the truth of the past is closer to literature's heterogeneous time, "the passion of patience, the passivity of a time without present . . . [the writer's] sole identity."[11]

Literary space is also related to a full rather than empty oblivion, one that guards "le caché des choses."[12] It is not on the side of knowledge, and certainly not of Hegel's absolute knowledge. But what exactly is forgotten, or watched over so impersonally that it is nescience rather than knowledge? In Plato's myth of reminiscence, the soul descending to this world from a world of essence must forget its origin. Similarly, the historical specificity of Blanchot's "disaster" disappears into an immemorial suffering, "suffering as an event."[13] Literature's "errance" within that oblivion is less an anamnesis (the undoing of a forgetfulness) than a purification *from* essence, the acceptance of a negativity that cannot be dialectically completed and produces no new beginning, no identity principle "enriched by the repeated experience of defeat."[14]

I suspect that Blanchot's referential vagueness is bound up with this elision of originative or datable events. When he does offer a date, it is as mysterious as the "1807" in his quasi-autobiographical *L'Instant de ma mort*. The narrator of this story is saved from a firing squad at the last moment; Blanchot too, as a writer, is marked permanently by the consciousness of death, yet he remains unable to convert it into personal or historical significance.[15] But the reader is left with an enigma. What moves the writing on? What is the motivating *spirit* of this repetitive corpus? Can it be the survival, the legacy (though useless) of one unspecified traumatic event? Or, in historical terms, what animated Blanchot during his idealist-terrorist phase of the 1930s, and what remains now of that life/death force or fire-portion ("la part du feu"), the violent rhetoric that exalted him and led to a culpable action, hardly separate in retrospect from the consuming fires of the Holocaust?

If what happened in history is undeniable, the spirit once active in the young Blanchot is also undeniable. To break with that spirit, I speculate, required a counter-spirit, drawn from the same source (the rapture that produced the desire for rupture) yet antithetical to it and without hope for retroactive justification. Blanchot's later writing, in theory at least, embodies this counter-spirit: its chiaroscuro of reference and absence of a logical or dialectical progression do not violate human time. Blanchot does not fire, that is, at clock-towers, like the revolutionaries cited in Walter Benjamin's thesis 15 "On the Concept of History." Benjamin uses this poetic image to illustrate the difference between the calendar of a revolutionary historical consciousness and ordinary history writing; but it also suggests an attempt to abolish time, or to make this

moment determining for all time. But in Blanchot, nothing is over-
turned in the name of an absolute separation of the future from the past
or of a decisive spiritual revolution. If Blanchot's "disaster" is undatable
it is because it does not install itself in history with apocalyptic specificity. Rather, it elides parousia and salvation as reference points or discloses that a violent temporal demarcation is itself the disaster.[16]

For Blanchot, then, writing cannot reference its own authenticity.
The role of the reader enters here, as a modality of the Other; but since
reading at its most intense is also a writing, the theoretical issue of an au-
thenticating reading is never clarified. Blanchot seems to opt for the notion of an "entretien infini," but without so absolute an intimacy or
interiority that it could not find itself outside, estranged, face to face
with what I would have to call an "extralocutor." Autobiography is thus
a questionable literary genre precisely because its motivating spirit is
justification. Writing's essence is linked to the nonessential, the errant,
the uneventful, the strangeness at the heart of even the most intimate relationship.[17] Even hope in the past—to bring in Walter Benjamin's paradoxical concept, guarding against simplistic theories of progress and
happiness—is unfaithful to a patience that will not allow us to act in
hope. "When we are patient, it is always in relation to an infinite misery
[*malheur*, literally "bad luck" or "mis-fortune"], which does not impact
on us in the present except by linking us to a past without memory. Misfortune of the other and the other as misfortune."[18] Time is the perpetuity of this *malheur*, "the horror of a suffering without end, a suffering
time can no longer redeem, that has escaped time and for which there
is no recourse; it is irremediable."[19] We can think of the situation of
Ahasuerus, the Wandering Jew, or of a hell without any devilish torment except a time that does not pass and which subjects us to others
without any hope of redeeming them or oneself.

Here a link with Levinas becomes obvious. Levinas, following Heidegger, introduced the question of how we enter into relation with
time, given that meaningful action and the possibility of presence are always undermined by both a past or an *à venir* whose horizon is death.
While Levinas does not neglect the factor of language, no one has artic-
ulated as clearly as Blanchot its character as temporal medium. (Perhaps "medium" is too cold a word, but "mediation" would be too
warm.) To concentrate on the moment of writing is, for Blanchot, to experience Levinasian time, but he always exposes the writer's entrapment in a worldly and visual vocabulary centering on self and other.

Writing is the perpetuity of a *malheur;* even literary impersonality, which dis-identifies the self, cannot get beyond a *moi sans moi;* yet that destituted self remains submitted to the *regard* of the Other and continues to feel a responsibility impossible to bear.

How can we judge this concept of responsibility? Blanchot focuses strictly on the writer's unmediated struggle with words and the accompanying recession of self-identity, its kenosis. The paradox of the writer is therefore not unlike the paradox of the actor. Blanchot affirms a *moi sans moi*[20] as the seat of a suffering, inexpressive itself (lying too deep for tears) yet the basis of all expression, of all empathic writing. Yet how can we judge a concept of responsibility that seems to reduce writing to a task blinder than that of the synagogue in Christian iconography?

As long as our concept of suffering remains activist, oriented toward achievement, we have no choice but to question Blanchot's position. Because Blanchot (like Paul de Man, and like a large number of European writers) contributed to an atmosphere that made persecution normal, we expect of him avowal or explicit acknowledgment. Only an *act* of this kind, we believe, can have redemptive or remedial force.

Yet where we tend to view Blanchot's silence as a form of mastering (that is, evading) the past, he implies over and over again that the past cannot be mastered: its temporality is such that it can only be endured, not redeemed. The patience, suffering, and labor of the negative, of which Hegel talked so movingly in the preface to his *Phenomenology,* has no progressive historical visibility. There is nothing to see except the repetitive *sufferance* of the self-other relation, or the writer's entrapment in a worldly and visual vocabulary. Even that "scene" is not passive enough, insofar as it becomes manifest, a "phenomenon," unable to forgo an existential need to appear, to become a symbolic action or to aspire to authentic being by taking on itself the mystery of things.

As Blanchot withdraws from visibility, time changes direction: "le temps a radicalement changé de sens."[21] The double entendre here, since "sens" denotes meaning as well as direction, indicates that meaning itself has changed, for it is no longer archaeological or teleological. Time loses, that is, its totalizing or redemptive aspect; it is not *événementielle,* a present extended between significant beginning and significant end, or a history of disasters in whose aftermath we live and which gives us importance by that fact. We glimpse a temporal condition without such punctuation, and so without the possibility of a *récit.* The withdrawal, in any case, can never be the effect of an act of will,[22] for it moves us away from such agency, as from the world-stage on which human power is displayed. Trying to describe this passive state of being, Blanchot cannot use the older spiritual vocabulary and has to say, incongruously, that we "fall prematurely out of the world, out of being."[23]

It is clear that Blanchot wants to evoke a spirituality that cannot be confused with triumphalism in any of its ideological configurations: Christian supersessionism, or Western imperialism, or fascism's "triumph of the will," or other movements aiming at "spiritual revolution."[24] The labor of having to transform rather than abandon spiritual words tainted by the ecstasy of violence (including the word "spirit") makes *The Writing of the Disaster* a cryptic and yet moving book in search of a post-Holocaust spirituality. Blanchot, at the very least, sensitizes us to how desire, meaning, and expectation invest the commonest words— "beginning," "end," "now," "come," "see"—with a pathos strong enough to provoke disaster.

The issue faced by Blanchot (one is reminded of Pascal) is the seduction of style: the potential complicity of style, visibility, and power. In the aftermath of the Shoah, literary extroversion leads to an impasse, because narrative art "uses language as a tool to master the past; it thereby becomes both too reductive and too sovereign to do justice to the ultimate powerlessness of the victims and to the void of disaster."[25] There should be instead a rebirth of language out of the spirit of powerless utterance, out of that which could not manifest itself in the camps. Robert Antelme's note on *The Writing of the Disaster* characterizes Blanchot's style as "parole désarmée" and adds: "Aurore de la 'faiblesse humaine,' souveraine."[26] The activism of the citizen-writer is one thing; the integrity of art—the integrity of literary space—is another, and often harder to bear in its marginality or extreme patience.

Notes

1. Theodor Adorno, *Negative Dialectics*, trans E. B. Ashton (New York: Continuum, 1973), 367.

2. The most thorough account of these engagements and withdrawals is Philippe Mesnard's *Maurice Blanchot: Le sujet de l'engagement* (Paris: L'Harmattan, 1996).

3. See "Le refus," republished in *L'Amitié* (Paris: Gallimard, 1971), 130–31.

4. Maurice Blanchot, *Etretien Infini* (Paris: Gallimard, 1969), 46ff.

5. The intricacies of refusal are carefully followed by Gerald Bruns (*Maurice Blanchot: The Refusal of Philosophy* [Baltimore: Johns Hopkins University Press, 1997]), who integrates them under the heading of "The Refusal of Philosophy" and anarchism.

6. Philippe Mesnard talks of "une chute d'éléments biographiques dans l'oubli" (86) and associates this not only with Blanchot's "retreat" into literature but also with his acceptance of the Hegelian discourse of negativity between 1947 and 1949 (*Maurice Blanchot: Le sujet de l'engagement* [Paris: L'Harmattan, 1996]). As Mesnard also points out, the identitarian issue already surfaced in Blanchot's early fiction with the theme of the stranger, of outsideness or outsiderness. (From there a thematic line leads to the Jew as stranger.) In a previous essay, based on Blanchot's writings to 1960, I described his dilemma as that "of a mind that seeks to overcome itself from within, to pass into reality rather than more and more consciousness," and that through art (or as Blanchot would say, *écriture*) it intended to become real rather than more conscious. See "Maurice Blanchot: Philosopher–Novelist," in *Beyond Formalism* (New Haven: Yale University Press, 1970), 93–110. It is possible that Blanchot alludes to the identity-unity complex demanded by political engagement, and the contrary pressure exerted by "writing" that leads to an indirect or nontransparent self-inscription, in two axioms following each other in *L'Écriture du désastre* (Paris: Gallimard, 1980): "The 'false unity,' the simulacrum of unity, compromises more than its direct contestation [mise en cause] which, moreover, is not possible" (8). "To write, could it be, in this book, to become readable for everyone, and for oneself indecipherable?" (8) (translations mine). Not even Mesnard has managed to disentangle completely the way Blanchot melds contestation/(Hegelian) negation/autonomous literary space/the expenditure of self as depersonalization/asceticism. Blanchot's prewar fiction, of course, had already jettisoned realism of the conventional sort and was experimenting with a mode of cryptic self-estrangement close to Kafka's as well as the *Kunstmarchen* of the German romantics.

7. Blanchot, *Après coup: Précédé par Le ressassement éternel* (Paris: Editions de Minuit, 1983), 86. My translation.

8. "Parler, ce n'est pas voir. Parler libère la pensée de cette exigence optique qui, dans la tradition occidentale, soumet depuis des millénaires notre approche des choses et nous invite à penser sous la garantie de la lumière ou sous la menace de la lumière." Blanchot, *L'Entretien infini*, 38.

9. Since my tenor in this essay is more expository than critical, I should indicate that Blanchot, in theory, renounces any instrumental use of words, as if the instrumentalizing of language would fatally lead to words' becoming instruments of power. This clearly does not follow, yet it inclines him toward

absolutizing Mallarmé's concept of radically different types of verbal discourse: poetry (including literary prose) and . . . all the rest, including journalism. When Blanchot writes, "Language is the undertaking through which violence agrees not to be open, but secret, agrees to forgo spending itself in a brutal action in order to reserve itself for a more powerful mastery" (*The Infinite Conversation,* trans. Susan Hanson [Minneapolis: University of Minnesota Press, 1992], 42), he remains caught in the power dialectic, even if he intends "powerful mastery" to suggest a more radical withdrawal, an ascesis that opens onto the impossible horizon where conversation is so selfless that each companion is "Celui qui ne m'accompagnait pas."

10. Blanchot, *L'Entretien infini,* xxvi.

11. Blanchot, *The Writing of the Disaster,* trans. Ann Smock (Lincoln: University of Nebraska Press, 1995) 14.

12. Blanchot, *L'Entretien infini,* 460.

13. Compare Emmanuel Levinas, *Le Temps et l'autre* (Paris: Presses Universitaires de France, 1983), 71, on "la souffrance comme événement."

14. Thus does Paul de Man distinguish Blanchot from Mallarmé in his seminal essay "Impersonality in the Criticism of Maurice Blanchot," in *Blindness and Insight: Essays in the Rhetoric of Contemporary Criticism* (New York: Oxford University Press, 1971), 60–78.

15. The "1807" is marked on the castle in the story, but in the *histoire événementielle* elided by Blanchot it is the date when Hegel, completing the *Phenomenology,* saw Napoleon in Jena. In Blanchot's "undatable" or immemorial development, then, it may stand for a deadly impact on his consciousness, antithetical to Hegel's "refusal of death" (or his acknowledgment of it, but as a perpetually transcended negativity in the dialectic). Hegel's impact on Blanchot's mental world, moreover, is not necessarily confined to a single moment in personal space, and it has its vicissitudes in French intellectual history from Kojève on.

16. See also the essay on Jabès, in *L'Amitié,* from which I take (253) "cette rupture du pouvoir violent qui veut faire époque et marquer une époque." Blanchot's "là parle la catastrophe encore et toujours proche, la violence infinie du malheur" shows how close he already is to the concept of a disaster in writing. Blanchot's "disaster" is also adumbrated in earlier essays by citing Hölderlin's understanding of a "withdrawal" of the gods, which Heidegger elaborates as "*Entzug.*" This cannot be literalized as an "event," however, without introducing either a mythic speculation or a false mode of temporal reckoning that, seeking a return to essence, an event that is an advent, turns everything else into an inessential non-event. Compare Blanchot, "Hölderlin's Itinerary," in *The Space of Literature,* trans. Ann Smock (Lincoln: University of Nebraska Press, 1982), 269–76. I discuss the issue of historical dating, of epochalism, in *The Fateful Question of Culture* (New York: Columbia University Press, 1997), chap. 4, "Language and Culture after the Holocaust."

17. Essentialism would also include, at the most mundane level, the will to meaning, or negation as the source of new meaning. Compare Blanchot, *L'Écriture:* "Écriture (ou Dire) précédant tout phenomène, toute manifestation ou monstration: tout appraître" (23), and "Vouloir écrire, quelle absurdité: écrire, c'est la déchéance du vouloir, comme la perte du pouvoir, la chute de la décadence, le désastre encore" (24).

18, Blanchot, *L'Écriture,* 44–45. The last two sentences read in French: "Lorsque nous sommes patients, c'est toujours par rapport à un malheur infini qui ne nous atteint pas au présent, mais en nous rapportant à un passé sans mémoire. Malheur d'autrui et autrui comme malheur." If "patients" is construed as a noun, it would be the opposite of "agents" or "actants."

19. Blanchot, *The Infinite Conversation,* 172.

20. The same thought is relevant to the case of de Man, whose essay on Blanchot in *Blindness and Insight* seeks to make a case for a self distinct from the empirical self.

21. Blanchot, *L'Écriture,* 30. Blanchot, in short, is drafting a counter-phenomenology.

22. "The renunciation of the first-person subject is not a voluntary renunciation." Blanchot, *The Writing of the Disaster,* 29.

23. Blanchot, *L'Écriture,* 46ff. He also talks of "an interruption of being . . . between man and man there is an interval which should be neither that of being nor that of non-being, and which bears the Difference of the word *[parole]*" *L'Entretien infini,* 99. Blanchot keeps redefining, often as awkwardly as here, that "Difference," a "rapport du troisième genre," as he calls it, although this relation is a nonrelation, in the sense that it gives value to an absolute respect for the Other in others, for a quality of othernesss that cannot be reduced to samenesss or unity. Such insights, which struggle against the sentimental aura of common moralistic terms coming from the ideology of humanism, seek to define, as does Levinas, "l'autre humanisme." One often feels that Blanchot's enterprise is a revision of Buber's *I and Thou,* where the two contrasted fundamental relations, the I-Thou and the I-It, are called "words" *(Grundwörter).* Blanchot's "Autrui," however, is not *in relation* to the I, as Buber posits. Because of its link to the neutral "Il," who is "le sans 'Je,' le sans nom, la présence de l'inaccéssible" *(L'Entretien infini* 94–105), there can be no fundamental affinity.

24. Blanchot precedes in this Derrida's inquiry, *De l'espirit: Heidegger et la question* (Paris: Gallimard, 1987).

25. Vivian Liska on Sarah Kofman, in "Last Words: Sarah Kofman between Theory and Memory" (unpublished manuscript).

26. *Robert Antelme: Textes inédits / Sur L'espèce humaine / Essais et témoignages* (Paris: Gallimard, 1996), 68. Compare *The Writing of the Disaster,* 11: "May words cease to be arms, means of action, means of salvation."

II

Shoah and the Origins of Teaching

DAVID METZGER

A historian, in my estimation, has to do two things, especially when dealing with a subject such as this one [the Holocaust]: one, research and analyze; and two, remember that there is a story to be told, a story that relates to people's lives. So a real historian is also a person who tells (true) stories. This does not mean that the main task lies outside documents and their interpretation—anyone who has ever head my friend and colleague Raul Hilberg pronounce the word d-o-c-u-m-e-n-t will know what I am talking about—but a historian must also be a teacher, and teachers have to remember that their pupils, and indeed themselves, are just like the people they talk about in their telling of history.[1]

At first blush, Professor Bauer seems to be evoking something quite familiar to scholars: their responsibilities to their discipline and to their students. But he does something else as well: the sharp distinction he proposes prompts us to consider how our approach to historical work (particularly if we are not historians) might change if we were to place the accent on *the* teaching. At least, we should begin to talk about the work of the classroom as well as use the classroom as a place to talk about *the* work. But how are we to talk about the teaching if not as the work? On the one hand, the work differentiates what we (students and teachers) do in one classroom and what we might do in another. On the other hand, the teaching/the telling (and, by implication, the learning/the listening) prompts us to liken our experiences—our participation as agents and instruments in the world—with the experiences of others. The middle ground proposed by Professor Bauer is helpful and succinctly expressed: we tell (true) stories. But how does this remark relate to the experiences of our students?

Let's say that we have asked our students to read Langer's *Holocaust Memories*, or something by Primo Levi, or Cynthia Ozick's "The Shawl." Then the class takes the train to the Holocaust Memorial Museum in Washington, D.C. One of our students uses a credit card in the museum shop, and he or she remembers the numbers tattooed on a survivor's arm; the student thanks G-d that he or she has a name to go with his or her (credit card) number. What has the visit, the student's reading, the class accomplished? Has this student learned something? Here's another example. At the beginning of one of our courses, a student tells us that the Holocaust is another example of "man's inhumanity to man." Then, at the end of the semester, the student tells us that we must distinguish between Shoah as a trope for disaster, playing a role in a totalizing history of history, and Shoah as a unique, historical occurrence. Is this an example of learning? Have these students begun to tell (true) stories? If so, is this telling of a (true) story the mark of how well these students have listened? It would not be difficult for many of us to say, "Yes, there is learning/listening, here." But I would argue that we need to take our analysis of the situation one step further. Our obligation to the material may be, in part, satisfied by these expressions of learning/listening, but I am not so certain that our obligations to the students have been equally satisfied. The students have heard; they are telling (true) stories: I felt such and such; I said such and such. But are they obligated to do so? And, without the obligation to tell (true) stories, how "true" are the stories that we have prompted them to share?

If the Wilkomirski affair has taught us nothing else, it is that there are (true) stories and there are "true" stories. That is, there are stories that are true because of our obligation to history, and there are stories that are true because of our obligation to a personal history, some pathology. We accept the former and reject the latter. Even those who have studied or written about the value of Wilkomirski's text have done so by linking his personal history (which is a lie as history) to the (true) story of his personal trauma or to the (true) story of the Shoah's place in the imaginary economy of twentieth-century Europe.

What is at issue here? How we are to map our work as "teachers" and "historians" to the field of ethics, the field of our obligations? Professor Bauer's identification of the tensions between the work of the historian and the work of the teacher is related to another tension: the tension between rhetoric (understood here as the art of telling stories) and teaching (the art of telling [true] stories). In the repetition of the term "story" we find the source of our difficulty. Stories offer us "satisfactory" answers to questions, and—if satisfactory—there must be some form of satisfaction. Levinas expresses the problem very well: the goal of teaching is to objectivize the world (that is, we become obligated to the world); the goal of rhetoric is to make the world an I (where we are obligated only by the I of the speaker and/or the I of the audience). With just cause, we are comfortable with the discomfort that results from the former and suspicious of the comfort offered by the later. Over the course of this essay, we will come to see how Levinas helps us to explore the pedagogical implications of our "uneasiness" with some, but not all, discussions where the Shoah is concerned. As Saul Friedlander has pointed out, "The problem is neither narrowly scientific nor blatantly ideological: one cannot define exactly what is wrong with a certain representation of the events, but . . . one senses when some interpretation or representation is wrong."[2]

At first, Levinas's discussion of teaching and rhetoric may not seem very helpful, if only because it is difficult to understand. "Teaching," Levinas tells us in *Totality and Infinity*, "is the thematization of phenomena," and "to receive a response" is the promise of thematization.[3] As we try to come to terms with these brief statements by Levinas, it is not too difficult to understand that a proposition is directed to someone: what we would call an audience. It is also not an unfamiliar move to acknowledge that an audience is derivable from a given proposition or series of propositions (to see, for example, that a particular cigarette ad is directed to minors). But to what extent is our rhetorical construction of audience as a semiotic derivative related to the directedness of a proposition in its relation to what Levinas calls the Other?

In order to respond to this question, we will need to see how far rhetorical commonplaces can be stretched to accommodate the social contract proposed in Levinas's discussion of teaching. For Levinas also tells us that a proposition is not itself a sign; rather, a proposition carries in it a sign within which one can find the key to interpreting the proposition. The key is "the presence of the [other] who can come to the assistance of his discourse, the teaching quality of all speech."[4] All of these terms (proposition, key, sign, other) will need to be explained before we can see whether Levinas can help us answer the question of what it means to teach and learn (about) the Holocaust. For the purposes of illustration I will juxtapose two scenes: the first, a family boating tour of the Elizabeth River with Aristotle and Levinas; the second, a section from the "Holocaust testimony" of a Jesuit priest.

Why propose this curious juxtaposition? The association of these two examples (one taken from a holiday with my family, the other from Langer's *Holocaust Testimonies*) is not unlike the experiences of many of our students—that is, our teaching may encourage them to speak or listen in a language that opens their everyday lives to what is revealed in these testimonies. The students then speak; they tell their true stories: "For half a second, I thought of *Maus* when I was watching this year's Purimspiel *(The Megillah according to Disney)*." "When I was at the mikvah, I wondered how long a Nazi would have to be kept under the water to be cleansed; I thought I might hold him down a very long time."

The "I" of Rhetoric

Imagine we were taking a boat tour of the Elizabeth River and someone told us not to lean over the railing while the boat is making a turn. This advice might immediately make sense to us. But if we really wanted to lean over the railing while the boat was turning, we might ask why. It would be a surprise to us if the person pulled out a white board and a marker and began an explanation of Newton's laws of motion. It would even be a surprise if the captain of the ship (Shema Israel! Who is piloting this thing!) began such an explanation. We would expect and, more than likely, be satisfied with the statement, "In my twenty-five years as a river boat captain, I've observed that everyone who leans over the railing while the boat is making a turn falls into the water." Now, from the previous statement, can we assume that the riverboat captain knows or does not know something about Newton's laws of motion? It is quite possible that the riverboat captain knows what he or she knows, takes responsibility for what he or she knows, and is obligated by his or her knowledge only in terms of an ethical appeal: the "I" that knows is the

"I" that speaks. But, for Aristotle, the "I" that speaks only knows insofar as it "knows" something of Newton's laws of motion. That is, Aristotle seems to propose a model where the "I" of knowledge—even if Newton is not born yet—*necessarily* knows Newton's laws of motion, while the "I" of speech *possibly* knows; ethos is simply a close-enough-for-government-work version of a knowledge that may or may not be known by a given party of speakers.

We can now revisit our boating tour with Levinas. Remember that Levinas's discussion of teaching provides us with the following: (1) the one who receives the proposition; (2) the proposition within which there is the key to interpreting the proposition; and (3) the key to interpreting the proposition that is the other to whom the one who receives the proposition will address his or her questions expecting an answer. The proposition, in this case, would be "Don't lean over the railing while the boat is turning." Who receives this proposition? Those leaning over the railing, those of us observing someone doing so, those considering such an action, those who are below deck buying a soft drink while the captain proposes the interdiction over the intercom.

And the key to the proposition? Below deck, we might address our questions regarding the prohibition to the individual working the concession stand. Leaning against the rail, we might ask the person holding the mike or one of our travel companions who is also leaning over the railing. Who would we ask if we were just thinking about how nice it would be to lean over the railing and shout, like Leonardo DiCaprio in *Titanic*, "Top of the world, Ma!"? We might ask ourselves or someone standing beside us. Or, we might laugh in the silence our absent interlocutor affords, making fun of those who just got in trouble for leaning over the railing.

We seem to have a wealth of recipients and keys in this example. But this is only because we have applied Levinasian terminology to a language event defined as such by an as-yet-unspoken complex of assumptions. We have simply invented a collection of others to whom a rhetorical construct (the intersection of the set of all possible addressees with the set of all those who are on the boat) might address its request for clarification. What is more, we have assumed that the fundamental response to the proscription ("Don't lean over the railing") is "On whose authority do you make such a proscription?" We are left then to interpret the stage direction that concludes this rhetorical scene (Enter ethos followed by a bear) by equating history (Who was really on the boat?

What boat? What river is the boat on?) with the bear. Note that in our little rhetorical exercise, there is no recipient for the proposition, and there is no key. Where Levinas would suggest there should be (are) two different entities (key and proposition), we are forced merely to repeat our shopping list of others—at one moment identified as recipients of the proposition, at another moment identified as history. And note, this time without any humor, that ethos enables (warrants) this evacuation of others into history and history into others.

However, if we receive the captain's imperative as a form of "Thou shalt not kill," we are led into a different direction. That is, "Don't lean over the railing" may mean "Those who fall over the railing may endanger the lives of those who will be obliged to save them." Then we may decide to lean over in the hope that somebody does, in fact, die (I kill you), or we decide that we will not lean over the railing even if we do not know whether others may be required to follow after us.

The railing, then, is a call to look, and it is a substitute for touch: look at the sea; it cannot touch you if you hold on. But, more importantly, the railing also promises that if you turn and walk away from it, you have saved a life. You may be alone at the moment you walk away, but you will soon enter into the company of others who are also alone. Of course, this is not everyone's experience of the railing; it is only the experience of those who have received the captain's imperative as a proposition, a thematization of the world that renders the world ("the river") as an object ("the railing") that is a-part, that cannot touch consciousness (what "walks away"). Walking away, consciousness can be touched (by itself) either as world or as object. The choice to be touched as object makes consciousness its own object; the choice to be touched as world makes consciousness shiver with being. Why? This is a question addressed to the Other, but this question requires an answer at the level of the same (which is the walking away of consciousness)? There is a "why" here?

Such talk may seem more phenomenological than pedagogical, so let us return to one of the statements that initiated this discussion of the "I of rhetoric." One of my students tells me that he thought of *Maus* when he saw children dressed like mouseketeers for his temple's Purim-spiel, *The Megillah according to Disney*.

Masks are a part of the Purim festival, the celebration of a victory detailed in the Book of Esther. Although the deity's direct intervention in the Jews' victory over Haman and his pogrom may be hidden *(hester)*—just as Esther's Jewish identity is hidden from her husband,

King Ahashverosh—the victory itself and the fortuitous set of circumstances leading up to the disclosure of the deity's actions on behalf of the
Jews is not. At the end of the story, Haman and his sons are hanged
from their own gallows. So, I asked the student, "What are you saying
when you put on a mask at Purim?" He replied, "God is hidden in
people's actions." "What does it mean for us to see the masks and not
see the masks in *Maus*?" "God is hidden, but people are hidden too;
when people hide behind masks, they are twice removed from God."
"And when we don't see the strings, when the characters are the masks,
are we only once removed from the deity?" "No, without the masks,
there is no God." "Were the four-year-olds dressed like Mickey and
Minnie Mouse saying that God is hidden from the world?" "No, they
just liked the masks." "Have you thought to catalog in *Maus* when we
see the string ties behind the masks and when we don't? I wonder if
Fackenheim ever shows us the ties behind the masks. Ever shows us the
mask." "Yes, I was wondering that too. I thought I might do that for my
research project." "Sounds good," I said.

In this instance, the student noticed that a part of his experience
touched on the Shoah, and in some way this touch of history made his
experience meaningful, something to talk about. Purim became a call to
look; it became a railing that allowed the student to look at something
without fear of running away. Recall that in our previous discussion I
suggested that the boat railing is an "object" that thematizes the world;
it is an object that calls us to the world. In this instance, then, what is the
world for the student? We might say the world is *Maus*, or we might say
that, looking at the mouse mask at Purimspiel, the student shared the
world of *Maus*. And what is the appeal of the railing? As Levinas would
put it, "That one might turn away and save the life of the I." Did the
student's I also experience this? The student was telling me that Purim
saved a life, the life of the Jews at that time, but he was also telling me
that Purim saves God: God is hidden, he said, not non-existent. But did
the student save God by turning away, by not leaning over the railing or
looking behind the mask? I did not realize it at the time, but my question about what the four-year-olds meant when they put on masks implied that the student had not looked behind the mask, that, in some
sense, the I of the student had run away at that moment—saving itself
(and not some other) in the name of God. The student was saying that
there is a part of himself that is untouched by the world (*Maus*, Shoah),
and the name he gave to that world was God. But is the "untouched of

consciousness" the same as "Thou shalt not kill," or is it "There is a part of me that can't be killed"? Or when the student asserted that there was a part of himself that could not be touched by the world, was he also saying—at least by implication—that there was a part of himself that was being touched by the world (understood, here, as the threat of death)? Throughout our discussion, both the student and I spoke about the "masks" and the "ties." These were the names that were given to the origins of our discussion; without them, we would not have had a discussion; we would not have understood each other. Even when I introduced another body of reading into the discussion (signified by Fackenheim), there seemed to be a sense of understanding. My comment about Fackenheim was even something the student had predicted; we seemed to be going down the same path.

But the crucial point, from a Levinasian perspective, is making a distinction between the "Thou shalt not kill" and the "There is a part of me that can't be killed." The first statement is the beginning of ethics as Levinas understands it; the second is the beginning of rhetoric, opening us onto a ferocious power that can be identified with the glory of a people or the purity of one's blood. The first equates the world with humanity; the second equates the world with the I. Which do we choose to deploy in our teaching? And how can we know which choice we have made when we are working in this "teachable moment"?

Teaching and Ethics

As I suggested earlier, our trip on the Elizabeth River, our example of the riverboat captain, may open us to another, less welcome association that levels our experience of the railing, the captain, and the river:

> They built a tall wooden fence there, and nobody was permitted to approach the fence; the word was out that they had machine guns lined up alongside the fence in the street which paralleled the railroad tracks. . . . I did not have permission to sneak up on the railroad station. . . . But I sneaked up to the fence . . . and I found a hole there . . . and that was the day when I saw my train, my deportee train. . . . It was a cattle train, and right in front of me, just about two tracks from the fence . . . it was opened by an SS soldier. And the impression was terrible because it was terribly packed.

> I literally saw what you see in pictures, mothers with children, and people, and old people . . . and one man immediately jumped off, and I always remember his face because he looked a little bit like my father. . . . I did not hear what he said to the German soldier . . . but his behavior was polite. What I made out, that he was asking for water. And immediately that SS soldier with the club of his rifle clubbed him down, and several times, to insensitivity. Whether he died or was later put on the track [I don't know]. And then I ran away, I was so scared and I was so upset, I never saw anything like this in my life. I simply ran away.[5]

In his subsequent discussion of this testimony, Professor Langer finds the image of the fence and the hole to be highly suggestive. We dare to approach the hole in the fence because of the distance and the anonymity that the fence affords us. Yet what we observe through the hole draws us in; this is knowledge for which we can be held responsible. For Father S., whose testimony this is, there is the prohibition of nearing the fence ("I did not have permission"). So, he "sneaks" unobserved. There is a certain ethical economy already presumed at this point: we can only know who he really is by watching him when he believes himself to be invisible. And what is he? He is a sneak. But looking through the hole, he finds that he sees someone else: first, the "my" of "my train," and second, the "my" of a man who looked a little bit like his father. The I of this testimony identifies with both the German soldier and the man who may have asked for water. But his identification with the German soldier seems more stable, since he can only identify (with) the man by way of a third party ("my father"). To be the third party in this instance requires that Father S. participate in what he is seeing. At one level, this participation reinforces his identification of himself as a sneak insofar as he can only know what the victim has said by observing the pragmatics of the situation and creating a set of possible needs, one of which is more likely than the others. At another level, he can only know the man as if he were like "my father." Yet this identification becomes tainted because this association might have been prompted by the sneak's desire to fill in the gaps in his perceptual field ("I did not hear what he said to the guard"). The identification of the man with his father then supports Father S.'s own identification with the German soldier, and this identification is unwanted and unbearable; that is, he—like the guard—was not obligated by the face that the victim turned to him: he ran away; he was a "sneak." It is possible, then, that Father S. runs away not because of the brutality of the scene but because his act of witnessing makes him complicit.

It is very difficult to find an object (something real) in this passage if we presume that the real is always prior to the representation of it. Notice that Father S. authorizes his speech with a reference to a photograph ("I literally saw what you see in pictures"). What did he see? He saw what you see in a photograph; what he saw was real because it has been represented. When was he a sneak? Before or after he became a witness? Professor Langer uses this passage for the purposes of teaching us something:

> Unintentionally, Father S. bequeaths us a pair of images that will pursue us throughout our investigation. The fence and the knothole blockade and invite us simultaneously, excluding us from the terrain where we dare not venture and do not "belong" while offering an apparently secure post of observation for our role as witness. But as "what" we witness makes inroads on that fragile security, as "distance" provides less and less defense, we are sucked through that knothole and forced to find our moral bearings shorn of prior visions of the noble human spirit under duress.[6]

To do so, Langer must put a fence around the testimony. He does this by means of the word "unintentionally." Would we think differently of Father S. if he had intentionally bequeathed to us "a pair of images"? Langer's point may simply be that Father S. could not have intentionally bequeathed to us a pair of images because Father S. had no knowledge of how Langer was going to use those images in his book or how these images would resonate with the experiences of those who "study" testimony. But there is something else at work here. Langer identifies with Father S.; he sees in this man's testimony a problem that Langer has had to wrestle with while studying other testimonies. Langer has found a hole (Father S.) in a fence (other testimonies). Insofar as these other testimonies are presented in Langer's work, Langer is drawn to watch; he is driven to discover if he is obligated by the Other or by the I. And Levinas would ask, "Does this obligation touch the I as an object or the I as a world?" Why should the other testimonies be a fence and Father S.'s a hole? He can only be touched by the fact that he cannot be touched—except by his own I. On the one hand, Professor Langer tells us that these testimonies challenge our sense of the heroic human spirit.

On the other hand, he salvages that sense of the heroic for the reader: "In our quest for valid principles of survival, we surface once more with a contradiction, a clash between the value of choosing wisely and in time."[7] The reader quests; the reader clashes; the reader surfaces (like Beowulf?). The key to his book is the question "Why study this material?" And his answer comes from the I ("It persuades") and is addressed to the I. His answer keeps us at the hole, not because we are obligated to study but because Langer presents an I that we can live with. My concern with Langer's exposition of Father S.'s story is that it resuscitates an obscene question ("Why were the Jews killed?") as an answer to a pedagogical question ("Why study this material?"). His (ethical) answer: because it challenges us. Why does this material challenge us? Because there are no heroes in this story. Again, why study this material? His (rhetorical) answer: Because this material is so challenging, because those who study this material are truly heroic.

Levinas, I think, takes us in a different direction. Yes, there is a why here, and it takes the form of "Why me?" Consider the Passover seder. If we ask "Why is this night different from all the other nights?" then we are acknowledging the presence of the other. We know the answer, and we are obligated by this answer because we know to whom our response will be directed. If we remove the "why"—asking "Is this night different from all other nights?"—then we could be asking anyone. Yet, even if someone were merely to repeat the "why" form of the question to anyone else, our acceptance of the answer will not simply be a matter of believing the *anyone* we have asked. We would still need to return to ask the other signed by this why, this key, if this anyone's answer is correct.

How does all of this relate to the ethics of teaching? Quite simply, we know we have done something wrong when we have asked our students (as anyone) to study. If we employ the rhetoric of the anyone in order to convince some I to study, then the student might simply restrict his or her statements to those instances where the other is absent; that is, we can train our students not to say certain things in our presence or in the presence of others. The student may even choose to speak only in his or her fantasies where the status of the key as sign is assured because the other is killed or absent. That is, the student holds onto a key for which there is no longer any door. Because there is no door, the proposition is not the key's vehicle: we are then no longer dealing with the student but with the student's ethos. And the ethical scene, as Levinas describes it, becomes "rhetorical": a "true" story rather than a (true) story.

I would like to dismiss the abstract character of these expressions by re-evoking an example that I casually presented earlier. A student comes to me at a break in a night class, and she tells me: "When I was at the mikvah, I wondered how long a Nazi would have to be kept under the water to be cleansed; I thought I might hold him down a very long time." I was shocked, disturbed, perhaps even delighted, by the juxtaposition of the mikvah, the place of ritual immersion, mikvah, a word related to the Hebrew root for "hope," and the student's expression of a "purity" only accomplished by the death of another. I almost laughed, but I decided not to. I said, "Good point." But was I being asked a question? I've come to think that there was no question there; the student's statement, rather, held the possibility of an other who might answer a question that was not to be expressed. What is more, since the question was not to be asked, the sign, the other to whom the question might be directed, was unclear: the mikvah or the Nazi, or a position held by both? The student and not her proposition held the key for which there was no question. Let us turn to another example, keeping in mind a possible distinction between a "true" story and a (true) story, between ethos and ethics.

Imagine the following scenario. Just before Kristallnacht, a young German girl locks the door of the Reform temple where she practices playing the organ. The temple is destroyed shortly thereafter, but the young girl still has the key. Years later, the daughter of the young girl donates this key to a museum; a card tells us the young girl's story. It is (a horror) for anyone who holds the key. But no one does; the key is kept in a display case. The key is now a part of the world; it is (a horror) for anyone, but this anyone is possible only because no one holds the key. We see the glass case, the hole in the fence; we walk to see what it is so prominently displayed, and we peer in: "To be sure, the knowing of the world—thematization—does not abandon its case. It works towards, and succeeds in, reducing the disturbance of the Same by the Other. It reestablishes the order troubled by Evil and by the Other through the history which it agrees to enter."[8] Imagine that, decades later, the young girl's daughter visits the museum. She sees us reading the card, and she tells us that the key belonged to her mother. Then we ask the daughter if her mother, once "the young girl," is still with us. Why did we ask such a question? What did we hope to learn from it? I am not certain that her answer teaches us anything more about the key, but the way we look at that key will be shaped by the daughter's answer. Locked behind a glass case, the key is something that might touch us, but there is a part of us that will never be touched by the key; we can never hold it. Perhaps the presence of the daughter reminds us that the key was held by someone. Yes, but the card told us as much. Outside the box, on the other side of the railing, the key reaches out to us. And we are obligated to care for those who held the key. If her mother is no longer with us, we must help the daughter sanctify the memory of her mother. If her mother is still with us, then we hope that her life is blessed; we may even hope that the daughter is happy and well. Of course, we could have other reactions as well. The card does not tell us the location of the temple. It does not tell us about how the key was spoken about in the family, where it was kept, what it meant for the mother. Did the daughter decide to give it to the museum, or did the mother? Was the key a bequest? Would the daughter have preferred to keep the key in the family? All of this is to say that we do not know what to do with this key. But we think we know what to do when we see the daughter.

Why is that? Because, eventually, we will need to walk away; there is so much more to see, and our bus will be leaving shortly. We become daunted by the fact of our flight from the exhibit. Unafraid, undaunted by the suffering our questions might provoke, we ask, not why, but where it is happening. Here! At that point, we move from the primary position of "Thou shalt not kill" to the secondary position of "Death." Emerging from the position of "Thou shalt not kill," death is no longer the I's confused rage over its own finitude (Is this happening or not? Am I dying at this moment or not? How can this be? I exercised. I never smoked. I was clever. I never volunteered for anything. I always volunteered for everything. Or, even, the I of the young girl managed to leave the temple just in time). In the "It happened," we see a movement beyond death as an (in)appropriate choice anchored in history. The space of death is now occupied by the "You shall not kill." We care for the "young girl"; we care for her daughter. The I's fear is transformed into mourning, and the "tour bus," perhaps even the very idea of a "tour," strikes us as an abomination. For Levinas, this is the end of teaching—the end proposed by the telling of a (true) story. Without a name for the origin of the "that which is precisely not an abomination" (the mikvah in our previous example), our teaching will always fail to thematize the world of the Shoah, and the impossibility of forgiveness will be only understood as the possibility of murder. We will hold the Shoah as if it were a key without a lock or a door. We must then introduce another end to the story, and this end ("It happened!") will serve as a sign for the other to whom we will address our question. This end (this true story) is the origin whose name is teaching.

Notes

1. Yehuda Bauer, *Rethinking the Holocaust* (New Haven: Yale University Press, 2001), ix–x.
2. Saul Friedlander, introduction to *Probing the Limits of Representation,* ed. Friedlander (Cambridge: Harvard University Press, 1992), 1–21, 3–4.
3. Emmanuel Levinas, *Totality and Infinity,* trans. Alphonso Lingis (Pittsburgh: Duquesne University Press, 1969), 96.
4. Ibid.
5. Quoted in Lawrence Langer, *Holocaust Testimonies: The Ruins of Memory* (New Haven: Yale University Press, 1991), 30–31.
6. Ibid., 32.
7. Ibid., 33.
8. Emmanuel Levinas, "Transcendence and Evil," in Phillipe Nemo, *Job and the Excess of Evil,* trans. Michael Kigel (Pittsburgh: Duquesne University Press, 1998), 165–82, 182.

12

Teaching (after) Auschwitz

Pedagogy between Redemption and Sublimity

MICHAEL BERNARD-DONALS AND RICHARD GLEJZER

We begin by asking a simple question: what do we think we teach when we write about, or give classes on, the Shoah? In the years since 1945 we have heard a lot of answers: so that we never forget; so that something like this could never happen again; so that we can heal or redeem the damage done to the world through anti-Semitism or racial hatred or any number of other symptoms of genocide. We would like to suggest that although these answers, and others like them—answers that focus our attention on knowing or understanding the events of the Holocaust and its broad ethical consequences—are compelling and useful, they are nevertheless wrong. They are wrong for two important and con- nected reasons. The first is that what we have come to understand as knowledge and learning do not so much provide access to an event as they occlude access to it by allowing us to believe that the event—or any object of knowledge for that matter, but certainly this particular event—can be retrieved. The second is that the objects through which we do have access to the event—testimony, documentary evidence, mu- seums and memorials, poetry and fiction—are representations of a traumatic, sublime object that are themselves resistant to knowledge.

245

Let us take as an example the fifty-year-old response to the question of why we should teach or write about the Shoah: to remember, so that it will never happen again. One rendering of this response is in terms of redemption: we study and read about the Holocaust so that we, or history, or Judaism, or the lives or memories of the lives of the six million, may be redeemed. This is the response by Irving Greenberg and Emil Fackenheim, the latter of whom went so far as to claim that we must add a 614th commandment that takes the form of an imperative not to grant Hitler a posthumous victory: to survive as Jews, to remember the horrors perpetrated upon the victims. Greenberg's dictum is to incorporate the pain of the victims and survivors into the hope that leads to the rebuilding of a better, more humane world. Both Fackenheim's and Greenberg's responses rest on the notion that it is possible not only to remember the events of the Holocaust but also to establish upon that memory the dreary and yet glorious work of rebuilding a sound Jewish community. From the ashes of destruction rises a new people. In this rendering, the Shoah and the Final Solution become objects of knowledge from which we can learn, objects of knowledge that, if viewed appropriately, will teach us how to act differently under similar circumstances by recognizing the logic or the elements that lead to genocide.

However, the Holocaust as an event complicates this notion of redemption resting within historical knowledge. The events that comprise the Holocaust, inasmuch as they compel people to learn about and to teach the circumstances that produced the events, are too fragmented to know, let alone teach, ultimately depending on the knowledge one already has in order to give it shape and coherence. In part this is due to the difficulty in having access to documentary evidence of the Shoah itself. One of the reasons Holocaust deniers have been as effective as they are is that the German government, during the closing months of the war, was successful in destroying many of the records they so systematically kept of the Final Solution. Himmler's assertion that the Final Solution was the never-written and never-to-be-written page of glory in SS history has been borne out not by Germany's success in hiding the annihilation from its citizens but, more importantly for us now, by the fact that the remaining records of the annihilation have been spread to archives and to attics all around the world. (And even in archives they are unavailable: Yad Vashem still has a significant portion of its archives untranslated and unavailable in boxes in warehouses.) How do you know that which cannot even be retrieved?

More importantly, though, history itself resists retrieval, not because the records are sketchy but because history itself is not inherently redemptive, redeemable, or knowable. This was the point that got Hayden White, among others, into trouble during the 1989 conference on "History, Event, and Discourse" when he noted that there is no such thing as transparently realist, historical writing.[1] It is not just the writing of the historians that is at issue here. Certainly it is true that, as writers, historians provide representations of events, events that are no less actual for their unavailability except as representations. But it is also the case that the records themselves—Reichsbahn double-entry columns recording the fares to be paid by the government for the transportation of fares to the killing centers in the East; camp commandants' reports to superiors of the inelegance and inefficiency of early models of the crematoria—do not provide access to the events that comprise the Holocaust but are representations of its fragments, fragments that do not comprise the suffering, or the injustice, or the bafflement of the individuals whose lives are between the lines of such records. If we think of the history of the Holocaust as a singular set of events that involves not just our capacity to write those events but to have some sense of the lives that were caught up, one by one, in those events, then history itself is a response to a demand for explanation that in turn complicates the possibility of explanation. Put another way, although history demands a knowledge of the bafflement, injustice, and suffering of individual victims of the Holocaust, it does not tell us how or where we derive such knowledge.

One response to this placing of the limit of knowledge within learning is to accuse us of taking away the very possibility of teaching a history or literature or political science of the Holocaust, of a certain kind of academic postmodernity. However, the object of our investigation is not to claim an end (as in eradication) to history or knowledge but rather to examine how an end (as in limit) becomes a necessary subject of teaching, just as it is a necessary end to witness testimony or any representation of trauma. We would like to suggest ways to understand the events of the Shoah that may do justice to the event's complexity but which will force us to reconsider what we mean by "learning." In other words, rather than eliminate any investigation focusing on a knowledge of the event, we want to shift the object of such investigations to a different kind of knowledge that is embedded in such historical or literary or sociological investigations. Rather than eliminating this traditional knowledge, the pedagogy we suggest treats it as a necessary means toward what we see as the more important kernel of the event.

The more fruitful, and more interesting, criticism of our consideration of knowledge, sublimity, and redemption comes from scholars like Dominick LaCapra and Berel Lang, who see the kind of sublime intrusion and redemptive return that we posit as potentially framing a response to the Shoah that does not acknowledge the possible traumatic acts such a prioritizing of the sublime may engender, how the violence of the Holocaust rested on just such a sublime intrusion. It is this critique that we will address at length below before moving on to the pedagogical stakes of considering a redemptive and sublime object of knowledge.

Redemption and the Sublime Object of Knowledge

In the *Critique of Judgment*,[2] Kant describes the relation between what we are able to perceive and to think and our capacity to perceive and to think. From the beautiful we learn how the demand for an end, the demand for a name or for learning, can be suspended in favor of a self-consciousness about learning itself. Aesthetics begins, once and for all, to lay the foundation for the universality of the human ability to think and to know: it is through the ability to bring the imagination and the understanding into agreement that we also have the ability to say something about the a priori capacities that enable us to do so.

Such a harmony bears a resemblance to the notion of redemption that is commonplace in rabbinic theology. The aim of redemption (*tikkun*, restoration) is to release the divine spark through human activity and especially the act of speaking and of prayer. Through utterance and righteous action, we may experience the completed aspect of the divine—pleasure/pain, order/chaos—if only momentarily, and in that act or utterance glimpse what exceeds the merely human. Thus, redemption works through discursive representation: following Scholem's understanding of the various Kabbalistic literatures, Walter Benjamin described the moment of Adam's fall as that in which the world and its elements, previously governed by the Tree of Life in which the divine and the mutable were in communion, become differentiated. Though the world was created through an act of divine language, "the Fall marks the birth of the human word, in which the name no longer lives intact, and

which has stepped out of the language of names . . . the word must communicate something (other than itself)."[3] And yet it was still possible to
glimpse the originary link between the heterogeneous human language
and the divine *Ursprache*, and the task of revealing the shape of this link, if
not the link itself, was given to redemptive criticism. Redemption is "a
work of remembrance: it is a process of preserving the truth content or
idea of a work [or an object] from the ever-threatening forces of social
amnesia to which humanity has over the ages become inured."[4]

This does not mean trying to recuperate the events that, in Pierre
Vidal-Naquet's terms, "precede discourse," if by that we mean getting
the historical moment, the minutiae of the Holocaust's horror, right.
Events of history are heterogeneous because their interpretive significance and their effect upon the participants' and the observers' lived
lives are by definition incommensurable. Any point of history is a disor-
derly intersection of moments—of pleasure, pain, logic, and chaos—
that resist narrative closure. Representations of such historical moments
will show the pressure of this historical incommensurability, despite
their attempts to do otherwise, in their effects upon readers or their figural displacements, but they do not provide access to—stand in for—
the events. What can be written is the impasse between what we can
imagine and the conventions available to us to express them. It is this
impasse—in Kabbalistic terms, "the strait gate through which the Messiah might enter"[5]—through which we have a sense of something simultaneously human and beyond the human, of something both distress-
ingly recognizable (providing us comfort or pleasure) and impossibly
painful as well. In Susan Handelman's terms, "for Benjamin the stripping or the mortification of the works," either of history or of literature,
"was only one part of the dialectic of allegory; in making things 'other,'
there is a countermovement toward redeeming them as well. On another level, Benjamin could be said to be endeavoring to relate the sacred and profane."[6]

Though the epistemologies of theology and phenomenology have
distinct aims, Kant is quite clear that he is concerned with humans' relation to the divine, and this connection is one that has been advanced
by Geoffrey Hartman, among others.[7] In the aesthetic moment, though
we are not able to understand the relation of the divine and the human,
we are nonetheless able to bring into accord (if not commensurate) rational capacity, that which makes us human, and the sensible world.
That accord allows us to understand the perfection that is achievable

through human capacities to know and to do but which is a perfection that has little to do with the divine of the supersensible, because that supersensible realm is simply not something we can make sense of. It may be there, and we must trust that it is there, but we ought not try to reason the divine, just as we ought not try to reason the theodicies about which midrashim were written and told after the destruction of the temple in the first century, and after the diasporas of the fourteenth century, or after the destruction of European Jewry in the twentieth. The nature of divinity and the Messiah are not our concern, though a reconciliation of the human and the natural law are.

But the sublime is different. Whereas the apprehension of the beautiful has to do with the form of the object and our ability to make sense of it, the sublime is the "exhibition of an indeterminate concept" that is "unbounded" (II.§23.244). Kant goes on: "what is sublime . . . cannot be contained in any sensible form . . . which, though they cannot be exhibited adequately, are aroused and called to mind by this very inadequacy" (II.§23.245), and "carries with it, as its character, a mental agitation" (II.§24.247), an agitation that is not harmonious but is rather irritating, troubling, traumatic. If the imagination's tendency is to organize sense data, and understanding's is to bring those data under a concept, then the mind is presented with something it simply cannot do in the sublime: it is forced to deal with something completely boundless. In a feeling of the sublime, "our imagination strives to progress toward infinity" (I.§26.252): as Russian and American troops entered the camps in Poland and central Germany in late 1944 and early 1945, they were confronted with the most unimaginable sense data—walking corpses, bodies piled upon bodies, the smells of decay and defecation and the sounds of suffering, and of death, and of birds, and breezes, and the vaguest feeling of warmth that comes after the edge of winter has been tempered. In comparison to what these soldiers may have seen in their travels toward the camps—in wartime, with the atrocities associated with the belligerence of nations—these "data" were infinitely more difficult to organize, because they were unassociated with the war: whose enemies were these, and by what combination are the chills of typhus and the warmth of earliest spring to be brought under a concept or unified such that they can be combined with understanding? But this is not to suggest that what American soldiers did at the liberation of Dachau—the immediate execution of SS officers without trial—is a proper response to a moment of sublime intrusion. Rather, it suggests that it is at just such a moment when one must choose to learn rather than identify with knowledge, choose an ethics over what might seem immediately "true."

Connecting sublimity to the disaster of the Shoah, particularly in its implications for the annihilation of historical time and its bringing together of pleasure and pain, runs certain risks, among them silence and the dissolution of particular horror into the ether of a broadly defined "discursivity," in which—with reference to Lyotard—"the Shoah is transcoded into postmodernism."[8] We want to briefly address these risks, because the fears directly expressed by LaCapra, as well as indirectly by Berel Lang[9] and to some extent by Saul Friedlander,[10] are essentially a fear that by naming the Shoah—either as sublime object or as redeemable—we domesticate it and sidestep the unnameable horror that it was. (Lang goes further, linking Kant's metaphysics to the logic of the Final Solution, although, interestingly, he says little about sublimity as such.) But this fear does not account for the pedagogical implications we are outlining here.

For the sake of brevity, we will address LaCapra's concerns. In an analysis of Lyotard's *The Differend* and *Heidegger and "the Jews,"* he argues that Lyotard's view "of the 'excess' of the Holocaust, whereby one is recurrently confronted by the need to put into language what cannot as yet be acceptably 'phrased,'" is convincing.[11] He goes on, however, to suggest that this same confrontation leads ultimately to a sublime silence, whereby one "'trope[s]' away from specificity and evacuate[s] history by construing the caesura of the Holocaust as a total trauma that is un(re)presentable and reduces everyone (victims, witnesses, perpetrators, revisionists, those born later) to an ultimately homogenizing yet sublime silence."[12] In later work, LaCapra wonders whether the Kantian sublime, in its theorizations by Lyotard and others, offers different modalities, in which silence, terror, and elation are but three distinct manifestations of sublimity.[13] Here the question, and it is an urgent one, is whether in speaking of the sublime in relation to the Shoah we are not finding a way to name it, but negatively; finding a way to make of the Shoah a divinity—not Steiner's negative divinity, but a divinity in the face of which we dare not speak, as Moses did, one whose negative presence calls forth silence, or flight, or pleasure. As LaCapra once put it to us, what does the sublime obligate one to do?

A careful reading of Lyotard suggests, however, that his understanding of the sublime—one closer to Blanchot's disaster than to the "uncanny" of the Rausch, the thrill of killing (in Friedlander's terms), or a secular displacement of the sacred—involves an obligation to utterance rather than an insistence upon silence.[14] The section of *The Differend* entitled "Obligation" makes this clear: when faced with the differend—the sublime object, that which exceeds understanding—the "addressee," the subject, is obligated to respond, not in the form of narrative, but in the form of rupture. Lyotard provides the biblical example of Abraham: the impossible command to kill his son is responded to ethically and discursively, but that response, the willingness to destroy his son whom he loves, is utterly excessive. The response cannot be understood; yet Abraham does respond affirmatively and in full grief, and this excess points both to the radical otherness of the character of Abraham and to the impossibility of hermeneutic closure in the narrative.[15] The act of witnessing to the voice of God, or the confrontation with the event of the Shoah, obligates individuals, in Kant's terms, to obey the moral law while recognizing that there is something that exceeds it that will abrogate it and potentially lead to its undoing.[16] Sublimity does not call forth "'appropriate' response[s]"[17] because it is experienced uniquely, with each individual responding to the event or object differently from every other individual. The "silences" so important to Lyotard in the section of *The Differend* entitled "Result" are the silences of Blanchot's disaster, but they are silences that precede what we think of as experience, that precede the understanding that allows us to name the event or to respond sensibly to it. Those silences that "interrupt the chain that goes from them"[18] are written in the language of representation and provide the glimpse, the divine spark, the potential for destruction and completion, inherent in redemption. Though LaCapra is right to worry about the ethical consequences of understanding the Shoah and representations of it as sublime, then, it is likewise true that we simply cannot guarantee that instances of sublimity or trauma will call up "appropriate" reactions. This is what Benjamin meant when he suggested that we can never know whether an instance of historical time that any one of us may experience is the one in which the Messiah will arrive or whether it will be the moment of catastrophe. Framed pedagogically, the ethical demand of the Messiah, like that of the sublime, must always be answered by learning rather than by an equation with knowledge. In these terms, the only "appropriate" response is one unlike what came before, unlike what one "knows" to be true.

It could be argued, we think, that the sublime is par excellence a discursive dynamic rather than a cognitive one precisely because it is the elusiveness, and the horror in the face of that elusiveness, of the attempt to match the infinite sense data of our lifeworlds to the capacity of reason which would hope to bring some kind of pattern or unity to it. It is the elusiveness of what Blanchot has called the "disaster," the "force of writing [which is] excluded from it, is beyond the pale of writing or extratextual," because it is what writing—that most reasonable of the capacities that organizes knowledge—comes after while at the same time it is the thing that writing hopes to bring to the present.[19] Particularly when that force of writing originates with the events we have come to name (but whose name we realize is inadequate) the Shoah, it is imperative that we recognize the potential for writing to generate the excessive, perhaps traumatic effect: the unease of the sublime, the potential and simultaneous risk of redemption.

The Ends of Learning

Edward Linenthal recalls the project undertaken by Yaffa Eliach that eventually became the wall of photographs at the United States Holocaust Memorial Museum. Eliach traveled to Lithuania to document the history of Ejzsyszki, a shtetl destroyed by Einsatzgruppen in 1941, and spent nearly eight years collecting photographs salvaged from family members who survived the liquidations of that year. Speaking of those photos saved by family members, Eliach characterizes them this way: "many were buried in the ground or stashed in unusual hiding places. . . . The photos [have] the weightier task of restoring identity and individuality to the otherwise anonymous victims of the Nazis." Linenthal goes on to say that the photos redeem the victims from "ashes, smoke, and pits filled with bodies."[20] Cindy Miller, the museum's project director, described the family photos' "scalloped edges . . . [c]ut in the shape of hearts to become part of cards, birthday cards and greeting cards," as stunning her with the vibrancy of the shtetl.[21] But it is one thing to understand these photos, and the life of the shtetl they evoke, as having an effect upon the viewer that stuns, that works beyond our capacity to describe them, and another to suggest that they redeem the lives of the four thousand Jews killed in Ejzsyszki, as though the four thousand might be anything other than irretrievably lost in spite of the imagined lives we might provide any one of the individuals pictured in Eliach's collection. The events that took place in Ejzsyszki between September 21 and September 26, 1941, let alone the moments of life that came to an abrupt end on the evening of the twenty-sixth, simply cannot be retrieved or saved, let alone be seen clearly enough, to be put into the context of law or human relations or language so that they could be enumerated or taught.

But in one sense, the images remaining from Ejzsyszki do demand something from us; it is a pedagogical imperative that demands knowledge. In this way the aim of all teaching is to produce knowledge of the object or the event that is the focus of the inquiry. What we have come to learn again and again is that knowledge is never complete, never wrought so well as to replicate or even directly represent that object or event. So it is with the events comprising the Holocaust—there is clear documentary evidence available to suggest to us the operations of the mobile killing squads that followed behind the invasion of the Russian and Polish pale, for instance, and there is enough testimonial evidence to suggest to us the experiences of individuals involved in the killing (both survivors and collaborators). That evidence does not provide us with a foundation solid enough to build a comprehensive knowledge of the events and the experiences of the Einsatzgruppen, but it does provide (or so we would like to believe) pieces of a puzzle, fragments—in the words of Walter Benjamin—of a broken vessel that, when pieced together, may not retrieve the vessel itself but may allow us to glimpse its shape before it shattered. To put this another way, though we realize that the imperative to learn or to know events like the operations of the Einsatzgruppen or the lives of individuals in a shtetl in Lithuania cannot provide access to those events, the admittedly partial knowledge that we have may allow us to approximate a sense of the event. To return to the imperative often attached to studies of the Holocaust, we need to produce a knowledge of the events that is as complete as possible so that we may prevent such events—events that we may recognize now because we have knowledge of their shape, of their texture, of their chronology—from happening again.

But knowledge of the Holocaust cannot possibly bear the weight of such an assumption, primarily because learning does not work that way. When we teach—and when we learn—we engage in a naming operation, regardless of whether we think of learning as transmission or as creation of knowledge. Augustine puts it this way when discussing his own teaching:

So it is that we bear these images in the deep recesses of the memory as witnesses, so to speak, of things previously experienced by the senses. . . . But these images are only witnesses to ourselves. If the one who hears what I am recounting has seen these things for himself and was there on the spot, he does not learn them from my words, but recognizes them himself by the images he took away from him from these things. But if he has not experienced them with his senses, then it is clearly a matter of his believing my words rather than of learning.[22]

We are at pains to avoid understanding an object or experience in terms of objects or experiences we have already understood and experienced on our own terms, or to avoid understanding them in terms of a paradigm or conceptual scheme of one kind or another. Of course, this is nothing new or controversial: that which we know we know in terms of either disciplinary or communitarian senses of the world. We may avoid the myopia of a single discipline's paradigm through what Sandra Harding and others have called "standpoint epistemology," an examination of an object or event from the perspective of more than a single conceptual scheme, but in the end the tendency is to provide the event (or its components, or its facets) with a name. The implications of learning as naming are especially severe for those of us who were not "there on the spot" and who have no point of experience to ground that which we learn: the destruction of a shtetl or the desperation of realizing that there will be no one alive to say kaddish for you can only be learned by understanding these events or moments in terms of events or moments we have already named, or experienced, or learned. Learning about the destruction of Ejzsyszki, or even learning about its residents' lives by viewing photograph after photograph of individuals, or groups, or families, only provides knowledge founded upon names—the Holocaust, murder, Shabbat, the Shema—already well established. More dangerously, perhaps, such a knowledge is also founded upon the particular terms to which an individual viewer unconsciously adheres, names that then intrude upon another's story—mother, father, sister, brother, cousin, grandfather, and so forth. When we see a photograph of a family lost to the destruction of Ejzsyszki, we necessarily see our own family, filling in what has been lost with a memory that is ultimately our own. We cannot but forget because we cannot retain a memory that is not ours to begin with. As Augustine reminds us, such knowledge cannot take us out of what we know, since the very inquiry into what we do not know can only be situated through what we do know. Knowledge cannot recover the lives of the six million, let alone allow us to understand the fact of their murder so that nothing like it ever occurs again, because even the recovery of the fragments of the vessel cannot recover the vessel itself, nor can it retrieve the moment of its shattering.

Pedagogy after Auschwitz

What this means for teaching is complicated and potentially troubling. The assumption we generally make is that a course's pedagogical goal should be the production of knowledge of the events of the Shoah and, whenever possible, to connect that knowledge with other knowledges — of the dynamics of poverty, or of racism, or of other disasters or genocides. But while there is clear documentary evidence available to, for example, suggest to us the operations of the mobile killing squads that followed behind the invasion of the Russian and Polish pale, and though there is enough testimonial evidence to suggest to us the experiences of individuals involved, that evidence cannot bring knowledge into accord with the events themselves. The problem is in part an ethical one: the severity of the events witnessed defies the historically transparent writing we generally assume to be the best vehicle for reporting them. The testimony of even the most reliable witness succumbs to the displacement of the events from the language of the narrative, and the effect of such a narrative — of its intransitivity — is what Saul Friedlander has called, in another context, "uncanny." Through it, "we are confronted with [an uncertainty brought on by the representation] of human beings of the most ordinary kind approaching the state of automata by eliminating any feelings of humanness and of moral sense. . . . Our sense of *Unheimlichkeit* [uncanniness] is indeed triggered by this deep uncertainty as to the 'true nature'" of the referent of the narrative itself.[23] The effect of the uncanny upon reading is that, faced with the enormity of the events as described in halting, incomplete, and yet horrifying testimonies and documents, our students often have a very difficult time evaluating what they read, let alone trying to find language with which to write themselves. How can you possibly assess the authority of the sources you read, and the character of the witnesses who have written them, when you are absolutely shattered by their effect? What is there to learn in this act of shattering?

To take only one recent example of this problem, Andrea Freud Loewenstein writes that during the spring semester of 1996 at CUNY's Medgar Evers College, her introduction of Spiegelman's *Maus* in a second-semester writing course produced some startling reactions from class members. In addition to seeing the book as a way to prompt her students to writing, she also saw the section of the course in which she used the book as an opportunity to "challenge the anti-Semitism I heard from my students" and to "think more widely about the origins and effects of stereotypes and prejudice, to see themselves not only as victims of stereotyping and prejudice, but also as perpetrators."[24] Loewenstein's students, through being asked to write about the book and about their identities as "minorities," began to find a language with which to express knowledge of Judaism, of the events of the Holocaust, and of their own very complicated positions as individuals defined by color, or ethnic category, or gender, or various combinations thereof. Loewenstein concludes that several of her students "embarked on their own projects: writing comic-strip texts, making films, or writing creatively about their own family situations."[25] She also includes transcripts of her students' conversations and some excerpts from their writing. One student passage reads, in part:

> We were both [blacks and Jews] packed like sardines and sent away from our homelands, the Jews by trains and the Blacks by boat. . . . [T]he German solution for the Jews was total destruction; the White solution for the Blacks was total utilization. . . . Unlike the Jews, Blacks were considered more useful alive than dead. Now whenever I pass the intersection of New York Ave. and Eastern Parkway I can observe the Jews with new insight, comprehension, and realization of our common experience.[26]

Though the student expresses a sense of her "common experience" as an African American student with those of Jews during the Holocaust, there is clearly more going on here: an expression of anger, a sense of discontinuity between the historical circumstances of the Shoah and the Middle Passage, a connection between the geography of New York and the machinery of destruction in Europe and the Atlantic. The student's conclusion is an attempt to forge a knowledge from her particular and very difficult position in the midst of an experience she is at pains to fully understand. What she has written, in other words, responds to the disciplinary demands of the course and to the pedagogical demands of a teacher whose trajectory for this section of the class is to foster a sense of diversity and to work against stereotypes. But the language of this passage marks a limit to these imperatives by writing against them, by exerting a pressure upon them that cannot be contained by the essay's language. To press the point a little, it is also possible to suggest that the student's writing marks a universal knowledge that stands in place of a particular one, that it substitutes a conventional knowledge for a more traumatic, complicated, and unwritable sense that is impossible to know except as a moment that precedes language altogether.[27]

While we may glimpse a trace of the event's horror, we do so at the expense of knowledge. Or, to put this another way, writing the disaster may indicate the event that ruptures narrative, but it does not build knowledge of it, and in fact it works against knowledge's grain. The injunction to see the Holocaust as an event that must never be forgotten, an event that functions as a paradigm for race hatred, or anti-Semitism, or the cultural logic of fascism, seems to insist upon finding a language with which the events of the Holocaust can be written, understood, identified with or against. But if the events of the Shoah are paradigmatic of the intransigence of events to knowing or of the way testimony both creates and destroys the language of witnessing, then any attempt to integrate the Holocaust into a pedagogy needs to deal with the possibility that in asking students to know (something about) the Holocaust we are asking them to do something utterly impossible, or at the very least traumatic. And such an act on their part—an act that demonstrates learning—cannot be scripted into a necessarily appropriate response. To suggest that our object be to construct a response for our students, to situate the event in universal terms, necessary precludes them from learning, from arriving at a point that demands something from them that whatever knowledge we give them is insufficient to offset.

Pedagogically, this means that we need to resist the temptation to think of writing or other media as historical markers for events. This is true both of the texts our students read—in testimonies, histories, films, and other narratives—and of the texts our students produce. Identification of the kind evidenced by Loewenstein's students is only one example of what happens when one attempts to bring the traumatic effect of figural displacement (in her case, in Spiegelman's *Maus*) under a universal knowledge. What the Holocaust shows, perhaps more clearly than other traumatic events, is that discourse cannot represent what has been seen, and that at best it indicates the effect upon the witness of what he or she saw. Even the most explicit attempt to regularize the horrible particularity, to elide what resists naming with knowledge, indicates, in its incommensurabilities, what lies behind it; "Unlike the Jews, Blacks were considered more useful alive than dead. . . . [I realize] our common experience."

Blanchot worries that by reading the testimonies of events as The Holocaust, we destroy the effects of the particular: "Fragmentation, the mark of a coherence all the firmer in that it has to come undone in order to be reached, and reached not through a dispersed system, or through dispersion as a system, for fragmentation is the pulling to pieces (the tearing) of that which never has preexisted (really or ideally) as a whole, nor can it ever by reassembled in any future presence whatever."[28] There is, in the disaster, the beginning of an ethics: the disaster occurs when one's particular implication in the event is held up as everyone's implication, making it a universal experience and producing a knowledge of the whole in contrast to the impasse itself. We are better off focusing our attention on those impasses and deferring our students' desires to produce knowledge of the event, to act as though we can ourselves make sense of an event we did not see and did not experience. If we see learning as an indication of an event rather than a representation of it, then perhaps the best we can hope for is that our students produce some record that makes clear the gap or impasse between the representation and the represented, and see their response to such incongruities as the site of knowing and teaching that keeps horror itself recognizable.

In the end, any attempt to represent—or teach—the disaster fails to provide us with access to the circumstances that lie at its source, and it may or may not accord with the historical record. It is only in the obliteration of events, in effacing them from the realm of the sayable and by acknowledging them as irretrievably lost to knowledge, that the witness is brought to language. The language to which he or she is brought does not necessarily adhere to what we think of as the historically accurate, or the verifiable, or even the circumstances of the witness him- or herself. But this is a troubling fact about history and memory that makes it very difficult to adjudicate the traumatic experiences we read in memoirs, in diaries, or in other narrative accounts of the Shoah. The gaps in a narrative cannot be said simply to represent inaccuracies; rather—as Cathy

Caruth suggests, speaking of Freud—they represent and "preserve history precisely within this gap in his text."[29] Each encounter with the event repeats the initial trauma, but by other means that are constantly interrupted by a "gap" of both memory and experience. What we are left with is the possibility that the gap between the historical record of the irretrievable event and the rhetorical memory built to fill it can never be closed.

Teaching in terms of the sublime object—in terms of redemption—works against knowledge at the same time it tries to inscribe it. For us and for our students, who were not there, we cannot possibly write into knowledge an event to which we have no access or experience, let alone understand it well enough to connect it conceptually to other events or experiences to which we do have access. Writing itself, though, shows something like a structure of disaster—we do not know the Shoah so much as we catch a glimpse of it in the disfigured language of testimony and of remembrance. And this uncanny effect—this displacement of knowledge—is disruptive of our own attempts to write in response to the Shoah. It stands in the way of our attempts to write disaster as much as it does the diarist's. But if it also forestalls turning the Shoah into a certainty to be filed away or made sacred, so much the better.

Notes

1. See Hayden White, "Historical Emplotment and the Problem of Truth," in *Probing the Limits of Representation: Nazism and the "Final Solution"*, ed. Saul Friedlander (Cambridge: Harvard University Press, 1992), 37–53.

2. Immanuel Kant, *Critique of Judgment*, trans. Werner Pluhar (Indianapolis: Hackett, 1987), hereafter cited parenthetically in the text.

3. Walter Benjamin, *Reflections*, trans. Edmund Jephcott (New York: Harcourt, Brace, Jovanovich, 1978), 327.

4. Richard Wolin, *Walter Benjamin: An Aesthetic of Redemption* (Berkeley: University of California Press, 1994), 45.

5. Walter Benjamin, *Illuminations* (New York: Schocken; 1969), 264.

6. Susan Handelman, *Fragments of Redemption* (Bloomington: Indiana University Press, 1991), 128.

7. See Geoffrey Hartman, "The Book of the Destruction," in Friedlander, *Probing the Limits of Representation*, 318–34; Maurice Blanchot, *The Writing of the Disaster* (Lincoln: University of Nebraska Press/Bison Books, 1995).

8. Dominick LaCapra, *Representing the Holocaust: History, Theory, Trauma* (Ithaca: Cornell University Press, 1994), 98.

9. Berel Lang, *Act and Idea in the Nazi Genocide* (Chicago: University of Chicago Press, 1990), 165–202.

10. Saul Friedlander, *Reflections of Nazism* (New York: Harper and Row, 1984).

11. LaCapra, *Representing the Holocaust*, 97.

12. Ibid.

13. Dominick LaCapra, *History and Memory after Auschwitz* (Ithaca: Cornell University Press, 1998), 27–42.

14. Saul Friedlander, *Memory, History, and the Extermination of the Jews of Europe* (Bloomington: Indiana University Press, 1993); his discussion of the elation associated with mass murder is on pages 80–114.

15. Jean-François Lyotard, *The Differend: Phrases in Dispute* (Minneapolis: University of Minnesota Press, 1988), 107–15.

16. See ibid., 125–26.

17. LaCapra, *Representing the Holocaust*, 106.

18. Lyotard, *The Differend*, 106.

19. Blanchot, *The Writing of the Disaster*, 7.

20. Edward Linenthal, *Preserving Memory: The Struggle to Create America's Holocaust Museum* (New York: Penguin, 1995), 180.

21. Ibid.

22. Augustine, "De Magistro," in *Fathers of the Church*, vol. 59, trans. Robert P. Russell (Washington, D.C.: Catholic University of America Press, 1968), 53.

23. Friedlander, "'The Final Solution': On the Unease in Historical Interpretation," in *Lessons and Legacies: The Meaning of the Holocaust in a Changing World*, ed. Peter Hayes (Evanston: Northwestern University Press, 1991), 48–72, 60.

24. Andrea Freud Loewenstein, "Confronting Stereotypes: *Maus* in Crown Heights," *College English* 60, no. 4 (1998): 419.

25. Ibid.

26. Ibid., 411.

27. For a more troubling view of this same point, see Philip Gourevitch's "What They Saw at the Holocaust Museum," *New York Times Magazine*, February 12, 1995, 44–45.

28. Blanchot, *The Writing of the Disaster*, 60.

29. Cathy Caruth, "Unclaimed Experience: Trauma and the Possibility of History," *Yale French Studies* 79 (1991): 190.

13

Approaching Limit Events

Siting Agamben

DOMINICK LACAPRA

At issue in many approaches to the Holocaust and other extreme or limit events, situations, and experiences are two perspectives with problematic relations to one another. One affirms a notion of redemption as absolute recovery with no essential loss, even with respect to so traumatic a past as the Shoah. The second involves the denial or absolute negation of such redemption and a view of redemption in general as unavailable, absent, or repeatedly and aporetically in question. An initial way to see these perspectives is as formulations of working through and acting out—working through as redemption of meaning in life and transcendence of problems toward mental health and ego-identity; acting out as often melancholic, compulsive repetition in which any notion of redemption or full recovery is out of the question and problems reappear in disguised or distorted form. If there is any hope of recovery in this second perspective, it is through radical negation of hope in redeeming the past or making sense of it in the present. Instead one affirms a decisive disjunction vis-à-vis the past, pure utopian possibility, creation *ex nihilo*, and a (post)apocalyptic leap into an unknown future or state of being. One may even apprehend a glimmer of a totally other form of life—even a redemptive *Augenblick*—in the shadow cast by radically negative critique itself. What tends to be excluded in both perspectives (neither of which I agree with) is a view of working through not as full redemption, total recovery, or unmitigated caesura but as a recurrent process that, with respect to extreme trauma or limit events, may never totally transcend acting out or compulsive repetition but that does provide a measure of critical distance on problems and the possibility of significant transformation, including desirable change in civic life with its responsibilities and obligations.

In changing registers in a manner that does not imply total discontinuity with the previous considerations, I would observe that another way to view these two perspectives is as approaches to the sacred or to the sublime. I would like briefly to explore this other way (if only because I have discussed more thoroughly the earlier one—that in terms of acting out and working through—in my writings).[1] Here I am suggesting that the sublime and the sacred can be seen as displacements of one another—one in a secular, the other in a religious key—or at least that, in discussions of the sacred and the sublime, one may have a comparable role for the distinction between the immanent and the transcendent. Indeed, in discussions of limit events or situations that invariably seem to bring up (if only to resist) issues typically related to the sublime, one may often be moving in the difficult and somewhat uncomfortable area of secular or displaced theology even when one attempts to give to that theology the name—perhaps the misleading name—of ethics, of literature as an ethics of writing, or even (as in certain discussions of Claude Lanzmann's film *Shoah*) of autonomous art.

In the first perspective (involving full redemption or recovery) we have a modality of the immanent sublime, and in the second perspective (denying the very possibility of such redemption or recovery—even seeing it as taboo, sacrilegious, or "barbaric"), a modality of the radically transcendent sublime that at the limit (with the "death of God") may be erased or repeatedly held in abeyance (for example, in the form of a messianism without a Messiah or messianism as a structure of expectation that intrinsically requires continual deferral). Yet both perspectives intimately relate trauma and the sublime. The sublime involves a transvaluation or transfiguration of trauma with more or less destabilizing effects for any conventional or harmonizing notion of sublimity and perhaps for any normative conception of ethics or politics whatsoever. The sublime is related to excess or, conversely, lacuna or

lack—that which is disconcertingly, perhaps ecstatically other and aporetically beyond (or beneath) any ability to name or to know. It may also
be related to radical transgression, at times in sadomasochistic and/or
sexual form. It may even approximate disaster and be approached only
in a self-effacing writing of disaster marked by a repeated recourse to
the paradox, double bind, and *mise en abîme.*

I would note that the immanent sublime finds one of its most unsettling manifestations in what I would term the Nazi sublime. This variant
can be detected in the words and actions of at least certain perpetrators
during the Shoah. Indeed, I think the primary locus of the sublime during the Nazi genocide itself was in this group of perpetrators. A much-
discussed document in which it is active is Himmler's 1943 Posen speech,
and one finds traces of it in the endlessly repeated, at times elated or
even carnivalesque dimensions of killing and torture in the Einsatzgruppen and their affiliates. One also finds it in certain forms of activity in
the camps or the forced marches at the end of the war. Such "sublimity"
involved a fascination with excess or unheard of transgression, endlessly
repeated yet adamantly endured traumatic scenes, a code of silence (or
unsayability), and a quasi-sacrificial quest involving regeneration or redemption through violence and purification for the self and the community by eliminating "contaminating," phobic, even ritually repulsive
presences. Here I shall cite some relevant passages from Himmler's
Posen speech given to upper-level SS officers (hence intended for the initiated and not as propaganda for the general public):

> I also want to make reference before you here, in complete frankness, to
> a really grave matter. Among ourselves, this once, it shall be uttered
> quite frankly; but in public we will never speak of it. Just as we did not
> hesitate on June 30, 1934 [the purge of Ernst Röhm and his SA leader-
> ship], to do our duty as ordered, to stand up against the wall comrades
> who had transgressed, and shoot them, also we have never talked about
> this and never will. It was the tact which I am glad to say is a matter of
> course to us that made us never discuss it among ourselves, never talk
> about it. Each of us shuddered, and yet each one knew that he would do
> it again if it were ordered and if it were necessary.
>
> I am referring to the evacuation of the Jews, the annihilation of the
> Jewish people. . . . Most of you know what it means to see a hundred
> corpses lie side by side, or five hundred, or a thousand. To have stuck
> this out, and—excepting cases of human weakness—to have kept our
> integrity [or decency: *anständig geblieben zu sein*], that is what has made us

hard. In our history this is an unwritten, never-to-be-written page of glory.[2]

Paradoxically, one may also find another variant of the immanent sublime in the belated reactions of certain survivors or commentators who attempt to provide a redemptive, awe-inspiring, at times even sacralizing account of the Shoah itself and to convert it into a founding trauma that furnishes an affirmative identity for self and community. This gesture cannot be assimilated to, or viewed as simply "contaminated" by, the Nazi sublime; it is complex. In one sense it is an attempt to take back the Shoah from the perpetrators and make it serve the victims (perhaps figured as martyrs) or their descendants. In significant ways, however, the gesture remains within a certain logic of redemption and has many dubious dimensions, especially in the case of nonsurvivors who find sublimity through a transfiguration of the suffering of others. The transfiguration of trauma into a founding experience or occasion for saving sublimity may have a political and ethical role in justifying policies or practices that are open to question—from Holocaust memorialization in the United States to certain Israeli figurations of the redemptive nation and its hard-line right to defend itself in any way it sees fit.

The transcendent sublime, which may be hesitantly intimated or under erasure, has the appeal of counteracting the lure of the immanent sublime, which may include regeneration through violence and a quasi-sacrificial or totalizing logic. Indeed, the transcendent sublime would seem to serve as a bar to any mode of sacrifice, but at the cost of eliminating all forms of the immanent sacred, including the limits it sets on human assertion and its protective function for nature or human and other-than-human beings. There is also a sense in which the transcendent sublime remains within an all-or-(almost)-nothing "logic" of the absolute and a displaced theological frame of reference. It too stresses excess or what is (perhaps transgressively) beyond the limits of representation, naming, and normativity. The supplementary stress is on lacuna, lack, or loss and what is beneath representation. Such an orientation may be accompanied by a bracketing or even denigration of knowledge (except for learned ignorance in which knowledge aporetically returns time and again to its own limits and forms of undoing); it may have a dismissive, demeaning, or begrudging view of this-worldly activity *(divertissement)* in general—or at least it seems to provide little viable space

in which to develop such knowledge and activity. In a sense an orientation to the transcendent sublime remains fixated on the absolute in its
very elusiveness, unavailability, or unpresentability. Jean-François Lyotard, at least in certain aspects of his thought, would perhaps be a paradigmatic figure here, but he is not alone.[3]

Whether Maurice Blanchot's writings, insofar as they bear on the
Shoah, can be seen as engaging considerations associated with the sublime may be debatable.[4] Still, in Blanchot a simultaneous attenuation
and intensification of the contemplative life and a hesitant, allusive intimation of what might seem to be an effaced or erased transcendent sublime are related to endless waiting, patience, and an ascesis of style (or a
self-effacing ethic of writing), even harrowing isolation in the wake of
disaster. Blanchot's writings, insofar as they pertain to the Shoah, may
be defensible as a personal, anguished response—a modality of impossible mourning undecidably close to (or sharing a threshold of indistinction with) endless melancholy and (im)personal bereavement. In a sense
they may be read as based on an extreme, posttraumatic, empathic response to the abject plight of victims, even to the point of self-erasure.
But one may doubt whether they should be taken as exemplary or
whether their import for the response to limit events should be generalized. It is unclear whether they become exemplary in Derrida's rein-
scription of them. In any case, the understanding of ethics in the complex constellation of thought that includes Blanchot and Derrida (for
example, in the latter's "The Force of Law: The 'Mystical' Foundation
of Authority'" or *The Gift of Death*) tends in significant ways to be linked
to the sublime—ethics in terms of excess or what is beyond the limit of
normativity that articulates relations of people in groups or institutional
settings such as the family, the school, the workplace, or the polity.[5]

Here what was traditionally seen as the supererogatory virtue—that
which is above and beyond the call of duty or ordinary obligation—
seems at times to lessen or even obliterate the significance of the latter or
to cast it at best as a necessity made as a pragmatic concession in order
to carry on in the world (just as human rights or the subject may be radically criticized in principle but conceded as a necessity of contemporary
forms of political and social action). Civic life may even become ghostly
or virtual—a spectral hope with at best a virtual agent or bearer, a question of an unavowable or coming community, or, in Derrida's recent
formulation (in *Specters of Marx*) of endless longing, a seemingly blank
utopianism that denies its own utopian status, a messianism without a

Messiah.[6] The relation to every other may even be figured on the model of the radically asymmetrical or nonreciprocal relation (or nonrelation) between the agonized individual (or singularity) and the radically transcendent divinity. This relation involves absolute respect for the Other in others, yet this respect in the seeming register of sublimity provides little sense of how to relate to others in terms of daily commitments, obligations, and mutual rights and duties. It provides a sense of justice not in terms of measure or limits but as an invariably supererogatory virtue that seems to take relations out of institutional settings and even make them transcend or systematically exceed institutions. Justice here is closer to grace or the excessive gift—the *acte gratuit* or the potlatch—than to norms and judgment related to a network of normative limits. The sense of normativity I am invoking should not be conflated with positive law, construed as amenable to programmation and rigid codification, or collapsed into normalization (or taking the statistical average or the dominant as normative). Rather, it would relate to articulatory practices that would be open to challenge and even at times radical transgression but would nonetheless set limits to personal and group assertion that ideally would be affirmed and could be argumentatively defended as legitimate.

I think there is greater appeal in the second (transcendent) perspective on the sublime than in the first. But the problem that is occluded or at least insufficiently addressed in the second perspective is that of the transitional "space" or mediating and mitigating (but non-totalizable) links between absolutes or sublimities, that is, the sublunar or subastral space of ethical and political life. This is the space in which the primary question is the variable relation between limits and excess, including transgression and the limit event or situation, in various institutional settings and sociopolitical forms of activity. It is the space in which the distinction between the human and the nonhuman (which invariably serves invidious functions that often underwrite victimization of the other) may be radically problematized but not become a deceptive, self-defeating object of fixation—a space in which such problematization is related not only to a notion of the split or disjunctive subject but also to a notion of the human animal or being as a compromise formation of complex, interacting forces. It is also the space for developing forms of knowledge and understanding (involving affect, notably in the form of empathic response) that do not pretend to be identical with things themselves but that do provide some orientation in behavior and have a bearing on ethical judgment. (Hence empathy in the sense I am using the term involves not identification but respect for the other as other even when one's response is, in relation to the traumatic, itself unsettled and to some extent uncontrolled.) In this civic space, the ethical is not fully calculable or a matter of accounting, but it does involve the mutual ability to count on others in terms of one's fallible knowledge of how they have behaved in the past and may be expected to behave in the future.

Such knowledge is not fully redemptive, but it may confront the problem of transmitting trauma (or rather unsettlement) in a mitigated way that both indicates empathy with victims and—at least with respect to the Shoah—questions (without peremptorily dismissing) a "logic" of the sublime that transfigures trauma. Such constitutively limited knowledge may also help create the readiness to feel anxiety in the face of the unexpected or the uncanny in a fashion that does not assure nonrepetition of the past but that may provide some basis for a nonparanoid response to its displaced repetitions or reconfigurations. Moreover, I do not see the possibility of an ethics of daily life—an ethics with a critical distance on theology—that is not based on a sense of legitimate limits, however much such a sense may be problematic, tested by forms of excess, or open to continual questioning and supplementation (for example, by necessary economic and political concerns). It is in terms of ethics in this nonsublime or subastral sense—a social and civic sense that is remedial but not fully redemptive—that one may ask for an explicit acknowledgment of one's past, for example, in the (different) cases of de Man, Heidegger, or Blanchot. I think ethics is misconstrued as, or even sacrificed to, sublimity when Derrida, in what would seem to be an unguardedly transferential act of projective identification, writes these startling words: "Perhaps Heidegger thought: I can only voice a condemnation of National Socialism if it is possible for me to do so in a language not only at the peak of what I have already said, but also at the peak of what has happened here. He was incapable of doing this. And perhaps his silence is an honest form of admitting he was incapable of it."[7]

Without denying one's own implication in the ambivalent "logic" of the sublime and even recognizing its almost compulsive appeal, one may still insist on the need to develop thought and practice in the transitional civic "space" or modality that at times seems reduced to a vanishing point in an emphasis on either an immanent or a radically transcendent sublimity. Or to put the point in deceptively simple nominal terms: after a generation devoted to exploring what was gained in the paradoxical mode of pure waste or excessive expenditure *(dépense)*, it may now be time to ask whether something important was obscured or lost yet may still be recoverable (or "redeemable") in readings of Bataille, notably with respect to his response to Durkheim, to wit, a sense of legitimate limits not only or even predominantly as a pretext for, but rather as a strong countervailing force to, excess and the allure of transgression.[8] (Of course the challenge would be to articulate such limits, not in the abstract but in specific, variable, contestable situations.) And the question I would raise is whether and to what extent, with respect to the Shoah and perhaps to other limit events, one should, in one's own voice, resist a "logic" of the sublime and, more generally, whether one should engage in a careful, differentiated critique of an aesthetic of sublimity. One may raise this question without subscribing to an indiscriminate hostility to the sublime, especially when its role — notably in art and religion — is explored in its tense, mutually questioning relations to an affirmation of legitimate limits (including ethical and political limits).

I would like to turn now to the work of Giorgio Agamben, particularly his recent *Remnants of Auschwitz*, in the light of the problems I have evoked.[9] Agamben has recently risen to prominence in the field of critical theory, and there is a sense in which he seems constrained to raise the stakes or "up the ante" (which is already astronomically high) in theoretically daring, jarringly disconcerting claims if he is to make a significant mark as a major theorist. This seemingly inevitable process of vying with, or even trying to outdo, predecessors is one of the more problematic aspects of the "race for theory" in the recent past, an inclination that becomes increasingly tempting to the extent that critical theory, both in general and in its significant variations, is subjected to impatient dismissals or misinformed understandings. (This context makes it all the more important to try to develop informed and nuanced — albeit at times forceful — readings, interpretations, and critiques.) In Agamben, moreover, a sustained intricacy of formulation and an insistently paratactic or "poetic" style in philosophy make it both difficult to understand him in a way that enables critical exchange and possible for a sympathetic (or perhaps extremely generous) reader (or overwriter) to gloss questionable passages in a quasi-theological manner that always displaces attention to other, less dubious passages, even if they are to be found in another work. The fact that Agamben is a writer who seems to

elicit this response in some readers (even to generate a discipleship) is itself of interest, but it shall in general not characterize the approach I
take. Rather, I assume that through critical analysis and exchange at
least aspects of Agamben's thought will be disclosed that might otherwise escape attention.

Agamben adamantly rejects the first perspective on limit events that
seeks redemptive meaning, and he often seems to move toward the second perspective. But there are at least intimations of a transitional
"space" or non-binary network of possibilities—a "threshold of indistinction"—that cannot be reduced to the options allowed by my two
perspectives or even conceived in spatial terms. (A closer analysis would
disclose comparable dimensions in the thought of Blanchot or Derrida.)
In *Means Without End* such a threshold of indistinction seems related,
however problematically, to the form of life involving open possibilities
that Agamben defends and opposes to the nexus of sovereign power and
bare or naked life. The allusive status of this dimension in *Remnants of
Auschwitz*—where, if anything, it should have been elaborated further
with respect to Agamben's notion of ethics—is unfortunate. Moreover,
Agamben in the latter book also refers to a state of exception (also invoked in his earlier works) and to a gray zone (a move made with reference to Primo Levi's *The Drowned and the Saved*) whose relations to the
threshold of indistinction and to one another are not explicitly thema-
tized and explored as a problem.[10] The larger question that arises is that
of the way in which the transitional "space" or "threshold of indistinction" (close to Derrida's notion of undecidability) operates historically
and transhistorically as well as empirically and ideally (or normatively);
the way it problematizes, or even undoes, existing concepts or norms—
indeed entire conceptual and normative orders, perhaps even the very
concept of normativity; and the way it may help to generate newer conceptual and normative articulations explicitly recognized as problematic but nonetheless in important ways affirmed as legitimate.

Agamben clearly (and, I think, rightly) rejects the idea of any full recovery, redemption, or use of the Holocaust (a term he rejects for etymological reasons) for spiritual uplift or as proof of the essential dignity
of the human being and the ability of the human spirit to endure all
hardship and emerge on a higher level of spirituality.[11] Indeed, he even
sees Auschwitz (a metonym he employs and apparently finds unproblematic) as radically undermining or delegitimating all preexisting ethics and all postwar discourses relying on traditional notions of ethics as
well as any and every ethics related to dignity and conformity to a norm.

Auschwitz marks the end and the ruin of every ethics of dignity and conformity to a norm. The bare life to which human beings were reduced neither demands nor conforms to anything. It is itself the only norm; it is absolutely immanent. And "the ultimate sentiment of belonging to the species" cannot in any sense be a kind of dignity. . . .

The atrocious news that the survivors carry from the camp to the land of human beings is precisely that it is possible to lose dignity and decency beyond imagination, that there is still life in the most extreme degradation. And this new knowledge now becomes the touchstone by which to judge and measure all morality and all dignity. The *Muselmann,* who is its most extreme expression, is the guard on the threshold of a new ethics, an ethics of a form of life that begins where dignity ends. And Levi, who bears witness to the drowned, speaking in their stead, is the cartographer of this new *terra ethica*, the implacable land-surveyor of *Muselmannland.* (69)

In a sense, the provocation and promise of, as well as the problems involved in, Agamben's approach are condensed in this passage (including the unfortunate, dissonant use of "guard"). It signals the way Agamben offers what might be seen as a powerful but questionable conception of the relation between the post-Auschwitz and the poststructural (or perhaps the postmodern) that is of world-historical and fundamental philosophical importance. I shall begin with the issue of the relation of the historical to the transhistorical. Often Agamben seems to subsume Auschwitz as a complex historical phenomenon in a theoreticist or high-altitude discourse that eliminates its specificity and uses it to make points (for example, concerning the role of paradox and aporia) that might have been made without it. In any case, his understanding of the relation between history and theory does not set up a sustained, mutually interrogative relation in which questions are posed in both directions without the hope of a final synthesis or reduction of one term to the other. In another sense, however, Agamben attributes uniqueness to Auschwitz that goes beyond any notion of specificity or distinctiveness and is related to the world-historical, even apocalyptic significance he attributes to it both in placing in question and even eliminating the relevance of all preexisting or conventional ethics (whose nature he does not really investigate) and in posing the problem of rethinking ethics from the ground up, indeed from an indistinct point of virtuality that undercuts any conceivable ground.

Here I would mention a number of other features of Agamben's thought that one may accept, reject, or have mixed reactions to on the basis of one's own (often unexamined) assumptions. Indeed, how one describes these features or tendencies depends on how one reacts to them (my own reactions are mixed). Agamben has a sense of the apocalyptic and a penchant for the all-or-nothing response that help to induce the figuration of Auschwitz as a radical rupture or caesura in history.[12] This radically new state of affairs, signaled by the advent of the *Muselmann*, creates a sense of urgency and extreme insistence that might also be described as lending itself to a rhetoric of histrionic hyperbole—one that contrasts significantly with the general tone of understatement broken only at times by emotional upset and stylistic hyperbole in Primo Levi, who has a privileged place in Agamben's study of the remnants of Auschwitz. The privileged position is, however, somewhat equivocal, in that Levi is both taken as a paradigm and employed as an object of projective identification whom Agamben ventriloquates, just as he sees Levi ventriloquating or speaking for the *Muselmann*. In the former respect, Agamben can write: "Primo Levi is a perfect example of the witness" (16). In the latter respect, Levi serves Agamben as a prosthetic device (not to say a dummy-figure) in a covert process of identification with, and speaking for, the ultimate victim and instance of abjection, the *Muselmann*.

Agamben is concerned not with delimited historical research that uncovers new facts about Auschwitz but with its "remnants" or remainders construed in terms of the problem of the possibilities and limits of understanding it—"the ethical and political significance of the extermination" and "a human understanding of what happened there—that is, . . . its contemporary relevance" (11). One question, however, is whether certain forms of specificity are eliminated by the overly homogeneous view of Auschwitz as a *unicum* that marks a radical break in history or at least in the history of the ethical and political. For example, Agamben insists quite rightly on the need for a sustained inquiry into the *Muselmann* that has not as yet been undertaken. He relates and contrasts the *Muselmann* and the witness. The *Muselmann* is one who cannot bear witness for him- or herself and hence needs to be supplemented by the witness who nonetheless is paradoxically forced to bear witness to the (*Muselmann*'s) impossibility of witnessing. And the *Muselmann* is Primo Levi's drowned victim, the only true witness, the bereft witness unable to give testimony or bear witness. He or she is also the Gorgon whom others could not bear to behold but upon whom Agamben gazes and enjoins us all to gaze. The Gorgon is the *antiprosopon*, the prohibited face that does not give itself to be seen (53). And "the Gorgon designates the impossibility of seeing that belongs to the camp inhabitant, the one who has 'touched bottom' in the camp and has become a non-human" (54). (Here one broaches the question of the turn to a discourse of the sublime in the attempt to account for the most extreme form of abjection and victimization—a *coincidentia oppositorum* or meeting of extremes.) Yet there are a number of dubious dimensions in Agamben's ambitious and admirable attempt to affirm the importance of, and somehow come to terms with, the *Muselmann*.

Agamben takes the *Muselmann* in isolation from his or her context— the historical conditions of emergence which cannot be seen only in terms of a homogeneous idea of Auschwitz or a few restricted references to the SS. Indeed, Agamben almost seems to come upon the *Muselmann* as one might discover a creature in the wild or on another planet—what has sometimes been called planet Auschwitz to distinguish it from anything we have hitherto known on planet Earth. And in Agamben the planets collide and interpenetrate to the point of indistinction. The difficulty is that Agamben offers no sustained inquiry into the ideology and practice of perpetrators in the creation of the historical state of affairs that brought the *Muselmann* into being. One gets almost no sense of the perpetrator-victim dynamic that was crucial in the emergence of, or the erosive process leading to, the *Muselmann*. One would think that the perpetrators and their role in the genesis of the *Muselmann* would also be among the remnants of Auschwitz that are deserving of contemporary understanding and relevance. Indeed, Agamben's use of the historical for transhistorical purposes postulates the *Muselmann* as the prototype of the split or divided subject, and in the process Auschwitz itself tends to become a paradoxically abstract counter or philosophical *Lehrstück*.

Agamben has a general conception of the modern age as one tending toward or even embodying the combination of sovereignty and mere, bare, or naked life—of unlimited power and the reduction of the human being to a being denuded of possibilities and in a condition of ultimate abjection. (One might compare naked life to Heidegger's conception of the *Ge-stell*, or reduction of all things to a standing stock or reserve of raw material, perhaps even to Marx's notion of abstract exchange value.) Auschwitz and the *Muselmann* are the fullest realization to date of this extreme or excessive state of affairs which Agamben both severely criticizes and at times seems to approximate or even replicate at least in part in his own all-or-nothing, insistently evacuating, post-apocalyptic assumptions or assertions. Indeed, in Agamben the immanent sacred is denuded of all traditional dimensions of the sacred (its ambivalence, its attraction-repulsion, its elation or ecstasy, its limit-setting and limit-transgressing power).[13] It is reduced to bare or naked life. Instead of seeing this reduction as one important effect of recent history (related to developments within religion and to modes of secularization, including capitalism and positivism)—an effect nonetheless countered by other significant forces—he at times seems to postulate it as a general theory of the sacred in transhistorical terms. Insofar as this postulation occurs, he discloses, apparently as a belated, posttraumatic effect of Auschwitz, what putatively was the case all along. The begged question is whether, to what extent, and in what specific ways it is the case even now.

Elaborating this theory is a basic project in *Homo Sacer*, where Pompeius Festus's *On the Significance of Words* becomes the basis of a conception of the "sacred man" as a victim or outsider subject to being killed at will by anyone but not to sacrifice (in any traditional sense) or homicide (in any criminal or legal sense). The result in that book with respect to the Holocaust is a rather reduced understanding of it in terms of biology, medicalization, and eugenics related to a Foucauldian notion of biopower and biopolitics. This line of argument continues in *Remnants of Auschwitz* (see, for example, 82–86), and as in the earlier book it leads to an excessively one-sided or analytically reduced understanding of the victim as mere or naked life. Hence the camps are "the site of the production of the *Muselmann*, the final biopolitical substance to be isolated in the biological continuum. Beyond the *Muselmann* lies only the gas chamber" (85). Agamben's notion of mere, bare, or naked life may in important ways apply to the reduced state of the *Muselmann* and to one dimension of other victims (insofar as they were considered as mere raw material or stock, treated as pest or vermin, or hunted as "mere" game by perpetrators and bystanders). But, as I shall try to indicate, it eliminates or ignores other aspects of Nazi ideology and practice with regard to victimization. Agamben himself, moreover, also sees the *Muselmann* not as mere life but as a threshold figure: he or she "marks the threshold between the human and the inhuman" (55). How the notions of *Muselmann* as naked life and as marker of a threshold relate to one another is not clear, but in any case, for Agamben, "the sight of *Muselmänner* is an absolute new phenomenon, unbearable to human eyes" (51). In the *Muselmann* we presumably behold and bear witness to

the absolutely, blindingly, even apocalyptically new. And in our relation to Auschwitz and the *Muselmann*, we are decidedly within a post-
apocalyptic condition of existence, a condition of remnants or perhaps
of ruins.[14]

Here one may mention the importance for Agamben of Carl
Schmitt's notion of the state of exception.[15] He does not examine to
any significant extent Schmitt's ideas on secularization as the displacement of the religious in the secular, which, I think, might in certain
ways inform a treatment of the sublime, including unthematized dimensions of Agamben's own thought, including its insistence, if not fixation, on the dubious human/nonhuman opposition and its relation to
the sublimely apocalyptic and post-apocalyptic. In the runaway state of
exception (which seems close to Schmitt's state of emergency), the exception becomes the rule (hence the distinction between rule and exception becomes blurred or breaks down), and preexisting normative and
legal orders are suspended. (At the limit one is in a "state" of anomie or
Hobbesian war.) The sovereign is one who declares and decides on the
state of exception. Agamben sees this condition as generalized or rampant in the post-Auschwitz world, and this allows him to assert that the
camp is the prototype of modern life and that Auschwitz is now everywhere. As he puts the point in one of his more resounding declamations:
"Behind the powerlessness of God peeps the powerlessness of men, who
continue to cry 'May that never happen again!' when it is clear that
'that' [Auschwitz] is, by now, everywhere" (20). The post-apocalyptic
Auschwitz-now-everywhere hyperbole is one insistently repeated and
variously reformulated feature of Agamben's account that lends itself to
an elated, seemingly radical, breathlessly ecstatic discourse of the sublime. Hence in his chapter on "The Witness," after putting forth a
pathos-charged, participatory evocation of Levi's discussion of the
wordless child Hurbinek (who utters an "obstinately secret" word whose
meaning is undecidable—the word *mass-klo* or *matisklo*, which Agamben
approximates to "the secret word that Levi discerned in the 'background
noise' of Celan's poetry" [38]), he ends with these intricately straining
(unsayable?) words (reminiscent of certain passages in Foucault's *Histoire
de la folie*): "The trace of that to which no one has borne witness, which
language believes itself to transcribe, is not the speech of language. The
speech of language is born where language is no longer in the beginning,
where language falls away from it simply to bear witness: 'It was not
light, but was sent to bear witness to the light'" (39).[16]

One might, however, also argue that the hyperbole (even the cryptic prophetic mode) allows for a justifiable sense of urgency and indicates the limitations of ethics or politics as usual or indeed of any useful, easy approach to problems. Indeed, if one agrees with Agamben, he is not being hyperbolic but rather lucid in the arresting manner of the child who sees that the emperor has no clothes—that the post-Auschwitz world is itself utterly bereft or bankrupt and in dire need of some inconceivably new politics and ethics. In any event, one (or at least I) would like to know more than Agamben provides about the usual or conventional state of ethics and its relation to traditions. One result of his procedure is that he offers little room for immanent critique or deconstruction based on a careful analysis of the past and the "unredeemed" possibilities it may offer for action in the present and future (the possibilities that interested Walter Benjamin in his historical and critical dimension— Benjamin's more decidedly apocalyptic-messianic moments are the ones that captivate Agamben). One may well argue that Auschwitz itself provided no such possibilities either in itself or in its aftermath, and this would seem to be Agamben's view. But one may contest this view without going to the other extreme of spiritual uplift or fixation on the moments of resistance (the Warsaw ghetto uprising, for example) or mutual aid in the most dire of circumstances (some instances of which Levi recounts and which appear in many survivor testimonies). One may also contest Agamben's view while recognizing the importance of sustained reflection on the *Muselmann* and, more generally, on the question of posttraumatic repetition of the conditions and experience of victimization, including extreme disempowerment and harrowing isolation, even in survivors who have in certain significant respects reconstructed a life "after Auschwitz."[17]

One reason for what might be seen as a deficit of historical understanding and of immanent critique is Agamben's reliance on etymology, which tends to substitute for both historical analysis and argument. Agamben will often provide an etymology, at times lending it greater certainty than it may warrant, or he will cite some authority who has provided such an etymology and then proceed from the putative etymology to a conclusion, thereby omitting any analysis or argument linking the etymology to the point he wants to assert. This is a feature Agamben shares with Heidegger, the philosopher who has probably had the most formative role in his thought. Etymology, however putative or even fictive, can be thought-provoking when it opens up a line of investigation or reflection. But can it substitute for historical analysis or argument?

I would like to look closely at the way Agamben invokes etymology to dismiss any use of the term "Holocaust." He is not alone in doing so, although he declares his dismissal in peremptory tones that seem to imply an unawareness of the extensive discussion of usage in this matter. But the more important point is that his appeal to etymology not only substitutes for historical analysis and argument but also ignores the way usage over time may deplete or even wash away etymological sediment in the meaning of a term. I think this process has occurred for many people who employ the term "Holocaust" largely because it is the one having currency in their society and culture, not because of any invest-ment in a certain idea of sacrifice.

Agamben rehearses the well known etymology of "Holocaust" in terms of a burnt sacrificial offering, and then he adds many less known, erudite details. The telos of his account is that the term is "intolerable" and he "will never make use of this term" (31). (The apodictic nature of his statements might suggest that his analysis and critique function sub-textually as a ritual of purification with respect to a "contaminated" usage.) The intolerability of the term "Holocaust" derives from its am-biguity as a euphemism and an intimation that the events in question could possibly have sacred meaning. Agamben also makes reference to the use of "Holocaust" as a component of anti-Semitic diatribe. One may agree with these excellent reasons for suspicion and still question whether the use of the term necessarily entails them. One may also raise a question about a term Agamben seems to use as if it were unproblem-atic. "The Jews also use a euphemism to indicate the extermination. They use the term *so'ah*, which means 'devastation, catastrophe' and, in the Bible, often implies the idea of a divine punishment" (31). But what about the term "extermination"? Was this not a term employed by the Nazis—a term that is far from unproblematic? Is it not a component of the discourse of pest control, if not bare or naked life? The point I wish to make is that no term is unproblematic for "the events in question." The best (or "good-enough") strategy may be both to recognize that there are no pure or innocent terms (however "purified" by critical analysis) and to avoid fixation on one term as innocent or as taboo. In-stead, while being especially careful about unintentional repetitions of Nazi terminology, one might employ a multiplicity of terms (Holocaust, Auschwitz, Shoah, Nazi genocide, and so forth) in a flexible manner that resists fixation while acknowledging the problem in naming. More-over, as I intimated earlier, the banalized use of the term "Holocaust" may be beneficial in eroding any sacrificial connotation not only with respect to "Auschwitz" but even more generally—a process Agamben might also see as beneficial (and that could be taken as the desirable "demystifying" or delegitimating dimension of his own conception of *homo sacer* and bare or naked life). It is also noteworthy that the term "Holocaust" is used not only by anti-Semites, as Agamben seems to imply, but also by Jews, including survivors, and this could be another reason for its use more generally. (In a comparable way, the broader population of those who try to avoid prejudice or even to be "politically correct" tends to follow usage in self-designation within a relevant group, say, of "African Americans" or "Latinos" and "Latinas.") Agamben notes that Levi used the term "Holocaust" reluctantly "to be understood" and that he believed that Elie Wiesel "had coined it, then regretted it and wanted to take it back" (28). But whether or not Wiesel "coined" it (which I doubt), it came into general currency among survivors, Jews, and the general population with the varied effects I have tried to touch upon.[18]

I have noted that Agamben moves from a rejection of an immanent sublime or a redemptive reading of Auschwitz to a more transcendent sublime that is nonetheless complicated by certain movements in his thinking. Particularly problematic is his use of Primo Levi as privileged witness (or "example") in relation to the *Muselmann*. Agamben at first supplements his rejection of redemptive readings with a critique of the view that Auschwitz is unsayable (32). He also criticizes Shoshana Felman, who is often associated with an extremely sophisticated variant of this view. But his criticisms are, I think, local disagreements within a more general accord. Felman traces a labyrinthine paradox or aporia whereby the witness cannot bear witness from either inside or outside the events of the Shoah but can only at best bear witness to the breakdown of witnessing. For Agamben, Felman does not interrogate "the threshold of indistinction between inside and outside" the Shoah, and she aestheticizes testimony in appealing to the song as a performative event that "speaks to us beyond its words, beyond its melody" (36). But Agamben is in fundamental agreement with the view she elaborates in *Testimony* of the Shoah as an event without witnesses or an event that paradoxically bears witness to the breakdown of witnessing, thereby leading to endless aporias.[19] He also invokes Lyotard's *The Differend* in noting that "there is something like an impossibility of bearing witness" (34). And like Felman and Lyotard he stresses the excess and the lacuna at the heart of the limit situation or event. The question here is how his critique of the appeal to unsayability relates to his affirmation of what seems to be very close to it, indeed even within the same "threshold of indistinction": the notion that the Shoah in its excess and its lack (its supplementary uncanniness and disconcerting challenge) bears witness to the impossibility or breakdown of witnessing. In Lyotard and at times in Agamben, this paradoxical view prompts a dual movement: both toward the insistence on the paradox as paradox and in the direction of the necessity of working or playing out new formulations to respond to the excess/lack that continually requires rearticulations that can never reach total closure. At other times, however, there seems to be a compulsively repetitive return to, or even presupposition of, the paradox or aporia to which one moves as does the moth to the flame.

Let us look more closely at these complex movements. While relying on the unexplicated notion of uniqueness, Agamben nonetheless puts forth a relatively rare appeal to caution:

> Those who assert the unsayability of Auschwitz today should be more cautious in their statements. If they mean to say that Auschwitz was a unique event in the face of which the witness must in some way submit his every word to the test of an impossibility of speaking, they are right. But if, joining uniqueness to unsayability, they transform Auschwitz into a reality absolutely separated from language, if they break the tie between an impossibility and a possibility of speaking that, in the *Muselmann*, constitutes testimony, then they unconsciously repeat the Nazis' gesture; they are in secret solidarity with the *arcanum imperii*. (157)[20]

Agamben probably means "survivor" or "witness" rather than "*Muselmann*" in the last sentence. But such slippage aside, he elsewhere restricts the possibility of testimony to bearing witness to the impossibility of witnessing, or speaking "only on the basis of an impossibility of speaking," which, *mirabile dictu*, presumably will be the ultimate rejoinder to negationism. In the light of such "undeniable" testimony, "Auschwitz— that to which it is not possible to bear witness—is absolutely and irrefutably proven" (164). In addition, "the witness attests to the fact that there can be testimony because there is an inseparable division and non-coincidence between the inhuman and the human, the living being and the speaking being, the *Muselmann* and the survivor" (157). What Agamben adamantly resists is relating the threshold of indistinction to an understanding of the human being as a compromise formation between biological life (not reducible to mere life) and political or ethical life—a supplementary understanding that contests without simply negating the idea of an "inseparable division and non-coincidence between the inhuman and the human" and allows for more complex, non-absolute interaction between the two.

At times Agamben formulates problems in a manner that itself seems to eradicate the paradox in paradox and to lead to a pure, all-or-nothing antinomy that eventuates in a stark decision and eliminates any tension between a disjunction, radical difference, or internal alterity within the human and an understanding of the human as a compromise formation:

> When one looks closely, the passage from language to discourse appears as a paradoxical act that simultaneously implies both subjectification and desubjectification. On the one hand, the psychosomatic individual must fully abolish himself and desubjectify himself as a real individual to become the subject of enunciation and to identify himself with the pure shifter "I," which is absolutely without any substantiality and content other than its mere reference to the event of discourse. But, once stripped of all extra-linguistic meaning and constituted as a subject of enunciation, the subject discovers that he has gained access not so much to a possibility of speaking as to an impossibility of speaking— or, rather, that he has gained access to being always already anticipated by a glossalalic potentiality over which he has neither control nor mastery. . . . He is expropriated of all referential reality, letting himself be defined solely through the pure and empty relation to the event of discourse. *The subject of enunciation is composed of discourse and exists in discourse alone. But, for this very reason, once the subject is in discourse, he can say nothing; he cannot speak.* (italics in original; 116–17)[21]

Such a formulation deprives one of an ability to ascribe responsibility and agency. It vastly oversimplifies the problem of language in use. And it amounts to a philosophical analogue of both the political idea of a postwar *Stunde Null* (point zero) and the theological concept of creation *ex nihilo*. It also indicates Agamben's proximity to a variant of existentialism as well as a variant of structuralism.[22] One finds a comparable formulation in *Means Without End* (141), where options are restricted to the poles of the antinomy between the view of humanity as having one fully unified identity, telos, essence, or ergon and its construction in Agamben himself as pure possibility related to the absolute bankruptcy of the past and the irrelevance of every preexisting value (an enumeration of these values on page 124 lists "freedom, progress, democracy, human rights, constitutional state"). Such an antinomic and antinomian formulation eliminates the mediations provided by history in its relation to theory.

In *Remnants of Auschwitz*, via the universalization of the *Muselmann* and his or her identification with the divided or split subject, Agamben goes on to assert that "the living being and the speaking being, the inhuman and the human—or any terms of a historical process . . . have not an *end*, but a *remnant*. There is no foundation in or beneath them; rather, at their center lies an irreducible disjunction in which each term, stepping forth in the place of a remnant, can bear witness. What is truly historical is not what redeems time in the direction of the future or even the past; it is, rather, what fulfills time in the excess of a medium. The messianic Kingdom is neither the future (the millennium) nor the past (the golden age); it is, instead, a *remaining time*" (159). One may agree with Agamben's criticisms of teleology, foundationalism, and modes of redemption as fulfillment at the beginning or end of time but still raise questions about what he affirms (insofar as it is understandable) as a fulfilled time (in the key of excess) or perhaps an always already available remnant. Indeed, he seems to redefine the "truly historical" in terms of transhistorical, theoreticist notions of an "irreducible disjunction" and a paradoxical time-fulfilling excess that entail a construction of all history as a post-apocalyptic remnant whose terms both bear witness to the apocalypse and hold out a saving grace in the form of an ever-present *Jetztzeit* ("remaining time").[23] Agamben's conception of the "truly historical" may even be residually indebted to a sacrificial logic involving substitution, in which the part that remains somehow saves or redeems the whole in however paradoxical or aporetic a manner.

Other movements in Agamben's account would seem to invalidate any notion of redemption or salvation.[24] The witness (Levi, for example) bears witness to the *Muselmann*, hence to the most extreme or abject impossibility or breakdown of witnessing. (Is the difference between the unsayability Agamben criticizes and such paradoxical witnessing one of reflexivity: one now repeatedly says that there is unsayability rather than just saying the event is unsayable? Is Agamben's approach different from one—which I would accept—that does not begin with, or become fixated on, breakdown or aporia but is open and alert to such break-down or aporia when it occurs in the witness's attempt to recount trau-matic experience and perhaps in the commentator's empathic attempt to render such an attempt?) Such paradoxical or aporetic saying or wit-nessing, as Agamben discusses it, often seems close to a discourse of the sublime which Lyotard has elaborated, and Felman enacted, in more explicit terms. Except for the sacrificial form the analysis at times seems to take, the sublime here is radically transcendent in that one can bear witness to it only indirectly or paratactically by indicating time and again, and in various repetitive formulations, the impossibility of acced-ing to it through representation. And it is now radically disjoined from any positive or affirmative senses of the sacred, from any intimation of the martyrological, or from any unspoken promise of parousia in the mode of negative theology. Yet the lowest of the low, the *Muselmann* as the limit of abjection, seems to evoke a discourse that, in its own excess and its insistent, at times intolerant, struggle with the aporetic limits of thought, seems at least like a specter of the sublime. If one may refer to sublimity at all (and one may conceivably argue that one may not), it now seems like the horizonless pale shadow of a god that has not died but been recognized as absent, perhaps endlessly.

Still, there are times in Agamben when the *Muselmann* him- or her-self becomes sublime in effulgent yet chiaroscuro terms that outdo, while recalling, passages in Kant:

> This is language of the "dark shadows" that Levi heard growing in Celan's poetry, like a "background noise"; this is Hurbinek's non-language *(mass-klo, matisklo)* that has no place in the libraries of what has been said or in the archive of statements. Just as in the starry sky that we see at night, the stars shine surrounded by a total darkness that, accord-ing to cosmologists, is nothing other than the testimony of a time in which the stars did not yet shine, so the speech of the witness bears wit-ness to a time in which human beings did not yet speak; and so the tes-timony of human beings attests to a time in which they were not yet human. Or, to take up an analogous hypothesis, just as in the expand-ing universe, the farthest galaxies move away from us at a speed greater than that of their light, which cannot reach us, such that the darkness we see in the sky is nothing but the invisibility of the light of unknown stars, so the complete witness, according to Levi's paradox, is the one we cannot see: the *Muselmann*. (162)

Even aside from the question of whether the *Muselmann* can or should serve as the occasion for a dark-winged lyrical flight into sublimity, one may ask whether there is a crucial dimension of bearing witness and giving testimony that Agamben occludes. He discusses the *Muselmann* as the ultimate victim, the one who died or was completely crushed, and yet who is also the true witness, the sublime witness whose testimony would be truly valuable but who cannot bear witness. He also discusses the survivor-witness as ultimately bearing witness to the *Muselmann*. What he does not investigate with care is the arduous process whereby bearing witness and giving testimony are themselves crucial aspects of the movement (however incomplete and subject to remission) from the victim—indeed the potential *Muselmann*—to the survivor and agent. Agamben concludes his book with a series of quotations from former *Muselmänner*, and one may ask how it is even possible to refer to oneself as a *Muselmann* in the past tense given the utterly abject, disempowered position from which one has to emerge, at least to some extent or momentarily, to make this usage possible. Indeed, one might argue that part of the process Agamben elides is crucial in understanding the witness who performatively is not only a victim but a survivor who lives on in part precisely by giving testimony or bearing witness.

This process is obscured, perhaps even devalorized (whether intentionally or not), by the relentless insistence on the aporias and paradoxes of bearing witness to the impossibility of witnessing—aporias and paradoxes that may indeed arise but should not be presupposed or converted into a vehicle for a repetition compulsion. In Agamben one often has the sense that he begins with the presupposition of the aporia or paradox which itself may at times lose its force and its insistence in that it does not come about through the breakdown or experienced impasse in speaking, writing, or trying to communicate but instead seems to be postulated at the outset. In other words, a prepackaged form seems to seek its somewhat arbitrary content. And the paradox and the aporia become predictable components of a fixated methodology. Indeed, the terms in which the aporia as assumed, self-negating telos are sometimes (not always) formulated may be rather unconvincing. For example, near the beginning of the book, one has the following:

> What is at issue here is not, of course, the difficulty we face whenever we try to communicate our most intimate experiences to others. The discrepancy in question concerns the very structure of testimony. On

the one hand, what happened in the camps appears to the survivors as
the only true thing and, as such, absolutely unforgettable; on the other
hand, this truth is to the same degree unimaginable, that is, irreducible
to the real elements that constitute it. Facts so real that, by comparison,
nothing is truer; a reality that necessarily exceeds its factual elements—
such is the aporia of Auschwitz. (12)

This formulation may give one an indistinct sense of a problem, but
an indistinction that is more vague than indicative of one's implication
in a threshold of indeterminacy or undecidability. "The only true
thing," "irreducible to the real elements that constitute it," "facts so
real," "a reality that necessarily exceeds its factual elements"—these
formulations gesture offhandedly without evoking an aporia. Or, if the
aporia is evoked, it is in rather routinized terms with reference to an excess in the limit event that others (notably Lyotard and Saul Friedlander) have discussed extensively.[25]

The relations between and among the threshold of indistinction, the
gray zone, and the state of emergency are not elucidated in *Remnants of
Auschwitz*—indeed the three seem at times to be conflated, at least "after
Auschwitz."[26] The lack of elucidation may be abetted by post-
apocalyptic assumptions, the acting out of posttraumatic symptoms,
and the fragmented, paratactical nature of Agamben's approach.
(Reminiscent of Wittgenstein in the *Tractatus* and the *Philosophical Investigations* or Lyotard in *The Differend*, he employs numbered paragraphs.) I
would suggest that the "threshold of indistinction" is a transhistorical
concept that is evoked in variable ways by historical phenomena or
"cases," while the gray zone and the state of exception as rule refer to
more historically determinate situations that may nonetheless become a
basis for transhistorical reflection, just as the historical figure of the *Muselmann* may become a basis for a general or transhistorical reflection on
abjection. I would also suggest that the threshold of indistinction has an
affirmative or at least an undecidable valence that both problematizes
norms and may help in the generation of newer normative articulations.
When approximated to or conflated with the state of exception, it is
generalized and given a political and juridical inflection. As such it may
be related to a condition of normative dislocation which the sovereign,
through a decisionist gesture, is supposed to determine and resolve.
One may of course argue that a goal of social, political, and civic life is
to avoid the rampant state of exception or to see it at best as an extreme

condition in an intolerable state of affairs that may be a prelude to revolution. Hence one might even want to bring about something at least close to a state of exception in oppressive regimes, but the judgment concerning what regime falls into this "category," and whether collapse, panic, and disarray are more likely than revolution in any desirable sense, is debatable. The post-apocalyptic Auschwitz-now-everywhere hyperbole would eliminate this problem in judgment by generalizing the state of exception along with the gray zone and the threshold of indistinction. Hence the routine yet surrealistic soccer match in Auschwitz between the SS and Jewish members of the Sonderkommando "repeats itself in every match in our stadiums, in every television broadcast, in the normalcy of everyday life. If we do not succeed in understanding that match, in stopping it, there will never be hope" (26). How would one go about stopping that match, and if one accepts the limited value of the afterimage of unsettlement projected forward by the match at Auschwitz but objects to the shrill yet leveling logic in Agamben's exclamation, is one condemned to hopeless complacency and business as usual?

One might also contend that the gray zone in its historical sense (as used by Primo Levi) is not so much a threshold of indistinction or even a state of exception as a condition of extreme equivocation that is created largely through the practices of perpetrators and imposed on victims, typically in the form of double binds or impossible situations. Moreover, as a historical condition, the gray zone need not be generalized but at least at times may exist as an intermediary zone between relatively clear-cut cases or groups of perpetrators and victims. Indeed, one may argue that the gray zone and, in different ways, the rampant state of exception may obviate confrontation with the threshold of indistinction as it exists and poses problems for everyone. This is because the gray zone and the state of exception (particularly when it gives way to an anomic state of emergency) typically involve, or devolve into, a binary opposition between self and other (perpetrator and victim, friend and enemy, us and them) in which anxiety may be projected from the (oppressing) self onto the (oppressed) other as well as localized invidiously in those placed in equivocal or double-bind situations (particularly perpetrator-victims or collaborators). Moreover, the generally applicable threshold of indistinction creates anxiety that normative orders may help mitigate but never entirely eliminate. It relates to the manner in which decisions, especially extremely difficult decisions, are never entirely predetermined by norms, although norms may indeed help guide decisions in many cases and to some extent in all but the most difficult and problematic cases. In addition, one may defend as desirable a condition of society in which the threshold of indistinction exerts pressure on everyone but is not generalized as a state in which the exception becomes the rule—a state that is of direct political consequence. The legitimate normative articulation of life in common would be such that one could in general distinguish between the exception and the rule and not expect everyone to live according to the extreme or excessive demands placed upon the exception (something that may be argued to occur in the state of exception). Within any concrete situation, one would of course have to further articulate these general considerations, for example, with reference to questions of equality and hierarchy involving specific economic, political, and social issues. The considerations on which I have touched all too briefly seem to have little role in Agamben's discussion, in *Remnants of Auschwitz*, of the gray zone, the threshold of indistinction, and the state of exception.[27]

Agamben not only sees Levi as speaking for the *Muselmann* but generalizes the gray zone in a manner that threatens to undo significant distinctions and to eventuate in a view of all existence in terms of the limit event or situation as a state of exception if not emergency or crisis in which the exception becomes the rule. I have noted that, from Agamben's post-apocalyptic perspective, "Auschwitz marks the end and the ruin of every ethics of dignity and conformity to a norm" and "Levi, who bears witness to the drowned, speaking in their stead, is the cartographer of this new *terra ethica*, the implacable land-surveyor of *Muselmannland*" (69). Of Levi, Agamben also writes: "He is the only one who consciously sets out to bear witness in place of the *Muselmänner*, the drowned, those who were demolished and touched bottom" (59). The problem here is not the argument that Auschwitz, or the *Muselmann* in particular, poses distinctive problems for ethics or that it is dubious to impute essential dignity to the *Muselmann*, especially for self-serving reasons. What is problematic pertains to the synecdochic *use* of the *Muselmann* as a theoretical cipher to disprove human dignity and to discredit all preexisting (perhaps all presently conceivable) forms of ethics. What remains of ethics (if it still can be called ethics) in Agamben is dissociated from law and voided of all forms of normativity (including responsibility and guilt). It seems to eventuate in an empty utopianism and a form of political romanticism ("as Spinoza knew, the doctrine of the happy life" [24]). In any case, Agamben takes a potential in humanity and, rather than examining closely its historical role in Auschwitz and comparing it carefully with other situations and possibilities, actualizes it in universal terms by generalizing the *Muselmann* as the prototype or exemplar of humanity. This *condition humaine,* as "life in its most extreme degradation," becomes "the touchstone by which to judge and measure all morality and dignity" (24).[28] The result is an unsituated, extreme mode of victimology or identification with the abject and utterly disempowered—something which, despite its transhistorical cast, might most generously be seen as a radical reversal of, or perhaps an overcompensation for, extreme victimization under the Nazis.

In his brief but trenchant reflections on ethics, Agamben apparently takes Auschwitz as an apocalyptic divide between past and present which delegitimates all uses in the present of past ethical assumptions or discourses. He even attributes such a view to Levi: "The *Muselmann,* as Levi describes him, is the site of an experiment in which morality and humanity themselves are called into question" (63). Moreover:

> The unprecedented discovery made by Levi at Auschwitz concerns an area that is independent of every establishment of responsibility, an area in which Levi succeeded in isolating something like a new ethical element. Levi calls it the "gray zone." It is the zone in which the "long chain of conjunction between victim and executioner" comes loose, where the oppressed becomes oppressor and the executioner in turn appears as victim. A gray, incessant alchemy in which good and evil and, along with them, all the metals of traditional ethics reach their point of fusion. (21)

There are many contestable features in these statements to which I shall return. Here I would point out the dubiousness of seeing total ethical meltdown in Levi, who drew from traditional culture and ethics both to provide him with sustenance in the camps and, in a manner that was, if anything, perhaps insufficiently informed by the concerns that preoccupy Agamben, to inform his postwar reflections on his experience.

If one recalls the quotation from Himmler's Posen speech, one may well sympathize with Agamben when he asserts of the *Muselmänner:* "To speak of dignity and decency in their case would not be decent." Sympathy wavers when he adds, in his prevalent turn to a kind of free indirect style or middle-voiced usage: "The survivors [including Levi as

Agamben speaks with(in) and for him] are not only 'worse' in comparison with the best ones—those whose strength rendered them less fit in
the camp—they are also 'worse' in comparison with the anonymous
mass of the drowned, those whose death cannot be called death. This is
the specific ethical aporia of Auschwitz: it is the site in which it is not decent to remain decent, in which those who believed themselves to preserve their dignity and self-respect experience shame with respect to
those who did not" (60). Auschwitz epitomizes the absolute impossibility of "death with dignity" in the modern world, the way in which death
gives way to the fabrication or manufacture of corpses. "This means
that in Auschwitz it is no longer possible to distinguish between death
and mere decease, between dying and 'being liquidated'" (76). More
generally, in the modern world one's unease about dying is related to its
privatization, deritualization, and concealment from public view.

Agamben is touching upon important issues here—issues that
should not be obliterated by any reservations about his approach. Still,
he is so concerned with the problem of death that he pays scant attention to processes of killing among the Nazis and their relations to specific objects of victimization. In the relatively few references to the SS,
even they undergo, rather than activate, processes and are often framed
in the passive voice or in something approximating a bystander position
or even a position that almost seems to place them (as in the soccer
game) on a gray-on-gray, level playing field with victims. "The SS could
not see the *Muselmann*, let alone bear witness to him" (78). Or again:
"Both the survivor's discomfort and testimony concern not merely what
was done or suffered, but what *could* have been done or suffered. It is this
capacity, this almost infinite potentiality to suffer that is inhuman—not
the facts, actions, or omissions. And it is precisely this *capacity* that is denied to the SS" (77).

There may be a worthwhile shock or scandal induced by accusing
the SS of an incapacity to be inhuman—a shock relating to an attempt
to rethink the threshold between the human and the inhuman or nonhuman and to reposition ethics as other than purely humanistic. Agamben
does not make explicit and explore the implications of this unsettling,
seemingly paradoxical idea, for example, concerning the "rights" or
claims of other-than-human animals. (Indeed, one danger of Agamben's
sharp binary between the human and the inhuman or nonhuman,
which he maps onto the opposition between the speaking being and
mere or naked life, is the exclusion or even scapegoating of nonhuman

animals who, by implication, seem reduced to mere life or raw material.) Moreover, *pace* Agamben and whatever may be the case concerning almost infinite potentiality, the capacity to suffer is something humans share with other animals, and it is related to empathy, which the SS did not have with respect to victims. But this capacity (or Agamben's postulated incapacity, for that matter) was not simply denied to the SS as passive recipients. It was actively countered, blocked, or eliminated through ideological and related practical forces as well as through the dynamic of victimization that brought victims to the abject state which Nazi ideology, in circular and self-fulfilling fashion, attributed to them. A particularly questionable feature of Agamben's orientation is that the deficit of the SS, in terms of a lack of inhumanity, is itself construed in terms of an almost infinite (quasi-divine?) capacity or potentiality for suffering. No known being, human or otherwise, has this infinite capacity. Beyond a certain threshold of suffering, one blacks out, and it would seem that Agamben strives to write from, or even from beyond, that threshold. Once again we seem to be in the vicinity of ethics understood in paradoxical terms as supra-ethical, supererogatory excess rather than in more socially and politically viable terms. Does empathy with respect to both human and other-than-human beings require an infinite capacity for suffering, or does the latter radically transcend empathy into an ecstatically indistinct realm of sublimity that would itself seem, in any social or political terms, to be isolating? (Almost involuntarily, I think of the unimaginably suffering but transfigured Christ ascending into heaven.)

Agamben's related understanding of the meaning of Himmler's Posen speech is curious at best. He sees it in line with his idea of the SS as not having the inhuman, almost infinite capacity to suffer. He relates the latter to another passive position with a paradoxical twist: the *Befehlnotstand*. "The executioners unanimously continue to repeat that they *could* not do other than as they did, that, in other words, they simply *could* not; they had to, and that is all. In German, to act without being capable of acting is called *Befehlnotstand*, having to obey an order" (77–78). Agamben then relates the perpetrator's claim to undergo orders that one must obey, thereby acting without really acting, to the passage from Himmler's Posen speech (which I quoted earlier in a somewhat different translation): "Most of you know what it means when 100 corpses lie there, or when 500 corpses lie there, or when 1,000 corpses lie there. To have gone through this and—apart from a few exceptions caused by human weakness—to have remained decent, that has made us great. That is a page of glory in our history which has never been written and which will never be written" (78).

Himmler himself has here a preference for passive or indeterminate constructions which veil somewhat the fact that those whom he addresses not only have beheld a scene but are responsible for having brought it about. One may analyze the functions of such a construction but not simply repeat it transferentially in one's own analysis. Moreover, Himmler in this passage is not altogether like Eichmann on trial appealing to a distorted Kantian sense of duty in doing one's job and obeying orders; he does not simply appeal to a *Befehlnotstand* or the inability to do otherwise. There are in his words an appeal to the sublime (notably a mathematical sublime in the geometrically increasing expanse of corpses), to the fascination with excess and radical transgression in the form of unheard-of mass destruction, to the glory which the uninitiated will never understand, to the quasi-sacrificial allure of victimization in the absolute injunction to kill all Jews without exception (by definition there is no such thing as a good Jew), and to the superhuman ability to become hard (interestingly mistranslated in the above quotation as "great"—"absolute greatness" characterized the sublime for Kant) by enduring *(durchstehen)* the aporia or combining in oneself the antinomic features of decency and radical transgression.[29] In other words, for Himmler, Nazis did look the Gorgon directly in the face, and this "sublime" gaze made them hard in a sense they desired. What is interesting is Agamben's inability to detect these aspects of the Posen speech and to focus instead on what would seem unaccentuated in, if not projectively inserted into, it.[30]

There is also a problem with respect to what might be termed, for lack of a better word, subject positions. For Levi as survivor to say that not he but the *Muselmann* is the true witness is, I think, an acceptable hyperbole. For Agamben to identify with Levi and hence speak for (or in the stead of) Levi and hence for the *Muselmann* (as he believes Levi does) may be hyperbolic in an objectionable sense. Moreover, the idea that Auschwitz radically delegitimates all preexisting ethics and all present appeals to them, including all notions of decency and dignity, paradoxically runs the risk of granting a posthumous (post-apocalyptic?) victory to the Nazis. In any event, it obviates a careful inquiry into the uses of such concepts by victims and survivors themselves as well as their attempts to preserve some sense of dignity and decency in impossible situations. It also risks handing the concept of decency over to Himmler as his heritage rather than struggling for and rethinking it (for example, by criticizing any invidious use of it to distinguish the human from the other than human, including the animal that cannot itself be reduced to bare or naked life or be understood in neo-Heideggerian terms as not having a world or a form of life).

One important feature of Agamben's notion of ethics is its radical disjunction from law—with responsibility and guilt placed squarely on the side of law. I would agree that ethics may not be identified with or reduced to law (or vice versa) and that protesters are evasive if they claim moral but not legal responsibility for their actions (22). But this does not imply a total disjunction between ethics and law or a relegation of responsibility and guilt to law and their elimination from ethics. Responsibility and guilt are concepts that are differentially shared by ethics and law, and Agamben does not provide any idea of a form of social life in which ethics would not involve these concepts. Nor need responsibility as answerability be reduced to a rigidly codified, quasi-legal formula, as Agamben seems to imply in his etymological analysis of *sponsa* and *obligatio* as well as in a pseudo-historical just-so story which at most would apply to a restricted idea of the subject and subjectivity ("Responsibility and guilt thus express simply two aspects of legal imputability; only later were they interiorized and moved outside the law" [22]). The unstated horizon of his view would seem to be an ecstatic, anarchistic utopia that remains *terra incognita* and whose relevance to present problems or commitments is left utterly blank. Indeed, not only is it dubious to make Auschwitz the bomb that explodes the status quo; the sublime negativity and the hope against hope that combine to inspire such a gesture may all too readily become a license for evasiveness with respect to responsibilities and commitments in the present. Moreover, in Agamben's approach one loses sight of the tense, mutually engaging relation between the "law" or the strength of norms and what it fails to encompass—what indeed remains both as remnants and as possibly valuable irritants that indicate the limits of the law and areas demanding change. And generalizing the ecstatic, including the ecstatically transgressive, threatens to dissipate or neutralize it, eliminating the very force of its challenge. As I have intimated, one may recognize a tendency in modernity, perhaps accentuated in the recent past, for the sublimely ecstatic and the transgressive to be generalized and banalized but not repeat and aggravate it to the point of hyperbole in one's own voice.

I have indicated that it is indeed important to reflect in a sustained manner on the extremely disconcerting phenomenon of the *Muselmann*, the living dead or hopeless being on the verge of extinction who was the object of disdain and avoidance among camp inmates themselves. But here one could maintain that the *Muselmann* should not be directly identified with, universalized, or spoken for—something that Levi, despite a reference Agamben quotes ("we speak in their stead, by proxy" [34]), at times resists doing, even as he presents the *Muselmann* as the true witness.[31] Rather, one might argue that the *Muselmann*, an actuality in Auschwitz, represents a potential that may become a real possibility for anyone in certain conditions, and the possibility may be related (as Agamben indicates) to split subjectivity and the "real" as analyzed by Lacan. This may be why the *Muselmann* provoked anxiety and avoidance, not simply indifference or curiosity, in the camps. One might also see Beckett as having had the daring to stage, in an incredible series of radically disempowered beings, the—or at least something close to the—*Muselmann*'s experience of disempowerment and living death—a view that would give a different perspective on Adorno's paradoxical attempt to present Beckett as more politically relevant and radical in his seemingly autonomous art than was Sartre in his defense of committed literature. Here something Zizek writes of the *Muselmann* as paradoxically beneath or beyond tragedy and comedy is apposite: "Although the Muslim is in a way 'comic,' although he acts in a way that is usually the stuff of comedy and laughter (his automatic, mindless, repetitive gestures, his impassive pursuit of food), the utter misery of his condition thwarts any attempt to present and/or perceive him as a 'comic character'—again, if we try to present him as comic, the effect will be precisely *tragic*."[32]

One should certainly acknowledge the importance of Levi's gray zone and recognize that it often presents the most difficult cases for analysis and understanding. But (following Levi rather than Agamben) one need not construe it as all-encompassing even in the camps much less in present societies figured as the covert, post-apocalyptic embodiment of the concentrationary universe. Although one may mention still other cases without utterly blurring the distinction between perpetrator and victim, Levi restricts his discussion of the gray zone to the Sonderkommando and the Jewish Council, notably the case of Chaim Rumkowski of the Lodz ghetto. The Auschwitz-now-everywhere hyperbole is itself provocative only as a prelude to a differential analysis of how and to what extent, in Benjamin's phrase, "the exception is the rule" in contemporary societies—an analysis Agamben does not provide. While Levi certainly did, in trying circumstances, get carried away and returned at least verbal blows in a manner that brought him close to his sometime adversary, Jean Améry,[33] I have noted that the gap between Levi and Agamben is marked by the distance between typically careful reserve or even cautious understatement and prevalent, at times histrionic, hyperbole. There is even a paradoxical sense in which the Auschwitz-now-everywhere hyperbole eventuates in a banalizing rhetoric (or a rhetoric of banalizing hyperbole in which almost every sentence seems to be followed by a virtual exclamation point) bizarrely reminiscent of Ernst Nolte's normalization of the Holocaust, during the 1986 *Historikerstreit*, through an appeal to the prevalence of genocide in modern times.[34] Indeed, one finds the Auschwitz-now-everywhere hyperbole in surprising quarters. It is, for example, invoked by radical antiabortionists in the self-styled "Army of God" that even contains a "White Rose" faction. For those in the "Army of God," abortion is tantamount to the Holocaust, and they are resisters and rescuers for whom violence, including the murder of supposedly SS-like doctors practicing abortion, is justified. Of course Agamben would not seem to mean "that," but what he means—and how one stops the putatively omnipresent soccer match—is often unclear.

I would simply note in passing that the fact that perpetrators may be traumatized by what they do does not make them victims in the relevant sense. The very term "trauma victim" may invite confusion, and there is still much to be done in perpetrator history and theory. Hence Levi's gray zone should not be made into an oil slick or radically deregulated and generalized threshold of indistinction that covers everyone indiscriminately. It is inaccurate and perhaps projective to write of Levi, as Agamben does: "The only thing that interests him is what makes judgment impossible: the gray zone in which victims become executioners and executioners victims" (70). With respect to the Shoah, the gray zone for Levi exists between relatively clear-cut "zones" of perpetrators and victims, and as Levi himself writes in his very chapter on "The Gray Zone":

> I do not know, and it does not much interest me to know, whether in my depths there lurks a murderer, but I do know that I was a guiltless victim and I was not a murderer. I know that the murderers existed, not

only in Germany, and still exist, retired or on active duty, and that to confuse them with their victims is a moral disease or an aesthetic affectation or a sinister sign of complicity; above all, it is precious service rendered (intentionally or not) to the negators of truth. I know that in the Lager, and more generally on the human stage, everything happens, and that therefore the single example proves little.[35]

Levi goes on to qualify but not to retract these emphatic comments made with some degree of exasperation.

Without fully agreeing with all of its aspects, one may also quote another passage from Levi that Agamben himself quotes without engaging its critical implications for aspects of his own approach. It concerns the poetry of Celan:

This darkness that grows from page to page until the last inarticulate babble fills one with consternation like the gasps of a dying man; indeed, it is just that. It enthralls us as whirlpools enthrall us, but at the same time it robs us of what was supposed to be said but was not said, thus frustrating and distancing us. I think that Celan the poet must be considered and mourned rather than imitated. If his is a message, it is lost in the "background noise." It is not communication; it is not a language, or at most it is a dark and maimed language, precisely that of someone who is about to die and is alone, as we will all be at the moment of death. (37)

A crucial reason Agamben believes the *Muselmann* invalidates all previous ethics and notions of dignity and decency is that the latter prove not to be universal since they do not apply to the *Muselmann*. He is also at points alert to the danger that his own views may approximate those of the SS, although he does not seem effectively to counter or perhaps even mitigate that possibility. He even asserts that "the SS were right to call the corpses *Figuren*" (70). He also writes:

Simply to deny the *Muselmann*'s humanity would be to accept the verdict of the SS and to repeat their gesture. The *Muselmann* has, instead, moved into a zone of the human where not only help but also dignity and self-respect have become useless. But if there is a zone of the human in which these concepts make no sense, then they are not genuine ethical concepts, for no ethics can claim to exclude a part of humanity, no matter how unpleasant or difficult that humanity is to see. (63–64)

The logic of this paragraph is dubious. One does not counteract the danger of transferential repetition with respect to the SS by claiming that it is the *Muselmann* him- or herself who "moved into a zone of the human where not only help but also dignity and self-respect have become useless." Indeed, this view would seem once again to avoid the role of the perpetrators as agents (not simply spectators, commentators, gesticulators, or judges) in creating the conditions Agamben tries to understand. It might seem to involve blaming the victim in a manner not that different from "gestures" of the SS. The *Muselmänner* did not simply "move" into a zone of abjection; they were kicked, whipped, and beaten into it. And the SS and their affiliates were the ones who conducted the "experiment" that Agamben seeks to replicate in his own way.

Moreover, one may claim that certain values are general or even universal in their relevance while nonetheless maintaining that in certain extreme situations, such as that of the *Muselmann* as well as other inmates of concentration and death camps, they are not applicable. Being placed in such a genuinely paradoxical position with respect to relevant, at times pressingly insistent, but inapplicable values or norms may be a reason why survivors felt "shame"—a reason Agamben does not entertain. Instead, the dominant note he strikes in his chapter on shame is the largely asocial idea that shame is ontological and constitutive of subjectivity. Shame is presumably the way, according to Heidegger, "we find ourselves exposed in the face of Being" (106) or, in a quotation from Levinas, "what is shameful is our intimacy, that is, our presence to ourselves" (105). However one may respond to this understanding of shame as Agamben employs it (I think it diverts attention from social interaction and ethicopolitical issues), one may insist that the nonapplicability of values or norms with respect to the *Muselmann* would be primarily the responsibility of the perpetrators, and it is only from a questionably skewed perspective that the *Muselmann* could be invoked to invalidate them.

The nature of this perspective is indirectly illuminated by a comment Agamben makes about philosophy: "Philosophy can be defined as the world seen from an extreme situation that has become the rule (according to some philosophers, the name of this extreme situation is

'God'") (50).[36] Here philosophy itself becomes a post-apocalyptic, post-Auschwitz perspective of conceptual and ethical meltdown, or radical blurring of distinctions, wherein the threshold of indistinction, the gray zone, and the rampant state of exception seem fully to meld. And, in Agamben's understanding, this perspective, at least "according to some philosophers," is a God's-eye view—a god who is decidedly astigmatic if not cockeyed. But does anyone have the right to speak on behalf of, or as proxy for, this god?

Put in less polemical terms, one might say that writing from within the limit situation or the state of exception in which the *Muselmann* is everyman, Auschwitz is now everywhere, and the exception becomes the rule is in a sense to write *in extremis* as if each moment were the moment of death. One question is how general this exceptional writing should be and whether it should function to provide the perspective from which all else is approached "after Auschwitz." In what I would see as its most general form of pertinence, Agamben's threshold of indistinction might be related to transference and one's transferential implication in the object of study with the tendency to repeat symptomatically the forces active in it and, as well, to react to the formulations of others in a highly "cathected" or charged manner. My own response to Agamben has not escaped this pattern. As Agamben himself at times intimates, the challenge is not how to escape it but how to come to terms with it—how to work it through and acquire some critical perspective on it and some enlarged sense of possibility without ever entirely transcending its at times compulsive force. A question Agamben leaves one with is how to understand the historical and transhistorical, as well as the empirical and normative, relations between and among the threshold of indistinction, the gray zone, and the state of exception (and emergency), as well as the possibilities of a rethought (but not entirely new or sublimely post-apocalyptic) ethics and politics. Another crucial question is whether utter abjection can be construed as both the end of all previous ethics and the beginning of a radically new ethics ecstatically linked to the sublime. I have tried to argue that utter abjection is the end or limit point of ethics in that ethical norms do not apply to the behavior of the utterly abject and disempowered but, paradoxically, still remain relevant to it. I have also argued that the sublime does not suspend, or configure a radically new, ethics for sublunar beings such as humans for whom the specific conditions of possibility of ethics are not ontological but instead concrete social, economic, and political conditions. And I have resisted the attempt to conjoin abjection with, or transfigure it into, sublimity, particularly on the part of those who have not experienced the abjection in question, those who "were not there," except perhaps in their imagination and in their rhetoric.

One may be in a better position to come to terms critically with Agamben's own perspective on these questions, as well as my response to it, if I gather together and make explicit what I have represented as basic aspects of his orientation or framework that I find both problematic and worthy of further thought:

1. Modernity, especially after Auschwitz, is bereft, bankrupt, and within the age of accomplished nihilism.

2. Thought is to push this putative condition to the limit and make its vacuousness evident. In other words, thought is to engage in unyielding, radical critique of the present in its relation to the past. Hence the key role for aporia, paradox, and hyperbole as "in-your-face" strategies of provocation.

3. Especially in the present, one has only two real choices: a mystified view of full identity, rights, essence, and telos or a vision of the human as pure potentiality related to the bankruptcy of the past and all preexisting values with the reduction of life to naked, bare, or mere life.

4. The consequence of Agamben's choice of the latter option is an elimination or downplaying of a view of the human being as a compromise formation (in a sense even a "threshold of indistinction") between body (not reducible to naked or mere life) and signifying practices that are social, political, and ethical in various ways.

5. The further consequence is the unavailability of immanent critique with respect to the past or the present. Rather, one is in a position of *Stunde Null* (point zero) requiring creation *ex nihilo*.

6. The only true "ethics"—in contrast to a derided "morality" of responsibility, guilt, repentance, and perhaps normativity and normative limits in general—is an ethics of pure potentiality, openness, and exposure.

7. The only true "politics" is a form of blank utopian, messianic (post)apocalypticism that combines Heidegger and a certain Benjamin.

In this intellectual context, the ultimate in traumatized abjection, the *Muselmann*, becomes a figure of sublimity, and Auschwitz emerges as a transhistorical *leçon de philosophie*. The formula here—whether paradox or one of the oldest of Christian doxa—seems to be that only by descending to the depths can one ascend to the paradisiacal heights of revelatory language.

Notes

1. See *Representing the Holocaust: History, Theory, Trauma* (Ithaca: Cornell University Press, 1994), *History and Memory after Auschwitz* (Ithaca: Cornell University Press, 1998), and *Writing History, Writing Trauma* (Baltimore: Johns Hopkins University Press, 2001).

2. Lucy Dawidowicz, ed., *A Holocaust Reader* (West Orange, N.J.: Behrman House, 1976), 132–33.

3. See especially *The Differend: Phrases in Dispute*, trans. George Van Den Abbeele (1983; Minneapolis: University of Minnesota Press, 1988).

4. See, for example, *L'Entretien infini* (Paris: Gallimard, 1969) and *The Writing of the Disaster*, trans. Ann Smock (1980; Lincoln: University of Nebraska Press, 1986).

5. "The Force of Law: The 'Mystical' Foundation of Authority," *Cardozo Law Review* 11 (1990): 920–1045, and my response to it in the same volume; *The Gift of Death*, trans. David Wells (1992; Chicago: University of Chicago Press, 1995).

6. *Specters of Marx*, trans. Peggy Kamuf (New York: Routledge, 1994).

7. "Heidegger's Silence," in *Martin Heidegger and National Socialism: Questions and Answers*, ed. Gunther Neske and Emil Kettering, trans. Lisa Harries, intro. Karsten Harries (New York: Paragon House, 1990), 148.

8. For two important readings of Bataille, which were crucial in setting the tone of poststructural approaches to him, see Jacques Derrida, "From a Restricted to a General Economy," in *Writing and Difference*, trans. with an intro. and notes by Alan Bass (1967; Chicago: University of Chicago Press, 1978), 251–77; and Michel Foucault, "A Preface to Transgression," in *Language, Counter-Memory, Practice*, ed. and intro. Donald F. Bouchard, trans. Donald F. Bouchard and Sherry Simon (1963; Ithaca: Cornell University Press, 1973), 29–52.

9. *Remnants of Auschwitz: The Witness and the Archive*, trans. David Heller-Roazen (New York: Zone Books, 1999), hereafter cited parenthetically in the text. Any larger study of Agamben would have to include an extensive discussion of at least his *Homo Sacer: Sovereign Power and Bare Life*, trans. David Heller-Roazen (1995; Stanford University Press, 1998), and *Means Without End: Notes on Politics*, trans. Vicenzo Binetti and Cesare Casarino (1996; Minneapolis: University of Minnesota Press, 2000). Agamben conceives of these works, along

with the more recent *Remnants of Auschwitz,* as composing a series. One may note that *la nuda vita* is translated as "bare life" by Heller-Roazen and as "naked life" by Binetti and Casarino. Moreover, the *Muselmann* in *Remnants of Auschwitz* is conceived as the extreme form or instance of the *homo sacer*, who is interpreted by Agamben as the bearer of *la nuda vita* and is reduced to this condition by sovereign power. It is open to debate whether and to what extent the notions of bare or naked life and *homo sacer* as Agamben understands them provide an adequate account of the sacred or even of the status of the Jew as victim under the Nazis. I would argue that this view accounts only for one dimension of the complex figure of the Jew for Nazis—the dimension related to the Jew figured as pest or vermin fit only for extermination. It does not, I think, account for the more ambiguous dimensions of the Jew (which Agamben rejects in the sacred itself at least as it is conceived in Roman law) whereby the Jew was also an object of quasi-ritual or phobic repulsion as well as invested with world-historical, conspiratorial powers of evil and made an object of quasi-sacrificial scapegoating and victimization. One of the difficulties in understanding Nazi ideology and practice involves the role of the shifting registers of pest control and quasi-sacrificial response with respect to the Jew. However, I shall later suggest a sense in which Agamben's view may itself be symptomatic of an exhaustion or depletion of the sacred and sacrificial in the recent past which I would see as beneficial insofar as it counteracts victimization as a crucial dimension in the appeal of sacrifice. Agamben does not see how the banalized use of the term "Holocaust" may be in part defended as itself symptom and performative force in the erosion or active depletion of the sacrificial and its attraction.

10. *The Drowned and the Saved* (1986; New York: Random House, 1989).

11. Agamben does not comment critically but only in (dubious) etymological respects on a term that is crucial to his account: *Muselmann*, or Muslim (44–45). This prejudicial appellation was camp slang for the absolutely exhausted and beaten down who had given up hope in life and led a living death. The use of such a term would seem to illustrate the tendency of the oppressed and abject to locate invidiously a presumably even more abject group, and the history of strained relations between Jews and Arab Muslims renders particularly dubious the choice of *"Muselmann"* as the term of distancing and denigration.

12. In *The Coming Community* (trans. Michael Hardt, 1990; Minneapolis: University of Minnesota Press, 1993), Agamben contrasts an ethics of pure possibility and openness (which in certain ways seems close to the early Sartre's notion of pure, evacuated *disponibilité*) with a conception of morality. "Morality" is castigated and would seem to include any normativity including repentance, responsibility, and guilt—perhaps any normativity at all. The correlate of Agamben's "ethics" is an apocalyptic politics of the coming community of totally open and substitutable "whatever" singularities. The nature of

this putative ethics is elaborated via an analogy to the cabala in a fully apocalyptic-messianic manner reminiscent of aspects of the thought of Walter Benjamin:

> In the society of the spectacle [that is, modern society], in fact, the isolation of the Shekinah [the word of God] reaches its final phase, where language is not only constituted in an autonomous sphere, but also no longer even reveals anything—or better, it reveals the nothingness of all things. There is nothing of God, of the world, or of the revealed in language. In this extreme nullifying unveiling, however, language (the linguistic nature of humans) remains once again hidden and separated, and thus, one last time, in its unspoken power, it dooms humans to a historical era and a State: the era of the spectacle, or of accomplished nihilism. . . .
>
> The era in which we live is also that in which for the first time it is possible for humans to experience their own linguistic being—not this or that content of language, but language *itself,* not this or that proposition, but the very fact that one speaks. Contemporary politics is this devastating *experimentum linguae* that all over the planet unhinges and empties traditions and beliefs, ideologies and religions, identities and communities.
>
> Only those who succeed in carrying it to completion—without allowing what reveals to remain veiled in the nothingness that reveals, but bringing language itself to language—will be the first citizens of a community with neither presuppositions nor a State, where the nullifying and determining power of what is common will be pacified and where the Shekinah will have stopped sucking the evil milk of its own separation.
>
> Like Rabbi Akiba, they will enter into the paradise of language and leave unharmed. (*The Coming Community*, 82–83)

13. For an account of the sacred that focuses on these features, see Julia Kristeva, *The Powers of Horror,* trans. Leon S. Roudiez (1980; New York: Columbia University Press, 1982). Kristeva does not apply her analysis of the sacred to the Nazi genocide, in part because, in her often apologetic understanding of Céline's anti-Semitism and sympathy for fascism, she focuses in an analytically isolating manner on aesthetic issues and even construes Céline's anti-Semitism in the narrowly biographical terms of a personal need for identity. And Kristeva is close to Agamben in bringing together the abject and the sublime (with the sublime functioning as a secular displacement of the sacred).

14. For an extensive, critical, yet sympathetic account of the postapocalyptic mode, see James Berger, *After the End: Representations of Post-apocalypse* (Minneapolis: University of Minnesota Press, 1999). In certain important respects, Agamben's sensibility and approach to problems may be compared to

that of Bill Readings in *The University in Ruins* (Cambridge: Harvard University Press, 1997). See my discussion in "The University in Ruins?" *Critical Inquiry* 25 (1998): 32–55 as well as Nicolas Royle, "Yes, Yes, the University in Ruins," *Critical Inquiry* 26 (1999) and my rejoinder ("Yes, Yes, Yes, Yes . . . Well Maybe") in the same issue. See also Royle's ecstatically post-apocalyptic *After Derrida* (Manchester: Manchester University Press, 1995).

15. See Carl Schmitt, *Political Theology: Four Chapters on the Concept of Sovereignty*, trans. George Schwab (1922, 1934; Cambridge: MIT Press, 1985).

16. Compare the sober words of Levi, which, despite their own dubious aspects (for example, the facile invocation of pathology or the decisive opposition between humans and other animals with a limited idea of language serving as an invidiously differentiating criterion), may raise the question of the unexplored relations between certain forms of existentialism and of poststructuralism:

> According to a theory fashionable during those years [the 1970s], which to me seems frivolous and irritating, "incommunicability" supposedly was an inevitable ingredient, a life sentence inherent to the human condition, particularly the life style of industrial society: we are monads, incapable of reciprocal messages, or capable only of truncated messages, false at their departure, misunderstood on their arrival. Discourse is fictitious, pure noise, a painted veil that conceals existential silence; we are alone, even (or especially) if we live in pairs. it seems to me that this lament originates in a dangerous vicious circle. Except for cases of pathological incapacity, one can and must communicate, and thereby contribute in a useful and easy way to the peace of others and oneself, because silence, the absence of signals, is itself a signal, but an ambiguous one, and ambiguity generates anxiety and suspicion. To say that it is impossible to communicate is false; one always can. To refuse to communicate is a failing; we are biologically and socially predisposed to communication, and in particular to its highly evolved and noble form, which is language. All members of the human species speak, no nonhuman species knows how to speak. (*The Drowned and the Saved*, 88–89)

On Foucault, see my discussion in *History and Reading: Tocqueville, Foucault, French Studies* (Toronto: University of Toronto Press, 2000), chap. 3.

17. See Lawrence Langer, *Holocaust Testimonies: The Ruins of Memory* (New Haven: Yale University Press, 1991), and my discussion of the book in *Representing the Holocaust*, 194–200.

18. For one chapter in the use of the term, see Gerd Korman, "The Holocaust in American Historical Writing" (first publ. 1972) in *The Nazi Holocaust*, vol. 1, ed. Michael Marrus (Westport, Conn.: Meckler, 1989), 284–303. For Korman, Wiesel did not coin the term "Holocaust" but with "other gifted writers and speakers" helped to make it "coin of the realm" (294).

19. See Shoshana Felman and Dori Laub, *Testimony: Crises of Witnessing in Literature, Psychoanalysis, and History* (New York: Routledge, 1992). I comment extensively on Felman's contributions to this book in the three works mentioned in footnote 1.

20. I indicate ways Agamben himself seems to "unconsciously repeat the Nazis' gesture." This transferential repetition, which is often invoked dubiously as an ultimate "knock-down" argument, confronts all discourses on the topic, and the problem is not whether it threatens to occur but how one comes to terms with it in more or less explicit fashion—to what extent and how one acts it out and works it through.

21. Here the reader may allow me a thought experiment concerning the response of an individual (or rather "singularity") who, after reading Agamben, is caught by a spouse or partner in bed with another "singularity": "The subject who made a commitment to you is a shifter, and the one you find in bed is a psychosomatic individual who is expropriated of all referential reality and is reduced to glossalalic potentiality that cannot speak." Does this scenario move too quickly from theory to practice for the sake of a joke?

22. The variant of existentialism to which I refer is pronounced in one important dimension of Sartre's *Being and Nothingness* wherein the for-itself has a nihilating relation of disjunction and transcendence with respect to the in-itself, a relation that aligns the for-itself with pure possibility or *disponibilité* and with the imaginary. A variant of structuralism, while it may downplay or deny the freedom and agency of a "for-itself," nonetheless stresses a relation of radical disjunction or epistemological break between structures.

23. For a different articulation of the relations between the transhistorical and the historical, one that does not collapse them or evacuate historical specificity by deriving the historical from the transhistorical, see my "Trauma, Absence, Loss," *Critical Inquiry* 25 (1999): 696–727, a version of which is chapter 2 of *Writing History, Writing Trauma*.

24. The background noise in the following passage might seem to drown out any meaning, but the passage in its reference to the "non-coincidence of the whole and the part" might conceivably be read as countering a sacrificial logic: "In the concept of remnant, the aporia of testimony coincides with the aporia of messianism. Just as the remnant of Israel signifies neither the whole people nor a part of the people but, rather, the non-coincidence of the whole and the part, and just as messianic time is neither historical time nor eternity but, rather, the disjunction that divides them, so the remnants of Auschwitz— the witnesses—are neither the dead nor the survivors, neither the drowned nor the saved. They are what remains between them" (163–64). Is the philosopher, in Agamben's vision of him as one who sees the world from an extreme situation that has become the rule, one of these remnants?

25. Along with Lyotard's *The Differend,* see especially Friedlander, *Memory,*

History, and the Extermination of the Jews of Europe (Bloomington: University of Indiana Press, 1993).

26. In *Homo Sacer*, Agamben explicitly links the state of exception and the threshold of indistinction: "The situation created in the exception has the peculiar characteristic that it cannot be defined either as a situation of fact or as a situation of right, but instead institutes a paradoxical threshold of indistinction between the two" (18). The question is whether the converse is also the case and whether the threshold of indistinction always creates a state of exception. The more important question is whether, in modernity and especially "after Auschwitz," the exception becomes increasingly the fundamental political structure and ultimately the rule.

27. For a careful, thought-provoking discussion of related issues, see Etienne Balibar, *Masses, Classes, Ideas: Studies on Politics and Philosophy before and after Marx*, trans. James Swenson (New York: Routledge, 1994), esp. part 3.

28. See also Slavoj Zizek, *Did Somebody Say Totalitarianism?* (London: Verso, 2001), chap. 2.

29. The Eichmann who is more like Himmler in his Posen speech is evoked by Saul Friedlander:

> Could one of the components of "Rausch" be the effect of a growing elation stemming from repetition, from the ever-larger numbers of killed others: "Most of you know what it means when 100 corpses are lying side by side, when 500 lie there or 1000." This repetition (and here indeed we are back, in part, at Freud's interpretation) adds to the sense of *Unheimlichkeit*, at least for the outside observer; there, the perpetrators do not appear anymore as bureaucratic automata, but rather as beings seized by a compelling lust for killing on an immense scale, driven by some kind of extraordinary elation in repeating the killing of ever-huger masses of people (notwithstanding Himmler's words about the difficulty of this duty). Suffice it to remember the pride of numbers sensed in the Einsatzgruppen reports, the pride of numbers in Rudolf Höss's autobiography; suffice it to remember Eichmann's interview with Sassen: he would jump with glee into his grave knowing that over five million Jews had been exterminated; elation created by the staggering dimension of the killing, by the endless rows of victims. The elation created by the staggering number of victims ties in with the mystical Führer-Bond: the greater the number of the Jews exterminated, the better the Führer's will has been fulfilled. (*Memory, History*, 110–11)

Friedlander also observes that "for further analysis, we would need a new category equivalent to Kant's category of the sublime, but specifically meant to capture inexpressible horror" (115). The question of course is precisely how one invokes this category, including the role of critical precautions concerning the possibility of transferential repetitions particularly when an appeal to some aspect of the discourse of the sublime is undertaken in one's own "voice."

30. In his earlier discussion of Heidegger (73–75), Agamben does not quote the most notorious passage of the Bremen lecture of December 1949, which seems close to aspects of Agamben's own Auschwitz-now-everywhere perspective: "Agriculture is now a motorized food industry: in its essence it is the same thing as the manufacture of corpses in gas chambers, the same thing as blockades and the reduction of a region to hunger, the same as the manufacture of hydrogen bombs" (cited by Wolfgang Schirmacher, *Technik und Gelassenheit* [Freiburg: Alber, 1983], 25). Agamben goes on to argue that Auschwitz "calls into question the very possibility of authentic decision [particularly with respect to death] and thus threatens the very ground of Heidegger's ethics" (75). The apparent implication is that one must have an ethics that goes beyond even Heidegger in its fundamental radicality and break with the past—an ethics that Agamben seeks.

31. As Levi, in markedly nonsacrificial terms, puts it in *The Drowned and the Saved*, "one is never in another's place" (60).

32. *Did Somebody Say Totalitarianism?* 85.

33. See the discussion in Nancy Wood, *Vectors of Memory: Legacies of Trauma in Postwar Europe* (Oxford: Berg, 1999), chap. 3. See also the contributions to the special issue of *Cultural Critique* 46 (2000) on "Trauma and Its Cultural Aftereffects," ed. Karyn Ball.

34. Ernst Nolte, "Vergangenheit die nicht vergehen will," *Frankfurter Allgemeine Zeitung*, June 6, 1986; translated as "The Past That Will Not Pass" in *Forever in the Shadow of Hitler: Original Documents of the Historikerstreit, the Controversy Concerning the Singularity of the Holocaust*, ed. James Knowlton and Truett Cates (Atlantic Highlands, N.J.: Humanities Press, 1993), 18–23. See also my discussions in *Representing the Holocaust*, chap. 2, and *History and Memory after Auschwitz*, chap. 2.

35. *The Drowned and the Saved*, 48–49.

36. In *The Coming Community*, Agamben formulates what might be read as a view of the sacred as radically transcendent: "What is properly divine is that the world does not reveal God" (91). Paradoxically, he also has a notion of what could be termed transcendence from below: "The world—insofar as it is absolutely, irreparably profane—is God" (90).

Contributors

Index

Contributors

JANET ALSUP is assistant professor of English and curriculum and instruction at Purdue University. She has written on teacher authority, critical pedagogy, and teaching the Holocaust, with recent essays in *Pedagogy* and *English Education*.

ELIZABETH JANE BELLAMY is associate professor of English at the University of New Hampshire. She is the author, most recently, of *Affective Genealogies: Psychoanalysis, Postmodernism, and "The Jewish Question" after Auschwitz*.

MICHAEL BERNARD-DONALS is professor of English and Jewish studies at the University of Wisconsin–Madison. He has written essays on the problems of Holocaust representation and the rhetoric of the witness and is the coauthor (with Richard Glejzer) of *Between Witness and Testimony: The Holocaust and the Limits of Representation*.

SUSAN DAVID BERNSTEIN, associate professor of English and Jewish studies at the University of Wisconsin–Madison, is the author of essays on Victorian literature and women's studies and of *Confessional Subjects: Revelations of Gender and Power in Victorian Literature and Culture*.

RICHARD GLEJZER is associate professor of English at North Central College. He has written essays on medieval rhetoric, gender studies, and psychoanalytic theory and is the coauthor (with Michael Bernard-Donals) of *Between Witness and Testimony: The Holocaust and the Limits of Representation*.

GEOFFREY HARTMAN is Emeritus Sterling Professor of English and comparative literature and a director of the Fortunoff Archive of Holocaust Testimonies at Yale University. He has written a number of essays and books on the Holocaust, including *The Longest Shadow: In the Aftermath of the Holocaust*.

REINHOLD HILL is assistant professor of English at Ferris State University. He is the author of essays and reviews on folklore and the problem of insider research.

DOMINICK LACAPRA is the Bryce and Edith M. Bowmar Professor of Humanistic Studies at Cornell University and the director of the Society for the Humanities. He is the author, most recently, of *Writing History, Writing Trauma*.

DAVID METZGER is associate professor of English and rhetoric at Old Dominion University. He has published widely on rhetorical theory, Jewish rhetoric, and psychoanalytic theory and is the author of *The Lost Cause of Rhetoric*.

SHARON OSTER is a doctoral candidate in English at the University of California at Los Angeles.

ALAN ROSEN is a lecturer in the English department at Bar-Ilan University in Jerusalem. He is the editor of *Celebrating Elie Wiesel* and the author of *Dislocating the End*. He is at work on a book-length study of the Holocaust and multilingualism.

JAMES E. YOUNG is professor of English and chair of Judaic studies at the University of Massachusetts at Amherst. He has written extensively on museums and memorials, has curated exhibits on memorials, and is the author, most recently, of *After-Images of the Holocaust*.

Index

309